Her Day in Court

Women's Property Rights in Fifteenth-Century Granada

Harvard Series in Islamic Law

Maya Shatzmiller

Her Day in Court

Women's Property Rights in Fifteenth-Century Granada

Published by the
Islamic Legal Studies Program, Harvard Law School
Distributed by Harvard University Press
Cambridge, Massachusetts
2007

Library of Congress Control Number: 2007924952

Printed in the United States of America
ISBN 978-0-674-02501-1

CONTENTS

Acknowledgments vii
Abbreviations ix
Introduction 1

Part One: Rights and Their Acquisition
1. The Ṣadāq 19
2. The Inter Vivos Gift 41
3. Inheritance 61
4. Delayed Acquisition 77

Part Two: Body and Soul
5. The Body As Property 93
6. Property Rights in Conversion 118

Part Three: Economy and Class
7. Labour and Wages 149
8. Sales and Loans 176

Conclusion 197
Notes 201
Bibliography 249
Index 269

ACKNOWLEDGMENTS

... I want our day to come. (Joan Kelly's *Cancer Journal*, 1982)

The title *Her Day in Court* for a study of women's property rights in Islamic law and society was suggested to me by my son Ron Shatzmiller, now M.D., when he accompanied me some years ago to Istanbul, during my search for Arabic gynecological manuscripts for Chapter Five, "The Body as Property." Since then the importance of the court of law for women's rights has only increased, and not for Muslim women alone, and therefore it remains highly appropriate.

While I worked on the study, I benefitted from institutional and individual support, which I am pleased to acknowledge here. I am grateful to the Canadian Social Science and Humanities Research Council, which provided me with funds through research grants in 1994–1996 and 1999–2002. My university, the University of Western Ontario, has also given me several research grants at different points in time that enabled me to pursue this project. The Dean of the Faculty of Social Science granted me a research leave in 2000–2001 which made it possible to devote my entire time to the project. The year I spent as a fellow at the Davis Center in Princeton in 1995–1996, was enriched by the interaction I had with other scholars who, like myself, were studying a variety of questions related to women's economic activities. The Hannah Institute for the History of Medicine gave me a grant in 1997–1998. This, together with the year I spent at the Department of the Social Studies of Medicine at McGill University, 1999–2000, was instrumental in allowing me to understand and formulate the Islamic legal concepts of the body as property. I wish to thank Dr. Allan Young for offering me the fellowship in the department. At McGill University, the late Don Bates, M.D. was a dear friend and a guide in the field of the History of Medicine, who made my two-year stay in Montreal very special. At McGill University I also benefitted from long discussions of the legal aspects related to women with Professor Wael Hallaq of the Institute of Islamic Studies, and I am grateful for these. Many colleagues in Spain were extremely generous in putting at my disposal publications that were unavailable to me in Canadian libraries. My warmest thanks go to María Jesus Viguera Molins, Mercedes García-Arenal, Delfina Serrano Ruano, and Manuela Marín in Madrid, and lately to Miquel Forcada and M. Merce Viladrich in Barcelona, each of whom was extremely gracious with their time and efforts.

During the years I worked on the project I presented lectures, workshops, and seminars at various centers and universities. I thank colleagues and students at the University of British Columbia, the University of Toronto, Cornell University, the Institute for Advanced Study in Princeton, the Davis Center at Princeton University, Exeter University, Haifa University, the Oriental Institute in Naples, and many others, for comments and criticisms. I am grateful to Susan Merskey and Robert Lewis for editorial work at different stages, but mostly I am indebted to Peri Bearman, Associate Director of the Islamic Legal Studies Program at Harvard Law School, who accepted this book for publication in the series. Only she and I know the extent of the work she has undertaken in shaping the manuscript, in clarifying the obscure, and in eliminating the inconsistencies that had escaped me. If in spite of all her admonitions I have persisted in my erroneous beliefs, all faults and mistakes are mine and mine alone.

ABBREVIATIONS

Abrégé	Khalīl b. Isḥāq, *Abrégé de loi musulmane selon le rite de l'imām Mālek*, trans. G.-H. Bousquet, 4 vols. (Alger/Paris: Adrien Maisonneuve, 1961).
Documentos	*Wathāʾiq ʿarabiyya gharnāṭiyya: Documentos arábigo-granadinos*, ed. and trans. Luis Seco de Lucena Paredes, 2 vols. (Madrid: Instituto de Estudios Islámicos, 1961).
EI^2	*The Encyclopaedia of Islam*, New Edition (Leiden: E.J. Brill, 1950–2004).
Kitāb al-Wathāʾiq	Muḥammad b. Aḥmad Ibn al-ʿAṭṭār, *Kitāb al-Wathāʾiq: Formulario notarial hispano-árabe por el alfaqui y notario cordobes*, ed. Pedro Chalmeta and Francisco Corriente (Madrid: Instituto Hispano-Árabe de Cultura, 1983).
Maqṣad	ʿAlī b. Yaḥyā al-Jazīrī, *al-Maqṣad al-maḥmūd fī talkhīṣ al-ʿuqūd*, ed. Asunción Ferreras (Madrid: Consejo Superior de Investigaciones Científicas, 1998).
Miʿyār	Aḥmad b. Yaḥyā al-Wansharīsī, *al-Miʿyār al-muʿrib wa 'l-jāmiʿ al-mughrib ʿan fatāwā ʿulamāʾ ifrīqiya wa 'l-andalus wa 'l-maghrib*, ed. M. Ḥājjī et al., 13 vols. (Beirut: Dār al-Gharb al-Islāmī, 1981–82).
Mukhtaṣar	Khalīl b. Isḥāq, *Mukhtaṣar*, ed. Aḥmad Naṣr (Cairo: Dār Ihyāʾ al-Kutub al-ʿArabiyya, 1988).
Muqniʿ	Aḥmad Ibn Mughīth al-Ṭulayṭulī (d. 459/1067), *al-Muqniʿ fī ʿilm al-shurūṭ: Formulario notarial*, ed. Francisco Javier Aguirre Sádaba (Madrid: Consejo Superior de Investigaciones Científicas, 1994).
Qawānīn	Muḥammad b. Aḥmad Ibn Juzayy, *al-Qawānīn al-fiqhiyya* (Beirut: N.p., 1967).
Traité	Yvon Linant de Bellefonds, *Traité de droit musulman comparé*, 3 vols. (The Hague: Mouton, 1965–73).

INTRODUCTION

This book is a study of the historical record of Muslim women's property rights and equity. Based on archival documents of a unique historical distinction, those of the Islamic court of fifteenth-century Granada, the book examines the legal entitlements of females to acquire property as well as the social and economic significance of these rights to Granada's female population and, by extension, to women in other Islamic societies. The Granadan collection of court documents covers the years between 1421 and 1496, the last century of Islamic political independence in the Iberian Peninsula, with a strong concentration of documents for the 1480s. These are records of private transactions—that is, family and commercial deeds that Granadans registered in the Islamic court. The incoming Christian administration recognized these deeds for their binding legal power and, eager to safeguard documents relating to property in the city, took care to preserve them.[1]

Reverence for legal procedure was a trait of Andalusian society, and Granada's citizens continued to register their property transactions in the Islamic court even during the last five years that the court was allowed to function following the 1491 conquest.[2] The ninety-five Arabic files became an archival collection when they were edited, translated into Spanish, and published by Luis Seco de Lucena Paredes in 1960,[3] but unlike other court records, they show a higher degree of women's involvement in Granada than anywhere else.[4] Ninety-five per cent of the documents refer to a female either transacting family and business deals in some capacity or exercising one or several of her legal entitlements to property.

The strong showing of Granadan women in the documents is intriguing for the sheer number of women represented and for the scope of their property-related activity. The most probable explanation for this strong showing is the role played by the demographic conditions in fifteenth-century Granada, a society at war. The battles of the Reconquista, raging in al-Andalus since the thirteenth century, had reduced the male population of Granada to the point where, by the time the city surrendered, there were only 1,250 horsemen left to defend it. The Spanish armies' continual onslaught had decimated the productive capacity of the countryside by destroying crops and fields, thus leaving a concentration of land and property in limited hands, many of them female. A large number of refugees from the conquered Andalusian cities also lived in Granada, enlarging its population to an estimated 100,000, including many families, most of which were without property.[5] These demographic conditions are depicted in several generations of small-family archives that show multiple transactions by female members only. At the high end of the spectrum was the property left in the hands of the female members of the royal Nasrid family—the mother, the sisters, and the wife of Granada's last king, Boabdil—which included ovens, stores, and inns located in the Alpujarra region. But many other women of the middle and lower classes also amassed equity.[6] The need among women of all classes to assume a more active and public role in property matters made their participation greater than under normal circumstances. However, the women in Granada clearly could not have done what the documents indicate they did unless their property rights were already in place. Thus the demographic conditions magnified the effect of women's property rights but did not create them.

Property rights, both individual and institutional, have emerged in recent years as an important factor in the economic prosperity of any given society. In particular, economists have identified such rights as incentives that lead to better economic performance. Not to be confused with property itself or with rights to the land either in Islamic or in other medieval societies, property rights are legal provisions that entitle an individual to acquire, keep, and use property in a secure social and legal environment. Most economists who focus on property rights employ economic theory to determine their effects.[7] By comparison, for historians, who are methodologically more interested in evidence than in theory, the appeal of this economic theory lies in the innovative way that it explains economic history.[8] Among historians, viewing property rights as an incentive to engage in economic activity suggests a new philosophy of economic history, one that favours targeting the interactions of humans and institutions over employing technical and mathematical models. The potential usefulness of the concept of property rights to Islamic historians cannot be ignored, even though the concept is not easily defined within the framework of Islamic law (*Sharīʿa*). As Farhat Ziadeh notes, following Johansen, there is no general theory of property law in the Shariʿa.[9] For the most part, the right to land ownership has been the focus of scholarly work that has drawn on classical law and on the medieval theory of land ownership through land taxation.[10] Elsewhere, I have used institutional property rights to conduct a historical analysis of economic performance in the Islamic context[11] while looking for ways to approach women's property rights, which are not given their own chapter in the law manuals. Here, by comparison, the Granadan evidence offers a unique opportunity to study the historical and legal context of women's property rights.

An underlying assumption of this book is that women's property rights were not a novelty in the Middle East, where Islamic law was formulated, but a concept with which the ancient Near Eastern societies were familiar. In 1400 B.C. women in the city of Nuzi could hold title to real estate and took part in property transactions.[12] During the Hellenic period, like the women of Athens, a woman in the Middle East owned her dower and any other property that she had inherited, even though males, including her father, brother, uncle, husband, son, or son-in-law, were authorized to administer her property on her behalf and to represent her in legal proceedings, ostensibly to safeguard her interests.[13] When Roman law was enacted in the region, these legal provisions were maintained, thus permitting a woman to inherit property but only from her agnatic relatives. A woman's power to control her property also varied as she either remained under the guardianship of her father or other male relatives after marriage or chose to be transferred to her husband's guardianship. A Roman wife could not perform any transactions without the involvement of a tutor.[14] Her only freedom lay in her right to request that the senators appoint one for her or to ask for a different tutor. Another regional model of female property rights is suggested by the rights afforded Jewish women in the first century A.D., when Jewish women held their property, including their dowries, separately from that of their husbands, to whom they could lend money.[15] Although in Europe the practice of Roman law saw the guardian's role become a mere formality, his consent was nonetheless needed in order to validate a woman's contract. By contrast, under Germanic law of the early Middle Ages, which summarily replaced Roman law in Europe, women could not take legal action, appear independently before a court, or manage their own wealth, and, unlike men, they were disadvantaged by the law of succession.[16] However, when the first legal manuals were written in the eighth and ninth centuries in the Islamic Middle East, all women's property rights—*ṣadāq*, gifts, inheritance, separation of assets in matrimony, freedom from male guardianship, and control over property—were already present.

The historical process that facilitated the articulation of women's property rights in Islamic law involved a certain evolution within the legal institutions of Arab society at the time. Arab nomads, whose tribal legal system initially recognized only the concept of collective property, were not completely unaware of private property, as shown by the shift in the status of property in Meccan society.[17] Women's property rights can be associated with what was hailed as the birth of "Islamic capitalism" in Mecca, where the first females associated with property resided, not only the Prophet Muḥammad's wife Khadīja, but also others. The transition from collectivism in property ownership to individualism, which involved also holding private property, has been linked as well to the end of the matrilineal system, in which women did not have the right to own property, which was held collectively by the family and administered by the women's brothers.[18] Yet some legal historians, such as Noel Coulson, see in the advent of women's property rights an "historical change" in the legal construct of filiation: "According to the traditionally accepted picture of this tribal law, women occupied the position of childbearing chattels, generally deprived of proprietary or other rights and sold into a loose sexual liaison with their husbands for a price which was paid to the wife's father or other close male relatives . . . The treatment of *nasab* [filiation] in the law indicates a historical change in family relations from the situation before Islam, where the father was the sole basis of legitimacy, to a new situation under Islam, where the maternal connection is as important as the paternal one."[19]

Joseph Schacht argues that the arrival of property rights marked a great improvement in the status of women: "The legal position of women is not unfavorable. The woman is, it is true, considered inferior to the man . . . But as regards to the law of property and obligations, the woman is the equal of the man; the matrimonial regime is even more favorable to her in many respects."[20] But according to Jules Roussier, "the Qur'an encourages the Muslim woman to marry. As long as she is married, she does not need property because her husband is supposed to provide for her. Yet the Qur'an accorded inheritance rights to women because it was necessary to address the property needs of unmarried women, whether divorced or widowed. In order to encourage women to remarry, their inheritance rights were limited."[21]

Other legal historians focus on the dichotomy between "equity" and "equality." While women's property rights were clearly formulated, the image of parity was illusory given the presumed incompatibility of women's rights, especially those related to property, with the Qur'an's dictum that men are superior to women (Q 2:228). Barbara Stowasser insists that the women's reduced share was a sign of inferior status and evidence of patriarchy: "The Qur'anic laws of inheritance where the female's share is half of that of the male in a number of cases ([Q] 4:11, 4:12, 4:176) also fit a patriarchal family framework."[22]

Hamilton Gibb adopts a similar view: on the one hand, certain basic positions stem from Qur'anic prescription, but on the other hand, the bulk of the actual operative rules either derive from or are influenced by non-Qur'anic practices.[23] Linda Schatkowski Schilcher, who suggests that the patriarchal family is not only a comparatively recent (i.e., eighteenth-century) development in the Middle East, but also "just a family phenomenon" expressed solely in marriage patterns, relegates judicial practices to the order of social norms, thus excluding from the equation the legal and economic paradigms so central to the concept of property rights and their effect.[24] For his part, Yvon Linant de Bellefonds dismisses the entire construct, arguing that consulting the Qur'an for juridical purposes is useless: "These contradictory interpretations of the sacred text made any direct consultation of the Qur'an for juridical purposes useless and mistaken."[25] He judges Qur'anic interpretations respecting women's rights to be devoid of interest.

Regardless of the debate about the origins of women's property rights in Islamic law, evidence of female property ownership surfaces regularly in historical sources for the early centuries, the formative period of Islamic law. Women appear as property owners in the wake of the first conquests, when wives, mothers, and sisters of Arab generals and soldiers bought and owned land in the newly conquered territories of lower Iraq.[26] Egyptian papyri from the ninth and tenth centuries also show that women's property ranged from slaves and houses to commercial products, fields, date plantations, and orchards.[27] The legal mechanisms by which women's property ownership was constructed and by which their property rights were formulated cannot be fully teased out except by means of a comprehensive examination of the entire corpus of relevant laws, including those affecting marriage, divorce, inheritance, guardianship, property rights, gifts, endowments, sales, and hirings. There is no better context in which to undertake this endeavour than that presented by the legal history of Muslim Spain.

The process by which Andalusian society became subject to a framework of laws was evolutionary and produced a judicially obsessed and litigiously minded populace. By the tenth century, the development of legal awareness had permeated the fabric of society. At the political level, institutional legal advisory groups, such as the *shūra*s, which served as adjuncts to the courts for the legal councils, also participated in legal activities involving numerous jurists fervently engaged in the discussion of legal matters. These discussions often took place informally in the mosques and were carried on in an animated manner that distracted the Friday worshipers in the mosque in Cordova. Even worse, they resulted in legal opinions formulated by individuals who were unqualified to produce them, at least in the eyes of the official jurists. Soon the practice earned itself a legal rebuke in a *fatwā* (solicited legal opinion, henceforth fatwa) from the officially appointed jurists.[28]

Recent research done in Spain in the field of legal studies has documented these activities, and profiles of the legal schools of thought in cities such as Toledo,[29] Cordova,[30] and Granada[31] now exist, together with descriptions of their institutions, jurists, and writings, all of which exhibit a distinct legal character. However, the greatest merit of the Maliki school of North Africa and Muslim Spain lies in the sheer volume and comprehensiveness of its sources, which range from law manuals (*fiqh*) and notarial manuals (*kutub al-wathāʾiq*) to fatwas, together with the enquiries that elicited them, all incorporating elements of local custom in addition to the law. New editions of legal sources have been published, several of which have been instrumental to this book's systematic study of women's property rights. In their capacity as a legal historical source, the Granadan documents represent 800 years of Islamic legal practice in al-Andalus and can thus be meaningfully contextualized with reference to other legal historical records. In an article calling on historians to use legal documents as historical sources, Claude Cahen singled out the Maliki school of Spain as providing the richest cache of legal source material among all the regional schools. Focusing on this school has made it possible to reconstruct a more accurate picture of the historical evolution of women's property rights and their practice under the law.[32]

Beginning with the *fiqh*, I have chosen texts by two Maliki authors of the fourteenth century because of their chronological or geographical proximity to the Granadan documents. The first was written by Muḥammad b. Aḥmad Ibn Juzayy of Granada (d. 1348)[33] and the second by Khalīl b. Isḥāq of Egypt (d. 1365).[34] Despite using different approaches, each provides a picture of the Maliki school, and together they form the source material for the rules on women's property rights treated in this book. Khalīl specifies that he was writing for the benefit of jurists engaged in delivering fatwas.[35] Ibn Juzayy chose to detail the Maliki view in comparison to the views of the three other schools, the Shafiʿi, Hanafi, and Hanbali, stating that in doing so, the "gain is more complete and the benefit much greater."[36] The concise manual was a popular legal genre because it attempted to address "the problem of indeterminacy" (*ikhtilāf*) within the Maliki school by establishing a set of binding rules that would limit the independent rulings of unqualified *muftī*s (issuers of fatwas, henceforth mufti) or *qāḍī*s (judges, henceforth qadi).[37] The texts by Ibn Juzayy and Khalīl differ in style and structure but not in content. Both authors use a systematic list of abbreviations, which they describe in their respective introductions. Khalīl uses key words that, when mentioned, allude to earlier authors such as Ibn Qāsim, Ibn Yūnis, Ibn Rushd, and al-Māzarī.[38] Ibn Juzayy uses abbreviations to indicate legal concepts—for example, *ijmāʿ* when referring to "community consensus" and *al-arbaʿa* ("the foursome") when referring to the opinions of the four eponymous school founders.[39]

Both contemporary and past users of Khalīl's manual deserve our sympathy. Bousquet, who translated the text, remarks that "one cannot think of a more uninviting, and more absolutely incomprehensible work than this text, if not helped by a commentary."[40] Mohammad Fadel, author of a comparative study on Khalīl's manual, remarked: "Indeed, one cannot accurately describe the 'concrete' rules in Khalīl as actually being rules: instead Khalīl may cite concrete examples as instances of a general rule."[41] Nonetheless, since he was a contemporary Maliki jurist, whose reputation was acknowledged in Granada, authors saw in his manual a yardstick with which to gauge the independency of the legal rulings issued by Granadan jurists.[42] It offers little social history, unlike Ibn Juzayy's manual, which provides useful social and economic context, especially when his text is studied together with other sources from Granada. Ibn Juzayy wrote a coherent legal manual that exposes the principles without losing sight of the problem and that provides a comprehensive and systematic presentation of the legal issues. As a member of the dynamic legal community of Granadan jurists, his discourse is closer to the legal practice of Granada during its last two centuries of Islamic independence.

A comparison of how the manuals by Ibn Juzayy and Khalīl addressed women's property rights provides a comprehensive view of what was considered essential in the Maliki school, but also allows us to see how each of the two approached the issues at hand. For a general comparative and synthetical analysis of the legal rules, I have relied on Yvon Linant de Bellefonds's three-volume study of Islamic law, *Traité de droit musulman comparé*. This excellent study, which draws on source material by both Muslim and non-Muslim scholars, provides a thematic analysis of all four schools and their legal sources alongside a discussion of modern Islamic legislation.

The notarial manuals are the kind of source that Claude Cahen regarded as "rendering in their own way the sociology of the milieu that produced them."[43] Equally used in other regions,[44] these Andalusian notarial formularies, which have survived in relatively large numbers, simplified application of the law by issuing blanket documents to fit many and different events and situations. Their practical application is beyond doubt.[45] While a single document found in the archives represents a single event, the model notarial collections from Muslim Spain and the Middle East are unique in offering templates for many events. Thus their value as historical evidence is no less important than that of documents known to have been written for a specific case. They have gained universal recognition for providing useful documentary evidence of Islamic legal theory and norms. Those materials compiled by Muḥammad b. Aḥmad Ibn al-ʿAṭṭār in the tenth century,[46] by Aḥmad Ibn Mughīth al-Ṭulayṭulī in the eleventh century,[47] and by ʿAlī b. Yaḥyā al-Jazīrī in the twelfth century[48] have been of most value to this book. Thanks to new studies linking law manuals and notarial formularies, a source once seen as fragmented, contradictory, and unrelated to reality has now been accepted as an authentic, legitimate historical interpretation of the legal discourse.[49] While the earlier formularies reflect local influences, the later ones reflect court practice and judicial decisions that were extracted from court records or fatwas and incorporated into the legal manuals.[50]

Not unrelated to the legal articulation of women's property rights are questions about whether these rights were upheld by jurists. In an effort to establish the historical record, I have turned to the fatwas in a previous study as well as to notarial manuals of model contracts, although the result has not been entirely satisfactory.[51] In answering these questions, the Granadan documents also provide information on the practice of the law and on lawyers that is important to the study of women's property rights.

As with notarials, the place occupied by fatwas, our third category of legal documents, as providers of historical data was slow to be recognized. Methodological concerns dominated the discussion, and fatwas were seen as chronologically obscure and obfuscating.[52] A fatwa was described simply as "a non-binding advisory issued to an individual questioner whether in connection with litigation or not,"[53] a description that, though accurate, fails to highlight the importance of the genre with regard to the historical conditions it describes. Until very recently, this preoccupation with the question of the fatwa's authenticity had all but paralyzed any attempt to treat it as a historical source, a project began by López Ortiz, who has shown that turning to muftis was a norm among Granadan judges and courts.[54] Ortiz's study confirms a process of incorporation of fatwas into the legal theoretical body, which began as early as the eighth century and occurred continuously in the work of later Andalusian jurists until the end of Muslim rule in Spain. His study of the Granadan fatwas in the fourteenth and fifteenth centuries specifically shows how they addressed the changes in the social and economic conditions in Granada.[55]

For the purposes of this book, I have used a selection of fatwas taken from the large collection of decisions by Maliki muftis compiled by Aḥmad

b. Yaḥyā al-Wansharīsī in the sixteenth century.[56] Collected in volumes according to their legal subject matter, the fatwas present cases of private and institutional conflict and thus offer an account of legal and social norms. Despite having gone through an editing process before coming to us in a shortened form and with some of their details eliminated, they remain indispensable for historical studies.[57] The collection's fatwas have already demonstrated their potential to provide information on the history of Islamic marriage and family.[58] The foregoing three categories of legal sources—*fiqh* (law manuals), *kutub al-wathāʾiq* (notarial manuals), and fatwas (legal opinions)—provide the context within which the legal issues raised by the Granadan documents are discussed. I have approached women's property rights from different angles and in a comprehensive way that treats not only those rights commonly addressed as women's rights, such as marriage gifts, other gifts, and inheritance, but also those rights that are less obvious, such as women's rights respecting their bodies.

Given the array of subjects covered, the study is divided into three parts: Rights and Their Acquisition, Body and Soul, and Economy and Class. Each part treats not only property rights enacted between individuals related to one another in myriad family relationships—that is, individual rights—but also rights to which males and females were equally entitled but when exercised by women in the context of social and economic transactions were subject to special conditions.

Chapter 1 examines the *ṣadāq* (money, or property converted to money, promised to the bride upon marriage), focusing on the legal framework by which it is acquired in two instalments and on these instalments' timing and consequences. The chapter treats the *ṣadāq*'s operational uses and practices, the family relations involved in its acquisition, the form in which it came into the hands of wives, and the cultural perceptions of marriage, family, and property that could be gleaned from the legal records and from the jurists' discourse. Because marriage marked a wife's acquisition of other property rights, there is a risk that the *ṣadāq* may be seen as an organic part of property devolution. In fact, as the comparative context makes clear, the Islamic *ṣadāq* differed in both theory and practice from the European dowry and was not part of Islamic property devolution, to which it was sometimes compared.

Chapter 2 deals with the modes, timing, and content of various gifts as well as with the motivations for giving them and with the rights to which women were either entitled or subjected as donors and recipients of property gifts. The lingering power of parents, mostly fathers, over their daughters' property was maintained through gifts to minors, which afforded parents access to property income based on guardianship. The chapter shows that gender influenced the timing of property acquisition and that, in the case of a gift to a minor, this timing delayed, curtailed, and shortened the potential economic return from the asset in question. The right of the inter vivos gift was exercised by wives wishing to trade particular rights in exchange for men's property rights. Unlike the *ṣadāq*, the timing of the inter vivos gift was not mandatory but could be triggered by accidents or occasions, such as an unexpected death in the family, payment of a debt, or marriage to an elderly man.

Chapter 3 deals with the inheritance law, which enabled a family's female members to inherit, acquire, retain, and use a share of the family's inheritance. The Granadan documents provide good examples of how the inheritance law was used to accommodate family needs in times of demographic decline, such as occurred during the fifteenth century. They show that the Islamic inheritance law inadvertently played a major role in guaranteeing women's property rights and in establishing their status as independent property holders. The importance of the female inheritance right was its part in ensuring that all other property rights could be acquired and safeguarded, which it did by facilitating the passage of property to the next generation of males and females.

Chapter 4 studies the guardianship of minor females and parents' control of young married daughters, which was motivated by their desire to maintain access to property income for as long as possible, thus submitting the sometimes very young and inexperienced wife to her parents' authority well into marriage. At the same time, the law of guardianship also benefited women by enabling them to receive property through different channels at a young age and by making it legally more attractive for family members to transfer property to them. The separation of a couple's property in marriage facilitated giving property to the wife without fear that it would necessarily come under the husband's control, even though it could be lost in the case of a *khulʿ* divorce—that is, a divorce initiated by the wife and accepted by the husband in exchange for some form of compensation. The potential for abuse, numerous examples of which can be found in the sources, should also be recognized, while the prolonged control of daughters by their parents also highlighted the ambiguity of marriage as a determinant in the acquisition of property rights.

Chapter 5 looks at the wife's rights over her reproductive activity as property rights. These include the right to choose whether to practice birth control, the right not to breastfeed, the right to wages for breastfeeding, and the right to wages for childrearing. It reveals that the law regarded procreation as a matter of property relations and that husband and wife had rights respecting each other's body that had to be acquired for both to fulfil their respective roles in procreation. The comparative context is provided by Islamic medicine and the ways that Muslim physicians treated the female body and women's reproductive health. Taking the comparative approach one significant step further, I compare the Muslim physicians' discourse to that of their teachers, the Greek physicians, particularly those in the misogynous Hippocratic medical corpus. The comparison reveals an unfailingly positive Islamic medical discourse that took a compassionate view of women and their reproductive lives. The similarity of this positive medical discourse on the female body to that of the jurists can be explained by the fact that a legal framework existed that gave the female body an independent legal status and that recognized the body as a repository of property. This conclusion is reaffirmed by the correlation between the pseudo-legal context and the attack on the little girl's body through female circumcision. The significance of bringing the medical view of women's bodies to bear on the study of women's legal property rights over the body lies not in establishing a textual link between them, as has been previously attempted, but in adding depth and comprehensiveness to this study by approximating the cultural and historical context that they shared.

Chapter 6 deals with property rights in the context of religious conversion by looking at what conversion to Islam meant in legal terms for women and by showing how it affected their property rights in two circumstances: when the conversion was of their own volition; and when their husbands or fathers demanded it. A cluster of five conversion documents—three for Christian, Jewish, and pagan males and two for Christian and pagan females—from a notarial manual composed in tenth-century Cordova has been used here to place the results of the investigation within the analytical framework of the study of Muslim women's legal status and, further, into the emotional and psycho-social environment of women's conversion to Islam and its significance as a life event.

Chapters 7 and 8 examine two categories of economic practice: wage labour and commercial activity. The study of women's wage labour as a woman's property right focuses on two issues, her right to engage in wage labour and her right to keep her wages. Of particular concern are the social and legal implications of women's acquiring and activating these rights. Remuneration for productive labour was acquired and kept in a similar manner to the wages received for services rendered by the female body. The right to engage in wage labour was upheld by the jurists in absolute terms as a universal property right, but in practice the acquisition of this right appears to have been subject to additional considerations.

The right was challenged in two instances: when it collided with other property rights and when the standards for women's conduct within the marriage rendered it socially unacceptable. The marriage contract, which had become a vehicle for articulating and guaranteeing arrangements of all sorts, failed to secure women their right to engage in wage earning under moral and social pretexts. Putting this in a historical context, the massive employment of women in the textile industry made women's wages a common and regular event, and the legal system, jurists, courts, and the social scene all needed to adapt to these new conditions.

Chapter 8 examines women's freedom to engage in financial transactions and to keep the proceeds. Activities such as selling and buying land and real estate, tax farming and brokerage, small-scale local commerce, and investment in long-distance trade by loaning capital or credit are investigated here as they appear in the legal records. The degree of women's participation in business and loans varied from a strong showing in sales and purchases of real estate and land to a more limited involvement in extending credit to family members, a limited physical participation as sellers in local markets, and an almost total absence from long-distance trade. Investment in trade was another area where women benefited from the combination of women's property rights and the intrafamily nature of Islamic business. Paradigms studied include motivation, access to the markets, identity of partners, size and nature of the property exchanged, and the frequency of transactions. The study also shows that the negative image currently attached to the intrafamily pattern of investment in trade could stand a correction to the extent that it favoured women's participation. The opportunity to invest their resources with brothers and fathers in trade, the essence of the intrafamily system, meant that the limitation on women's exposure to public space did not stop them from moving idle capital into fruitful venues. Nonetheless, the Granadan evidence shows a rather limited spectrum of involvement by women in the business sphere relative to the potential offered by their property rights.

The historical evidence furnished by the Granadan court documents provides an example of "history from below." Our heroes, women known to us by name and family affiliation, were otherwise silent. We find them frozen in a single moment of legal procedure before their disappearance from the annals of history. While the trajectory of their legal narrative is fully contextualized within the framework of the Maliki legal sources, I have looked in vain for a "female voice" in the literary sources. I am not alone in my disappointment at this absence; literary critics have judged these sources to be insincere, unauthentic, and manipulative. On the nature of the Arabic and Hispano-Arabic literature, James Nichols has this to say: "There is a kind of literalism that appears and reappears in works of historical criticism devoted to Arabic and Hispano-Arabic literature. The root of the evil is the failure on the part of historians to grasp the principle that poets borrow, steal and lie."[59]

With the exception of the slave poetesses of the ʿAbbasid court, an unpropertied and marginal group whose cultured and skilled voices were heard,[60] this judgment was not restricted to Muslim Spain's literature alone. Louis Pouzet accuses the medieval Arabic sources of being "elitist and aristocratic, making it very hard to see in them the daily life of regular men and women."[61] As for the attitude of male writers toward women, Huda Lutfi asks: "Could it be also due to a certain attitude of the Muslim man which has led to his continuous squelching of woman's presence in public life and in 'his literature'?"[62]

In the absence of the female voice, the answer to the question of Muslim women's property rights and their role in the economy must ultimately consider legal and regional variables and the economic structures of medieval Islamic society. For this reason I have examined the microhistory of women's property rights in fifteenth-century Granada in a comparative historical, social, and economic context by using three blocks of evidence: Islamic legal documents from earlier and later periods, legal evidence from Jewish communities then living in the Islamic lands, and legal evidence from medieval Christian Europe. For the Islamic historical practice, I have used comparative data from other regions and periods in order to determine how unified or diverse it was, including court records, collections of fatwas, records of *waqf* (charitable endowments), and studies based on documents from the Ottoman archives, which become more readily available as my examination progresses chronologically and which feature all the issues dealt with in the Granadan records.[63] The historical experience of the Jewish communities, whose legal system developed in proximity to and in contact with Islamic law, offers a closer context for comparing Muslim women's property rights to those of Jewish women. The Geniza documents provide much of the historical data on the practice of these rights, while a recent detailed comparative study of Islamic and Jewish law provides information on the larger scope of the law itself.[64] Documentation of the legal systems in medieval Europe, particularly the extensive legal records for the Italian Renaissance cities, which were contemporary to fifteenth-century Granada, has made it possible to highlight the substantial differences between the European and Islamic cases. Expectations of some affinity between the European and Islamic legal and social systems were not always borne out; instead, similarities to the Islamic model surfaced in the most unexpected contexts, such as in the case of an eighteenth-century Russian noble women and in the Chinese system before the Mongol conquest.[65]

In addition to the comparative historical context, the subject of women's property rights also belongs in the realm of gender studies, pointing to the need for a theoretical framework in which this book's conclusions might coexist with the Islamic feminist discourse on the law as a patriarchal system. Locating such a framework was relevant to me both as a scholar and as a woman. I felt the need to situate my findings within a more universal framework, one that would combine the effect of women's property, women's property rights, and the role of jurists in women's acquisition of these rights. The variety of theoretical interpretations of women's property rights runs the gamut of disciplines from anthropology to history, most frequently within the economic paradigms of marriage. Sometimes evidence from primitive societies is used that documents the view of women as property, as was seen in rural societies, where women's labour was recruited through marriage.[66] For later periods, a Marxist interpretation is favoured, one that links the loss of the means of production to the decline of women's status. In the capitalistic societies of nineteenth-century Europe, women were rendered subordinate when the industrial means of production were transferred to private ownership.[67] Valuable as each of these theories is in its particular context, none lends itself very well to an account of the unique relationship between women's property rights, as documented in the Islamic sources, and the involvement of the judicial milieu, the courts, and the jurists in determining their acquisition.

In contrast, such a theory has been presented by Carole Rose of Yale University Law School, whose work analyzes women's loss of property as a result of interactions between women, social mores, and the actions of judges.[68] Rose argues that the differences, real or alleged, of the mental and behavioural patterns of men and women affect how they bargain with each other over property. Through a subtle process of coercion, women are pressured to give in to men's demands. Through what she terms "a real or assumed taste for cooperation," women's property rights are eroded.[69] Women's perceived or real weakness in negotiating with related males is encouraged by the law and by the jurists and judges who apply it, leading to systematic inequalities and to the liquidation of women's assets.[70] Rose's study establishes questions about the construction of the relationship between women, property rights, and the law that can be applied to Islamic sources. For example, did Muslim society expect women to surrender their property in defiance of their property rights? And did Muslim jurists, the Islamic courts, and the Islamic legal system help men to defraud women, thereby curtailing the benefits that the law had given to them? The historical accuracy of portraying Islamic law as patriarchal is scrutinized by bringing Rose's theory to bear on the documented evidence. Each chapter addresses these questions and also raises the question of links between women's property rights and society's economic performance.

Finally, in relation to the foregoing questions, when applicable I have ended each chapter with references to contemporary Islamic societies. I have done so because the laws governing women's lives, including women's property rights, continue to be widely shared by societies that are subject to Islamic law. The historical experience of the Granadan community offers a model of the strength of women's property rights and their positive effect on women's social status and economic progress. The historical evidence demonstrates the importance of maintaining these rights. Given that the issue of women's rights has become, along with jihad, the public face of the Shariʿa, it seemed appropriate to introduce this kind of evidence into the debate on women's rights. Two examples of the contemporary relevance of the historical material will suffice.

While I was writing this book, an unsuccessful attempt was made to introduce into the Province of Ontario's Arbitration Act, 1991, the option of turning to Islamic arbitration in matters of family and inheritance. If successful, this attempt would have given standing to Shariʿa rules within a Western country's legal framework for the first time.[71] Enforcement of the Shariʿa in recent years by several Muslim countries—for instance, Iran, Nigeria, and Pakistan—has already alerted the public to how such enforcement, in particular when women have no say in its interpretation, can negatively affect women's treatment at the hands of the law.[72] Thus for Western observers, women's rights under Islamic law have become the tool by which women's status and their level of education are measured.[73] Some Muslims trained in both Islamic and Western legal thought have advocated abandoning the Shariʿa altogether, turning instead to contemporary legal systems vetted by international standards.[74]

The second example of the historical evidence's bearing on the present relates to issues of the female body. The task force on female circumcision in Egypt reports that large numbers of women are still routinely circumcised there.[75] But as I point out in Chapter 5, which deals with the body as property, legal justification for the practice is not sustainable with reference to the historical sources. This finding would be useful to governments attempting to bring the practice to a halt. Women's rights to bear children and to access new reproductive technologies, as well as the legitimacy of birth control and abortion, are equally debated in Islamic societies, which are battling a population explosion that has placed constraints on their economic progress.[76] In these debates, because the Qur'anic verses relating to women's rights and the commentaries on them are open to various interpretations, the law will remain strictly interpretive unless the historical record is taken into account.[77] Only a truthful and intellectually honest understanding of the past is likely to affect the status of women in the present, which the evidence presented here will surely enhance.

Part One

RIGHTS AND THEIR ACQUISITION

One

THE ṢADĀQ

Contracting a Marriage in Granada

On 20 October 1488, four years before her city, Granada, fell to the armies of the Catholic kings, Umm al-Fatḥ celebrated her marriage to Abū Jaʿfar Aḥmad b. Muḥammad al-Fakhkhār.[1] People needed a great deal of courage and optimism to build a new household in besieged and war-torn Granada. The threat of the Reconquista had become more imminent since the Christian armies tightened their grip on areas around the city in 1485, and the suburbs were filled with thousands of refugees from the neighbouring conquered towns. Inside Granada civil war decimated the city, as the supporters of Boabdil, Granada's last king, clashed with those of his uncle, al-Zaghal, in the populous quarter of Albaicín.[2] Granada's jurists, among them the preacher (*khaṭīb*) and jurist Abū ʿAbd Allāh Muḥammad al-Fakhkhār, who was probably related to the groom, took a political stand by issuing a fatwa against Boabdil's supporters.[3] Yet, judging by her marriage contract, Umm al-Fatḥ, her groom, and their families handled this special event in their lives with poise and confidence.[4] By registering their marriage in the Islamic court, following the Andalusian notarial formula as generations before them had done, the couple and their families gained a sense of continuity and legitimacy, if not security.[5]

The marriage contract followed Granada's notarial Maliki norms. Umm al-Fatḥ is described in eloquent terms as the "blessed [*saʿīda*] virgin," and her groom is described as the "esteemed, admired, honoured, and respected vizier,"[6] all conventional superlatives that the notary attached to the names of people contracting transactions of this sort.[7] The list of properties given to both bride and groom, who were cousins, shows that both were members of well-propertied families.[8] Umm al-Fatḥ's *ṣadāq*, together with the list of properties either gifted to her at the moment of marriage or previously owned by her and now released by her brother, reveal both her own and her female relatives' status as property owners in Granada. Her *ṣadāq* consisted of 6 pure gold dinars from the current mint, which, her brother stated in the contract, had been received from the groom, and 2 gold dinars from the same current mint, which were to be handed over to her six months later, together with a *farda* (outer garment) made of silk and linen. In addition to the money, she received silk fabrics and headgear, made in the style of the Andalusian cities Abla and Murcia, and the customary tray of perfumes and ornaments.[9] She was gifted land and estates by the female members of her and her groom's families, and these were also registered in the marriage contract. Abū Jaʿfar's mother, Umm al-Fatḥ's aunt, gave her an entire house in the neighbouring village of Buliyāna as a *niḥla* (marriage gift). She also gave Umm al-Fatḥ both her own share in the estate of her late brother Abū l-Qāsim, the bride's father, and the share that she had inherited from her other brother, the late Aḥmad, the bride's uncle, land that was situated in the suburb of Qarbasāna al-Qanb and that measured approximately eight square kilometres.[10] Abū Jaʿfar's mother gave him half of the land in al-Jabāsin outside Granada—his brother, Muḥammad, owned the other half—as well as half of an olive grove, which he would also share with this brother. The groom's sister, ʿĀ'isha, gave him her share in a house in the old Qasba in Granada, which belonged to their late father's estate and which the notary judged to be too familiar to require a description. At the moment of marriage and independently of her gifts, Umm al-Fatḥ gained complete control and sole power over all the property that she had been given in previous years. Her brother Aḥmad stated for the record that she owned cash and property and proceeded to enumerate four different estates that belonged to her: half of a country estate in Buliyāna, which she shared equally with him; a plot of land in Buliyāna near the village of Chaun, in its entirety; an olive grove adjacent to his own in Buliyāna, also in its entirety; and another property planted with olive trees, which he currently owned. Aḥmad stated in the document that he had completely and ultimately divested himself of his sister's properties and had surrendered and delivered them all to her, including the shares, which she now controlled.

Only one additional marriage contract, written for a couple in very different circumstances, is preserved in its entirety in the Granadan collection.[11] Fāṭima, daughter of ʿAlī b. Mūsā b. Ibrāhīm b. ʿUbayd Allāh al-Lakhmī, and her groom, Abū Isḥāq Ibrāhīm, belonged to families whose members were refugees from neighbouring Baza now resident in Granada, and both were still under the guardianship of their respective parents. They were less well off economically than the first couple, and, as newcomers, were also at the margin of society. The marriage contract, which was signed on 11 November 1438, mentioned only one piece of property in addition to the *ṣadāq*.[12] Fāṭima, who was given in marriage by her father, was to receive a *ṣadāq* of 600 silver dinars, 375 of which she had already received, while the remaining 225 were to be paid to her two full years from the date of the document.[13] Her future mother-in-law, ʿĀʾisha bt. ʿAbd Allāh b. Mufaḍḍal, who was her son's property executor, gave Fāṭima an orchard bordering on her daughter's property as a *niḥla*. Unlike Umm al-Fatḥ, Fāṭima did not acquire, nor was she promised, any property from her family. She did not gain control over any property upon her marriage, nor does the marriage contract tell us whether she had any property under her father's control, even though we know from another document in the collection that she had indeed inherited property from her late mother in Baza.[14] Her future mother-in-law signed the marriage contract in her capacity as her son's guardian and undertook to fully execute the property transfer.

Another Granadan marriage, for which the contract has not survived but whose details were revealed during the division of the husband's estate following his death, united two scions of the city's prominent families: Fāṭima, granddaughter of the vizier Abū l-Nuʿaym Riḍwān,[15] and Abū Yazīd Khālid of the family of the Jāʾ al-Khayr. The *ṣadāq*, which sealed their union, was a fabulous sum of 110 gold dinars, together with a golden *farda* and a slave.[16] The first instalment of Fāṭima's *ṣadāq* was 525 silver dinars, but Abū Yazīd Khālid also left in his will a charitable bequest of 10 silver dinars as a *ṣadāq*, or wedding gift, for each of the poor and orphaned virgin brides of Granada. The will was signed on 18 August 1452, and the money was to come from the unencumbered third of his estate.[17]

The small number of marriage contracts found in the Granadan collection is not unusual when compared to other collections of court documents, but despite this relative paucity, these contracts constitute an ideal tool for introducing women's property rights.[18] Umm al-Fatḥ's marriage contract announced three of her property rights: the right to a *ṣadāq*, the right to gift and be gifted, and the right to inherit and bequeath. It also displayed two legal mechanisms in action that regulated her acquisition of property: guardianship and conveying and taking possession of property. For Umm al-Fatḥ, the marriage contract also inaugurated property control. Like any other woman in Granada, she was born into a world where women's property rights entitled her to acquire property, beginning with the *ṣadāq*. As the first right to be exercised and acquired by a young woman, the *ṣadāq* can be seen to inaugurate the process of acquiring female property rights.

Legal Framework of the Ṣadāq

Uniting all marriages and marriage contracts in Granada, as elsewhere, was the *ṣadāq*, a sum of money in the city's or region's currency that was given by the groom to the bride and specified in the contract. The *ṣadāq* was the first of many cash or goods transfers that could take place between spouses, but unlike other gifts, the *ṣadāq* formed a legal category by itself; it was a mandatory gift allotted only to females, and again unlike other gifts, it had to be gifted at a precise moment.[19]

The historiography of the *ṣadāq* as a woman's property right began with the Qur'anic dictum "Give to women their dowers willingly," a command that created a legal property obligation between future husband and wife (Q 4:4).[20] By the tenth century a fully developed legal framework for the *ṣadāq*, which included instructions for its acquisition, appeared in the law books. An early definition is found in a Maliki law manual known as the *Risāla*, written by the North African Ibn Abī Zayd al-Qayrawānī in 938.

> For a marriage to be valid, the bridegroom must give a *ṣadāq* in the form of property with a commercial value to his future wife prior to consummation . . . Any incorrect reference to the *ṣadāq* that has been introduced into the marriage contract invalidates the marriage . . . A marriage contract containing uncertainties concerning the *ṣadāq* should be cancelled before the marriage proceeds to consummation . . . If a marriage is consummated without it, it should proceed nonetheless, but a *ṣadāq* for the amount is due. A marriage without a *ṣadāq* is called an "empty" marriage and is only feasible under certain circumstances . . . A marriage can be concluded without a *ṣadāq*, but the husband has to fix for his wife a *ṣadāq* at a later point . . . If it is equivalent to what other spouses have received, she is obliged to accept it. If it is lower, she does not have to accept it . . . While a marriage to a man on his sick bed is not allowed, if it has been consummated, she can collect her *ṣadāq* from one-third of the estate, but she cannot inherit.[21]

The *Risāla*, believed to have been written when the author, who died in 996, was only seventeen, quickly became accepted and was used throughout Muslim Spain even though the author could have been suspected of lacking the influence of age and experience. Andalusians held the manual in great esteem and continued to use it even after the Christian conquest when the region was no longer under Islamic rule. As indicated by the many copies made when the community had *mudejar* status—that is, lived under the new regime that the Christian kings imposed on the Spanish Muslim communities after the conquest—it has become a veritable legal manual.[22] The *Risāla* shows that followers of the Maliki school adopted an all-powerful stand on the mandatory nature of the *ṣadāq*.[23] By the fourteenth century, the Granadan jurist Ibn Juzayy stated: "The *ṣadāq* is a necessary condition for marriage, and forgiving it voluntarily is not permitted, nor is it permitted to stipulate its forgiveness."[24] In our sources, for the notaries concerned with the status of marriages, which they registered in the contracts, for the jurists who adjudicated marriages in court, and for the muftis who deliberated on marriages in their legal opinions, a *ṣadāq* was the only property transfer required for a legally valid marriage, and the wife was its mandatory recipient.[25]

Acquiring one's *ṣadāq* was another matter. Despite what the legal manuals say about the unified nature of the *ṣadāq* as a gift, the records reveal the contrary. Unlike other gifts, the *ṣadāq* was split into two instalments, the first given immediately upon marriage and the second delayed, and again unlike other gifts, the content of its first instalment, denominated in coins, was legally converted in the process into household items. As a result, the *ṣadāq* also consisted of acquiring two different kinds of property: material goods in the first instalment and cash in the second. All legal sources, except the *fiqh* itself, show that only the first instalment (*naqd*) of the required *ṣadāq*, a sum of money denominated in the marriage contract and pledged in its entirety to the bride, was delivered at the moment of the wedding. Moreover, on delivery, this portion was transformed into household goods. The second portion became a *kāliʾ* (deferred instalment), also of a specified monetary value, that was paid later in cash. Although a definite date for its payment was entered in the marriage contract, no payment was made on this date. Since acquisition itself was divided and two acquisition dates were given, the wife acquired her *ṣadāq* under two different legal property regimes: the first when she was a minor and restricted in property matters and the second when most wives, but not all, were of majority status.

The legal status of the *ṣadāq*'s division into two instalments was ambivalent since it could not be traced to a direct Qurʾanic dictum, yet it seems to have been decided at an earlier date and universally adopted throughout the Islamic lands. The practice of not paying the second instalment on the date specified surfaced as early as the eighth century in marriage contracts from early Islamic Egypt, probably imitating local traditions or existing Mediterranean social structures.[26] The marriage contracts show that the deferred *ṣadāq* appeared at the same time as the early gift to divorcees disappeared, transforming the *kāliʾ* into a payment destined to guarantee the wife support at the moment when her husband's income was no longer available to her. The dual timing of the *ṣadāq*'s acquisition became the norm in the Maliki school, but since it was a deviation from the strict Qurʾanic rule, it could not go unmentioned by the jurists. Protest against the practice has been traced all the way back to Mālik, the eighth-century eponym of the school, while later generations of Maliki jurists were content simply to register their awareness of the objection in their law books *de rigueur*.[27] The fourteenth-century Ibn Juzayy was no exception, writing in his manual that "it is permissible that the *ṣadāq* be *naqd* and that a *kāli'* be paid at a given date . . . It is commendable, however, to combine the two."[28]

Acquisition of the First Ṣadāq Instalment: Daughters versus Fathers

The community's historical compliance with the instructions for the *ṣadāq*'s acquisition can be inferred from the model notarial contracts, which specify the details of acquisition, from fatwas dealing with cases of noncompliance, from the Granadan marriage contracts themselves, and from court cases. The sources indicate that in acquiring the first instalment a wife encountered a particular set of obstacles that recast the property relations between father, daughter, and future husband in an unenviable light. Most brides embarking on their first marriage were still under guardianship and therefore dependent on their fathers to physically acquire and administrate the *ṣadāq* for them. (Umm al-Fatḥ, an older and orphaned bride, who was entitled to take possession of all of her properties, including the *ṣadāq*, was an exception to the rule.) The father thus dominated the first half of the acquisition process of the first instalment, receiving the cash from the groom. He was also put in charge of acquiring the cash and buying the trousseau (*jihāz*) with it, purchasing household items, utensils, and clothes to make up the *jihāz*, which the Andalusian model notarial manuals insisted was his legal obligation.[29] Instead of a cash payment, the *ṣadāq* could be given in the form of a slave or a house, but such items were supposed to be sold and the proceeds used to purchase the goods for the trousseau.

Once complete, the trousseau had to be delivered to the bride's home so that it would be physically available to her prior to the consummation of her marriage, as required by law. No formal process of taking possession, normally required in all matters of property acquisition and transfer, could be performed since the daughter was usually young and still under the restrictions of her father's guardianship.

Since this part of the first instalment of the *ṣadāq* was the only gift to which the bride was legally entitled before the consummation of her marriage, problems abound. Both the model notarial manuals and the fatwas show that the acquisition of the first instalment pitted daughters against fathers. The notaries provided an array of model contracts to ease the process. The Toledan notary Ibn Mughīth drafted a model to be used by a father whose daughter claimed that she had not received the trousseau in its entirety. This was a model deposition in which the father enumerated the items that he had bought with his daughter's cash *ṣadāq* and stated under oath that he had delivered every item to her new home. The model reads as follows:

> When the father, or the property guardian, transfers the trousseau, which he has bought with her cash *ṣadāq*, to her husband's home, you [the notary] should write: So-and-so transferred to his daughter so-and-so's new home [whether she is under guardianship or an orphan] all that he has bought with her cash *ṣadāq*, which he took from her husband so-and-so. These include the following items: a cloth item of the following description, bought for so much, and another item, description and price, until he has accounted for everything. Then you will write: all this was delivered to the house of so-and-so for his wife so-and-so in the city of/quarter of by the person so-and-so and in the presence of a witness, whose name appears at the bottom of this document, and in the presence of the husband.[30]

In the commentary Ibn Mughīth explains: "There were cases when a married daughter approached her father claiming that he took her *ṣadāq* and did not buy her a trousseau with it, and if her husband supported her claim, she would be entitled to compensation, unless such a document was signed in advance."[31]

In cases where the trousseau's inventory was not recorded and where the daughter did not acquire her *ṣadāq*, jurists were expected to give the father the benefit of the doubt, even when the daughter testified against him. They would side with the father because a father's reputation was regarded as beyond dispute and unassailable. Ibn al-ʿAṭṭār wrote in his commentary: "A father may testify under oath that due to an unfortunate turn of events, his daughter's *ṣadāq* was ruined in his hands, and . . . her husband will be given the right to consummate his marriage to her without a *ṣadāq*."[32]

Why was the father given the benefit of the doubt? The reason, said one notary, was that all fathers were equally believed to be "righteous and pious" and thus enjoyed a status shared by the court witnesses (*ʿudūl*), whom no one would suspect of giving false evidence.[33] The father's privileged legal status with regard to his daughter's *ṣadāq* was defined by the celebrated Maliki jurist Ibn Rushd, grandfather of the philosopher, who wrote in twelfth-century Cordova that when divorce occurred before the marriage was consummated, the father was entitled to his daughter's share of the *ṣadāq*. He argued that if the marriage did not proceed to consummation, an outcome linked to the father's obligation to provide the trousseau, then the wife's right to a *ṣadāq* was overridden by her father's right.[34] He went further, arguing that a father had a claim over his daughters' *ṣadāq* even in cases when consummation took place but no cohabitation ensued. The father was entitled to his share of the *ṣadāq* presumably to defray costs.[35] Also the father had the right to request and receive compensation from the groom at the moment of marriage, over and above the *ṣadāq* given to his daughter. Ibn Rushd restated the Maliki rule that if such stipulations were made in the marriage contract, the payments were illegal, but when compensation was agreed to after the wedding, the father would receive his share without affecting that of the bride.[36] What was the historical framework for such stipulations? While we may see in this evidence that both the law and society resisted shaking off an earlier concept that recognized a father's property rights respecting his daughters, it is possible to see here an outcome stemming from the practice of concluding children's marriages before puberty, which was common in Muslim Spain as well as in other regions.[37] The law allowed that once the age of sexual majority was reached, both groom and bride had the right to contest not only the price of the *ṣadāq*, but also their consent to the marriage itself. In cases where such pre-puberty marriages fell apart, the law appears to have recognized the father's privileged status even though the expenses incurred were not specified.

The cases brought before jurists, judges, and muftis, as well as those discussed in the Maliki fatwas from North Africa and Spain, show that disputes between daughters and fathers over acquisition of the *ṣadāq*'s first instalment took place either immediately after the wedding or during the following protracted period of the young wife's guardianship.[38] Complaints reported in the fatwas against fathers include such violations as mishandling the cash or the goods, not remitting the full amount to the daughter, trying to regain control of the *ṣadāq*, returning all or part of the *ṣadāq* to the husband, or simply appropriating and using the *ṣadāq* money for other purposes rather than delivering all of it to a daughter's new home. At this stage the battle over acquisition might also have involved the husband. On one occasion a father repossessed his married daughter's property (*matāʿ*) and trousseau after it was delivered to her home, claiming that since she was under his guardianship, he had the right to do so. In his ruling, the mufti Ibn Lubāba (d. 914) had to navigate a narrow path between the competing rights of the father/guardian, the daughter/wife, and the husband:[39]

> Since the woman's husband had already benefited from his wife's trousseau for more than a year, as she was living in her husband's home for this time, her father had to have a very compelling reason for launching an attempt to regain

control of it. He could take possession only if this was done to benefit his daughter and not to injure the husband (*iḍār bi 'l-zawj*). If he demanded that he regain possession because of some enmity between himself and his son-in-law, such action was not permissible, except if the latter was unreliable (*ghayr ma'mūn ʿalayhi*); e.g., unscrupulous (*khalīʿ*), a sinner (*fāsiq*), or a spendthrift (*mitlāf*).[40]

In another fatwa, a father claimed the cloth that he had bought with his daughter's *naqd* under the law of guardianship, stating that she was a spendthrift (*safīha*), a clause used when denying women freedom from interdiction.[41] Other fatwas seem to point to a local practice whereby, under the pretext of benefiting the daughter, her *ṣadāq* was given to her husband, thus prohibiting her acquisition of the first instalment. The fatwas describe a variety of cases in which, after supposedly "consulting" with his daughter, a father purchased a house in which husband and wife would live together using her *ṣadāq* or other property that he had given her.[42] Abū Isḥāq Ibrāhīm al-Tūnisī (d. 1051) described this practice in the Ifrīqiyan towns of Zawīla and al-Mahdiyya and stated categorically that the father's use of his daughter's property in this manner was not permissible and would cause considerable strife in event of divorce. In yet another fatwa, we find evidence to the contrary. Here, a father used the *ṣadāq* agreement to insert a clause into the marriage contract protecting his daughter's property (*māl*) from being utilized by her husband without her permission.[43]

The law divided the acquisition process into two stages, which the notaries articulated by providing each stage with its own deed. The acquisition of the first *ṣadāq* instalment was a matter of considerable importance for all concerned—father, daughter, and husband—but the father was clearly the dominant figure at this stage and was able to hamper, even to challenge, his daughter's acquisition of this instalment. A very different family dynamic arose during acquisition of the second *ṣadāq* instalment.

Acquisition of the Second Ṣadāq Instalment: Wives and Husbands

All legal manuals agree that a specific date was required for payment of the *kāliʾ* and that this date was to be inserted into the marriage contract. Indeed, all marriage contracts have one. However, acquisition of the *kāliʾ* was a different matter and contravened the letter of the law. In fact, payment never occurred on the stated date but on the occasion of divorce or widowhood. The mufti and jurist al-ʿAbdūsī of fifteenth-century Fez confirmed that "the custom is to delay the *kāliʾ* request until the occasion of death or divorce."[44] Why, then, was the practice of entering a date maintained at all? This was done to create an obligation and to stipulate that from the specified date onward the debt would be available for collection. Without a definite date, the promise of a payment would not have been valid. Inserting a date into the marriage contract meant that the *kālīʾ* became a debt owed to the wife that could be neither conveniently forgotten by the husband nor overlooked by the wife, even if she were willing to do so. If no acquisition took place, the amount owed became part of the estate.

The notary Ibn Salmūn, who practiced at a time closer to the period of the Granadan documents, provided a model document to be used by wives that acknowledged acquisition of the *kālīʾ* without mention of its precise timing, a reference to the practice of acquiring the second instalment upon divorce or a husband's death.[45] Indeed, by the eleventh century, the practice of officially discharging the *kālīʾ* at such times was well established in al-Andalus, where a woman's right to the *kālīʾ* was exercised mostly during an estate's division, when it assumed priority, the amount being deducted and paid to the widow before the estate's division could proceed. The Granadan documents illustrate such cases of the second instalment's acquisition during an estate division. One such instance was the case of Maryam bt. Muḥammad b. Faraj, whose uncollected *kālīʾ* of 7.5 dinars was excluded from her late husband Aḥmad b. Muḥammad al-Ruffa's estate.[46] In another court document registered on 19 December 1467, Muḥammad b. Muḥammad Baḥṭān went to court to sue his stepfather for not excluding from his late mother's estate before division the outstanding *kālīʾ* of 15 silver dinars, to which he, as an heir, had a claim.[47] Fatwas from fifteenth-century Granada contain additional cases where children went to court to sue over this very same issue.[48] Court records from fourteenth-century Jerusalem show uncollected deferred payments of as little as 5 dinars and as much as 36 dinars in the estates of various women.[49]

The notaries were well aware of possible litigations over this issue. Ibn Mughīth instructed notaries on how to deal with discharging the payment in cases of estate division: "The *kālīʾ* is a debt, and you cannot include in the same document both its settlement and the settlement of the wife's claims on the estate; only the ignorant will combine these two in one document."[50]

Nonetheless, acquisition of the second instalment was not always easy for widows. Two fatwas, one from the Maghrib and the other from al-Andalus, show the challenges that faced women seeking to acquire their *kālīʾ* upon the death of a husband. The first fatwa states:

> The Tunisian mufti al-Waghlīsī (d. 1384) was asked about a widow who wanted to collect her *mahr* [or *ṣadāq*] from grain left by her husband in storage; the value

of the grain was estimated as equal to or less than the amount registered as her delayed *ṣadāq*. Was it admissible for the widow to accept this rough estimate of what she was owed, or should the grain be removed from storage and weighed so that its exact worth could be determined? The mufti replied that it was not lawful to pay the widow without weighing the grain and calculating her exact due; failure to do so would invalidate the transaction, which is similar to a sale.[51]

In the second fatwa, written in an unspecified locality in al-Andalus, a widow demanded payment of the rest of her *ṣadāq* upon the death of her husband. However, one of her sons had already sold a garden that was part of the estate. The mufti responded that the debt was payable upon the husband's death and before his properties were sold. The widow was entitled to block any attempt by the heirs to exercise their inheritance rights before she had exercised her *ṣadāq* rights.[52] The potential for the husband's heirs to challenge the widow's right to collect the *kāli'* from her husband's estate increased in cases of second marriages, but the jurists were adamant that widows negatively affected by the sale of her husband's estate were entitled to sue the buyer.[53]

Even though the *kāli'* was supposed to provide protection to the wife upon divorce or widowhood, a father could manage to acquire it while his daughter was still under guardianship and thus subject to *maḥjūra* (interdiction in property matters). A husband who appealed to the mufti al-ʿAbdūsī in fifteenth-century Fez complained that his father-in-law had collected the *kāli'* from him and was using it for his own needs, whereas he wanted his wife to buy clothes with it, making herself beautiful for his sake (*li-tatajammal bihi ilayhi*), which was more in keeping with how the first instalment was generally used.[54] Al-ʿAbdūsī replied that the husband had a claim only over the *naqd*, which could be used to enhance the wife's beauty, and that the father's motives and actions had to be trusted unless proven otherwise.

The legal protection accorded the *ṣadāq* as a woman's property right, as manifested in the acquisition deeds drafted by notaries for the first instalment, extended to acquiring the *kāli'*. The Toledan Ibn Mughīth provided in his manual several such deeds meant to accommodate the different circumstances that might affect payment of the deferred *ṣadāq*. The first deed addressed the need to renew a lost or a damaged marriage contract in order to verify the amount of the *ṣadāq* still owed to the wife. In this deed the husband recognized in the presence of witnesses that he had contracted to pay his wife a *ṣadāq* of a specified amount, that he had already paid the first instalment, and that the remainder was due on a given date.[55] Ibn Mughīth left it to the individual notary to decide whether to have the wife testify to the accuracy of the document, including its claim that there were no other property items mentioned in the original document. If a wife claimed more than the registered amount and no deed could be furnished, the husband would be required to take an oath confirming the accuracy of his deposition. The second deed included in Ibn Mughīth's manual was meant to accommodate a husband by providing a model document in which the wife could acknowledge, upon his request, past receipt of the deferred instalment.[56]

Because the *kāliʾ* was defined as the husband's debt, it was much easier to acquire and less frequently challenged in comparison to the *naqd*. However, the status of the *kāliʾ* as a debt also meant that the wife could forgive it in exchange for one of her husband's rights. This option inaugurated a new dynamic in the relationship between husband and wife.

Forgiving and Exchanging the Kāliʾ

On 17 July 1474 ʿĀʾisha bt. Abī ʿUthmān Saʿd b. Aḥmad appeared in court accompanied by her parents to register her *khulʿ* divorce from her husband, Muḥammad b. Aḥmad al-Ashkar. In accordance with the terms of a *khulʿ* divorce, in exchange for her release from the marriage, she signed away several of her property rights, among them her rights to the deferred *ṣadāq*, to maintenance for herself and her daughter, and to support for any future child that she might be carrying.[57] The notary consulted her *ṣadāq* contract and confirmed the renunciation of these rights, concluding with the formula "the wife is divorced in return for all the rights to which she is entitled by this marriage contract" (*ikhtalaʿat al-zawja bi-kull ḥaqq lahā fī hādhā l-ṣadāq*).[58] This phrase echoed the one used to seal the marriage contract: "with this contract, the marriage is contracted and sealed" (*wa-ʿalayhā inʿaqada al-nikāḥ al-madhkūr wa-bi-sababihā tamma*).[59] Her parents, Saʿd b. Aḥmad al-Muʾadhdhin and Fāṭima bt. Aḥmad al-Sharqī, signed the document as witnesses to the renunciation of their daughter's rights and had to specify that they would not sue for these rights at a later date.

The parents' participation clearly indicates that despite being a wife and a mother, ʿĀʾisha was still a minor under guardianship and that she had not yet acquired her property rights.[60] Nevertheless, their existence was not denied in the settlement of the *khulʿ* divorce. Ibn Juzayy referred to such an exchange of rights in his legal manual: "When she has gifted him any property for a divorce, she has divorced herself from him."[61] Of interest here is the principle behind the exchange, a provision that seems to be as old as the *ṣadāq* itself and that was probably inspired by the rest of the Qur'anic dictum, quoted earlier, that enshrined it: "Give to women their dowers willingly, but if they forego part of it themselves, then use it to your advantage" (Q 4:4). As a result, trading a property right or a property for another right in the sphere of family law was feasible and acceptable. In addition to making it possible to initiate and obtain a divorce, the *kāliʾ* could also be forgiven in return for the husband's relinquishing his right either to marry a second wife or to demand that his wife travel with him, leaving behind her hometown and family.

Once the principle was admitted, forgiving the *kāliʾ* expanded to other areas. In their manuals Ibn al-ʿAṭṭār and Ibn Mughīth each offered a model deed by which a woman could renounce the *kāliʾ* in other circumstances. Ibn al-ʿAṭṭār's deed enabled a widow to renounce the delayed part of her *ṣadāq* to the benefit of her dead husband's heirs.[62] A second deed enabled her to renounce her share in the estate altogether.[63] Ibn Mughīth provided only one model, which enabled a widow to forgive the *kāliʾ* to the benefit of the heirs,[64] but in another deed that he drafted, a wife could renounce the *kāliʾ* for much "loftier" gains—for instance, in recognition of the husband's fine conjugal treatment. Before him in tenth-century Cordova, Ibn al-ʿAṭṭār had drafted two model deeds, in the first of which the wife renounced the deferred *ṣadāq*, citing as the reason the "good treatment" that she had received during the marriage.[65] In their respective manuals, Ibn Mughīth and al-Jazīrī included the renunciation deed immediately following the model marriage contract.[66] Ibn Mughīth drafted a contract in which a wife signed a deposition (*waḍʿ*) renouncing her right to the deferred *ṣadāq* in recognition of what the jurist called "her gratification with his companionship and their admirable matrimonial relationship."[67] Ibn Salmūn, the fourteenth-century Granadan notary, extended this voluntary renunciation of the *ṣadāq* to a woman's father and incorporated both models into a single notarial deed.[68]

Registering such transactions was similar to acquiring any other debt. As recipient of the debt's forgiveness, the husband was required to be present and to claim the property right by performing a possession-taking ritual (*ḥiyāza*) that used the same phrases and reasoning mentioned by the tenth-century notaries.[69] Given the serious nature of the transaction, namely, the renunciation of property—not only alimony and support in the event of divorce or death, but also and primarily part of the wife's estate—it could trigger law suits by the wife's heirs. This explains why all the parties had to acknowledge the transaction in writing in the same document. It also fell to the notary approached by a wife seeking to release her husband from his debt to verify that she was indeed aware of her rights and of the implications of her decision. Ibn Mughīth required the witnesses to verify the wife's identity before signing the document testifying that she was of sound mind and body and that the husband had received the renunciation from her. Unlike commercial deeds, which could be recorded without the woman's physical presence, this act required both husband's and wife's presence and the witnesses' testimony. In fact, their presence served as evidence; in their absence, the document's validity could be contested.[70]

Since a monogamous marriage and a promise that the wife would not be forced to travel away from her hometown could have been imposed on the husband in the initial marriage contract, what could have motivated a wife to give up property in return for the intangible gift of having her husband's good "conjugal behaviour" recognized?[71] One reason was that marriages were concluded by fathers for minor daughters still under guardianship; imposing limitations on the husband was possibly not paramount in a father's mind at that time. Once a daughter was free of guardianship and had gained power over her assets and resources, different considerations could influence such decisions. Most prominent was the threat of another wife and more children with rights to shares of the estate. A monogamous marriage was a desirable objective for a wife not only because she did not have to share her husband with another woman, but also because she did not want her husband's estate divided among several wives and their offspring, thus diminishing her own share and that of her children. However, exacting a promise of monogamy from the husband would not necessarily have limited his sexual activities since he could avail himself of a concubine if he could afford one.[72]

Anthropologists suggest a link between property ownership and monogamous marriages, pointing to evidence that the conjugal relationship changed in favour of monogamy in societies where women were heirs to significant property.[73] The Islamic practice of renouncing a property right is also intriguing in other ways—for instance, because it contravened the rule that in all commercial transactions the value of the items exchanged had to be fully known and had to have a comparable market value. In the case of renunciation, this requirement was not fulfilled: whereas the *kālī'* was always stated in precise and recognized monetary units, this was not the case with "conjugal behaviour." Feelings of "happiness" or the husband's "good" marital conduct could not be expressed in monetary terms. Nevertheless, the constant existence in the notary manuals of legal deeds for the renouncement of the second *ṣadāq* instalment most likely points to a practice. While the service rendered by the notaries in these matters could well have been in use because it was what wives wanted, the discourse that accompanied the act of renunciation—namely, "in recognition of his kind behaviour"—is remindful of the modern feminist theory, mentioned earlier, explaining how women lose property rights. The legal discourse uttered by the notaries corresponds to Carole Rose's examination of the link between women's "taste for cooperation," their loss of property, and the role that jurists play in facilitating this loss.[74] Can the wife's voluntary renunciation of the second *ṣadāq* instalment be seen as the Islamic equivalent of this process?

The Ṣadāq As an Economic Agent

Within the framework of a study of economic history such as this one, evidence regarding the *ṣadāq* ultimately raises questions about whether it was a positive element that helped to promote economic development and whether it was an instigator of wealth accumulation. Of interest here is the *ṣadāq*'s potential as an economic agent. Given its status as a mandatory transfer of property to women, the *ṣadāq* was significant in terms of women's property ownership, although its exact magnitude cannot be verified. Few data are available for quantitative study, and Hady Idris, who collected some monetary evidence from fatwas, could not derive any conclusions from his findings for lack of both sufficient data and a comparative framework.[75] Nonetheless, some reflections can be offered on the potential economic agency that the *ṣadāq* payments afforded women. The practice of paying the entire amount in two instalments created two separate data items with two potential economic effects. When in the form of cash capital, the *ṣadāq* could, at least in theory, be invested with an expectation of return and growth. The value of the 6 gold dinars that Umm al-Fatḥ received was not insignificant, but this amount was dwarfed by the 110 gold dinars given to Fāṭima bt. Riḍwān, an outstanding sum of money that, when invested by her guardian, generated a substantial return.[76] If the return depended on the initial sum and the cash amount was small, its economic potential was reduced. By comparison, if substantial enough, this sum could be invested in merchandise bought for trade or in property to be rented out, or it could be loaned out in anticipation of a handsome return, all of which are activities that the Granadan women undertook.[77] However, the *ṣadāq*'s economic potential was affected not only by the amount of capital that brides received, but equally by their inability to invest it themselves for the duration of their minority status. Still, the question of the *ṣadāq*'s potential investment value is strictly theoretical given that the first instalment's potential was greatly reduced, or even eliminated, by the practice of converting the original cash capital into a trousseau consisting mostly of household items, including clothes, which were subject to considerable everyday wear and tear. The conversion of cash into goods left the wife in possession of property of declining value.

Because the second instalment was in fact a forced loan to the husband by the wife with a delayed and undetermined date of repayment, its investment potential was limited. In addition, the *kāliʾ* was always smaller than the first instalment, both in the Islamic West and in fourteenth-century Mamluk Egypt. Even if the money was invested, its economic potential was further reduced by young wives' limited exposure to the market.[78] If the *kāliʾ* was received upon divorce or widowhood, its investment potential was also reduced by the more limited time during which it could be invested. Nor was its use for everyday needs likely to produce a monetary return. Even when the *kāliʾ* was actually acquired and this small amount invested, it produced little or no return. Although the *ṣadāq* was a well-protected property right, it had limited potential as an economic asset in the hands of women. As we shall see, this potential was affected by additional legal factors as well as by individual and personal social and economic conditions.

The Ṣadāq in Comparative Historical Context

The first context to be examined is that of Islamic societies elsewhere. Court documents and other related sources from the regions falling under Hanafi law confirm that the *ṣadāq* retained the features observed earlier. Studies of records from the Balkan provinces, where the registration of marriages according to Islamic law was introduced as early as the sixteenth century,[79] from Anatolia, as represented by the seventeenth-century town of Kayseri, from the eighteenth- and nineteenth-century records of Rumelia, and from twentieth-century Palestine show that the prices of the first and deferred *ṣadāq* instalments were fixed using the monetary units in circulation (*akçe* and *gurus*) but that payment may have also included property, clothes, and jewelry, these presumably comprising the trousseau.[80] The records of the Hanafi courts also show careful attention to detail when recording the *ṣadāq* and its acquisition.[81] The Ottoman historians maintained and confirmed the singular status of the marriage gift: "The *mehr* [or *ṣadāq*] required by the *şeriat* [Shariʿa] seemed to be the only contractual obligation that consistently appeared in the registration."[82] The Ottoman courts also confirmed that the first instalment of the *ṣadāq* was to be transferred to the wife, while the deferred part was to be collected on the occasion of divorce or a husband's death.[83] Because non-payment of the *kāliʾ*

was taken seriously in the case of a *khulʿ* divorce, Ottoman husbands made their ex-wives come to court and take an oath that the payment had indeed been made.[84] The practice of renouncing the deferred *ṣadāq* in a *khulʿ* divorce was also common in Ottoman Kayseri and Rumelia, where wives also renounced maintenance rights, such as the *nafaqa* (financial support during the *ʿidda*, the period after divorce when a woman could not remarry).[85]

While the evidence seems to confirm the strength of the *ṣadāq*'s hold on Islamic societies, fitting the *ṣadāq* into universal models is not easy since most models approach the marriage gift as a transfer of funds or property between the contracting families, which the Islamic model was not. The Islamic version did not form the basis of conjugal property, as the European model did. Nonetheless, its historical origins were to be found in Roman and Middle Eastern legal precedents, and its universal practice in the Mediterranean world may offer some clues about where Islamic patterns originated. The practice of paying a brideprice predated Islam and was observed among the Arabs. Moreover, the Roman practice of paying "three annual instalments in the case of money or other fungibles" in the second century B.C., the Ciceronian age, could have inspired the Islamic pattern of instalments.[86] However, the Roman model used the dowry as one element in the process of the devolution of family property, which the *ṣadāq* was not.[87] On the contrary, what distinguished the *ṣadāq* was its status as an independent right rather than as an instrument in property devolution.

A comparative study of the evolution and divergence of Jewish and European marriage gifts does indeed show a relation between these gifts and inheritance rights. Evidence suggests that in the Jewish experience, the marriage gift and the status of marriage as a whole among Jewish communities living in the vicinity of Muslims acquired some features of the *ṣadāq*.[88] New rules, originally not found in the Talmud, appeared in the Geonic literature and in the Geniza documents, including the monogamy clause in the Jewish marriage contract (*ketubbah*), the wife's right to initiate divorce, and division of the marriage gift, as stated in the contract, into "advanced" and "delayed" payments.[89] Since both the Geonic and Geniza periods correspond to the time frame of Islamic rule in the Middle East, one can speculate that Islamic law influenced these provisions and that the patterns of implementation were borrowed from the Islamic *ṣadāq*. In discussing the question of why these changes to Jewish custom occurred, Gideon Libson hypothesizes that where Jews lived in proximity to those practising Islamic law after the eighth century, it became expedient to accommodate the customs of Islamic society. Whereas Jewish law had initially an influence on Islamic law, Jewish customs were now influenced by the latter.[90] This development is indeed striking: the *mohar* (money paid by the groom to the wife's father) of Biblical times was gradually replaced in Talmudic times by a *nedunia* (dowry) brought to the marriage by the bride, an arrangement facilitated by the *ketubbah*'s stipulation that the husband was required to compensate his wife if he divorced her.[91] The singular status of the wife's property in the Islamic marriage contract was not fully assimilated into the Jewish marriage, even though the wife's property, including the dowry that she brought to her husband and other property that she owned or acquired during the marriage, did not become conjugal property. The Jewish wife retained ownership of this property during the marriage, although she was expected to allow her husband to manage and invest it as he saw fit and to appropriate the income for the household. Nonetheless, the husband did not require her permission to conduct transactions using her property as long as the initial capital remained intact and available to be claimed in the case of a divorce. If the investment of the wife's property produced revenue, the value of the *nedunia*, plus an additional one-third or one-half, would be repaid to the wife.

An even more compelling example of the influence of Islamic society is that Jewish women who were satisfied with the new status of property relations in marriage did not attempt to contest their *nedunia* arrangements in the Islamic courts or to register them according to Islamic law, which they had done on other occasions when they stood to lose more—for instance, when they were deprived of their inheritance. Among the Geniza Hebrew court documents, Shlomo Dov Goitein found evidence that appeals were made to the Islamic courts in matters of inheritance and that Jews' wills were registered in the Islamic courts, a practice accompanied by an increased number of complaints from the rabbis.[92] This demonstrated an awareness among Jews of the strength of women's property rights under Islamic law. Moreover, because Jewish women could not inherit property unless they were the sole surviving heir, they appealed to the Islamic courts if male relatives denied them a share of their inheritance. Although Jewish women were clearly not shy about appealing to Islamic courts when the law benefited them, they did not seem to do so in matters involving complaints regarding *mohar* practices. Jewish men also appealed to Islamic justice when they could not obtain a divorce under Jewish law—for instance, when someone with the surname Cohen or Levy wanted to marry a divorced women, which was forbidden—as well as when they wanted to force a divorced wife to come to court to testify that no money was owed to her. To force an ex-wife to appear in court, Jewish husbands from Lucena, a town near Granada, used a *shtar* (notarial model) drafted in Hebrew that brings to mind models used within the Andalusian notarial practice.[93] The Geniza documents from Egypt also reveal that the rabbinical courts adopted an attitude similar to that of the Islamic courts in demanding the payment of the delayed instalment to a divorced wife.[94] Whether Jewish law voluntarily adopted the unique structures of the Islamic *ṣadāq*, seeing in it a beneficial or useful institution, or was forced to do so as a result of Jewish women's insistence, Jewish communities shared the practice with Islamic society and ensured its legal protection.

On the European side, the Germanic marriage gift (*Morgengabe*) from the husband to the bride, which had become quite considerable by the eighth century, was similar to the Islamic marriage gift in so far as the woman was the recipient but otherwise contradicted the Muslim women's property rights. The *Morgengabe* did not guarantee the bride entitlement to her dower after her husband's death but was subject to inheritance laws and to the demands of his heirs.[95] In the later Middle Ages the husband's generous *Morgengabe* to his wife became the father's gift to the husband.[96] In fifteenth-century Italian cities, as in the rest of Southern Europe, this shift to a dowry system, in which the bride's father made a donation to her groom, further eroded the rights of women in relation to the marriage gift and led to the disinheritance of daughters. In tracing the development of the dowry from its early stages in the Middle East, Diane Owen Hughes does not mention the Islamic case.[97] However, it is evident that the *ṣadāq* was distinct from the European dowry not only in its trajectory from the groom to the bride, but also in its implications for other property rights—notably, the devolution of property.

Italian daughters were regularly disinherited through their dowries, in contrast to the Islamic case, where the husband's gift to his wife corresponded to a growing recognition of the daughters' inheritance rights. The shift from brideprice to a dowry has been interpreted as an evolution toward higher civilization and alternatively explained as resulting from a shortage of men, but mostly it seems to reflect the privileging of patrilineal affiliation at the expense of the conjugal unit. A similar significance has been suggested for the appearance of filiation (*nasab*) in early Islamic law, but in contrast to what happened in Italy, filiation led to an improvement in Muslim women's property rights, especially those respecting inheritance. And the differences do not end there. While all models focus on the transfer of funds from father to husband, the model that Jack Goody terms an "indirect dowry" may be similar.[98]

The appearance in the Granadan marriage contract of the gifting of other properties alongside money, as was the case in Umm al-Fatḥ's marriage contract, has led some historians to conclude that the matter attended to in the marriage contract was in fact the devolution of a family's property. As a result, the *ṣadāq* has been seen as a sort of "generic dowry" meant to fulfill the role played by dowries in European societies.[99] However, the practice of registering additional properties seems unique to the Islamic West, where even the disputes and litigation documented in court records and fatwas indicate that when properties other than the *ṣadāq* were registered, they did not become legal components of the *ṣadāq* itself. None of the other Islamic regions shows a similar notarial practice of recording additional land gifts, nor do the marriage contracts from Mamluk Egypt or the court registers from the Ottoman lands testify to the existence of such patterns of gifting at marriage.[100] Further, the practice was controversial, and from a strictly legal point of view, uncalled for, since only the *ṣadāq* was mandatory for a valid marriage; hence the frequent appeals to muftis and courts to decide whether these gifts were valid under the law.[101]

To construct a complete system of property devolution, Islamic law incorporated two other property rights—the gift and inheritance—and applied the mechanism of guardianship to women's property rights. Whereas demands in Europe for a larger and larger dowry forced families to marry off only one daughter, relegating the others to nunneries, the social mores of Islamic law established a more humane and equitable socio-moral order. The Italian practice, which stressed the dowry's value to the conjugal estate, followed the ancient Mediterranean societies of Greece and Rome, which also commonly practiced endowment of women at marriage, but this was not the case with the Islamic marriage gift. Property devolution, in the theoretical and legal sense and in practice, was fulfilled by inheritance law. Women's property remained separate from that of their husbands for the entire duration of the marriage and was inherited by the wife's relatives, including her husband. When collaboration between husband and wife occurred, the economic benefit of both their properties was enhanced. However, there was no legal way to force them to cooperate.

While the unique features of Islamic female property rights will become clearer as we progress, at this stage it is sufficient to say that none of the systems that practiced dowry seems to have insisted as much on the woman's entitlement as did the Islamic one with the *ṣadāq*. That Islamic society in general adopted the *ṣadāq* as it did might therefore indicate recognition of social and economic conditions favouring its continuance. This is not to say that society as a whole was oblivious to the future needs of unmarried girls. All societies shared a concern to address their monetary needs prior to marriage, whether the marriage gift came from the bride's or the groom's side. In Jewish law, upon the father's death, the brother of a minor daughter was obligated to give her a minimum of 180 grams of silver as her future *nedunia*. Muslims looked after unmarried women by leaving them money in their wills, and in fourteenth-century Florence the institution

Monte delle doti was established to provide poor brides with financial support upon marriage.[102] However, the undeniable link between dowries and the devolution of family property in Europe stood in contrast to the *ṣadāq*, which established a legal and independent channel by which women could acquire property without depriving them of their share in the inheritance.

Conclusion

This chapter has dealt with questions about the *ṣadāq*, the first of a woman's property rights, focusing on its legal framework, particularly its timing and acquisition. Of interest are the *ṣadāq*'s operational uses, the family relationships involved in the process of acquiring it, the form in which it came into the wife's hands, and the cultural perceptions of marriage, family, and property that might be gleaned from legal records and juristic discourse concerning the *ṣadāq*. Marriage contracts have been shown to demonstrate only the first phase of the *ṣadāq*'s acquisition, while notarial manuals, court records, and fatwas have been crucial in providing evidence of the second and final phase. The evidence has confirmed that the *ṣadāq*'s legal status as a mandatory gift was in fact unchallenged in practice and that its central place was not obfuscated. Nonetheless, the evidence also shows that the process of acquisition was lengthy and sometimes convoluted, as it extended through the daughter's or wife's entire lifetime and could be disrupted during each phase of acquisition. Evidence that family members went to court to litigate for a share of any outstanding *ṣadāq* payment and evidence of the numerous issues involved in its acquisition indicate that although the *ṣadāq* was the wife's property, family members tended to regard it as a form of family inheritance and usually knew that they would be entitled to a share when the time came. For this reason, the practice was marred by legal challenges and noncompliance, but the actual numbers of such cases should not surprise us. Statistically, given the commonality of the *ṣadāq*, it is naturally represented in more disputes than are other property rights.

The *ṣadāq* represented property the acquisition of which was essential not only for husbands and wives, but also for their parents and children, making forgiveness of a *ṣadāq* debt dubious. When voluntary renunciation occurred, it was expected to benefit the wife materially and, in its own way, signalled the role of property rights in defining the conditions and status of a marriage. Renunciation sent the message that property rights were tangible assets, similar to property itself, that could be sold, purchased, or symbolically traded away in exchange for better treatment, love, companionship, and the like by either women or men. In the context of property rights, good conjugal treatment and emotional wellbeing had their market value. Through property rights, the law gave wives the distinct option of using their economic assets to create the kinds of conjugal relationships that they desired. Maintenance by jurists and the courts of the standards for registering marriage contracts and for resolving disputes was crucial to safeguarding the *ṣadāq*'s status as a property right and to ensuring the universality, resilience, and consistency of its acquisition.

Throughout this chapter I have used the term "*ṣadāq*" rather than the generic terms "dowry" or "Islamic dowry," as is sometimes done, in order to ensure a precise description of this particular entitlement and to distinguish it from the array of other forms of property exchange upon marriage. Because marriage inaugurated the wife's acquisition of her other property rights, there might be some impression that the *ṣadāq* was an organic part of property devolution. The comparative investigation has revealed that the Islamic *ṣadāq* was in fact different in theory and in practice from the European dowry, which played a role in the paradigm of property devolution. Neither the right to gift and be gifted in theory and practice nor the acquisition record of women's inheritance and the structure of women's property rights support a correlation between the European dowry and the *ṣadāq*. The uniformity of the Islamic practice and its paradigms—including its *longue durée*, its endurance in its current form, its mandatory nature, and its strength as a property right—, which is supported by records attesting to the *ṣadāq*'s constant acquisition, enhanced woman's rights to property. How additional property rights interacted with the *ṣadāq* to construct a woman's legal persona and propertied identity, how these rights were interpreted and handled by society, and how they were regarded by jurists and the courts are the focus of the next three chapters.

Two

THE INTER VIVOS GIFT

Gifts to Minors

On 8 February 1495, three years after the fall of Granada, a couple went to the city's Muslim court to register the gifting of a home to their minor daughter. The deed reads as follows:

> In the name of God, the kind and merciful, may his prayer be over our Lord, Muḥammad and his family. The most exalted and just spouses, Ḥakīm b. Ibrahīm [b.] Ghālib and Fāṭima bt. Abī Jaʿfar Aḥmad Musāʿid, are gifting their daughter, ʿĀʾisha, a youngster, under guardianship of her aforementioned father (*fī ḥajr wālidihā*), the whole house that they jointly own. The house is standing near the mosque al-Jawza in the Bayāzīn quarter in Granada. It is bordered on the south side by al-Ḥanīnī, on the north side by the road, on the east side by al-Shuwaykh, and on the west by the lane where the gate is situated. The house is gifted with all its rights and restrictions, contents, and adjacent parts (*maṣdarihā*), making it a complete, definitive, and final (*batāla*) gift severing all rights that the parents might have in it, such as ownership, money, or constructions. They surrender all this to ʿĀʾisha, making any money and property her possession. They no longer have any right in this house nor derive any income or benefit from it. They have vacated the above-mentioned house, and her father has transferred the property from himself and his previously mentioned wife to her and has accepted and taken possession of it on her behalf, to be in full control, until the daughter in question reaches adulthood. The witnesses identify the two parents and testify that they are in good health and of sound legal status. They signed the document on the twelfth of Jumādā l-ūlā, in the year nine hundred.[1]

When ʿĀʾisha's parents gifted their house to their minor daughter, Granada was a Muslim community with *mudejar* status—that is, no longer under Islamic rule but under a regime that had been negotiated for them in the capitulations of 1492. This status allowed them freedom of religion and protected their property from confiscation. The Muslim court continued to function, enabling them to register property transfers and business transactions.[2] Moreover, *mudejar* status guaranteed women's property rights: in Toledo, conquered in the eleventh century, the patterns of Muslim women's property ownership were the same as in Granada, even though women could no longer register their property in the Muslim court.[3] Notably, they could own houses and other real estate in equal shares with their husbands; lease, rent, and sell property, either alone or with their husbands; guarantee loans to their husbands; inherit from their male relatives; and make property gifts to family members. In an archival deed recorded in 1480, one Muslim woman, Doña Hebiba, gifted her son, Abrahen Alcaysi, a house situated near the city's mosque.

Thus ʿĀʾisha's parents could not have known that the Catholic kings would not keep to the terms of the capitulations and that within a few years, they and their daughter, together with the rest of the Muslims living under Catholic rule, would be forced to choose between conversion and exile.[4] Trusting in the court's power to ensure their daughter's ownership of the house, they acted like many parents before them and gifted it to her as a minor. When parents wanted to secure the transmission of property in its entirety to a daughter, they gifted it to her while she was still a minor, then vacated it for a while in compliance with the law, before taking possession of the gift on her behalf and continuing to live in it, thereby securing control of the property.

Earlier, on 18 January 1470, another father, Abū Jaʿfar Aḥmad, had registered the purchase of an irrigated field for 220 dinars on behalf of his daughter ʿĀʾisha, a minor, using money that he had gifted her.[5] The deed confirmed the transfer of all rights over the property to the daughter, stating that Abū Jaʿfar, like other parents of minor daughters, took possession of the property on her behalf. While he controlled his minor daughter's property, a father could carry out transactions with it. ʿAlī b. Mūsā al-Lakhmī, who, as was noted earlier, married off his minor daughter Fāṭima on 11 November 1438, came to court a few months later, on 10 February 1439, to register his house and garden as collateral for some transactions made using property belonging to his other minor daughter, Umm al-Fatḥ.[6] In the deed, the father acknowledged that the property used for the transactions was his daughter's share in her late mother's estate, which was under his control. On 14 December 1460, another Granadan father, Abū l-Ḥajjāj Yūsuf Ibn al-Sharāj, made a gift of two stores bought with money that he had gifted to his son, a suckling baby (*raḍīʿ*).[7] Both the buyer and the seller, Abū l-Qāsim b. Riḍwān Banigash, were members of powerful fifteenth-century Granadan families whose roles in Granada's final years were recorded in both Muslim and Christian chronicles.[8] The writs of these deeds have survived, along with several similar acts and the records from Toledo, providing a final testimony to the strength of the court system and of women's property rights in al-Andalus.

Property gifts to minor females could precede the *ṣadāq*, and therefore could be seen as inaugurating a gifting process that not only continued throughout a woman's life, but also saw her gain possession of various properties at different times. Legally speaking, the rights to gift and to be gifted were not gender-related, being equally enjoyed by males. However, in practice, the timing of, motivations for, and goals of gifting to females, as well as the patterns of gift acquisition, differed greatly. In fact, the various paradigms of giving the inter vivos gift to females were so distinctive from those respecting gifts to males that the inter vivos gift can be seen not only as a separate female property right, but also as an independent factor in the social and economic dynamics of a community's life. For this reason, a detailed discussion of the rules for giving and acquiring gifts is necessary.

The Legal Framework of Property Gifting

Several modes of property gifting were defined in the law under the terms *hiba, niḥla,* and *ṣadaqa,* with the gifted property moving either horizontally among family members or vertically from one generation to another.[9] The *hiba* is a gift given in perpetuity, unrestricted by either duration or destination, unlike gifts such as the *ʿumrā* (a gift given for the duration of a lifetime) and the *ṣadaqa* (a charitable gift); all of these gift forms are found to have been used in practice. The *hiba* is defined in Islamic law as an inter vivos transfer of property without either benefit or remuneration for the donor. It could consist of a tangible piece of property, such as real estate, but could also comprise forgiving a debt or granting another the right to derive enjoyment and income from a property, such as a building or a field, or the right to use water for irrigation.

The actual act of gifting was a complex process involving several steps. It began with the donor's declaration of his or her intention to give a gift to the recipient. This declaration consisted of making an offer of a gift (*ījāb*) and then receiving the recipient's acceptance of the offer (*qabūl*). Acquiring the gift was accomplished by following another set of steps: the donor made the property available to the recipient by performing a conveyance (*ḥiyāza*), and the recipient completed the transaction by performing a possession-taking (*qabḍ*). Not all legal schools required a strict physical possession taking for ownership to be transferred, but the Malikis and the Hanafis did.[10] Maliki law was particularly adamant about scrupulous acquisition and insisted that all steps be performed. Indeed, all the Andalusian notarial models for gift transactions reminded both donor and recipient that a gift transaction was not legally binding until the *ḥiyāza* and *qabḍ* had been performed.[11] Any infraction of these rules could invalidate the act of gifting, although this outcome could be mitigated by the presence of witnesses (*shuhūd*) to the donor's declaration of his or her intention to give a gift, which was seen as equivalent to an effective conveyance leading to possession-taking. Nevertheless, taking physical possession of the gifted property was still required in order to seal the transaction.[12] The donor's mere abandonment of the property was also regarded as signalling a valid conveyance, thus allowing the recipient to take possession.[13]

The method of possession-taking varied according to the nature of the gift. Once possession taking had been made possible—for example, by handing over the keys to a box of jewellery—the recipient's possession-taking was valid. The process of conveyance and possession-taking served as a public declaration of intent and alerted potential heirs, as well as the general public, to the change in a property's ownership status.[14] However, when a donor offered a gift and the recipient accepted it (*ījāb wa-qabūl*), the right of acquisition was created, meaning that the recipient could take possession even without the donor's permission since the donor had, in effect, merely abandoned the property. Nonetheless, the donor was entitled to rescind his decision and revoke the gift in response to changed circumstances. Any attempt to gift a property immediately before death was problematic, as the death of the donor before a conveyance was completed created an obstacle for possession-taking, as did bankruptcy, madness, a fatal illness causing death, or dispossession of the gift.

The desire to either circumscribe, avoid, or counter the inheritance law was the prime motive behind any gift since the law did indeed require that property be divided according to strict rules, thus preventing the exercise of personal wishes.[15] Jurists admitted that no rule prohibited a donor from exercising his or her gifting rights in a manner favouring one member of a family at the expense of others. Indeed, the Granadan jurist Ibn Juzayy noted: "A donor of property (*wāhib*) could be any healthy individual who is not under property guardianship . . . and the recipient could be any human being, and it is permissible to give one's entire fortune to a stranger by mutual agreement . . . however, giving the entire estate to one child in preference over another or benefiting some children over the others is reprehensible according to the majority of jurists, but, if it happens, it is legal nonetheless."[16]

Despite this acknowledgment of legality, deprived heirs regularly went to court to contest gifts, claiming abuses of the complicated mechanism of gifting and possession-taking to cast doubt on the validity of gifts. Because gifts to minor females were numerous and common, the disputes over these cases appear more frequently in the fatwas. I will now trace the historical record of gift acquisition during three stages of a woman's life: (1) when of minority status, (2) at the moment of marriage, and (3) when of majority status. The chronological periods highlight the social and economic paradigms of gift acquisition.

Acquisition of a Gift to a Minor

Since minor females could neither legally acquire their gifts nor exercise control over them, the practice of gifting property to minor daughters was popular among property owners who wanted to exclude the gifted property from the estate. Being their daughters' guardians, the donors continued to control the property for all practical purposes as though they were the full owners. The long period (up to seven years after marriage) of the recipient's guardianship under the father's or mother's control allowed the parents to continue using the property in question, to derive revenue from it, and even, in blatant disregard for the law, to maintain control over it beyond the daughter's release from interdiction.[17] Since the law did not differentiate between recipients based on gender, the Andalusian notarial manuals provided general, non-gendered models for giving a gift to a minor.[18] Nonetheless, the disputes reported in the fatwas seem to indicate that minor girls were more frequently made the recipients of property than were minor boys and that the high incidence of litigation surrounding the practice was a reflection of the many challenges to females' acquisition of property gifted to them as minors. The main reason for challenging a gift to a minor seems to have been the delay of several years which usually separate the moment of gifting to a minor girl and her official release from guardianship. The longer the period, the more obscure and dissipated became the details of the deed. Consider the two disputes submitted to Ibn al-Makwī, a twelfth-century Cordovan jurist:[19]

(1) Ibn al-Makwī was asked about a father who summoned witnesses (*ashhada*) to attest that (a) he had given all his possessions, including both jewellery and clothes, as a gift (*hiba*) to his two minor daughters; (b) that one chest containing clothes was to go in its entirety to one daughter, that another chest was to go to another daughter, and that he kept for himself only the shirt on his back (*kiswat ẓahrihi*); and (c) that he was giving a silo to one daughter and all the food in the house to the other. The

witnesses did not examine the property in detail and did not ascertain the exact quantities of the different items, except to see that the silo was full of food, that the house had food in it for the second daughter, and that the daughters were wearing jewellery prior to their father's death. The sender asking the question, the *mustaftī*, wanted to know if the gift was lawful. In a brief response, Ibn al-Makwī said that everything belonged to the daughters.

(2) Ibn al-Makwī was asked also about a father who gifted and took possession of jewellery and clothes on behalf of his daughter who was under his guardianship; the items were placed in a locked chest under the supervision of the girl's mother, his wife. After his death, the man's heirs claimed a share of the jewellery and clothes. Ibn al-Makwī responded that if it was widely known that the deceased had intended the property to be a gift to his daughter, the heirs had no claim to it.[20]

In both instances, the donor was accused of noncompliance with the legal requirements. The heirs contested the gift, claiming that the legal procedure had not been followed in so far as the witnesses had not examined the contents of the gift and thus could not attest to its exact value, had not actually been present, or had not been given the opportunity to verify the gift. But Ibn al-Makwī defended the legitimacy of the gifts on two counts. First, he concluded that compliance with the technicalities had indeed occurred. The act of gifting in the first dispute was deemed valid because the donor-guardian had divested himself of everything ("he had kept for himself only the shirt on his back"), whereupon he could take possession on behalf of the minor, and, in the second dispute, because the means of taking possession were made available by giving the mother the keys to the box containing the gifted property. Second, Ibn al-Makwī validated the gift on the grounds that the parents' intention to gift their daughters was clear.

The disputes revealed in these two fatwas confirm, if nothing else, the legal complexities and manipulations of the clauses regarding taking possession of gifts. The considerable number of fatwas dealing with gifting property to minor daughters shows that it was a common practice and that it clearly satisfied the needs and preferences of parents. The jurists had no difficulty upholding such transactions, which were a common and accepted practice, because the act of gifting expressed the will of the parents and because the purpose of gifting minors was to place property in the hands of children.

Marriage Gifts

The next phase of property gifting to women could take place at the moment of marriage, although, according to the available records, not all regions shared the North African and Andalusian practice of registering gifts in the marriage contract. The value and legal status of such gifts varied. The marriage contracts in the Granadan collection specify gifts of considerable real estate property, including houses and orchards, as well as very small pieces of property, which were listed next to the mandatory *ṣadāq* and gifted to brides by the groom, parents, or other family members. The notarial formularies and the fatwas confirm this pattern throughout al-Andalus and North Africa. The term used to designate a father's gift to his daughter or son upon marriage was *niḥla*, and that used for the husband's gift to his future wife was *siyāqa*.[21] The *siyāqa* could comprise the husband's entire property, half of it, or any part of it, and the *niḥla* could consist of a house bought by the father, the price of which he could choose to deduct from the first *ṣadāq* instalment and, if given to him for her—as long as the daughter was still under guardianship—even from the second *ṣadāq* instalment.[22] Unlike the bride, the groom was often free of guardianship by the time of marriage and capable of legally dispossessing his property, which the bride could not do.

Ibn Mughīth's model deed made it legal for a father who gave a house as a *niḥla* to deduct the value of the house from both instalments of his daughter's *ṣadāq*.[23] The act of gifting bore all the signs of a perfectly legal transaction: it was a specific house of known value, was described in its entirety, and was shown to have been gifted, along with all its adjunct parts and rights of benefit and ownership, to his daughter under guardianship. The marriage contract was also a perfectly legal transaction, which concluded with the statement that the gift of this property sealed the marriage. As with all gifts, a legalizing act of possession-taking had to be enacted either by the father if his daughter was under guardianship or by the bride herself if she was a mature adult.

We cannot be sure when the Andalusian marriage contract became a vehicle for registering individual property gifts to either bride or groom. Such gifts have appeared in the marriage contracts since at least the eleventh century, and Ibn Mughīth's formulary contains a fully developed model for both the *niḥla* and the *siyāqa*. In his section on gifts, the twelfth-century notary al-Jazīrī provided abundant details on the nature of property gifts that the bride might receive from her father, mother, or future husband. While both the *niḥla* and the *siyāqa* were included in the notarial manuals and discussed in the fatwas, only the *niḥla* has actually been found in the Granadan documents. Nonetheless, we may assume that the *siyāqa* was also a reality in Granada since the Granadan notary Ibn Salmūn included a model deed for its registration in his manual written around the middle of the fourteenth century.[24] That both the *niḥla* and the *siyāqa* actually existed is borne out by the details that the notaries required for registration. Both the location and the size of the gifted property had to be precisely defined in the document, which named the properties adjacent to the gifted property's four boundaries and stated that this property was donated along with all its rights and benefits as well as with its extended internal and external parts, such as its hall, well, toilets, and flocks. The value of the property had to be specified and no conditions could be attached to the act of gifting.[25] Marriage gifts acquired legitimacy through their association with the *ṣadāq*, and the notaries in Granada, though they were not legally bound to validate a marriage contract specifying such gifts since only the *ṣadāq* was mandatory, nonetheless confirmed that a marriage was "contracted by this gift" (*ʿalayhā inʿaqada al-nikāḥ*).

As in the case of the *ṣadāq*, a marriage gift to a minor daughter was acquired (or kept) by the father. At issue, as with other gifts to minors, was when and whether this gift was eventually passed on to the daughter. The difficulty in asserting whether the wife had taken possession of her gifted property was related to the couple's situation. When the gift consisted of a house, as indicated in the *niḥla* deed discussed above, the couple would live in a house that was legally owned by the wife but, in reality, controlled by her father. The case of the Granadan *khulʿ* divorce in Chapter 1, when ʿĀʾisha bt. Saʿd b. Aḥmad signed away her property rights with her parents present, is a good example of these circumstances. When a piece of land was gifted, the case could well be even more complicated because cultivation of the land raised questions about who had cultivated it and who was thus entitled to the resulting income. A study of the fatwas has concluded that such income remained in the hands of the donor and that, when the donor was the husband, he and his family cultivated it. In practice, this meant that regardless of whether property was gifted by the bride's family or by the husband's, it did not leave its previous owner's possession for quite some time—probably only at the time of the estate's division. In either case, it would appear, a marriage gift was not transferred to its rightful owner immediately after the wedding but at a later, unspecified time.[26]

This conclusion is derived from the fact that most fatwas describe confusion and uncertainty surrounding the location or the ownership of the gifted properties. These complications were similar to those resulting from the young wife's prolonged period of guardianship, discussed below in Chapter 4. Legal challenges to such gifts were based on a lack of information regarding the precise location, size, and/or definition of properties gifted in marriage contracts.[27] In many instances, litigation arose when the estate was divided or when the status of the marriage changed, such as in cases of *khulʿ* divorce, which saw property used as compensation. A lack of information about the precise status of the property in question often brought the whole divorce into question, not only threatening the status of the marriage, but giving the heirs a reason to contest the gift. Similar legal wrangling at the time of an estate division was triggered by a husband's practice of cultivating his wife's land without obtaining a legal document attesting to her consent and without either arranging for her to receive the income from the field or dividing it into his and her shares. Typically, the fatwas do not show disputes between a husband and wife over ownership or cultivation of her land as long as the marriage was ongoing. The disputes that ensued were always initiated by heirs contesting the husband's right to income that he had derived from the wife's land.

Disputes surrounding the practice of giving gifts at marriage have led at least one observer to suggest that these gifts, whether the *niḥla* and the *siyāqa*, were in fact fictitious.[28] Given the legally prolonged period during which gifted land remained in the hands of its former owners, it has been concluded that such gifts were officially bestowed on the wife to take advantage of her curtailed power to control them, the intention being to pass the land to the wife's children upon her death, thus bypassing the husband. Regardless of whether a wife made a conscious decision not to claim the land on her release from guardianship, leaving her property unclaimed in the hands of the donors, her future heirs could use the inheritance law to ensure that she established her claim to gifted land at some point. A "fictitious" gift of property to a wife would have prevented the division of family property only in the short term. Upon the death of a woman's father or mother, the property would have been divided among the heirs based on a deed documenting the gift, which was usually contested if the land had remained in the estate for any length of time without having earlier been carefully excluded from the estate. The association of gifts with marriage also led to court appeals in other instances. Although not legally or implicitly specified as such, North African jurists considered a husband's contribution to the wedding banquet itself—that is, provisions such as food, animals, and so on—to be gifts to his wife that should be included with the other properties that she received at the moment of the wedding. The fatwas from North Africa studied by Zomeño Rodriguez show that the jurists there regularly regarded wedding-party gifts as part of the bride's estate, and thus as inheritable by her heirs, and that they consistently resolved disputes involving such gifts in favour of the wife.[29]

The Andalusian practice of recording gifts other than the *ṣadāq* in the marriage contract—and, in all probability, the practice also of North Africans—differed from what has been noted in the rest of the Islamic Mediterranean. In his discussion of marriage gifts, Hady Idris suggests that the difference was due to a substrata of previous practices in Iberian history.[30] Be that as it may, I contend that property gifted to a wife upon marriage was actually intended to be her property, that she would eventually acquire it, and that the appearance of marriage gifts in the marriage contract is probably a direct result of Maliki marriage laws, regardless of whether the *niḥla*'s prevalence in al-Andalus overshadowed the *ṣadāq* or whether the *niḥla* was linked to the amount of the *ṣadāq*. The uncertainties plaguing marriage gifts were not unusual in the overall picture of the gift as a woman's property right, and marriage gifts cannot be considered in isolation but must be viewed within the larger context of property transferred to women in a variety of legal deeds. This conclusion is borne out in the next chapter's examination of cases of estate division.

Gifts to a Wife of Majority Status

The third stage in the gifting process was inaugurated when a wife was liberated from guardianship. At this time, she could make her own gift decisions and receive gifts without her father's consent. The gifting pattern after marriage is illustrated by the property that the sheikh Abū Jaʿfar Aḥmad b. Muḥammad al-Mughannī, previously of Baza and later a resident of Granada, gifted to his young second wife, Mahjūna. In such cases, the act of gifting served the needs of property owners contemplating the division of their property before death. The deeds preserved in al-Mughannī's family archives indicate how the provision for the inter vivos gift was used in property devolution and estate planning in the later stages of life as well as the roles played by Mahjūna, al-Mughannī's in-laws (her parents, the al-Ḥakīms), and the al-Ḥakīm's in-laws (the al-Qirbilyānīs) in exercising this provision.[31] A series of deeds shows that al-Mughannī was preoccupied with the future of his estate for quite some time and that, as the guardian of her husband's mentally handicapped son, Mahjūna played a specific role in this future.

On 4 April 1481 al-Mughannī gifted his share in the estate of his first wife, the late Fāṭima, to his mentally handicapped son, Muḥammad, who was under his guardianship. The properties numbered in the document are a house and seven parcels of cultivated land in different parts of Baza. By means of this gift, the father united the properties in the hands of a single owner and proceeded to take possession of the gift on behalf of his son and to hold it in partnership with him.[32] Two years later, on 23 July 1483, he appointed Mahjūna to be the property guardian of her stepson, Muḥammad.[33] Her aging husband conferred upon Mahjūna the ultimate power to manage this son's affairs without supervision from anyone, nor did he impose on her the duty to provide the court with an account of her decisions in this matter or of the expenses that she incurred, as her sister ʿĀ'isha had to do respecting her daughters and as Tāj al-ʿUlā, whom we shall meet next, had to do respecting her niece.[34] Al-Mughannī stated that he had complete confidence in Mahjūna's ability and that he trusted her judgment.[35]

On 28 February 1485 al-Mughannī, who is described in the various legal deeds as suffering from a chronic illness due to old age that forced him to remain immobile for about a year but who remained in perfect mental health, signed a will dispensing "the third," or unencumbered share, of his estate.[36] He willed half of his current residence to his brother-in-law, ʿAlī b. Ibrāhīm al-Ḥakīm, Mahjūna's brother. He had previously gifted to Mahjūna the other half of the residence, a gift that might have been registered in her *ṣadāq*, although we do not have the deed for this particular gift. On 25 April 1485 al-Mughannī had the court register another deed, in which he gave his wife, the "blessed" Mahjūna, daughter of Ibrāhīm al-Ḥakīm, a cash gift (*hiba*) of 200 newly minted silver dinars (*ʿashrī fiḍḍī*). Mahjūna, who was now of majority status and thus released from guardianship, came to court and performed the possession-taking ceremony, thereby accepting the gift, which now remained in her possession, the money being "a legal and definitive gift made with God's will."[37] The witnesses to the transaction testified that the recipient was in good physical and mental state but that the donor, her husband, was weak in body even though his mental state was sound. This declaration was needed in order to prove that this was not a deathbed gift. The law required such a statement because a sick man on his deathbed was not entitled to give gifts or to make any other financial decisions. If he did so and died soon afterward, the gift would be taken from the unencumbered third of his estate in order not to harm the heirs.[38]

At the same time, Mahjūna received another gift from her husband, a piece of golden brocade cloth in the possession, perhaps for safe-keeping, of the teacher al-Rumaylī.[39] Four months later, on 10 August 1485, the court notary registered another act gifting property to Mahjūna. This time she received a house from her husband that he owned in the town of Baza, along with all its appendages, rights, and added assets, including its various contents, wheat and other food goods, and a stable near the house of Aḥmad al-Karīm.[40] The document states that this act of gifting was a final transaction that severed the house, which was now owned by her, from the rest of the husband's estate. The witnesses acknowledged that the recipient was in good mental and physical condition but noted that the donor was in a state of enfeeblement because of his advanced age, which had forced him to remain immobile for more than a year, although his mental faculties remained intact. In this case, Mahjūna did not take physical possession of the gift since the house was in Baza, but the document, registered in Granada, indicated that two male representatives in Baza took possession of the house on her behalf.

Properties left behind in Baza continued to figure prominently in the transactions concluded by the women of the al-Ḥakīm and al-Qirbilyānī families, who were related by marriage. On 27 November 1483 Umm al-Fatḥ bought from her son Yūsuf al-Qirbilyānī an enclosure (*ghalāq*) in Baza for which she paid 202 newly minted silver dinars. She gave him only 30 dinars on the conclusion of the deal, stating that the rest would be given in due course to ʿAlī b. Ibrāhīm al-Ḥakīm.[41] On 12 January 1486 a document issued in Baza was certified in the Granadan court. In this document, the Baza experts assessed the investments made in the vineyard of Mahjūna's and ʿAlī's sister, ʿĀ'isha bt. Ibrāhīm al-Ḥakīm, by the latter's husband, the late Muḥammad b. Aḥmad al-Qirbilyānī. The experts surveyed the property and testified that both the plants and the construction, including the wood, reeds, stones, and plaster used as materials, came to the amount of 134 newly minted silver dinars. ʿĀ'isha might well have required this document in anticipation of selling the property.[42] Baza fell to the Christian armies a few years later, on 28 November 1489, after a siege of six months.[43]

The gift law provided a convenient means for resolving concerns about property devolution before estate division, thus avoiding the strict inheritance law. The separation of property in matrimony enabled husband and wife to gift each other property. The possibility of achieving property resolutions in this manner could have played a role in the choice of marriage partners, particularly in cases of second marriages for men, which were seen in Granada and elsewhere.[44] As in the case discussed above, the gift provision helped to build equity in the hands of a younger spouse, enabling her to properly look after the interests of a mentally handicapped son. In other cases, it helped a propertied family member to safeguard property outside the estate for his wife and their children while preventing others, whether relatives or the state, from sharing in this property.

Gifting a Property Right: The "Rent-Free" Husband and Usufruct

Earlier, we saw that the law gave a wife the right to gift her husband the delayed part of the *ṣadāq*, the *kālī'*, in recognition of his "esteemed companionship" (*li-karīm ʿishratihi*). Or she could renounce the *kālī'* in return for her husband's surrender of his conjugal right to marry a second wife or to force his wife to move away from her parents.[45] But the provision respecting gifts of property was also used in two other instances: (1) when the husband was given the right to live "rent-free" in a family home that was the wife's property; and (2) when the husband was granted the right to cultivate land owned by her and to derive income from it (*ʿimtāʿ*), an instance of usufruct.

The dimensions of the phenomenon of the "rent-free" husband were part of the circumstances of ʿĀ'isha's *khulʿ* divorce. The document specified that as part of the property rights renounced in that divorce, the father absolved the husband from paying rent for the house in which he had lived with his wife. The status of the house in question was not specified. However, based on the practice as revealed in the records, mostly fatwas from al-Andalus and North Africa, we can conclude that it was most probably a gift to the daughter. And we can surmise that the father had extended his son-in-law the right to live rent-free in the house based on instructions drawn up by the notary al-Jazīrī for giving such a gift:

> If the father of the bride gave his son-in-law the right to benefit from a house that he had given to his daughter as a marriage gift (*niḥla*), either for the duration of the marriage or for any other length of time, you [the notary] should write, either in the *ṣadāq* contract itself or in another contract to be given to the husband, as follows: So-and-so gifts his son-in-law, so-and-so, the husband of his daughter, so-and-so, the right to enjoy the entire house, which is located in this quarter, with all its benefits, inside and outside, the upper and lower parts, its well and toilets, and to use it for habitation and profit for the duration of the marriage between them, because he likes him and befriends him, and for the wellbeing of family life with his above-mentioned wife. With this, he gifted his daughter the entire income of the house, designated an everlasting gift to the end of times.[46]

The notaries justified a father's actions with the same reasoning that they used to justify a wife's renouncement of the second *ṣadāq* instalment in return for good marital relations (although other jurists seem to have cast doubt on the legality of such a repeal of one's property rights). To quote al-Jazīrī: "This gift is given to the groom for reasons of friendship, to benefit him, and to win from him excellent companionship and dignified affection for his aforementioned wife."[47] A father did not have to consult his daughter about whether she agreed to allow her husband to live "rent-free" in her house since she was a minor under guardianship. In a fatwa written in fourteenth-century Granada, Ibn Lubb traced the history of the debate over the "rent-free" husband:

> He was asked whether a husband who lives in his wife's house is required to pay her rent if she requests it. Ibn Lubb answered: It is known (*mashhūr*) that a husband who lives in his wife's house is not obligated [to pay rent] (*lā shay'an ʿalayhi fīhi*). This is the current practice (*wa-bihi jarā al-ʿamal*) as attested to by Ibn Rushd in his *Nawādir.* This is the correct one (*ṣaḥīḥ*) of the two opinions (*min al-qawlayn*) on the matter. We follow here the predicament of a husband who cultivates his wife's land or vineyard and derives benefit from it. This does not entitle his legitimate heirs to the proceeds (*lā yaghram li 'l-waratha shay'an*). [In other words, they will have no share in this land when the inheritance is divided.] Based on this opinion, several of Cordova's jurists (*fuqahā'*) in the not so distant past made a choice, which has since become the practice [a majority ruling], that the husband does not pay rent because it is to the wife's advantage and in the best interest of their family life (*li-annahu min maṣlaḥat al-zawja wa-taḥsīn al-ʿushra*). Thus this became the custom (*ʿāda*), and a different decision today is inappropriate (*lā yanbaghī al-ḥukm bi-ghayrihi*). This is how the esteemed judge Ibn Rushd ruled in the last days of his life, considering it to be the correct and legal truth (*wa-rāyhu al-ṣawāb wa 'l-ḥaqq bi 'l-amr*). Nonetheless, the jurists who ruled against the elimination of the rent due from a husband who resided in his wife's house also based their decision on the predominant concept (*ʿalā 'l-mashhūr*) that the Shariʿa requires that the wife reside in the husband's house. But the couple disjoined and did not bind. The origin of this custom (*ʿāda*) was a ruling made by a judge who ignored what was predominant (*mashhūr*). It was subsequently followed by others, until it became a custom, because of the ruling of an ignorant judge. What is correct in the legal sense is what the practice has been, and this is that he does not have to pay rent.[48]

Legal squabbling over rent owed for use of a wife's property was at least several generations old. In the twelfth century, we find its echoes in the qadi (judge) ʿIyāḍ's collection of legal practices in al-Andalus, the *Madhāhib al-ḥukkām.*[49] It appears that allowing the husband to live rent-free was not always admitted precisely because of the complications that it could cause in cases where other property rights were involved, such as rights in divorce, inheritance rights, and rules of estate division. Allowing the husband to live rent-free could raise questions about ownership of the house or about the value of the contribution that should have been made. Objection to the practice was not necessarily raised by wives, even though a wife's challenge could be motivated by the desire for income, concern for the rights of heirs, displeasure with her parents' actions, or displeasure with her husband. Nonetheless, the "rent-free" husband did not seem to represent a problem in the conjugal relationship. During the marriage, both wives and husbands knew to whom the house belonged, as they knew all about separation of property in matrimony and knew that a husband who did not pay rent could be seen as an infringement of the wife's property rights. The jurists, who regularly debated the irregularity of the transaction yet allowed it to continue, knowing all the while that this kind of gift was bound to create legal problems, mostly at the moment of estate division, did so in all probability not because they cared about women in particular but because they cared about property rights in general. Thus the gift of living rent-free continued to be justified by the same reasoning that had previously been advanced for permitting renouncement of the second *ṣadāq* instalment, namely, that it was good for one's conjugal life.

Gifting a husband the right to derive profit from his wife's property (*imtāʿ*) was just as common and equally consequential. The practice was widespread not only in al-Andalus but also in North Africa, where it was described in a fatwa by Abū Isḥāq Ibrāhīm al-Tūnisī (d. 1051). The fatwa deals with the custom among the people of Qafṣa, a town in today's Tunisia, of allowing fathers to give their daughter's husband property belonging to her as a life gift (*ʿumrā*) for the duration of the marriage:

> Al-Tūnisī was asked about a father who gave as a life gift (*aʿmara*) his minor daughter's property (*māl*) to her husband for the good of the marriage (*ʿalā wajh al-irfāq*). It was the custom of the people of Qafṣa to gift their daughters' property to the husband. [He was asked to] tell us whether this is allowed and whether, when the husband divorces the wife, he is obligated to return it.
>
> He answered: It is not allowed to gift the husband usufruct respecting the daughter's property, and if it has been done over a long time, the revenue should be requested. If the husband is wanting, the father should take over.

The editor of the collection, al-Wansharīsī, also included here a comment by al-Māzarī (d. 1141), who described the practice as current in the Ifrīqiyan towns of Zawīla and al-Mahdiyya, where a house in which a husband would live with his wife was included in her trousseau.[50] In a separate fatwa, al-Māzarī, who was infuriated by the practice, warned that the inclusion of such a clause in a marriage contract would lead to the marriage's invalidation.[51] Ibn Juzayy also warned against the practice:

> It is not permitted for the wife to include permission for the husband to benefit from her property in the marriage contract because this will appear as a gift in exchange for the marriage, rendering it illegal. It is permitted to give the permission after contracting the marriage, and if the wife is free from guardianship, she can do so herself. If she is under her father's guardianship, he is allowed to draw up such a document, but if she is being married off by someone other than her father, then that person is not allowed to gift this right, unless he is willing to guarantee all losses, because it will be a gift made of property of someone under guardianship (which is not allowed).[52]

Al-Jazīrī also expressed some reservations in his commentary: "This kind of *imtāʿ* [use of the wife's property] benefitting the husband is common in Algeciras [where al-Jazīrī was writing] and in other places, and I have seen them drafting the gifting of the *niḥla* in the *ṣadāq* and the *imtāʿ* in a separate document and stating in this model that the *imtāʿ* in the wife's property is given of her own free will or that of her guardian, but this is incorrect because the *imtāʿ* should not appear as a condition in the marriage contract, unlike the *ṣadāq*."[53] Nonetheless, the practice continued, and the evidence shows a wide array of properties that could be used for the purpose of *imtāʿ*, among them use of a wife's irrigation rights. The following fatwa illustrates the legal complications that could result from this kind of gift when given by the wife:

> In a question addressed to Ibn ʿAttāb (d. Cordova, 1069), a wife gifted (*wahabat*) to her husband her irrigation rights in a pumping machine (*sāniya*) in the same document where she gifted him the delayed portion [of her *ṣadāq*] (*kāliʾ ṣadāqihā*). The husband used the water to irrigate land belonging to him and used the surplus water to irrigate land belonging to his wife. The fatwa-requestor asked whether the donation was invalidated by the husband's use of the water for the benefit of the donor. Ibn ʿAttāb responded that the husband's use of the water to irrigate his wife's field did not invalidate the gift, although it was reprehensible for her to benefit from it (*yukrahu lahā al-intifāʾ minhu*), citing, as support for his conclusion, an episode related to the Prophet Muḥammad (*ḥadīth*).[54]

According to Maliki legal doctrine, a gift became invalid if it was returned to the donor. The use of water in crop irrigation was a longstanding and important property right in Spain. A commutative contract (*muʿāwada*) bears witness to this convention: the contract between two brothers in Granada, dated 6 August 1485, dealt with a gift of one-quarter of the quota of irrigation water from the Grand Canal (*al-sāqiya al-kubrā*), located below the city, for the night of every fifth day in an eight-day cycle.[55] The fatwa indicates that the wife's gift of these irrigation rights to her husband was used to irrigate her field, and an argument could be made that the gift had been returned to her and was thus invalid.

Although it might be surmised from the fatwas that husbands regularly took possession of their wives' property by ruse, such was not the case. Regardless of whether the couple reached a verbal or written agreement about cultivation or a tacit understanding between them about the cultivation of her land, the practice of the husband using the wife's property gave rise to disputes over ownership only in the event of estate division. In the fatwas, the legal challenge to such gifts did not come from a husband challenging his wife's ownership, nor from a wife contesting her husband's cultivation, but from family members either during estate division or when stepchildren, who would otherwise have not been entitled to a share in the estate, felt dispossessed by the gift. Land cultivation by a husband could give the impression that he owned the land at the same time, but the court expected a wife to track gifted properties and to retain the legal documents of ownership. In fact, the Granadan court documents provide evidence of such a practice in two cases where a husband and son recorded their work on a wife's/mother's property.[56] Determining rights over income-producing property and the value of the work undertaken on a wife's property was necessary at the time of estate division and when selling the property in question. Khalīl b. Isḥāq, the fourteenth-century Maliki jurist writing in Egypt, distinguished between a gift to a spouse and any other gift: "Tangible things such as real estate or slaves may be gifted by a wife to her husband, and the transaction is valid even if the husband does not perform the legal requirement of possession-taking (*qabḍ*), as required in the case of a gift."[57]

The background of the debate around the conjugal gift is therefore related to everday life. Common sense dictated that the husband would cultivate his wife's property alongside his own and that doing so would benefit the conjugal unit in the long run. Since there was no conjugal property in marriage unless a couple registered in court their property's division into his and her equal parts, the property that the wife brought to the marriage remained hers, and consequently that of her heirs, and was never regarded as conjugal property. Disputes could arise, but a wife suffered no definitive loss of her property. Legally speaking, a husband's involvement in his wife's property was possible without her rescinding ownership, but the danger of presumed ownership by the husband existed if prolonged cultivation of her property occurred without records being kept. This was the background for most of the disputes, which were not between a husband and wife but among heirs. This kind of undocumented transaction between a husband and wife in matters of property was much less dangerous to women's property than the acts perpetrated by fathers. The property relations between spouses occurred between equals, with both parties enjoying equal property rights, whereas such relations between fathers and daughters occurred between non-equals, the daughter's property rights being legally within the father's purview for a prolonged period of time.

Gifts in Comparative Context

The role of Islamic law's gift provision in the construction of women's property appears more pronounced given the assumption that gifts were neither an independent nor a significant means of property devolution both in previous and in contemporary societies. In Roman law, "inheritance and dowry were the two primary vehicles for transfer of the patrimony to the next generation," whereas gifts do not seem to have had any discernible effect on women's property rights, on their ownership of property, or on family relationships.[58] Dowry and inheritance continued to play a central role in the process of property devolution in medieval Europe, while the disappearance of Roman law and the rise of feudalism created new conditions and two different sets of women's property rights, one for peasantry and the other for the landed gentry.[59] But gifts made to women did not disappear altogether from the European scene: property donations were made to women as pre-mortem gifts by their husbands; alternatively, pre-mortem gifts were also given to married daughters by fathers and mothers in addition to the original dowry. Most notably, property gifts were made by widowed parents in their old age on condition that they themselves would be looked after by the recipients in return. The overall assumption is that when gifts of property to women appear in the European legal sources, these properties were more likely assigned to them either as legacies, acquired upon or just prior to the donor's death, or in individual arrangements. In Europe gifts seem never to have played a particular role within the larger spectrum of property transfers.

Fifteenth-century Italy represents a unique case in this regard. In Italy the changes to the dowry's status had serious consequences for women's property ownership. The dowry settled the bride's claim on the estate, but the property itself passed into the husband's control for the duration of the marriage.[60] Theoretically, the wife's lack of control over her property was not complete since control of non-dowry assets was not given to the husband, whose use of such assets required the wife's legal consent.[61] In reality, however, husbands in Florence were still able to exercise control over all non-dowry assets during marriage, with or without their wives' consent, "in disregard to legal niceties."[62] The legal discourse offered by the Italian jurists to justify this encroachment on women's property rights highlighted its benefit to the conjugal relationship. For instance, faced with resolving the recurrent issue of whether a wife had in fact consented to the use of her property, the Italian jurist Albergotti stated: "[T]he fourth consideration [allowing usage without consent] comes from the joining of persons and its defining quality, namely, that between husband and wife there is a joining which is linked to deference of the wife's part, and there arises as a consequence of that docility the presumption of dissent or forced assent."[63]

The basis for the Florentine jurist's argument was shared by jurists across northern and central Italy and endorsed by scholars of Renaissance history. Julius Kirshner explains that both the need to alleviate the mounting financial burdens attendant on marriage and the struggle to maintain and enhance status informed the husband's demand to assert control over the wife's property. The jurist's only potential concern was to protect the wife's property from the husband's creditors.[64]

Although Italian jurists and their Muslim colleagues shared the argument that a husband's use of his wife's property facilitated better conjugal relations, the Italian context cannot be equated with the Islamic practice of granting husbands usufractory rights respecting a wife's property while she was still under her parents' guardianship.[65] The Islamic position on women's property rights was stronger precisely because there was no common property in marriage. Nonetheless, the Italian jurists' discourse was reminiscent of the Islamic stance on the relationship between the husband's use of the wife's property and "conjugal welfare." Both Muslim and Christian jurists seem to have claimed that the benefit of good matrimonial relations amply compensated the wife for the loss of control over property as well as for the loss of property itself, thus equating emotions and matrimonial happiness with property. In this way, both the Islamic and Italian discourses are consistent with Carol Rose's premise, described in the Introduction, that male jurists played an active role in depriving women of their property rights by legally supporting society's expectations that they sacrifice rights for the family's welfare.

Conclusion

Unlike the *ṣadāq*, the timing of gifts to women was not mandatory and could be triggered at anytime by changes in the family fortunes, by an unexpected death, by the need to protect a property from unwanted heirs, by the desire to escape a debt payment, or by the choice of a husband, such as in the case of marriage to an elderly man with special needs. Women could gift and be gifted at every stage of life, from childhood to widowhood. Parents could either gift property to or buy property with money gifted to a child under guardianship, and using the instruments of possession-taking, *qabḍ* and *ḥiyāza*, they could take control of the property on her behalf. Gifts were used by females to facilitate pre-mortem property devolution and to satisfy individual desires either to promote or to deprive an individual within the family. The lingering power of the parents, mostly the father, was visible in the several forms of gifts used in order to preserve power over and to derive income from a daughter's property. But mothers, too, employed the limiting power of guardianship. Not only were the types of gifts, *hiba*, *niḥla*, and *ṣadaqa*, distinct from one another and from the *ṣadāq* in terms of their timing, content, and the motivation behind them, but they also had more property value than the *ṣadāq* and enabled women to be recipients as well as donors of property throughout their lives. Unlike the *ṣadāq*, the nature of the inter vivos gift as a property right was not unique to women, but it was nonetheless unique in favouring females as recipients of gifts to minors, which enabled them to gift property to their husbands and to acquire male's rights in a manner that males could not. Although the process of acquiring such gifts, especially those given to minors, was more volatile than the process of acquiring the *ṣadāq*, the gift inter vivos was a more economically powerful tool than the *ṣadāq* because it was usually more substantial. However, given the difficulties involved in acquiring such a gift, its potential economic return could be delayed and curtailed.

The comparison of the European and Islamic systems shows how they differed. Islamic law made the gift inter vivos an integral part of the inheritance system and, in the face of this system's rigidity, allowed such gifts to play a wider and more significant role in the transfer of property. But how significant was it to women's property rights? As revealed in the sources, the range of legal activities surrounding gifts to and from women indicates the wide array of uses to which they were put. For instance, since the gift inter vivos was a property right, it could be used by wives in a variety of ways, from acquiring a husband's rights to concluding a divorce. Moreover, such a gift was more flexible than the *ṣadāq* as a legal mechanism for dealing with property, not only in cases of property transmission, but also as a means of meeting personal needs, making it easier for women to use. Because of its flexibility, the inter vivos gift can be seen as a mitigating link between the *ṣadāq* and inheritance, the first being a precise and mandatory gift to a woman, the acquisition and renunciation of which were subject to a variety of requirements, and the second being an equally mandatory allotment whose acquisition was not precisely timed. Their relationship is treated in the next chapter.

Three

INHERITANCE

Granadan Estate Divisions

On 7 February 1495 division of the estate of Fāṭima bt. Saʿd b. Lubb, the "blessed old woman" (*al-ʿajūz al-mubāraka*), took place in the Islamic court in Granada.[1] The deceased's granddaughter, Fāṭima bt. Aḥmad Musāʿid, went to court to collect the unencumbered third of the estate (*thulth*), which her grandmother had assigned to her (*ʿahadat*), even though the old woman died before she could register her will in court. In addition to the third, the estate repaid Fāṭima a loan of 60 silver dinars, which she and her husband, Ḥakīm b. Ibrāhīm b. Ghālib, had extended to the deceased. No property was sold for cash at settlement, and there was no physical division of real estate or fields. The notary specified that the debt and the willed third of the estate were settled in the form of a house valued at 75 dinars[2] and a vineyard valued at 4 silver dinars. The very next day, 8 February 1495, Fāṭima and her husband registered this same house, identifiable by the neighbouring properties indicated in both documents, as a gift to their infant daughter.[3] This act completed a cycle of four generations of uninterrupted ownership of the family home by its female members, each relying on Islamic female property rights to ensure smooth passage from generation to generation. The house and vineyard constituted all the real estate properties (*amlāk*) of the estate. The other heirs had to agree to their being used to satisfy Fāṭima's entitlement to the third of the estate and their agreement was duly recorded in the document before the estate division could proceed. The rest of the estate was left in the hands of two other women: the deceased's daughter ʿĀ'isha, who was Fāṭima's aunt; and Umm al-ʿUlā, who was the mother and guardian of a minor boy, Muḥammad, the great grandson of the deceased's brother, also named Muḥammad. All the heirs received items valuing 193 and eight-tenths dinars, which included silk and brocade garments, wooden furniture, leather objects, and even gold nuggets (*futūt*).

Nowhere was the impact of women's inheritance rights over their property holdings better displayed than in fifteenth-century Granada at the moment of estate division (*qismat tarika*). According to the Granadan records, estate division was the main factor determining the amount of a woman's property. Granadan courts were not unique in detailing the deceased's properties; these properties were recorded meticulously in all Islamic regions where an effective centralized administration was in place. Partly because all parties wanted their share of the estate correctly and legally attributed to them and partly because the state wanted to collect its own share, detailing men's and women's property at the time of death became a central part of court work.[4] Although united by the general rules of the Islamic succession law, estate registration varied according to region. Nonetheless, estate divisions in Granada, including those specified in wills, and instructions for the division of the unencumbered third of an estate were recorded in the documents in the same manner both before and after the 1492 conquest. The frequency of such records reveals regional legal and social patterns, especially those specific to women's inheritance in Granada. Between 1430 and 1495, such divisions were recorded in the Granadan collection in thirty separate documents.[5]

The Granadan documents confirm that registering estate division was a socially comprehensive affair practiced by both well-off and less-propertied families. Even members of the ruling Nasrid family, government officials, and court dignitaries registered estate divisions; all were submitted to the court for scrutiny. In terms of both social class and estate size, one Fāṭima bt. Abī ʿAbd Allāh Muḥammad b. Abī l-Nuʿaym Riḍwān led the group of women who inherited property in Granada.[6] The division of the estate of her late husband, Khālid b. Jāʾ al-Khayr, took place on 31 August 1452, leaving in her hands property and cash totalling 1,596 gold dinars and 3 dirhams, which included an elegant, marble-decorated house and a barn.[7] Khālid must have been much older than his wife, having registered his will in court as early as 1430, some twenty-two years before his death. In his will he disposed of one-third of his estate for the benefit of brides from poor families in Granada.[8] As Fāṭima was still under guardianship at the time of his death and did not attend the estate division, she was probably very young when she married Khālid and would have been married to him only for a short time before his death. Her aunt and guardian, Tāj al-ʿUlā, did not go to court either but was represented by a jurist named Ibn Kharshūsh.[9] There is no mention of children born to Khālid from his marriage to Fāṭima or from any previous union, and the young Fāṭima was his only heir.

An estate division registered at around the same time as Fāṭima's was that of Abū l-Ḥasan ʿAlī b. Aḥmad b. Abī l-Ḥasan al-ʿUndūq, who had two wives, Maryam bt. Nabīl and Umm al-Fatḥ bt. Faraj, the only polygamy case recorded in the documents. The other heirs were a son by Umm al-

Fatḥ, Aḥmad, and the deceased's parents, Abū l-Ḥasan and ʿĀʾisha bt. Muḥammad b. Naṣīr.[10] This estate, divided on 4 July 1452, included a parcel of land valued at 682 and one-half dinars, another property adjacent to that of the second wife,[11] Umm al-Fatḥ, valued at 750 dinars, a red mule valued at 120 dinars, and a variety of items, among them furniture, valued at 175 dinars and 4 dirhams. The deferred portion of each wife's *ṣadāq* was deducted before the shares were calculated, with the estate being divided among the heirs in the following manner: 115 dinars to Umm al-Fatḥ, a sum that included repayment of a loan that she had extended to her husband, and 15 dinars to Maryam.[12] In addition each wife received 57 dinars and 8 and three-eighths dirhams. Each parent received 154 dinars and 2 and three-eighths dirhams, with the son receiving 501 dinars and one-quarter dirham. The wives and each parent represented themselves in court, while the son was represented by another adult male. The legatees agreed among themselves to take their shares without physically dividing the property in the process: Umm al-Fatḥ received one part of the land, which she would share with her son, who was entitled to three-quarters of the land's value; the father received the other part of the land and the red mule; while the other wife shared the furniture and other valuables with the mother. The second marriage might have been related to the first wife's infertility, since Aḥmad, the son of Umm al-Fatḥ, is the only offspring mentioned.

When heirs were required to share an estate with the state treasury (*bayt al-māl*), the property had to be liquefied at auction in order to raise the necessary cash. An estimate of the property's value was prepared by experts and registered in a separate document prior to the estate division in court. Maryam bt. Abī Yaḥyā b. Jubayr, the sole heir to the estate of her husband, the merchant Abī Jaʿfar Aḥmad b. Dughnayn, had to split the proceeds of the house that constituted the estate with the treasury on 22 January 1458.[13] The house fetched 105 gold dinars at auction. For future reference, the court notary included the name of the purchaser in the record of the estate's division: it was Fāṭima bt. ʿUthmān b. Muḥammad b. ʿUthmān, whose signature therefore appears in the estate division's document. She paid for her purchase with her own money and property, not on behalf of a child.[14] ʿĀʾisha bt. al-Martushī and her daughter Fāṭima also had to deal with the state's treasury manager, master of the charity and inheritance state bureau (*ṣāḥib al-zakāt wa ʾl-mawārith*), on 14 November 1490, when division of the estate of their husband and father, Ḥasan Zurayq, took place.[15] This estate included a house jointly owned by the husband and wife, so when the value of the estate was calculated, only 50 per cent, consisting of a store, a house, and a plot of land, was divided.

Mother and daughter became partners, thus avoiding a division of the property.

An auction situation, which involved non-family members in the division of an estate, could end unfavourably, something that happened to two sisters-in-law. A fallow field, initially bought on 5 January 1481 for 26 silver dinars, was the only property that Muḥammad b. Muḥammad al-Ḥajjām left to his wife, ʿĀʾisha bt. Saʿd b. Ḥasan, to their daughter, Umm al-Fatḥ, and to his brother Aḥmad.[16] Aḥmad died soon afterward, so his wife, Fāṭima bt. ʿAlī b. Zāfir, and their three sons were to share in the estate. The two widows, appointed guardians of their respective children by their deceased husbands, went to court on 18 April 1484 for the estate division. They sold the fallow land back to its original owner, Muḥammad b. Ḥayy, for 20 silver dinars and split the proceeds. On the same day, the buyer sold the land to another purchaser, Muḥammad b. Ibrāhīm al-Ṣanāʾ, for 26 silver dinars, thus earning for himself a profit of 6 dinars.[17]

When Umm al-Fatḥ bt. Abī Bakr al-Shaqwashī and her stepson, Abū Jaʿfar Aḥmad, shared the estate of their husband and father, Abū ʿAbd Allāh Muḥammad b. Aḥmad al-Ruffa, which was divided on 25 March 1476, they also acted in agreement to prevent the physical division of the property.[18] This estate included a house and four parcels of land, one of recently planted vine. The notary recorded that the heirs appeared in court and reached an amicable division that gave them joint usufruct (*bi ʾl-murāḍāt muhāyaʾa*). They concluded that the wife would receive the house, even though its value exceeded her share. Attached to the estate division were records of two payments of 50 dinars, each made by the wife, one on 15 January 1477, the other on 5 April 1479.[19] When the son died seven years later, similar arrangements were reached to prevent the physical division of his estate.[20] On 16 November 1483, his wife Maryam and their two sons, Muḥammad and ʿAlī, divided the land and the house using partnership arrangements between a mother and a minor son and between the two brothers. One month later, on 25 December 1484, the older son, who was not under guardianship, sold his mother his share in the house, which he had previously shared in equal parts with his minor brother under her guardianship.[21]

Such goodwill and cooperation within the family in matters of inheritance were not always the rule in Granada. On 7 February 1464 Fāṭima bt. Aḥmad b. ʿAṭiyya was sued in court by her brother-in-law, ʿAlī b. Muḥammad al-Barīṭī, for misappropriating his share in his brother's and her late husband's estate by seizing 7 ounces of silver and 80 silver riyals, silk garments, linen coats, and more gold dinars. A few days later, on 12 February 1464, Fāṭima acknowledged that the charges had been read to her and that she held in her possession 15 riyals and some cloths, which in fact belonged to the other heirs (*waratha*). On 9 April 1464 she returned to court to officially account for the whereabouts of the property. In her deposition, she said that the 14 gold dinars were the proceeds from the sale of a Christian slave by her father-in-law, Muḥammad b. ʿAlī al-Barīṭī, to Aḥmad al-Shuwaykh. She had used the 14 gold dinars to buy land from her brother, Ibrāhīm.[22] The rest, 150 silver dinars, came from the estate of her late husband, which had been divided among the heirs. A month later, on 25 May 1464, Fāṭima went to court again, this time to receive her share in the estate of her own parents, her father Abū Jaʿfar and mother ʿĀʾisha.[23] Fāṭima divided the estate with her brother, Ibrāhīm, and the two agreed that she would receive all the land from her mother's estate, while Ibrāhīm received the house and the land that their father had left. Five days later, on 1 June 1464, Fāṭima surrendered the property that she had misappropriated from her husband's estate, and ʿAlī acknowledged in court that he had received the 14 gold dinars and the 150 silver dinars from her.

A second act of litigation was launched by Muḥammad Baḥṭān on 19 December 1467. He challenged the division of his mother's estate, which had taken place ten months earlier, on 11 February 1467.[24] The heirs were her husband, Aḥmad al-Minshālī, their minor daughter, Najma, and the plaintiff, her son Muḥammad by another husband. The deceased owed 122 dinars to both her son and her husband, and her estate included a house and a vineyard, which the heirs split, the house going to the husband, the vineyard to the son. They also agreed to split the value of the deceased's belongings, for which the son received 25 gold dinars. However, Muḥammad Baḥṭān blamed his stepfather for failing to include his mother's deferred *ṣadāq* of 15 silver dinars in the estate as well as another house attached to the one already included in the estate.[25] Muḥammad also alleged that his stepfather had excluded from the estate a vineyard that he had bought with 30 dinars that had belonged to his dead sister, Fāṭima, and that had been given to him by their mother to buy property on his sister's behalf.[26] Attached to his claim was his stepfather's reply, signed on 4 January 1468, stating that the vineyard had been purchased with his own money. The litigation continued for two years and was finally resolved on 18 August 1470, when the two reached an agreement, registered in court, declaring that they no longer had any quarrel regarding the estate.[27]

Several estate divisions reveal an astounding accumulation of property in female hands. One such was that of Fāṭima bt. Ibrāhīm al-Layṭī, which was divided in court on 17 August 1468. Her heirs were her husband and five young children, four of whom were still under guardianship when their mother died. Fāṭima left the following properties: a house, four parcels of land situated in different areas of the city, a vineyard, and more land recently planted with vines.[28] The land, the house, and the vineyard were divided in equal shares, first between the two male children and then among the three daughters, with the father supervising the division and renouncing his share in his wife's estate. Some estate divisions preserved in the Granadan collection disclose only female heirs. One example of this is the estate of Abū ʿAbd Allāh Muḥammad b. Faraj, which was divided on 17 March 1487.[29] The heirs were his widow, ʿĀ'isha, the daughter of Aḥmad al-Ashkar; his minor daughter by her, also named ʿĀ'isha; his sister, Maryam; his mother, the elderly Fāṭima, daughter of Aḥmad al-Shūbarī; and "no one else" (*lā ghayr*).[30] The court was provided with a financial statement of the estate's monetary value: two houses, one valued at 100 gold and 25 silver dinars, and the other at 300 gold dinars; an apartment valued at 30 gold dinars; a vineyard valued at 373 and one-half dinars; another valued at 32 dinars; and the rest of the deceased's belongings, including furniture and other objects, valued at 92 and four-tenths dinars. The whole estate was valued at 1,175 and nine-tenths dinars, from which the notary deducted the debts, the customary portion of the wife's *ṣadāq*, and a loan of 285 dinars that she had made to her husband. Other debts were also deducted, leaving a total of 628 and five-tenths dinars, to be divided among the heirs. The widow's share came to 77 and four-tenths dinars, and the daughter's to 300 dinars and 98 dirhams. The mother's share was 130 and five-tenths dinars, and that of the sister was 129 dinars. The houses were to be shared, one between the deceased's sister and mother, the other between the wife and the daughter, represented by her uncle, who also took possession of another rural property on her behalf.

The Banū Lubb were a large family who lived in al-Andalus for generations and whose members made their mark on Granada's legal community.[31] We have already met an older member, Fāṭima bt. Saʿd b. Lubb, at the moment of her estate division. The division of an estate belonging to one of the family's younger males, who was unmarried and childless, reveals a concentration of wealth in the hands of young members, whose heirs were mostly women and children, a demographic process accelerated by the war. Division of the estate belonging to the "young man" (*shābb*), Dhū l-Nūn b. Aḥmad b. ʿAbd Allāh b. Lubb, took place in Granada on 21 February 1482.[32] His younger sister, ʿĀ'isha, and his uncle ʿAbd Allāh split two-thirds of the estate, while his nephew Muḥammad, his aunt ʿĀ'isha, and another woman named Fāṭima bt. Muḥammad b. ʿAmr shared the willed third of the estate.[33] This was a large estate that included land in Granada worth 823 silver dinars, another parcel worth 570 dinars, irrigated land worth 525 dinars, a plantation (*mazraʿa*) worth 300 dinars, another plantation also worth 300 dinars, a third plantation worth 150 dinars, including the trees planted on it, a number of different objects worth a total of 41 and six-tenths dinars, and rent from an oil press and land that together valued 60 dinars.[34]

The Legal and Social Patterns of Women's Inheritance in Granada

Two main factors determined how and what property went to females in fifteenth-century Granada: the Islamic inheritance law and changing demographic conditions. Women's inclusion in the Qurʾan as legitimate heirs allowed wives, mothers, daughters, and sisters to acquire property-ownership status through inheritance, something that they had hitherto been unable to do. Imposing this group of "Qurʾanic heirs" on the customary agnatic heirs of the Arab tribes in pre-Islamic Arabia was contradictory to the tribal structures prevailing at the time and was seen as nothing short of a "revolutionary act" on the part of the Prophet Muḥammad.[35] Besides generating a complicated and convoluted system of mathematical calculations to determine the respective shares, it also brought a dramatic change to the overall structure of women's legal status. According to David Powers, who has studied the inheritance system in its early stages, changes to the inheritance law were implemented partly to accommodate changes in the needs of the nuclear family and partly because the inheritance law mattered very little in practice. He distinguishes between the inheritance law and the Islamic inheritance system, the latter of which brought the rules regulating the inter vivos gift, family endowments, and the inheritance law together in an integrated system that facilitated the devolution of property and accommodated the preferences of individuals. However, his conclusion that "[i]n pre-modern times, the application of the Islamic law of inheritance was often the last and least important stage in the process of transmitting property from one generation to the next" is not borne out by the patterns of female inheritance in Granada.[36] The estate divisions discussed herein show that it was normal for Granadan women to acquire the bulk of their property through inheritance from family members. From the evidence, we can also deduce that the spirit of cooperation among heirs with regard to shares was equally evident among men and women, who embraced it as a natural means of preventing the physical division of property.

The contribution of estate divisions to our understanding of the demography and social history of the Granadan family is as great as their contribution to our understanding of women's property ownership. The decline in male numbers, which is clearly evident in the estate divisions, indicates that the nuclear family had become smaller. Some families had no male survivors at all, whereas each estate division in the Granadan collection includes females. Females appear regularly in the documents as heirs, property owners, guardians of orphaned children, legatees, litigants, and heads of households. The difference between the survival rates of males and females affected not only the modes of inheritance, but, of course, also the amounts inherited. This situation had wide-reaching consequences for women's property-holding in the city.

Granadans made sparing use of the right to bequeath the unencumbered third of an estate to benefit non-family, with only a very small proportion going to strangers. Women used it for non-family to an even lesser degree,[37] but did benefit from it themselves.[38] Whether because of the prohibition against willing to a Qur'anic heir[39] or by social consensus, it seems that except for charity, no bequests were made to individuals outside the immediate family, nor were endowments (*waqf*) made for a single member of the family.[40]

The documents for inheritance division show that marriage patterns were also affected by property concerns. Many of the families named in the documents were connected through marriage; the property transactions that they conducted show that, as elsewhere, marriages between cousins were common.[41] Class, social status, and local origins were determinant factors in marriage, as illustrated by a cluster of marriages among people from the city of Baza. It was common for very young women to marry much older men and to inherit from them before they had children of their own. The numerous mentions in estate divisions of children from previous marriages point to frequent second marriages for both men and women. In many instances, women became property owners before they entered marriage, having exercised many of the property rights previously mentioned, and thus gained ownership after marriage. Although war conditions produced more widows, the rate of polygamous marriages did not increase. Instead, the rapid disappearance of Muslim men from Granada resulted in households headed by women, many of them young. However, calculations based on the Andalusian biographical dictionaries show that the average age of procreation for men was thirty-eight, which may suggest that those Granadan men who married much younger women did so not because of the war but because such marriages were common in Andalusian society.[42] As shown in the cases discussed earlier, this marriage pattern had an enormous impact on women's property ownership because women, like men, were often married twice, had children from previous marriages, and were rarely part of polygamous marriages. Polygamous marriage meant a diminished share of the inheritance for everyone, without more property necessarily being available for division, even if both wives had brought their own property with them or acquired some during the marriage. In fifteenth-century Granada, the advanced age of males in some of the marriages, a trend accelerated by the war, meant that a larger than usual number of females—wives, sisters, and mothers—also inherited larger and larger amounts of the family property.

That many females headed the nuclear family or were the de facto head of the household is also reflected in the many cases where females appeared as the executor (*waṣī*) of their husbands' property. As the heads of households, women were also required to assume an increaingly active role in property management.[43] The role of property executor on behalf of minors was granted to females in preference to males throughout the Islamic regions, but in Granada more women may have been appointed as property guardians, and the scope of their work may have been greater, because of the war.[44] Alternatively, that such appointments were common elsewhere, sometimes even despite the availability of male relatives, may reflect confidence that women were competent to take care of their wards' interests, especially their property, and may also be an acknowledgment of both their central role as transmitters of property and their higher survival rate. That they enjoyed this right with the compliance of men may be interpreted as providing stability in times of trouble. The only legal concerns regarding estate division and acquisition appear to have been over payment of the deferred portion of the *ṣadāq*, which had to be settled before the division itself could proceed.[45] While it is true that there were no problems of this nature in the estate division prompting Muḥammad Baḥṭān's litigation against his stepfather nor in a fifteenth-century Granadan fatwa prohibiting a husband from migrating to another Islamic land without paying off the *ṣadāq* or any other debt to his wife, these cases reflect exceptions that prove the rule.[46]

The Granadan documents may differ from those of other regions,[47] but from the inheritance transactions—which frequently involved individuals known to us from other transactions in the collection, including estate divisions—we learn of family affiliations, marriage patterns, and the accumulation of wealth over several generations. The fifteenth-century Granadan records of female inheritance show that large shares went to females; they also reveal responsibility, flexibility, and accommodation in estate division. The documents provide a record of the Granadan methods of female inheritance while also demonstrating the potential of the Islamic inheritance law to significantly enhance females' property ownership.

One may argue that family interactions portrayed in the Granadan estate divisions appear to have been too harmonious, even idyllic. Yet it seems that female family members agreed on who should receive what and that they accepted belated cash transfers in order to facilitate an estate's division in cases where real estate property exceeded the value of their share. Such cooperation and collaboration among heirs was a decisive element in assuring the continued economic vitality of an estate's properties, and the court clearly trusted heirs, registering individual agreements without objection. In doing so, they were responding to the need to keep property intact and capable of producing income. Property seems to have been transferred smoothly, both horizontally and generationally, and the discourse was uniform and steady.

Women's Inheritance in Comparative Context

The continuity and stability, or at least the "official stability and consistency,"[48] of the Islamic law governing women's succession differentiated it from the legal systems of pre-Islamic and contemporary Europe. Both the Roman law of succession and that of the Italian Renaissance cities were fluid, shaped by social pressures, and regularly redefined to include new legislation that prevented women either from inheriting or from controlling their inheritance. Roman law provided "an array of instruments . . . for a variety of goals" in order to accommodate property transmission through succession and dowry, but changes in the economy and in social perceptions of kinship affected and reshaped the law.[49] In the fifth century B.C., Roman women enjoyed inheritance rights equal to those of males, but the passage in 168 B.C. of the *Lex Voconia* prevented them from inheriting large estates, thus rejecting them as reliable transmitters of property.[50] The earlier customs of allowing women to use wills to dispose of their property and to inherit large estates that they could leave to their children became further limited when, three centuries later, new legislation restricted their power to will.

Contemporary European societies went through a similar process. The cities of Renaissance Italy began by extending inheritance rights to women but were soon engaged in enacting legislation designed to deny them the rights that they had been given earlier.[51] The fourteenth-century Italian jurists devised two categories of statutes, one to limit the type and quantity of women's inheritance and the other to impose some form of male guardianship over its disposal. The practice was unanimous and the rule consistent: as long as there were agnatic males alive, females could not claim an equal share in the inheritance allocated to them; "Cities of all sorts, large and small, commercial centres and agricultural markets, from Lombardy to Tuscany and beyond, all adopted such rules."[52]

In comparison, within the *longue durée* context of Islamic law, women's inheritance rights appear to have been stable and protected. There was no room for legislation to diminish women's share of estates or to prevent women from inheriting. Even the unencumbered third of an estate that could be willed was limited by its size. The identity of heirs was known in advance, and no manipulation of the shares could have taken place. Moreover, because of the fixed-share system, there was little room for pre-mortem manipulation or fighting, and it was not legally possible to favour any one of several siblings. The separation of property in marriage meant that an estate was individual rather than a "family patrimony," as in European societies. Muslim men and women had little freedom in the dispossession of their estates, and although threats to women's inheritance could emerge in response to changes in Islamic social mores and attitudes toward women, they could not have been activated through legal provisions.

Aharon Layish's study of the contemporary situation with regard to Arab citizens of the Jewish state of Israel who were allowed to register their estate division under secular law rather than Islamic law, found that the result was the wholesale denial of inheritance to women.[53] This development, of using wills to prevent female family members from inheriting, was attributed by Layish to the economic need of Israeli Muslims, living under unique political circumstances, to preserve an estate's land in its entirety. The freedom to abandon Islamic law also effectively eliminated charitable trusts (*waqf*) made for sons as the need to ensure the non-division of estates could be achieved through a will.

However, when compared to evidence about women's inheritance from other Islamic regions, the Granadan court documents do reveal some distinctive features of female inheritance. For instance, the legal style and notarial practice of the administrative court of fourteenth-century Mamluk Jerusalem[54] varied in that the authorities in Jerusalem registered, first, the inventories of ailing men and women and, second, the estate division.[55] In seventeenth-century Damascus these administrative patterns were matched by inventories registered in the court that listed the respective household inventories before and after estate division.[56] A study of the inventories of 449 Damascene women has revealed that women owned some real estate but mostly jewellery and household goods, trousseau items, linen, bedding, furniture, and the like.[57] While these records confirm the regularity with which women inherited their shares, it is interesting to note the conspicuous lack of land found among women's property in Jerusalem and Damascus in comparison to that belonging to Granadan women.

This regional dichotomy resulted from the respective land-tenure systems of each area. The prominence of private land ownership in Muslim Spain and North Africa, unlike in the East, is reflected in the fact that estate divisions in Granada dealt only with private ownership of land (*mulk*). Private land ownership made it possible to transfer land efficiently and legally from one generation to another and from one family member to another with security and with a guarantee of no state interference once the treasury's share, or taxes on inheritance, had been paid. Land sales and purchases by the Nasrid sultans and their families were registered by the court in a similar manner to the rest of the transactions. In the East, notably in Egypt and regions of the later Ottoman Empire, the paradigms of land tenure were different. Through an examination of the Hanafi legal sources, primarily the law manuals and fatwas, Baber Johansen has been able to describe the evolution of the status of arable land in these regions, where land ownership was transferred from the peasants to either the state or, in the language of the sources, to the imam, ruler of the Muslim political community.[58] Ownership, previously manifested through the payment of land tax, became separate from taxes and land rental, while leases became an expression of landholding but not of ownership proper.

These differences between land-tenure systems influenced not only the distinct content, but also the unique practice, of inheritance in each region. Small land parcels, which were found in the estate of every man and woman in Granada, disappeared from the estates of their contemporaries in Egypt and Syria, even though this change did not arise from any disruptions in the inheritance law itself. The image of the Granadan "Republic of Women" embodied in the amount of property in female hands in Granada during the last eighty years of Islamic rule, the number of families headed by females, and the commercial activity conducted by females in buying and selling property, which will be studied below, made the Granadan context significantly different from that of Syria and Egypt. Land ownership was all about politics, economy, and society, but its administration was facilitated by the law of inheritance.[59]

Female Inheritance and the Charitable Endowment (waqf)

The Granadan collection does not include any charitable endowment (*waqf*) deeds for property transfers to either males or females, but the documents do contain references to property that had previously been endowed as well as clear evidence from nonarchival sources that endowments both to family and for the public good were common in Granada.[60]

I will briefly address the historical link between *waqf* and women's property below, since this study seeks to elucidate the question of women's property rights. To do so we need to point to the dichotomy between inheritance and the two forms of *waqf*, family and public, in terms of property rights. The law of *waqf* allowed a property owner to dispossess property during his lifetime by pledging it to one family member while still deriving income from it in perpetuity. As with the bequeathing of one-third of an estate, expressly allowed by Islamic law, such an action diminished an estate by removing property from it, which in turn limited the shares available to the (other) heirs. Therefore, in terms of property rights, making a *waqf* was by nature an "antiproperty right" act because it abrogated the right to ownership. The two forms of *waqf*—endowments made for family members and those made for the public good—were equally responsible for eliminating property ownership and for infringing on the inheritance law.

Historians and economists disagree about the impact of the *waqf* institution on the economy and society. In terms of Islamic institutions and the *waqf* made for the public good (*waqf khayrī*), historians highlight its perceived contribution to supporting cultural and municipal institutions. As I have argued elsewhere, however, economists point to its value to the economy being diminished by the fact that no individual property rights over these assets were secure, making the *waqf* an inefficient institution in sustaining a thriving economy.[61] Properties that were made an endowment for the public good more often diminished in value because everyday operation of the *waqf* system could be conflict-ridden, the effects being on the whole increased costs, declining revenue, or no revenue at all. Most significantly, the *waqf* practice gave rise to institutional arrangements favouring the liquidation of property, which from an economist's point of view is an indication of the system's failure to fulfill its institutional mandate.[62]

On the matter of women and the *waqf* and whether they benefited from it, the debate has revolved around the benefit of both the public-good *waqf* and the family *waqf*. In investigating the former, most writers have studied conditions under Hanafi law, which allows women to assume roles as managers of the properties that they endowed and, like male managers, receive wages for their work. This aspect did not apply to the regions under Maliki law because donors could not retain any link to the property that they endowed nor become managers of the assets that they endowed. Yet, even in the Hanafi case, women did not truly benefit because the resulting profits were not a significant or viable source of income. Margaret Meriwether notes from her Aleppan study that "the income from small endowments, as most of them were, could not support an individual or a family, especially when divided among several people."[63] Meriwether also observes that in eighteenth-century Aleppo only "a tiny minority" of women were *waqf* managers. Endowments were not an investment in an economic sense, nor could management wages be claimed as an "investment" since they did not provide reasonable return as compensation for the loss of property.

The abundant documentation on *waqf*-making by wealthy women of Mamluk Egypt during the fifteenth and sixteenth centuries provides examples of women's access to large amounts of endowed property, access that enabled them to become property managers of large complexes. However, the concentration of such an enormous amount of wealth in the hands of a single class was not the legal, social or economic norm. Wealthy Mamluk women inherited or gifted capital, bought property with it, and endowed this property to avoid its confiscation and to guarantee at least some income. Their *waqf*-making as an economic venture still dispossessed them of their property, and diminished property ownership by women.[64]

Nor did the family *waqf* empower women with respect to property rights. The late Gabriel Baer, who normally regarded the *waqf* as a great social benefactor, had a change of heart when it came to women, concluding that a *waqf* made for a women actually weakened her economic position as a property holder. Baer pointed out the contrarian nature of the action as it applied to women: women inherited property or acquired it through other property rights, then practically gave it away as a family endowment (*waqf ahli*), with the property eventually finding its way back into the hands of males or being used to enhance males' income, outcomes that negatively affected several generations of females in the process.[65] Although there were certainly important religious reasons for endowing property, the endowment of property for either public or family use contributed voluntarily to the erosion of property rights.

In his study of fatwas dealing with family endowments made under the Maliki school of law, David Powers notes that the family *waqf* was more frequently made in favour of sons:

> Fathers outnumber mothers as founders by a ratio of six to one; of forty-three endowments created by a father for his children, sons are specified as the exclusive beneficiaries in 60 percent of the cases whereas daughters are specified as exclusive beneficiaries in only 19 percent of the cases. Sons and daughters are

> named as cobeneficiaries in the remaining 21 percent of the cases. Thus, fathers were three times as likely to create an endowment for sons as for daughters. By contrast mothers appear to have been more evenhanded. Of eight endowments created by mothers for the benefit of their children, three were created for a son, another three for one or more daughters, and the remainder for sons and daughters jointly.[66]

He concludes that,

> While several cases confirm a phenomenon [whereby family endowments were used to frustrate the inheritance rights of females] (albeit fewer than the secondary literature suggest) both male and female children were vulnerable . . . The specification of females as secondary beneficiaries of familial endowments suggests that Muslim society in the period under consideration was not as rigidly patriarchal as is often asserted. Indeed, my source indicates that the Maliki family endowments frequently were used to supplement the rights of females.[67]

The tendency to benefit certain male or female members and to disenfranchise others reveals the punitive effect of the *waqf* provision on property ownership. Given the large number of females affected, the *waqf* system tended to curtail women's property acquisition, but the effect of the *waqf* system on women was balanced out by its equal elimination of the property rights of men. Nevertheless, women behaved unreasonably as economic agents by following the trend of making endowments in an accelerated fashion. The notion that making a *waqf* somehow protected women's property is mistaken.

Conclusion

By the time the Granadan women described in the records appeared in court for estate division, the Islamic inheritance law had been in effect for 800 years. To judge by the Granadan practice, the right of females either to inherit or to acquire inheritance shares was not contested, nor did inheritance pose either legal or practical challenges for women. Other property rights, such as the right to hold independent property within a marriage, the right to gift and be gifted, and the right to a *ṣadāq*, did not seem to impede or threaten inheritance acquisition either.

The Granadan documents also demonstrate how cooperation within the family mitigated the impact of the law when physical division of an estate was required, whether the estate consisted of land or of houses. The Granadan court cases and the fatwas show that Granadan women dealt with the division of property according to the succession law as sound economic agents, negotiating with co-owners, buying shares, or shifting properties to create equity. Given the lack of detailed records about acquisition, it is hard to ascertain whether identical patterns were present throughout the Islamic lands. Where such evidence exists, it seems to point toward compliance but also reveals that the evolution of social and economic conditions exerted considerable influence on the content of the property that women inherited. In particular, land seemed to disappear from the generational transmission of property, a trend reflected in the content of women's estates. Rather, the succession law itself was the best protection for women's property and for the property of their future heirs, who were watchful of their wives', mothers', and sisters' property because it had direct consequences for their own property ownership. The intrafamily dealings so characteristic of Granadan property ownership can be seen as the antithesis of the *waqf* provision, which can be conveniently described as "suicidal" in terms of property ownership. The importance of the inheritance component to the entire system of women's property rights lies in the fact that since other family members were directly concerned about whether their mothers, wives, sisters, and daughters could inherit, this right was conscientiously safeguarded because it recognized the central role that women played in the transmission of family property.

We can safely assume that practising the inheritance law in Granada had a positive impact both on the position of women within the family and on their capacity to actively participate in economic activities. The high freqency with which women acquired their shares had an added effect on Granadan society: stability. However, women did not see the materialization of these benefits until they had emerged from guardianship, which is our next topic.

Four

DELAYED ACQUISITION

Tāj al-ʿUlā and Her Ward in Court

For Tāj al-ʿUlā, the daughter of the Granadan vizier Abū l-Nuʿaym Riḍwān, 1452 was not a very good year.[1] She had lost her father sometime previously, probably in one of the battles raging around Granada, since the documents refer to him as a martyr (*shahīd*). Soon afterward, Abū ʿAbd Allāh Muḥammad, her brother by the same father, also died. We would probably never have heard of Tāj al-ʿUlā, who appears in the collection of Granadan documents only in the transactions studied here, except that her niece's husband, Abū Yazīd Khālid, died sometime in August 1452, before his young wife, Fāṭima, could be officially released from guardianship. Tāj al-ʿUlā became Fāṭima's guardian either before these deaths occurred or soon afterward. We know about her trials and tribulations on behalf of her ward from a cluster of six deeds concerning the division of Abū Yazīd Khālid's estate, three of which concern Tāj al-ʿUlā's transactions on Fāṭima's behalf.

In the case of the first deed, written and signed on 18 August 1452, Tāj al-ʿUlā went to court to register a claim in Fāṭima's name (her ward: *maḥjūratihā*) for her share of her late husband's estate. The court duly recognized her as Fāṭima's legal guardian and authorized her to claim, handle, and sell the properties comprising Fāṭima's share. On 31 August 1452 Tāj al-ʿUlā again went to the court, this time to claim the remainder of her ward's *ṣadāq*. The division of the estate of Abū Yazīd Khālid, who was the son and grandson of a known Granadan family of notables (*qāʾid*s), the Jāʾ al-Khayr family, took place on 16 September 1452, and Tāj al-ʿUlā returned to the court to confirm, by signing the document, that she had indeed received Fāṭima's share of the estate. This action produced another notarial act, for according to Maliki law, the lack of other relatives meant that much of the inheritance went to the Granadan *bayt al-māl*, the Nasrid state's public treasury. The document states that the *ṣadāq* consisted of the sum of 121 dinars of pure gold and a slave. Fāṭima had previously received 70 dinars, and through the efforts of her aunt, her guardian, she now received the balance of the money as well as the slave. The witnesses testified that they knew Tāj al-ʿUlā and that she was in perfect mental health and a legal agent. Less than two years later, on 19 April 1454, Tāj al-ʿUlā returned to the court to account for the property that she had recovered on behalf of her ward. In the notarized and signed document, she stated that she had received 1,402 gold dinars and 39 silver dinars from the estate on Fāṭima's behalf. Part of this money was in the form of a debt, since Tāj al-ʿUlā had sold land belonging to Fāṭima to another woman and was still awaiting payment. In addition to the money that Fāṭima had received from her *ṣadāq* before the death of her husband and the money that her guardian had claimed for her afterward, Tāj al-ʿUlā accounted for another 1,000 dinars: this sum included four expensive silk garments that had formed part of her ward's trousseau. She described the different pieces of brocade and silk and gave the exact price of each. She also accounted for some surplus money that had remained after the purchases were completed.

The practice of keeping young married women under prolonged guardianship created a legal category of women, referred to in the documents as *fī ḥajr*, who were owners of property but unable to exercise control over it for some years after marriage.[2] In Granada the legal status of the virginal bride in property matters was stated in the marriage contract, where she was referred to either as a "virgin under guardianship" (*fī ḥajr*) if she was young, like Fāṭima bt. ʿUbayd Allāh al-Lakhmī,[3] or, as in the case of Umm al-Fatḥ bt. Abī l-Qāsim al-Ḥannāt, as "a virgin, mature in age and an orphan" if she was older.[4] The latter was granted immediate control of her property. Both of Umm al-Fatḥ's parents were dead, so she, like Fāṭima of Abū l-Nuʿaym Riḍwān's family, was under the guardianship of another member of the family, in her case a brother, who subsequently declared Umm al-Fatḥ released from guardianship and in control of the vast assets that she owned and that had hitherto been under his control. The bride's legal status at marriage had more impact on acquisition than on any other factor. In Granada, as elsewhere, the prolonged guardianship meant that a bride could not immediately acquire her property, be it fields, houses, jewellery, and furniture, whether previously gifted to her in the *ṣadāq*, inherited, or acquired on her behalf. Her property continued to be managed by her parents—usually by her father but, in his absence, by her mother or other close relatives—for some time after she had left home to live with her husband. As shown in Tāj al-ʿUlā's actions on behalf of Fāṭima, despite being married and presumably sexually mature and despite being the recipient of property given to her under her three property rights—*ṣadāq*, gifts, and inheritance—she continued to be under guardianship and was deemed unfit to handle her own property. The prolonged guardianship was unique to women and not only delayed acquisition, but also affected the size and nature of the property that could be passed on to them since time produces negative effects on the economic potential of land and real estate. It had general legal and social implications for women's status within the family and for their economic activities.

The Legal Framework of Guardianship

As minors, boys and girls shared the same property status and were under guardianship (*walāya*) regardless of whether the parents were alive, dead, or divorced, whether the minor was a female or male, or whether the guardian was a female or male.[5] As a result, from birth to majority, which the law established as age fifteen or thereabouts, the property of minors was controlled by a guardian (*walī*), usually the father or, in his absence, any related adult. The Malikis permitted the father to nominate a female—who could be the mother or another related female—as a testamentary guardian in all property matters and also permitted the mother to nominate a male testamentary guardian when the properties in question originated with her and no *walī* had been appointed.[6] However, gender came into play when it was time to be released from guardianship. For males, guardianship normally ended at majority or puberty, but for females it lingered much longer and could be prolonged indefinitely, as was also the case for the mentally impaired. Young females remained under legal guardianship in property matters for up to a maximum of eight years after the time of marriage. This is how Ibn Juzayy explained the rule of the young married woman's interdiction:

> There are three norms with regard to interdiction of females:
> 1. If a woman has a father when she becomes of mature age (*bāligha*), she remains under the interdiction (*fī ḥajr*) of her father until she gets married and lives with her husband, and she remains thus for a period after consummation (*wa-tabqā muddatan baʿda 'l-dukhūl*). There is disagreement over the limits of this period, which can range from one to seven years. It has been said that she is not set free until her father declares that she is mature or tests her reason (*rushd*). Al-Shāfiʿī and Abū Ḥanīfa said that if she is *bāligha*, she is in control of her affairs (*malakat amrihā*).
> 2. If she has a testamentary guardian (*waṣī*) and thus is under property guardianship, she is not to be released unless she has been declared of age (*tarshīd*).
> 3. If she is an orphan (*muhmila*, lit. neglected), it is said that she will be in control of her affairs if she is *bāligha*; others have said [that she will not be in control] until she has cohabited with her husband.[7]

The delayed release of married women from guardianship set the Malikis of al-Andalus and North Africa apart from other legal schools and other regions, a situation of which Maliki jurists were well aware and that they frequently discussed.[8] In Egypt, Khalīl b. Isḥāq defined the issue somewhat differently: "A father of a virgin daughter who reaches majority may lift an interdiction before the consummation of her marriage but preferably should do it afterward. Two conditions must be met: her marriage must have been consummated, and four witnesses (*ʿudūl*) should testify that she is capable of managing her property."[9] The timing of the release was not arbitrary, as the father was forced to terminate his daughter's guardianship after seven years of marriage. When this did not occur, the daughter was automatically released, regardless of whether her guardian released her. Other conditions equally influenced the timing of the release. These included age and whether the marriage had been consummated. The testimony of outsiders about the daughter's intellectual maturity was also needed. Since the initiation of a release from guardianship by a declaration of the necessary mental maturity (*tarshīd*) was up to the father, both sons and daughters depended on his goodwill. They could not gain control of their property until he issued the official declaration of release in court.

In his explanation of the terms used in the marriage contract, Ibn Mughīth explained: "When we say a virgin girl under guardianship (*bikr fī ḥajrihi*), we mean the guardianship that precludes the freedom to freely dispose of her wealth and person, or body (*jism*), which is similar to the father's right to marry off his virgin daughter without consulting her (*bi-ghayr muʾāmaratihā*)."[10] Later, after providing his own model for *tajrīd* (release, literally stripping of), Ibn Mughīth reflected on the reasons for women's lingering guardianship: "The *ratio legis* of being interdicted is extravagance in spending (*safah*). Thus if she is a spendthrift, the interdiction [imposed by] her father is binding [on her] as long as a period of seven or eight years, during which she is with her husband, has not passed. If this period of time, during which she is with her husband, expires without her father removing her interdiction, she is released from his guardianship (*wilāya*), except if he summons witnesses [who confirm] her [continued] status as a spendthrift. This is the practice with the elders."[11]

While all notaries provided in their manuals a model document for a declaration of mental acuity (*tarshīd*) regarding a son, only Ibn al-ʿAṭṭār provided a model for a father about to release his married daughter from interdiction: "The father will register with the notary his married daughter's new status by declaring in the presence of witnesses that, having taken notice of his married daughter's previous incompetence and current competence and her ability to look after her affairs, he, in his role as her guardian (*walī*), is releasing, in fact "stripping" (*jarada*), her of interdiction (*ḥajr*). The witnesses must acknowledge that she has been married to her husband for two or three years." In the portion of his text that deals with legal rules, Ibn al-ʿAṭṭār indicated that the father's interdiction of his daughter could continue until the eighth year of marriage, at which time it would expire, whether he officially released her or not.[12]

Nonetheless, a wife released from interdiction could be re-interdicted for committing irresponsible financial transactions with her property. Ibn Juzayy noted: "If she is married and she spends her property without collateralizing [it] and thus is unable to replace (*bi-ghayr ʿiwaḍ*) shares exceeding one-third [of her property], as in the case of a donation or manumission for which, contrary to the law, she has used more then one-third of her property, this might trigger a return to interdiction."[13] For Khalīl b. Isḥāq, two conditions could trigger the re-interdiction of a wife: pregnancy and recklessness.[14] The reason for interdicting a woman six months pregnant was the fear that if she died in childbirth, any transactions that she had concluded beforehand would become null and void, having been deemed deathbed transactions, which were forbidden by law. According to Khalīl, recklessness occurred when a wife spent in excess of the allowed one-third of her property or gave her property as collateral for her husband's deals. These actions endangered her estate and deprived her heirs of their rightful share. As with other property rights, the inheritance law and consideration for the rights of heirs weighed heavily in individual decisions, except that in this case, the outcome was much more serious: a wife could be re-interdicted.[15]

Guardianship in Practice

The prolonged period of a young woman's guardianship had a wide array of positive and negative implications in the long run both for her property acquisition and for her property ownership. The full historical significance of guardianship's impact on acquisition is not apparent in the sources until we come to the fatwas, which represent the underbelly of the practice as reflected in the model notarial deeds examined earlier. The fatwas studied in the previous chapters, those dealing with acquisition of the *ṣadāq*, of the inter vivos gift, and of inheritance, reveal the frictions inherent in the acquisition process when the parent (usually the father) exercised the right to control the daughter's property in a manner that infringed on her ownership rights. The potential for friction began on the occasion of a marriage, when guardianship was used either to gift the daughter's property back to her future husband as a life gift or to claim it for the guardian's use. In the case of gifted properties, the fatwas repeatedly refer to fathers and mothers who either refused to relinquish control over their daughter's property when the time came or continued to derive income from it without sharing it with their married daughter. Parents' acquisitions of the second *ṣadāq* instalment, destined to provide support in the case of widowhood or divorce, are also reported. The longer the guardianship lasted, the greater the potential for abuse.

A fatwa written by the Granadan mufti Abū Saʿīd Faraj b. Lubb (d. 1380) further demonstrates the dimensions of the power of guardianship. It deals with a father who acquiesced to or initiated the loss of his married daughter's property by allowing it to be made a charitable endowment:

> Someone asked him about a married woman who had made an endowment while she was subject to the guardianship of her father (*fī wilāyat abīhā*), who consented to the endowment. Ibn Lubb responded: There is no doubt in my mind that the endowment should be declared null and void (*yufsakh al-taḥbīs*). This is because the father may not cause his child who is under his interdiction to dispossess any property without compensation (*ʿiwaḍ*), and there was no compensation [in this case]. The practice of the Maliki school is that, if [a father] makes a charitable gift of a house or land belonging to his child, [the property] is restored to the ownership of the child irrespective of whether the father, at the time of the gift, was rich or poor. The court practice is the holding for nullification. [This applies to two contingencies]: if we hold that the father, by consenting to the creation of the endowment, is the creator of the endowment, there is no doubt about its nullification. Alternatively, if we hold that the daughter is herself the creator of the endowment, because she "put her hand" (*bāsharat*) directly on the property, then nullification is even more appropriate because [her action] constitutes a voluntary disposal of property on the part of a female who is under interdiction (*maḥjūra*).[16]

The record of mothers' guardianship was no better. According to the fatwas, when mothers were appointed guardians of daughters, they intervened just as much as fathers did, and in similar ways, in the management of their daughters' property. In cases where the mother was the guardian, the appearance of the daughter's husband in family disputes involving struggle over property was more pronounced, reflecting relations of antagonism and animosity between parents, their daughters, and their sons-in-law:

> Ibn al-Sarrāj [alternatively, Sirāj], a fourteenth-century Granadan mufti, was asked about a husband who had purchased properties (*amlāk*) from his wife and put them to use for a year, at the end of which the wife died. At that moment, the deceased woman's mother took possession of the properties and refused to release them, claiming that she was her daughter's property guardian. In his answer, Ibn al-

> Sarrāj cast doubt on the mother's intention. Why had she remained silent about her claim until her daughter's death? And why had she permitted her daughter, who, according to her claim, was subject to her guardianship, to sell the property to her husband and collect the money? The mufti advised the authorities to look for possible fraud and to carefully examine both the sale document and the document appointing the mother as her daughter's guardian. The matter was referred to a second mufti, al-Ḥaffār, who concluded that the mother's actions amounted to depriving her daughter's offspring of their legal share in their mother's estate. He recommended that her actions be checked carefully because they pointed to improper conduct on her part (*sūʾ taṣarrufihā*).[17]

A similar case was sent for consultation to Muḥammad al-ʿUqbānī, a fifteenth-century jurist from Tlemcen:

> He was asked about a man who gave his wife as her *ṣadāq* one-half of an orchard in joint ownership (*ʿalā l-ishāʾ*), and she purchased the other half from him. For the next seven years, the husband continued to derive income from the property in the manner of a legitimate owner (*taṣarruf al-mālik fī amlākihi*), with the knowledge of his wife's mother (*ʿalā ʿayn wālidat al-zawja*), until the wife secured a divorce (*khulʿ*) from him [ostensibly by surrendering the orchard to him in return for the divorce]. Subsequently, the wife's mother produced a document dated five years before the divorce, indicating that her daughter had transferred (*sayyarat*) the garden to her as payment for a debt. During the entire period, the orchard remained in the same hands. However, in the transfer document there was no mention of *qabḍ*, possession-taking, nor of the *ḥiyāza*, actual transfer, from daughter to mother, except for the acceptance (*qabūl*) of the mother's offer to purchase the orchard.[18]

The question asked is whether instead of the required *qabḍ* and *ḥiyāza*, the acceptance of the offer itself was sufficient to validate the sale. Al-ʿUqbānī answered that if the wife's mother was present during the divorce proceedings and did not object to trading the orchard before the divorce was settled in court, or if she did not attend the court proceedings but did not reveal her knowledge for that entire time, she has no claim over the property. The transfer is dependent on possession-taking, and if the property remained in the hands of the one who was transferring it, or that person's representative, the transfer would not be complete. Another opinion is that even if there is a transfer, a *khulʿ* divorce takes precedence over any other condition.

While it is hard to speculate what actually happened in the above case, the two cases are similar. They both deal with complications in instances where mothers served as guardians of married daughters. Both involve claims over property that belongs to the daughters, both mothers making use of their power as guardians, although in both cases the claims are rejected for reasons resulting from time delays and lack of adherence to the proper rules of transfer.

The motivation for keeping married women under prolonged guardianship in property matters was clearly a concern for the state of the property. Jurists were of the opinion that a young woman would spend recklessly and that the delay in releasing her from interdiction would prevent her from doing so. They believed that the law was intended to provide young women time to grow and mature and to gain experience in economic matters. The inexperienced young wife, ignorant in the "ways of the world" and unaccustomed to appearing and interacting in public places, needed to be shielded from circumstances where she could lose her property. Given the young age of some brides, this was not unreasonable. Making sound property decisions was indeed a concern, as expressed in the distinction made between puberty, or availability for sexual relations, and intellectual maturity (*rushd*). The consummation of the marriage, for which brides acquired the first *ṣadāq* instalment, was not sufficient when it came to making financial decisions.

Another reason for the prolonged guardianship could well have been the law's desire to prevent a daughter from altering the decisions made by her parents regarding the properties that they had gifted her as long as they were alive and deriving income from them. In this respect, inderdiction allowed parents to continue living in the paternal home, ensured the right of a daughter's husband to live in his wife's house rent-free, and protected the husband's right, granted by his wife's parents, either to work her fields or to derive income from property that they had gifted her. Because a daughter's property acquisition, or more precisely the timing of her access to property, lay in her father's hands, guardianship allowed parents prolonged control and long-term planning of property distribution and use. In other words, they could secure the property transfer and enjoy use of the property at the same time. Parents may have hoped that, released from guardianship, a daughter would allow them to live in the house that they had gifted her in return for eliminating the claims of other heirs, but they felt more secure about gifting property to a daughter as long as she remained interdicted, and the law provided parents with the legal tools to delay their daughters' liberation from interdiction.[19]

The husband's position in all of this was awkward and dubious. His legal status in disputes resulting from delayed acquisition was questionable, and his attempts to defend his wife's acquisition claims were usually rebuffed, as we saw in the case of the husband who protested his father-in-law's acquisition of the *kālī'*, the second *ṣadāq* instalment. For their part, the jurists frowned on the benefits that a husband frequently received from deals given him using a daughter's property, and the husband himself was denied any power over his wife's assets even if he tried to assume such power. If the couple lived off the revenue of property given to the husband by his in-laws, he remained dependent on their decisions or on those made by other members of his wife's family to guarantee the flow of income to the household. Any work done on his wife's property had to be recorded and the documents made available to the court in case of disputes.[20]

Nonetheless, the prolonged guardianship law had some positive effects on women's property ownership and thus on their social and economic status. The frequent appointment of mothers or other female relatives as property guardians empowered them to deal with economic matters and demonstrated a certain degree of confidence in their ability to act as administrators and managers and to make business decisions. Both the Granadan documents and the fatwas show that mothers who were appointed to act as guardians had power over considerable resources and assumed a great deal of responsibility. In addition to Tāj al-ʿUlā, other Granadan women who appear in the court documents acted as their children's guardians. One such woman was ʿĀʾisha bt. Ibrāhīm b. Thābit, who was appointed by the court to look after her five young children following the death of their father, Abū ʿUthmān Saʿīd al-Sulaymī, on 30 August 1421.[21] Once appointed, a guardian had to appear regularly in court to account for all expenditures and economic transactions undertaken on behalf of one's wards. ʿĀʾisha, whose sister Mahjūna we met previously as the appointed guardian of her mentally handicapped stepson, went to court to officially account for her expenses as the guardian of her children.[22] The language used by the court scribe to describe ʿĀʾisha was respectful and laudatory and confirmed the trust placed in her. The court's matter-of-fact attitude toward female guardians was indicative of a social norm, not of a rare occurrence.

In the long run, however, the most important impact of the prolonged guardianship of women was that it increased women's chances of receiving property from their parents. The law of guardianship made it attractive for parents to gift property to minor girls because of the prolonged control and concomitant benefits that they enjoyed. This beneficial effect is confirmed by the Granadan documents, which show that when parents came into cash or property, they preferred to gift it—or buy property with it to gift—to their minor daughters instead of registering it in their own names, where it would be affected by the inheritance law.

The many challenges to the acquisition of property gifted to women during their minority prove untrue the idea that marriage alone was a legal step toward emancipation in property matters. The practice of prolonged guardianship over married daughters, as described in the fatwas, is the underlying stressful factor in situations when, several years after the marriage, parents continued to control property, regardless of whether it was already in the couple's physical possession or still owned by the parents. Although on the one hand marriage affirmed sexual maturity, on the other it did not automatically effectuate the acquisition of property, confirming that the jurists differentiated between sexual and intellectual maturity, considering immaturity in property matters to be remedied by experience and age. The jurists did not regard the act of marriage itself as investing the woman with the necessary capacity for the acquisition of property rights, even though the law endowed her with such qualities. In this respect, the prolonged guardianship of women can be seen as a component in women's property ownership that was as important as the entire spectrum of their property rights.

Guardianship in Comparative Context

All propertied societies shared a concern for the protection of minors and their property, and this concern was addressed by granting guardianship rights to related adults. The evolution of women's guardianship as a legal institution—and its relationship to the rest of the legal systems in the Mediterranean region during the pre-Islamic period—has been shown here both in Granada, where guardianship of females continued, and among Granada's European contemporaries. Women's guardianship was a constant component of Roman law, which equated women with children and used this equation as social justification for their guardianship.[23] The similarities between the Roman tutor of minors and the Islamic guardian are striking, suggesting that even if there was no historical link between the two systems, they at least shared a strong social perception that the defence of women's rights justified their being placed under prolonged guardianship.[24]

In fourteenth-century Florence, a male tutor or legal guardian (*mundualdus*) was required to sanction adult women's transactions.[25] As with Islamic female guardianship, the Florentine father had early control of his daughter's property and activities, but in contrast to the Islamic custom, he had to relinquish this right at the time of his daughter's marriage as he transfered her dowry to her husband. Like the young Muslim wife, the Florentine married woman did not benefit from this transfer since she was not free to handle her own affairs or to contract on her own. Instead, she was required by law to have an adult male associated with her in any legal transaction. The Florentine legal practice showed a bias toward granting the husband the role of *mundualdus*, and if a husband was present at the time of his wife's legal transaction, he was assumed to be the *mundualdus*.

The difference lies in the fact that the Muslim wife was legally released from interdiction after seven years of marriage, if not earlier, while the Florentine woman remained a permanent ward.

Perhaps to balance the equation, Florentine guardianship of the adult woman appeared to be a looser practice, whereas prolonged guardianship in the Islamic context involved strict control of the young wife's property. The Florentine requirement for a male guardian was more a matter of form and the prominence of family members turned it into a fixture in family relations. In terms of the wife's property, the Florentine *mundualdus* was a flexible institution. The appointment of a *mundualdus* was a regular legal practice, and a judge could appoint one for a woman in the same way as he did for minors. The male guardian, whose possession of the wardship (*mundium*) lasted only for a single day or for the duration of a sequence of legal actions in a given day, discharged his duty by simply consenting to transactions made by a woman. Furthermore, in simple contracts and voluntary legal activities, a woman could designate her own *mundualdus*, subject to the judge's confirmation, and ordinary contracts were sufficiently valid without a guardian. In other judicial proceedings, a woman needed a procurator, who had to be a notary versed in the law, and the judge could appoint such a person as a *mundualdus*.

The two guardianship systems resembled each other in administration. Both offered the woman ample protection from her guardian by forbidding him to sign transactions from which he might benefit, and both provided women with the use of witnesses and agents, *procuratores* in Florence and *wakīls* in Granada.

Clearly differentiating these two systems was the European husband's greater empowerment compared to that of the Islamic husband. Some historians of the Renaissance have seen in women's guardianship during this period evidence of the restricted legal status of Renaissance women. Joan Kelly, for example, sees women's guardianship as reinforcing women's initial exclusion from the benefits of the new economy and society.[26] Thomas Kuehn sees in the "Florentine institution of the *mundualdus* a means of dealing with those potentially dysfunctional moments in the structure of male dominance when women entered the public arena."[27] Julius Kirshner sees granting husbands power over wives' property as part of a "wider pattern in which legislators across northern and central Italy were granting husbands broad control over all the wife's assets, non-dotal as well as dotal."[28] By disempowering the wife, the Eropean system of guardianship empowered the husband.

This interpretation of the European context serves to highlight the opposite position of the Muslim husband. The Islamic system gave the father or mother longer and stricter control over the daughter's property, thus limiting the husband's power. The Muslim husband remained legally irrelevant and practically distanced from his wife's property during her interdiction, and he continued in this condition for the duration of the marriage, since the separation of property in marriage enabled married women to maintain control over their property. The practice of interdicting a young married woman in the early years of marriage did not negate or limit her potential to be a recipient of property or to otherwise accumulate property during her interdiction. None of her property rights was curtailed, in fact they and those of her potential heirs were protected, and her guardian was forbidden from dispossessing or destroying her property. Only her capacity to initiate and execute property transactions, commercial or other, on her own during the period of guardianship was limited. Nor did the existence of the prolonged guardianship of the young married woman impair women's capacity to be guardians themselves. By comparison, the Florentine *mundualdus* had to be a male, and Renaissance jurists regularly advised against leaving property and children under women's care because the Florentine jurists saw women's incapacity and legal inferiority as a permanent state. The Muslim woman's legal capacity was immobilized only temporarily and her release from interdiction was guaranteed, making the female guardianship of minors possible under Islamic law.

Finally, comparing the Islamic arrangement to property devolution in premodern Portugal attests to the originality of Islamic guardianship as an arrangement for securing the care of older parents.[29] The Portuguese inheritance law closely resembled the Islamic law, with two-thirds of the property devolving to fixed heirs and one-third available for distribution according to the owner's preference. When gifting the unencumbered third to children, Portuguese parents wrote the children's obligation to care for them in old age directly into the document that recorded the transfer of property from them to the children. The condition became a standard clause attached to the gift of property.

Conclusion

The guardianship of females, including already married daughters, was not about the personal relationship between a daughter and her guardian, even though all shades of parental love and abuse can be seen in the legal documents examined here. The evidence shows that some fathers and mothers acted in ways that infringed on their daughters' rights. They refused to deliver the property after their daughters' release from interdiction and prevented them from deriving the full benefit of their property, making decisions that a daughter might later challenge in court. Keeping a daughter's property well after guardianship had ended was clearly in defiance of the law but was nonetheless frequent. However, we should not forget that fatwas, because they were often issued after litigation, are more prone to depict the abuse of the guardianship rule than its benefits. The law of guardianship protected against the dispossession of property by forbidding parents to harm their ward's interests, even though such practices as giving the daughter's property to her husband upon marriage, allowing him to cultivate and derive revenue from it, and permitting him to live rent-free in the house that she owned seem to have been not only common, but also accepted begrudgingly by the jurists.

Given the potential for misuse of property, the law of guardianship benefited women by prolonging the period during which property could be given to them without the donor's losing control over it. Guardianship enhanced women's capacity to receive property legally from various sources at a young age because it made property transfers from family members more attractive. Once gifted, this property remained the woman's possession and, in the long run, benefitted her and her children.

The foregoing examination of prolonged interdiction of women in the comparative context also highlights the unique nature of Islamic property relations between parents and daughters and between husbands and wives. The strict legal separation of property in marriage facilitated the gifting of property to the wife without the fear that it would end up under her husband's control, even though it could be dispossessed by the wife in the case of a divorce. The husband who lived in a house that was a gift to a daughter would have felt threatened by prolonged guardianship. In theory, gifting a house symbolized the creation of a new household, but in reality the power of the parent to repossess the house would have hovered like a cloud over the couple. Moreover, a wife's delayed release from interdiction and the resulting lack of control of her property prevented her from freely lending money to her husband and from gifting him the rights to cultivate her fields. The potential for the guardian to impose re-interdiction under the pretext that she was a spendthrift complicated the relations between husband and wife even further. The property relationship between parent and daughter was always one of inequality as long as she did not control her property, contributing to adversarial feelings between husband and parent-in-law. The wife's release from interdiction could inaugurate a new property relationship for the couple. She could easily lend him money, and he could work his wife's fields, represent her in public transactions requiring a public appearance, such as sales and acquisitions, and rent out her property. Women's property rights and the separation of property in marriage afforded a wife a great deal of potential independence, even a sense of equality with her husband. By combining their property, a couple could further enhance the household's economic conditions, but this could not be voluntarily realized unless the interdiction was removed. In the relationship between parent-in-law and husband, there was much potential for friction, which the custom of marriages between cousins could assuage.[30]

While women's prolonged guardianship during marriage could have ambiguous effects on the relationship between a daughter and her guardian, guardianship could also prove liberating in her relationship with her husband, whose rights respecting her body and its feminine functions were equally limited. The female body as property is examined in the next chapter.

Part Two

BODY AND SOUL

Five

THE BODY AS PROPERTY

Foster Parenting ʿĪsā

On 4 September 1494, three years after Granada surrendered to the Christian armies, Abū ʿAbd Allāh Muḥammad al-Baḥṭān—whom we met previously when he sued his stepfather over his mother's *ṣadāq*—and his wife, Umm al-Fatḥ bt. al-Shalubānī, went to court to record an orphan-fostering deed.[1] The male child, ʿĪsā b. Mahdī, was fatherless, but his mother, Umm al-Fatḥ bt. Yūsuf Ibn Ḥadīd, was present and signed the fostering act. The couple undertook not to ask for the maintenance (*nafaqa*), day and night clothing, shelter, and custody payment (*ḥaḍāna*) to which the young ʿĪsā was entitled, nor to ask for anything else for him from others (*khalq Allāh*). They promised in court never to ask for any payment or reward for their actions, as they were fostering ʿĪsā for the grace of God. They also committed themselves to returning the boy to his mother when he reached maturity (*bulūgh*) and promised not to prevent her from visiting him while he was in their care. The witnesses signed the document and testified that the couple were both of sound physical and mental health.

Even though they claimed that ʿĪsā's fostering was a charitable act, the couple were no strangers to the boy. They and the child's mother were related: the Ḥadīd family was al-Baḥṭān's family of origin. His mother, as we learn from other documents in the collection, was a member of the Ḥadīd family, and her name was identical to that of the child's mother, Umm al-Fatḥ bt. Abī l-Ḥajjāj Yūsuf b. Abī Ḥadīd.[2] The couple, who were probably childless (there is no mention of children in any of the many other court documents that they registered), were also responsible for another act of child fostering. Thirteen years earlier, on 17 January 1481, Umm al-Fatḥ, al-Baḥṭān's wife, had appeared before the court to sign a fostering deed respecting her niece, ʿĀʾisha, daughter of her late sister Zaynab.[3] Both she and ʿĀʾisha's father stated before the court that they would not use ʿĀʾisha's property, an inheritance from her mother, to pay for her needs while she was in the care of her aunt. These two children, ʿĀʾisha and ʿĪsā, were named as stepchildren (*rabīb, rabība*) in Muḥammad al-Baḥṭān's will, signed in Granada on 17 December 1493, in which he divided the unencumbered third of his estate.[4] ʿĀʾisha was to receive cloth worth 20 new silver dirhams, 30 dirhams were to go toward feeding the poor, and the youngster ʿĪsā was to receive the remainder, both cash and property. At the same time, and in the same document, Muḥammad al-Baḥṭān, who clearly had full confidence in his wife's financial acumen, appointed her the executor of his will.

ʿĪsā and ʿĀʾisha each had one parent alive, but when people like the al-Baḥṭāns wanted to help their relatives who were single parents by taking over the children's care, they had to register the action in a court document. They were obligated to do so because one had a right to payment for providing care to a young child (*ḥaḍāna*, or custody). This legal right, normally reserved for a separated or divorced mother or for other related females, could be transferred to foster parents only by means of a trip to the notary and to the court, where the foster parents had to either accept or renounce the payment before they could take over care of the children.[5] The Baḥṭāns renounced this right. In another case a few years prior, ʿĀʾisha bt. Abī ʿUthmān Saʿd b. Aḥmad al-Muʾadhdhin and her guardian father, whom we met earlier, also renounced this right, among other property rights, in order to obtain a *khulʿ* divorce from her husband.[6] The right to payment for childcare was well respected in Granada.

The custody payment was technically a property right, one of those created by motherhood but acquired only when the mother no longer lived in the same domicile as the father. However, the law also granted the right to payment to the mother's relatives or to the female relatives of the father when they took over the care of the child. Bestowing this right on a female was a sign that the law recognized the female body as possessing some unique qualities that should be compensated. In the above example, it was the capacity to provide physical care to the young child that warranted payment, but the recognition of the body as property also incorporated payment for such functions as intercourse and breastfeeding.[7] When studied within their respective legal frameworks, the distinct status given to intercourse, breastfeeding, and childcare might differ in terms of legal reasoning and provisions, but they nevertheless retain a common background: each was subject to remuneration when fulfilled and, when denied, necessitated that surrogates be compensated in recognition of the fact that the physical functions related to reproduction were subject to female property rights. An examination of how these rights were formulated in the law books, their translation into practice in the notarial manuals, in court documents facilitating their acquisition, and in fatwas detailing jurists' deliberations and opinions arising from challenges to them, show that jurists granted similar legal status to a select and well-defined number of physical states or outcomes related to reproduction: virginity, circumcision, a child's death at birth, the mother's milk bond, abortion, and childlessness. Each of these was implicated in dimensions of the legal and social standing of the female body and thus subject to women's property rights.

For comparative context, I have selected the practice of medicine, a discipline involving care of the female body. Similar to law, medicine was a contemporary scientific discipline that concerned itself with the body, and its precepts were written in a literary form. As such, it was an auxiliary discipline alongside laws that dealt with the reproductive functions. Its difference from law lay in the physical nature of its preoccupations and treatments. Given the many similarities in content and context between the two disciplines, certain questions arise: Did the two disciplines share a mutual awareness of each other? Were physicians aware of the legal aspects of women's bodies? Were jurists sufficiently knowledgeable about problems, treatments, and cures respecting women's reproductive organs, all of which could affect their property rights? Did property rights have a direct bearing on the legal status of the body? Understanding how each group of specialists regarded the female body has merit in itself, but it is also important in light of each discipline's affect on family and social status. As we shall see in a comparison of medical and legal discourse on the female body, the two disciplines interacted, providing the female body with a cultural context and social content—hence the body as the subject of property rights.

Intercourse

From a legal perspective, the first act of intercourse between bride and groom, usually referred to as the consummation of the marriage, was more than a mere physical act: "One can say without exaggeration that the whole regularization of the marriage is dominated by this idea of consummation."[8] For a daughter still under interdiction, consummation was the great trigger of property acquisition, for it inaugurated the actual acquisition of the *ṣadāq*.[9] All legal schools, except the Hanafis, agreed that the bride was entitled to refuse intercourse, and some even gave her the right to request that the marriage be dissolved before consummation had taken place, regardless of whether the husband had paid the *ṣadāq* to the father.[10] Moreover, once consummation had taken place, the wife was entitled to acquire financial support for maintenance (*nafaqa*), both in marriage and in divorce. In practice, however, the legal sources seem to agree that the issue of consummation was also associated with female physiological issues, such as virginity and availability for sexual activity, which were not in themselves subject to property rights but assumed such legal status by their association with consummation.

Virginity held a unique position in terms of rights over a woman's body, and the jurists, muftis, and notaries gave it full legal exposure in their discourse. Virginity may have acquired its legal standing in the context of property rights because of its inclusion in the marriage contract, which was formally worded. A bride marrying for the first time was routinely described in her marriage contract as "virgin under guardianship" (*bikr fī ḥajr*).[11] In this case, the lack of virginity was considered a physical defect (*ʿayb*) similar to other bodily defects, such as leprosy, which entitled the husband to request the annulment of the marriage.[12] A bride accused of not being a virgin ran the risk of having her marriage annulled or forfeiting the payment of the agreed *ṣadāq*. Amalia Zomeño Rodriguez has studied numerous examples of such occurrences described in the fatwas from North Africa and Spain.[13] They show that the legal challenges to virginity came in the form of complaints launched by husbands who claimed that their brides had been found wanting in this regard on the first night of the marriage. The jurists resolved such cases with the aid of expert women, either midwives or other female caregivers, who were asked to examine the young woman in order to verify her condition. One assumes that by examining the girl, an expert midwife could tell whether the girl's intercourse with her husband was her first act of intercourse. Depending on the result of the examination, the jurists decided who was responsible for making a false claim. It might be suggested that claims on the part of a first-time husband were due to his lack of sexual experience or that, more deviously, such claims were made simply to gain back part of the *ṣadāq*. In any event, the jurists took these claims seriously. If the wife's state of nonvirginity prior to the marriage was confirmed, the husband had the right to decide whether to divorce or to remain in the marriage, with the woman receiving a reduced *ṣadāq*. The notary al-Jazīrī provided a model deed by which a father could anticipate or counteract the accusation and the attempt to reduce the *ṣadāq*. In this deed, the father would declare and register in court before witnesses a statement regarding his daughter's virginity. With al-Jazīrī's model, entitled *ʿAqd fī suqūṭ al-ʿudhra* ("A deed for the loss of virginity"), a father could testify that his young virgin daughter had fallen from a ladder, a staircase or a step, thus sustaining an injury that might suggest the loss of virginity.[14]

Because the body was subject to intrinsic property rights, intercourse with an underage bride was equally seen as an infringement of her property rights. In this context, the legal discourse became more sophisticated. Unlike the legal status of virginity, which either existed or not, the legal status of sexual maturity for intercourse was neither clearly established nor forcefully stated in the law books; however, the common practice of child marriages put it to the test. Jurists of all schools agreed that signing the marriage contract was not sufficient to permit intercourse between bride and groom; rather intercourse was to take place only when the wife became physically or sexually available.[15] Under normal circumstances, several years would pass between signing a marriage contract and the marriage banquet that preceded the wife's arrival at her husband's house and her availability for sexual intercourse.[16] Jurists of all schools save that of the Hanafis agreed on the law's insistence that puberty was required before sexual intercourse was permissible.[17]

Intercourse with a minor, even when a marriage agreement had been signed, was thus not normally permitted but clearly could have occurred if the young wife was prematurely taken without parental consent to her husband's home. Such an incident is reported in Mamluk Egypt in 1470, where the judge al-Ṣayrafī was called before the court.[18] An orphaned twelve-year-old bride was married off by the qadi Nūr al-Dīn al-Khaṭīb to a Mamluk soldier and delivered to his house, where the offence occurred, while her aunt, with whom she lived, was out of town. The case was brought before the grievances court (*maẓālim*, where citizens could lodge complaints against wrongful government actions), which was presided over by al-Sayfī Yashbak, the Mamluk Grand Major-Domo, who interrogated the judge who had presided over the conclusion of the marriage. Regardless of the circumstances, the offending husband was convicted, forced to divorce the girl, and required to pay a fine. The girl's compensation at the end of the trial was the 7 dinars that had originally been paid by the girl's aunt to the husband in exchange for a *khulʿ* divorce and 4 dinars constituting the husband's payment of her delayed *ṣadāq*.

Beyond consummation, intercourse continued to retain its own legal status in the context of property rights, with (free) wives having the option to forbid the practice of coitus interruptus (*ʿazl*) as a means of birth control.[19] All legal schools agreed that the practice itself was authorized and lawful, and most agreed that it could not proceed without the wife's consent.[20] The Shafiʿi school was the exception, saying that since the practice was legal, the wife's consent was not required. Some of the legal schools, such as the Maliki and the Shiʿi schools, demanded that a wife be compensated for consenting to coitus interruptus. They ruled that a monetary compensation was due, but limited it to the duration of the consent, stating that the wife had the right to change her mind, reopen the contract, and withdraw her consent before the end of the period. In such a case, she had to refund either the entire amount paid to her or simply an amount proportional to the remainder of the period. Shiʿi law even permitted making the establishment of a woman's consent a condition in the marriage contract and charged the husband 10 dinars each time coitus interruptus was practiced without her consent. Basim Musallam, who has written a study of the issue, concludes: "Contraception became an issue in Islamic law because coitus interruptus was an act of male volition in conflict with these basic female rights. Remove the specific context of women's rights and there remains no apparent occasion for the discussion of coitus interruptus in Islamic jurisprudence."[21]

The "women's rights" that coitus interruptus was deemed to transgress were the right to children and the right to complete sexual fulfilment. While not all the sources registered sexual fulfilment as a legal entitlement in the couple's relationship, it was recognized as a property right by the Hanbalis, who regarded sexual enjoyment as a female right, even among slaves.[22] The consideration shown by members of this school for this aspect of female sexuality is noteworthy given some of their proponents' support of female circumcision, a procedure that, if anything, deprived Muslim females of sexual pleasure.[23]

It is important for our understanding of women's property rights in the law to reiterate that only a free woman could enjoy property rights respecting her body, as the case of intercourse well illustrates. As Musallam notes, the law treated coitus interruptus under three headings: "(1) with a wife who is a free woman; (2) with a wife who is a slave of another party, man or woman; and (3) with a man's own female slave, or concubine."[24] The rights to give and withdraw consent to coitus interruptus and to receive compensation for permitting the act were available only to the "free wife," whose rights were infringed by the practice. Since the slave woman was herself "owned," her body could not entitle her to the same property rights as those of a married free woman. A marriage between a female slave and a free man was allowed only if the man could not afford a *ṣadāq*, which would have prevented him from marrying a free woman.[25] Consequently, all schools of law permitted the practice of birth control with a slave without her permission. The slave woman's reduced control over her body was also displayed in her lesser claim to privacy during intercourse.[26] The Shiʿi compilation of prophetic medicine, entitled *Ṭibb al-āʾimma*, insisted that privacy was required for intercourse with a free spouse but not with a slave woman: "Do not have intercourse with one free-born woman in front of another. As for (intercourse with) one bondmaid in front of another, there is no objection (to that)."[27] If married to another slave, a woman did not have the rights of a free wife as long as she remained a slave but gained access to them once both she and her husband had been manumitted and had acquired their own property rights. Such was the case of the black woman Zumurrud, who, together with her husband, the black manumitted slave Mubārak, came to the Granadan court on 23 April 1479 to register the purchase of a house. The house was bought from Umm al-Fatḥ bt. al-Shalubānī, the caregiver of ʿĪsā and ʿĀʾisha mentioned earlier, which explains why the document was preserved together with the rest of the deeds relating to the Shalubānī/Baḥṭān family transactions.[28]

To sum up, engaging in intercourse with a wife was a property right, one that the husband acquired by paying the *ṣadāq*. Virginity was required to safeguard this property right, but intercourse was not allowed before sexual maturity was determined and compensation had been given. A woman was duly compensated for the use of her body by marriage and by an array of payments, such as for maintenance. And because of intercourse's unique association with both procreation and pleasure, it required that a wife consent to and be compensated for the practice of coitus interruptus, which infringed on her rights of both.

Breastfeeding

The legal status of breastfeeding, although not in reference to women's property rights, has recently been the object of two academic studies.[29] Unlike intercourse, breastfeeding was specifically articulated in the Qurʾan as a remunerated activity, and mother's milk as a commodity, thus establishing breastfeeding as a property right. The first passage (Q 2:233) deals with breastfeeding within the marriage ("The mothers should suckle their babies for a period of two years for those [fathers] who wish that they complete the suckling, in which case they should feed them and clothe them in a befitting way; but no soul should be compelled beyond capacity, neither the mother made to suffer for the child nor the father for his offspring. The same holds good for the heir of the father [if he dies]. If they wish to wean the child by mutual consent there is no harm. And if you wish to engage a wet nurse you may do so if you pay her an agreed amount as is customary."),[30] and the second (Q 65:6) after divorce ("When divorced . . . and if they suckle the child for you, then make the due payment to them and consult each other appropriately.").[31] As Linant de Bellefonds has commented, despite the clarity of these pronouncements, "which should have lead to a unanimity of opinion, they become the subject of great divergences."[32] The essence of the debate over breastfeeding, as reflected in *ḥadīth* collections, legal manuals, Qur'anic commentaries, and a variety of other literary sources, was about breastfeeding as a property right—in other words, about the status of mothers' milk whether mothers, married or divorced, could be required to breastfeed their own children.

According to the majority of Shafiʿi, Hanbali, and Imami jurists, the precedent of the divorced mother is binding and should prevail within the marriage as well. A mother should not be compelled to breastfeed her child, except when the father is unable to find a wet nurse or the baby refuses a stranger's milk.[33] These jurists are also of the opinion that the father should pay the mother for breastfeeding, since he would have had to hire a wet nurse for the duration of the lactation period of two years in any event had the mother not been willing to suckle the child. In this way, they highlight the Qur'anic dicta that the mother should not be required to sacrifice her interests for those of her baby, and that in the event of divorce, payment for breastfeeding should be given in addition to maintenance (*nafaqa*).[34] The Hanafi and Maliki schools differ in that they hold that the mother is morally obligated to breastfeed her child, meaning that if she does it voluntarily, she is not entitled to any remuneration.[35] The Maliki school, however, makes an exception in the case of women of a higher social class. According to Ibn Juzayy in fourteenth-century Granada: "While it is the mother's duty to breastfeed her child, if she is sick, has little milk in her breasts, or belongs to a social class where this is not done, and the husband can afford to hire a wet nurse, he should do so. A wife must perform only the chores of the inside (*al-khidma al-bāṭina*), such as baking, cooking, sweeping the floors, spreading the carpets, and drawing water, but not income-generating activities, such as spinning, weaving, and the like."[36] The recognition of breastfeeding as a wage-earning activity is here well articulated.

With regard to the practice in the Maliki Maghrib and in al-Andalus, the great number of fatwas in the *Miʿyār* dealing with payment for lactation (*riḍāʿ*) reveal that when mothers nursed their infants within a marriage, even in the upper classes they did not seem to request wages, but they certainly did request them when divorced from the infant's father. It was not the mother's right to receive payment that was most at issue; disputes centered on uncertainties regarding the amount of payment and the length of time for which it was due.[37] In a fatwa submitted to the fourteenth-century Moroccan jurist al-Yaznasānī, a father asked his former wife to accept a low payment for breastfeeding their child because "times are difficult":

> This qadi was asked about a man who had a daughter living away from him with her mother, his divorced wife. The court ordered him to pay his wife wages of 5 dirhams a day for breastfeeding, which he did. The period of breastfeeding is normally two years. However, after eight months, the mother demanded an increase in her wages, but the father begged her to endure because times were hard. He suggested that if she gave him back the wages, he would hire a servant or a wet nurse for the child.[38]

In his answer, the jurist wrote that the wages for nursing could fluctuate, for better or for worse, according to fluctuation in the market prices (which confirms the status of mother's milk as a commodity), and that the mother remained entitled to the wages even if the father found someone else to nurse the child for less or even gratis.[39] The fatwas confirm that the obligation to pay for breastfeeding was a legal and social norm, and that acquisition of this right was never in doubt.

The interpretation that the legal status of breastfeeding can be explained by the wife's body being the property of her husband is challenged by our findings.[40] The fact that many jurists accepted breastfeeding as a remunerated activity and allowed that mothers could not be compelled to suckle their children, even with the prospect of a fatal outcome, means that a woman's milk was not ipso facto her husband's property in the eyes of the law but was seen as a commodity. This would seem to be a direct outcome of the legal stand that the wife's body and its reproductive qualities were her property. The recognition of this can be seen also in the legal articulation of wet nursing, for which service there was a hiring contract, practically the only hire contract for females provided in the notarial formularies.[41] With this contract nursing mothers had the right to hire themselves out for the job and to keep their wages from their husbands in accordance with the separation of property within marriages. The husband's signature on the contract was necessary because he had to agree to give up his right to sexual intercourse with his wife during the period she was hired to breastfeed.

Not only the Qur'an but also contracts for hiring a wet nurse from Roman and Byzantine Egypt reveal that Islamic law's position on the issue reflected longstanding historical practice in the region. Once a direct legal link between breastfeeding and wages had been established, the right to monetary compensation for any kind of breastfeeding, including nursing one's own child, must have automatically followed.[42] With the law regarding lactation as a service rendered by the female body in conformity with its perception of the body as property, women could practice wet nursing as a lawful and independent occupation. Equally consequential was the law's position on the wages paid for nursing one's own child when a woman was divorced. A wife and a husband could acquire property rights respecting each other's bodies, but neither of them owned the other's body. In the end, any individual interpretation of the legal sources dealing with breastfeeding, whether by the medieval jurists or modern commentators, depended largely on whether the interpreter recognized the premise that women's property rights were a fundamental principle of the law.

Pregnancy and the Rights of the Unborn

The notion that a woman's body was intimately involved in property issues—even rights—is illustrated by the legal status given to an unborn child in the mother's womb. The jurists treated the question of an unborn child's paternity in anticipation of mishaps during pregnancy, such as the premature death of the father, the mother, or the unborn child, and the focus of their deliberations was property rights. For instance, the unborn child acquired inheritance rights respecting his father's or mother's property from the moment of conception, but since paternity could be contested, provisions had to be made available for establishing an unborn's relationship to its father so that the unborn could inherit if the father died before the child was born.[43] In his manual Ibn Mughīth offered two models for establishing paternity, both involving the mother's body. In the first, the husband acknowledged that on this date his wife's pregnancy was showing, that she was pregnant by him, that he was the father of the child, and that a notice to this effect had been given.[44] The second document addressed a situation in which both father and baby died, the father during the pregnancy and his newborn at birth. In this case, the notary was to ensure that midwives, women described by him as "known for their expertise and honesty," testified to having been present when the mother was seized by labour pains and when she delivered a live child who later died. The document reads as follows: "She was the wife of the deceased, whose name was so-and-so, who died while she was visibly pregnant (*dhāt baṭn*), on this day or night in this month. The child, a male or a female, began life by crying out loud and was alive until a certain hour and then died, and they sign the document."[45]

By signing the document, the midwives, whom the law already recognized in the case of contested virginity to be professionally competent and legally trustworthy, resolved the complicated issue of how to establish that the child had given signs of life, a requirement that had to be fulfilled if the child was to inherit.[46] In the section of his manual that deals with the jurisprudence, Ibn Mughīth explained that if the child was deemed to have been born alive, since it cried out loud, it could inherit from its dead father and thereby safeguard the rights of those entitled to inherit from the child.[47] This had significance for a Caesarean section resulting in the retrieval of a live child from its dead mother's womb, even though the procedure was sufficiently rare that it did not generate a specific legal provision.[48]

The focus of these model documents is the preservation of a property right, the right to inherit. Through them the view that the womb, and beyond it, the female body, are crucial instruments in its transmission and preservation, is expressed. While the act of intercourse generates the new filiation, the pregnancy in the womb is the transitory stage that makes the activation of individual property rights feasible. During pregnancy, the legal rights of the unborn are enshrined and preserved and the individual property right of both mother and father is transmitted to the unborn. Thus the female body, which contains and assures the development of the new person, is a critical participant in the process of the transmission of property rights.

Custody and Care of the Young Child

The Granadan document that introduced this chapter, entitled *Ishhād ʿalā tabannī yatīm* ("A written declaration about fostering an orphan") includes a renouncement of several rights, among them the mother's right to *ḥaḍāna*, the custody of her young child.[49] The fostering couple who took over the care of the young child from his widowed mother renounced the maintenance payment due them for the expenses custody would incur. In this case, the payment would have come from the child's property that was his share in his father's estate. In the earlier case of 1474, the mother renounced this payment in order to obtain the *khulʿ* divorce but not her right to custody. Her parents renounced their right to custody over the granddaughter as well as the maintenance payment owed to her.

When the maintenance payment was at issue in fifteenth-century Granada, the custodian of the child adhered to the legal requirement of accounting before the court. As we have seen in Chapter Four, ʿĀ'isha bt. Ibrāhīm al-Ḥakīm went to court to record in a document, unfortunately undated, the money she spent and the items she bought with the maintenance payment of her daughters, which included sifted grain, flax, seed, butter, honey, barely, flour, etc. The format of dispensing and receiving maintenance followed the notaries' manuals. Ibn Mughīth included three different model contracts, the first regulating the expenses to be paid by a father to a mother taking care of her own child, or to her own mother undertaking the task, which includes quantities measured in kind and cash: flour and dirhams to pay for clothes, all included in the child's maintenance,[50] the second specifying payment by the guardian to the female caregiver of an orphan, detailing how much flour, oil, wood, and dirhams for clothes were provided,[51] and the third accounting for the sales of the property of the orphaned son made by the female caregiver.[52] As far as the notaries were concerned, waiving the right to receive maintenance for a child was not something that should be done in ignorance. Al-Jazīrī, in twelfth-century Algeciras, paid due attention to the mother's relatives in the notary's model document that he drafted for waiving the right of custody in a *khulʿ* divorce settlement, as well as the child's maintenance: ". . . if the mother has a sister, or a mother [who are entitled by law to custody and therefore to receive and spend the child's maintenance], their renouncement should be included in the divorce document, after it is clear that they are aware of their rights in this matter."[53]

For our purpose, the fact that all legal schools agree that custody is predominantly a female's right associated with the female's capacity to dispense a unique physical and emotional care, makes the right of custody a woman's property right.[54] Its performance also requires the handling of property and payments, whether regarded as a wage (*ujra*) for exercising the right, which was the Hanafi position,[55] or as wages for services (*khidma*) related to the child's welfare, as held by the Malikis, or simply her entitlement to receive and spend the payments she receives and accounts for, as held by all schools.

The law never involved itself with the process of childrearing within a marriage, except for breastfeeding, but when separation, divorce or widowhood occurred, the change in the mother's legal status had implications for the rest of her property rights, including entitling her to payment for caring for her child. The need to regulate the child's custody emerges when the mother no longer lives in the same domicile as the father.[56] The failure of the law to determine whether custody was a mother's obligation or a child's right may have been the reason, according to Linant de Bellefonds, for the diversity of opinion on questions of duration, content, entitlement, and wages.[57] Custody is linked to the period of a child's physical incapacity to look after itself; for boys it is limited to between the ages of 5 and 7 years, but its potential length for girls in the Maliki school could extend to consummation of marriage.[58] Thus, the effect of having custody may last for many years. Under such circumstances, childcare was transformed from a task undertaken without much fanfare by a married mother into a multifaceted legal matter for a divorced mother, or her surrogate, the other female caregiver, which required attending court sessions frequently to discharge necessary duties.[59] To judge by the frequency of its appearance in notarized documents, notary models, and fatwas—the legal sources recording practice—custody was regularly administered by the courts.

Custody being a property right, its renouncement required a visit to the court. Ibn Mughīth provided a model deed to be registered in court entitled *Wathīqa bi-isqāṭ al-ḥaḍāna* (Deed for the elimination of the right of custody).[60] The witnesses to this deed were required to testify that the mother was unfit to assume the care of her children. If there was no one else to look after them and the children were not receiving sufficient care and shelter, their father was entrusted with the task. Ibn Mughīth explained that such a ruling entitled the father to not pay the mother the maintenance payment for childcare and to move the children away from her to a new location. Ibn Mughīth cautioned that such a renouncement could be contrived: "When a man appears before the judge and declares that the children's maternal grandmother (*jaddat banayhi li-ummihim*), has given up her right voluntarily and not under duress, and she is present and denies it, do not issue the renouncement document. It is the father's duty to prove his claim and the grandmother's right to take an oath."[61]

The rules regarding payment of wages for custody differed among the legal schools. The Malikis deny the mother any payment, whatever her marital status, while the Hanafis allow her payment only after divorce—the payment in question being actually a substitution for the maintenance payment to which the mother was entitled during marriage and the waiting period, and an assimilation into the payment to which the child is entitled after separation. The Shafiʿis and the Hanbalis rule in favour of wages to the caregiver, which may include the mother, whether married or divorced.

Only the Malikis were adamant about not paying wages directly to the mother or her relatives in cases of custody,[62] but according to Ibn Mughīth, the prohibition was not unqualified. He denied claims to wages on the part of the female caregiver, but reminded the notary that wages were due for providing service (*khidma*) to the child. This may have been a way to avoid the prohibition on wages in cases of hardship; judging from some of the fatwas dealing with this issue, the issue may often have been the destitution of the maternal grandmother, who could not care properly for the children without adequate support, and the unwillingness of fathers to provide her with resources. In a fatwa at our disposal, the mufti Abū l-Ḥasan al-Lakhmī (d. 1085) was asked his opinion in a dispute between a maternal grandmother, who asks for *ujra* for custody (the term used is *kafāla*, a term identical to *ḥaḍāna*), and the father of the child, who replies that he has already hired someone else to serve the child. Should she be offered custody of the child without wages? The mufti replied that if the grandmother is available, there is no avoiding giving her custody rights and payment for the service, even if the child does not stay at her house, which is one of the conditions for fulfillment of the task. Only if the child has no need for a servant, could she be denied wages. The mufti added that some of the later jurists supported such a rule, but that there was disagreement among the schools about it.[63] Another fatwa by the Tunisian jurist al-Rammāḥ (d. 1348) opines similarly: when asked about the wages of the caregiver for service to the child, he replies that if the child is in need of service, wages should be paid.[64] A third fatwa by Abū Muḥammad al-Zawāwī in thirteenth-century Tunis describes a grandmother's inadequate care because of her poverty and advises that the children should eat at their father's but spend the night at their grandmother's.[65]

The law admitted that the biological link uniting a child, his mother, and his maternal grandmother determined the order of the devolution of custody, while highlighting the need to establish a legal context when the natural filiation (*nasab*) was absent. The establishment of childcare as a context in which property rights could be formed can be seen in the case of a foundling (*laqīṭ*) and his rights of inheritance. In a notary document,[66] the property rights of the foundling were spelled out by means of a legal deed indicating that the relationship between the foundling and the man caring for him or her was not that of a father and a biological child. Unlike a biological child, a foundling was not automatically entitled to inherit from his or her foster father, but establishing the caregiving link in an official document gave the child a legal claim to a share in property left in the estate.

To sum up, the law recognized not only the female role in reproduction, but also the dominance and centrality of the notion of property rights in society, and thus the biological functions related to reproduction and the female capacity for childcare were brought into the legal sphere of property rights by a unity of purpose. Granting a wife property rights over the biological functions of her body reflected the existence of a strong and well-defined concept of the body as property. Rights over the body were publicly and officially asserted through acquisition of property resulting from these rights, renunciation in exchange for various considerations, registration in notarized deeds, and the resolution of related disputes before the courts. This legal stand represented the centrality of reproduction and women's bodies to family and society. The concern with bodily rights on the part of the law and the jurists was shared by the medical discipline and physicians, and the views that medical writers held regarding the female body were a component of the social and cultural context occasioning the legal view.

The Cultural Context of the Female Body in Medicine and Law

In comparison to the prosaic and official language used in the law manuals and in the notaries' model contracts for dealing with the functions of the female body, the medical literature was humane in its description of women in all stages of their reproductive lives, in their intimate moments of pleasure and great pain, and in their roles as partners in sexual relations, pregnant and birthing mothers, wet nurses, midwives, and child caregivers.

Despite this difference, lawyers and physicians did share a cultural framework. Both received a thorough education and training in their respective fields, which shared a methodology inherited from Greek logic and philosophy.[67] Both disciplines were fashioned by the legacy of the ancient world, whether Greek, Roman or Byzantine, and both displayed a fully developed theoretical framework within which physicians and lawyers dealt with physiological acts as part of an ideological system of the body's functioning. Each system combined theory and practice in equal amounts, incorporating ideas and skills, observations, and attention to detail in their respective writings. Physicians observed the body, carried out physical examinations, and undertook medical or surgical interventions when necessary, while lawyers wrote notarial documents, issued fatwas, and sat in judgment in specific cases. The physician, whom society entrusted with caring for the welfare of women, was, like the jurist, a learned professional as well as a Muslim husband and father. Both experienced the common intellectual background of the medieval, professional, cultured Muslim man.

The quest to establish the cultural context of the female body is complicated by questions of ideology, such as what image the two disciplines shared of the female body. In answering this question, we must first consider the relationship between Greek and Islamic medicine, dispelling the current notion that the second was a mere imitator of the first. Disproving this assumption is crucial to discounting the idea that the view of the female body in Islamic medicine mirrored that in Greek medicine, whose image of the female body was highly charged with negativity.[68] The components of their misogynous theory included the ideas that women's physiology was inferior to that of men and that the female body could attain its optimal goal only when used in regular sexual activity and reproduction.[69] This theory maintained that even the mere physical survival of females depended on such activities. This lowly image of women and their bodies led physicians to attempt to cure women by giving them such demeaning medications as dirt.[70] Greek medicine judged women incapable of interacting in a man's world because of their physical inferiority and forbade them to share public spaces and cultural or civic life with men.[71] Scholars who read Greek gynaecological texts in this vein regard the cultural notions about the female body in medicine as a reflection of women's lowly status in Greek society in general. This social status has led researchers to conclude that "what the medical texts provided were biological reasons for individuals to conform to their society's code of sexual behaviour."[72]

Reading the Islamic medical writers reveals a different image of the female body than that favoured by the Greek physicians. To begin with, the Muslim physicians' discourse on the female body, and on women in general, was not demeaning. When physicians discussed female biological functions in the medical writings, women were not depicted as weak, helpless or stupid. In fact, the female body was assumed to have both a physical and a spiritual nature. Ibn al-Jazzār describes the female's contribution to the foetus developing inside her womb: "Two things are required from the woman during the formation of the child. One is physical (*min al-badan*), and the other is spiritual, of the soul (*min al-nafs*). This is the basis upon which the foetus is fashioned, meaning that the mother should be healthy and well built, good natured, and mentally and emotionally strong."[73]

In discussions of women's skills as medical practitioners, there was no suggestion of incompetence or lack of intelligence. Physicians deferred to them as midwives, relied on them as helpers, and engaged in teaching them. Professional standards were just as high for female as for male practitioners. Al-Zahrāwī wrote in his chapter on training midwives: "So the midwife must have wisdom and dexterity and be skilled in all these cases and beware of failures and mistakes."[74] He explained to the midwife not only how to extract a dead foetus from its mother's womb, but also how to treat a live foetus when it was not brought forth in the natural manner, how to extract the afterbirth, and how to treat a fracture of the female pudenda, all medical procedures involving manipulation of surgical instruments and the insertion of the hand into the pelvic area. ʿArīb b. Saʿd wrote on the midwife's role in delivery: "Above all procure an intelligent midwife, who will constantly straighten the labouring women's legs and when she is placed in the delivery chair, will press hard on her stomach."[75] Ibn Khaldūn, society's keenest medieval observer, even saw the continuation of the human race as dependent on the trade of midwifery.[76]

Needless to say, the Muslim physician's access to the female genital area was limited, as in other societies. The result was an increased need to listen to women as patients and practitioners in order to create a flow of information from the female patient to the male physician, a need highlighted by the Muslim medical writers. Islamic gynaecology manuals were written by and for male practitioners, who were informed by their patients and female practitioners. First-hand experience had to be shared by the three participants—patient, midwife, and physician—and their collaboration produced a collective voice that was heard in the medical writings.

The positive medical discourse on women as patients and practitioners was matched by that of the jurists, especially the notaries, who were more concerned with practice. References to female medical practitioners and to their role and legal standing both in notarial manuals and in court documents are never anything but respectful and appreciative. Ibn Mughīth had complete confidence in the midwife's ability to discern the importance of her account in legal matters when she was required to give evidence in cases involving the property rights of infants and their families. The testimony of midwives in legal procedures concerning women's conditions even acquired a unique power compared to other testimonial evidence from women.[77] They alone, and not the male physician, had the legal power to give evidence in cases involving the female biological functions. But women generally had legal standing in the court. As shown above, the jurists and notaries regularly invested wives with legal power over children and over other incapacitated family members, and appointed them as executors of wills. The court documents from Granada also show that when women undertook such roles, they were consistently praised for their moral and financial knowledge and ability.

But evidence to the contrary also exists. G.H.A. Juynboll has traced examples of "woman-demeaning" sayings to various personalities, some living as early as the eighth century, and in al-Andalus, the highly misogynous Ibn Ḥabīb's *ḥadīth* collection from the ninth century remains the earliest, although not the only, such collection to have come to light in the region.[78] The early reports (*ḥadīth*) became legal sources in later years, and in terms of rights over the body, they represent an ideology endorsing a demeaning attitude toward female sexuality akin to the one expressed in Greek medicine, with serious consequences.

Greek medicine had endowed females with a voracious sexuality, which was seen as a threat to men, but it had also encouraged men to engage frequently in sexual activity for their own good.[79] The early *ḥadīth*s equally believed in the threat of women's desire but called for repressing and restraining their sexuality and for reducing the wife's sexual appetite by limiting her enjoyment of the sexual act through female circumcision (*khiṭān* or *khifāḍ*), which was also intended to ensure a woman's future chastity.[80] Jonathan Berkey has provided a rounded discussion of the legal sources, or what I would refer to as the extra-legal sources (e.g., the Ḥisba manuals), and the literary sources on the various issues surrounding female circumcision, but for our purpose here one aspect in particular matters, namely, the jurists' stand on the legal status of the procedure and whether the rights over the body were infringed by the practice. As Berkey has established, finding solid legal evidence for the practice of female circumcision or for justifying it is tricky.

The Qur'an makes no explicit reference to the practice, and no direct reference to female circumcision as a historical practice has been found in the regular legal manuals. However, references to female circumcision found in the early *ḥadīth*s represent a legal source regardless of whether we consider this literature suspicious or unauthentic.[81] Indeed, claims that female circumcision was performed at an early date endowed the procedure with a false legal framework. Because of the nature of the operation, the practice was associated with male circumcision, which was, and is, performed for reasons of personal ritual purity. The Maliki jurists ruled that male circumcision was obligatory and that female excision was recommended.[82] There are few direct references to the practice in Spain, where Ibn Juzayy wrote in the context of male circumcision that "Men perform the circumcision on boys (*ṣibyān*) and women on slave girls (*jawārī*)."[83] The reference to slave women, not to females in general, is similar to the one made by Ibn Rushd, an earlier legal authority who recommended that a slave owner circumcise his female slaves.[84] But the silence of the Andalusian physicians is significant, particularly that of the surgeon al-Zahrāwī, who did not shy away from addressing medical procedures respecting female genitalia. While he described surgical procedures such as extraction of a dead foetus, incision of an overgrown clitoris, and an operation to remedy hermaphroditism in females, there was no mention of female circumcision.[85] He did not regard circumcision, or excision, as a legitimate medical intervention, even in the case of boys: "Circumcision is nothing but a solution of continuity, like other wounds, but as it is a result of our deliberate action, and as it is done particularly to boys, we should plan in this case the very best operation and the easiest way that leads to safety."[86] He never referred to female circumcision when he warned the surgeon against cutting too much for danger of haemorrhage.[87]

This non-treatment of female circumcision in the sources should not lead us to assume that the process was limited in Spain either to free or to slave women. Their mention of the latter may simply refer to a foreign female group coming from outside, on whom the practice had to be imposed in order to bring them in line with local Muslim women, all of whom may well have been circumcised. Neither are we allowed to assume that referring to female circumcision only as a recommendation, never an obligation, may have targeted only slave women, not free ones,[88] for there were jurists, such as the Hanbali Ibn Qayyim al-Jawziyya in the thirteenth century and Ibn Taymiyya in the fourteenth century, as well as the fourteenth-century Shafiʿi Egyptian market supervisor (*muḥtasib*) Ibn al-Ukhuwwa,[89] who called for the practice.

We may not know whether female circumcision was performed regularly, but we do know that it never acquired genuine legal legitimacy or its own legal status, which would have made it a basis for discussion as a subject of property rights, unlike male circumcision. In the category of the legal sources that are relevant to the issue of property rights, there is no discussion of mutilation or accidental death as a result of the procedure for girls, whereas there is one for boys. The reason for the difference between the treatment of boys and girls might well have been a matter of property rights. A woman acquired rights over her body respecting birth control, breastfeeding, and custody at the time of marriage, and although a boy who was mutilated as a result of circumcision was entitled to a full blood-money payment (if he died as a result of a botched circumcision, only half of the blood money was due),[90] the procedure of female circumcision did not trigger any liability suits. The silence of the jurists, notaries, muftis, and judges, who were involved in the practice of the law and its administration and who regularly sought to apply the principles of the law and to adhere to them, is a statement of the lack of legal justification in this matter, not necessarily a statement of legal consensus respecting its sanction.

Despite the misogynous *ḥadīth* texts, law and medicine generally took a favourable view of female sexuality. Muslim physicians seem to have been preoccupied more with encouraging women to become enthusiastic about sex than with how to suppress their voracious sexual appetite. In their writings, they provided numerous remedies for a lack of desire for intercourse. Muslim jurists were equally concerned with protecting a woman from a husband who might attempt to deprive her of sexual satisfaction and offspring by practicing birth control with her. Once a woman was married, there was no reason to defend either herself or her husband from her sexuality. On the contrary, it was important to defend her against his sexual freedom, which entitled him to satisfy his appetite elsewhere, depriving her of her rights in the process.

The connection that has been drawn between Greek society and the misogynous stand evident in Greek medicine begs the question of the link between Islamic society and misogynous views. We know of only one historical event during the entire medieval period when religious misogyny resulted in political action. This occurred in Egypt during the plague of 1438, which the religious milieu saw as divine retaliation for adultery, alcohol consumption, usury, and other moral transgressions, including blatant prostitution. Following the advice of this milieu, Sultan Barsbāy and the council agreed to forbid women from going out into the streets. After much suffering, female slaves and old women were permitted to go to the market to get provisions and wash in the public bath. Ibn Taghrībirdī, who reported the episode, described the measure as inept.[91]

In our own time, those retrieving and reprinting classical misogynous texts have given a great deal of attention to the agenda behind them in an attempt to maintain men's control over women in Islamic society. The more recent of these *ḥadīth* texts, and other similar medieval writings, such as Ibn Taymiyya's fatwas, have caused Muslim feminists, notably Fatima Mernissi, to link the resuscitation of such literature to an explicit attempt by Islamic fundamentalists to misuse the past in order to rob women of whatever gains they have made.[92] In the interest of putting an end to this practice, it is important to highlight documentation that shows the historical and legal inaccuracy and misdirectedness of this view of female circumcision and its ideological discourse respecting women. Women's lack of status has allowed the practice to survive into the present without any basis in the law. Questionable as it was, it acquired an aura of legal status, when it was in fact a violation of women's rights over the body that are implicit in the law.[93]

The Historical Context of the Body as Property: Pronatalism

It is true that the Islamic cultural context of the female body, whether medical or legal, is deprived of a historical female voice. No female trained as a physician in the scientific medicine of the time or trained as a jurist has left behind any writings. We know of no Muslim equivalent of Trota, the twelfth-century female physician and writer on women's medicine from Salerno,[94] and no Muslim Hildegard of Bingen.[95] Very few female "doctors" appear in the sources. Umm al-Ḥasan, the daughter of a physician from Loja, Abū Jaʿfar al-Ṭanjālī (d. 1349), studied medicine as well as literature.[96] Muslim female physicians treated the king of Aragon in 1332,[97] and Shlomo Dov Goitein has found several female doctors in Cairo during the Geniza period, although he is doubtful about whether they were trained in the scientific tradition.[98] The females who were called "physicians" were in most cases popular healers and practising midwives; neither the Greek, Roman nor Arabic texts describe women who had learned the practices of Greek medicine. But in this respect, Islamic society was no different from previous and contemporary societies, and the situation in other regions where Greek medicine was practiced was no different. Female physicians in Rome might well have practiced more than folk medicine,[99] but they were not common there, and in the London of twelfth-century Norman England, there was a hospital with a maternity ward but no female practitioners.[100] The historical context of the status of property rights given to female biological functions in Islamic law, as well as the Islamic medical discourse concerning female fertility, are to be found elsewhere. Their historical context was society's pronatalist formulation in reaction to its demographic decline.

Archeological and literary studies of the medieval Islamic Mediterranean have strongly suggested that societies there lived through a particular set of historical circumstances of population decline and low birth rate.[101] Archival documents, surface estimates, and literary sources all describe a small Muslim family with 1.5 children per household together with a large population of single men and women.[102] The documents found in the Ḥaram al-Sharīf archives of fourteenth-century Jerusalem show an average family size of about 2.7 people.[103] It is also reasonable to accept a birth rate of 1 to 3 children in al-Andalus during the same period. This figure is based on the data provided in the estate divisions of fifteenth-century Granada and supported by the appearance of patterns of childless couples and of marriages between an older man and a very young woman, such as those of Mahjūna and Fāṭima, whom we met in earlier case studies, both of whom were childless at the time of their husbands' deaths.[104]

It was not uncommon for people in al-Andalus to live into old age,[105] but at the same time, child mortality was also high. The medieval Middle East saw many unborn children die in accidents during pregnancy and during childbirth, and newborn children also died, whether in the frequent epidemics or from the generally poor quality of food, sanitation, and medical conditions.[106] Hygienic and nutritional deficiencies contributed to pathologies of the reproductive organs, and other diseases further impaired the rate of reproduction, along with famines, wars, and plagues, all of which contributed to the population decrease noted in the Islamic regions around the Mediterranean.

Physicians reacted to the falling rates of reproduction by offering a lengthy list of medications designed to increase desire for intercourse, by attempting to prevent miscarriage through the care that they offered to the pregnant woman, by facilitating labour and birth, and by providing care to the nursing infant and to the growing child. The law reacted to the demographic crisis by giving women rights over reproduction. Even the Qur'anic revision of the tribal succession law at such an early time as that of the Prophet Muḥammad can be traced to this crisis. The inclusion of wives and other related females among the heirs was so dramatic as to be judged "revolutionary,"[107] but in fact the succession laws, which replaced the then current tribal system by including an array of female heirs, show that Islam adhered to the view that males and females contributed equally to filiation (*nasab*) and should be rewarded accordingly.

The idea that females and males contributed equally to procreation might well have been inspired by ancient medical sources, where both female and male semen were seen as essential to the formation of the embryo and where females had a role in conception similar to that of males.[108] The concept of mutuality in procreation was explicitly present in Islamic medicine, as illustrated by the treatment of male infertility, which physicians considered to be a problem as serious as female sterility.[109] The law appeared to reiterate this notion not only by reforming the succession law, but also by giving women the power to consent or object to the practices of birth control and wet nursing, these being subject to female property rights that could directly affect how many children a woman conceived. The practice of hiring a wet nurse is known to have generally contributed to women having more pregnancies and more children.[110]

Islamic law's recognition of the mutual contribution of males and females to filiation contributed greatly to its recognition that husband and wife had property rights respecting each other's bodies whose acquisition depended on the biological functions of these bodies—hence the right to sanction or refuse birth control. That the female body had legal status made it impossible for legal or medical writers to discuss a man's right to dominate a woman's reproductive capacity. Having legal rights and thus control over her body's reproductive functions made a wife a conscious participant in procreation. Such an image of women greatly contrasts with the Greek view, endorsed by Plato and others, that a woman was nothing but a womb.[111] The more modern concept found in the Islamic context was already present in Roman law, and its impact is evident in the law's treatment of abortion, which till the third century A.D. was not illegal in any part of the Greco-Roman world.[112] It was made a criminal offence because it infringed on the husband's right to have an heir: "In Roman law the woman could be punished only if someone felt injured by the abortion process, and this someone was almost invariably the woman's sexual partner."[113] In punishing the woman, the law recognized that the acquisition of the male's right to an heir was dependent on the female body, over which she had control, and the two sets of rights contradicted each other.

Historians of ancient and medieval medicine also seem to agree that there was a correspondence between women's social status and the medical and legal discourse concerning their bodies. For instance, Ann Ellis Hanson sees the switch from the misogynous Hippocratic view of women's physiology in Greek medicine to the more positive view of women in Soranos's gynaecology as resulting from a change for the better in the status and social and economic activities of women in Roman society.[114] Monica Green sees a link between Latin gynaecology and social and legal realities. The link between women's status and lived experience was also embodied in medieval Europe in the advice offered to women in *The Trotula* on how to restore "virginity". Green concludes: "If successful these recipes may well have made the difference for some women between marriage and financial security, on the one hand, and social ostracization and poverty, on the other."[115] Renate Blumenfeld, who has studied the Caesarean birth in the premodern European miniatures and in the literature of the Reformation period, has established a link between gynaecology and society's view of women. In particular, she has found a correlation between the misogynous attitudes of Christian society and the transfer of surgical practice to male surgeons from midwives, who were marginalized as medical practitioners.[116] The status of the female body in medicine and law was intricately linked to historical conditions.

The correlation between women's property rights in general and their rights over the body in particular can be argued against a background of societies where one or the other was missing. This was the case in the Jewish society of the Geniza period in Egypt, which has been investigated by Shlomo Dov Goitein. There, the weakness, even the absence, of property rights for Jewish women in marriage was accompanied by a lack of the right to consent or object to birth control and breastfeeding. Goitein remarks that the Geniza documents never mention wet nursing among female occupations, which led him to believe that the practice was not common among the Jewish community in Egypt, even though he discovered that a Jewish wet nurse was hired in a Muslim home.[117] Concurrently, Jewish women were obliged by law to breastfeed their babies, and coitus interruptus was also prohibited.[118] Jewish medical writings represented by the Judeo-Arabic medical manuscripts in the Geniza collection and Jewish gynaecological treatises from Europe show that Jewish physicians dealt with the same kind of women's diseases treated by Muslim physicians.[119] Subjects such as diseases of the womb, difficult labour, strangulation of the womb, flow of menses, childbirth during the Sabbath, infertility, vaginal abscesses, diseases of the female urinary tract, and the like were discussed, but materia medica on birth control was ignored.[120] Unlike Muslim women, Jewish women were expected to engage in work for the household. They had to stipulate in their marriage contracts whether they wanted to keep their wages and they frequently complained about husbands who claimed their wages regardless.[121] They were unable to manage and control their property in marriage, as Muslim wives did. In the Jewish context, women's lack of rights over the body—which was equally matched by a general lack of women's property rights in marriage under Jewish law—was accompanied by a lack of medical information on gynaecological issues.

Conclusion

If modern science has furnished the scientific background to explain human reproductive life, the Islamic legal sources analyzed in this chapter put forward a picture of historical behaviour embodied in the law. Female rights over the body covered the areas of reproduction and motherhood in a way that gave married women a good deal of control over the rhythm of pregnancies and financial compensation for fulfilling their reproductive roles. Wives could not be obligated to nurse and were guaranteed wages for breastfeeding and childrearing when divorced. Rights over the body were an additional dimension of the larger corpus of women's property rights, which were created and acquired through marriage and motherhood. Although reproduction and motherhood could occur outside of marriage, the biological functioning of the female body alone did not impart property rights to every woman. These rights did not exist in practice independently of marriage. Moreover, even within marriage or concubinage, the rights over the body were not universally upheld as women's rights but were exclusively the rights of the free wife. The enslaved sexual partner and enslaved mother did not acquire them. Thus these rights were not absolute rights given to all females, regardless of their legal conditions.

The issue of rights over the body had an additional legal dimension since the law saw reproduction as a question of property relations between husband and wife, meaning that the couple had equal rights respecting each other's body so that they could fulfil their inherent roles in reproduction. The regulation of reproduction was a social objective, and judges, notaries, and muftis made sure that the rights relating to reproduction were properly acquired. The reservation of rights over the body exclusively for free married women also meant that female circumcision fell outside the legal framework, as little girls had not yet acquired these rights. No matter how later jurists link female circumcision to early *ḥadīth*, it is nonetheless significant that the procedure was never discussed as a legal obligation in the early *fiqh*.

Not all segments of society and, for that matter, not all segments of the legal community were honest in applying the concept of women's rights over their bodies, nor was the law alone in circumscribing woman's rights over the body. Historical conditions and culture helped to shape these rights as well. The historical context of rights over the body and the medical discourse about women's rights over the body were consistent with a low birth rate and a decreasing population. In this respect, the historical context was no different from that of ancient medicine, which was equally pronatalist. The difference lay in the legality extended to pronatalism in the Islamic framework, which provided the female body with its own legal status and recognized the body as a repository of property rights that both partners could acquire, a concept shared by later Roman law.

In theory, the equal contribution of males and females to filiation and, in practice, the treatment of pathologies of the reproductive organs were unified in a legal framework of women's property rights over the body that was unique to Islamic law.

Six

PROPERTY RIGHTS IN CONVERSION

The conversion to Islam of Zoraya, wife of the Nasrid ruler Abū l-Ḥasan ʿAlī (Muley Hacén), in Granada in 1474 and the conversion to Christianity of his daughter, ʿĀʾisha, after the city's surrender to the Christian armies were the most significant conversions by women in fifteenth-century Granada, but they were neither the first nor the last acts of female conversion to and from Islam.[1] In fact, in Granada there was a high enough incidence of former Christian women marrying Muslims that the capitulations of 1492, which immediately followed the conquest, addressed them directly: "If any Moor had taken a renegade as his wife, she will not be forced to become a Christian against her will, but she may be questioned in the presence of Christians and Moors and be allowed to follow her own will."[2] A few years later, in 1499, protection of the Christian converts to Islam by their Muslim co-religionists in Granada against Christian clerics' attacks on them in anticipation of their reconversion to Christianity eventually provoked the forced conversion of the entire Muslim community.[3]

Outside al-Andalus, conversion to Islam was not a prerogative of royals or of women, as indicated by the frequent examples of conversion in the historical sources, enough to suggest that the question of conversion merits an independent historical foray. Yet al-Andalus was the only region where notaries made available deeds for conversion to Islam and discussed their legal implications. The conversion deeds on hand include five certificates in Ibn al-ʿAṭṭār's formulary. Three are for males, one treating Christian conversion, one Jewish, and one *majūsī* (Zoroastrian, but here denoting "pagan," or a non-adherent to a revealed religion, as distinct from the term *mushrik*, polytheist, used by earlier sources), and two are for females, one treating Christian conversion and one *majūsī*. Together, they comprise by far the most complete and detailed deeds ever found for the purpose.[4] Some or all of the model deeds also appear in a shortened and slightly altered form in Ibn Mughīth's *Muqniʿ*,[5] in the manual by al-Bunṭī (d. 1070), and in al-Jazīrī's *Maqṣad*.[6] Al-Bunṭī included all five documents, but Ibn Mughīth provided only two, one for the conversion of a Christian male and one for that of a Jewish male, and al-Jazīrī included only one model, to be used for the conversion of a Christian male.[7]

The deeds, and their implications, constitute an important source for studying women's property rights because conversion affected marriage, which, as we have seen again and again, was the event through which many of these rights were activated, acquired, and practiced. Since conversion determined the status of an existing and future marriage, it also affected the status of a couple's property rights. For notaries and jurists, defining the status of property rights was the issue at hand, secondary only to the act of conversion itself. In their discourse on the status of women's property rights as an outcome of conversion, they observe women at the moment of transition from one legal system to another. Analyzing legal reasoning provides new insights into the story of women's property rights that are not accessible through the other sources, highlighting how socio-religious dynamics affect the wife's and the mother's status in the family.

The Conversion Deeds

Ibn al-ʿAṭṭār's deed for the conversion to Islam of a married Christian woman reads as follows:

> The Muslim woman, so-and-so, the daughter of so-and-so, or ʿAbd Allāh's daughter, if her father's name is unknown, bears witness in the court of law and before the signatories of this deed that she, in a healthy state of mind and firmness of intellect, being a lawful master of her person, is willingly rejecting the Christian faith to which she belongs and entering the Islamic faith of her free will. She testifies that there is no God except Allāh, who has no associate, and that Muḥammad is his servant and messenger, the last of his messengers and Prophets, and the best of his creatures. He was sent down to show the right path and the true faith, to make it triumph over other religions, even though the polytheists attacked him. She testifies that ʿĪsā b. Maryam, God bless all his Prophets, is the servant of God and creature of his creatures and messenger of his messengers, and his word was sent to Maryam, as well as his spirit as God said. She should wash and pray and stand to perform Islam's laws and pillars of belief, ritual ablution before prayer, complete and pure intention, prayer, alms giving, and the fast of the month of Ramadan, in every year and the pilgrimage to the House when she is able to perform it. She fulfills all these obligations because she chose to do so and she desires to do so, and she thanks God for inspiring her, and she thanks him for bestowing it upon her because she desired Islam, obeying without being forced or coerced to do anything or being afraid of anything.
>
> Her conversion took place before (the magistrate) so-and-so, and she agrees that all is in accordance with what is in the deed, then you [the notary] say, "witnessed."[8]

Ibn al-ʿAṭṭār's conversion document consists of two parts. The first is the official record of the conversion, a copy of which was given to the individual convert for his or her records and personal use. The second contains legal discourse on the issues involved for the notary's benefit. The first part of the document is a standard formula, common to all conversion deeds, that combines a statement of creed (*ʿaqīda*) and describes the steps to be performed.[9] The first sentence states that the person converting is of sound mind. The second testifies that he or she embraces Islam out of sincere conviction, without coercion, and rejects his or her former religion in the same manner. The third indicates that he or she has recited the Muslim profession of faith (*shahāda*) and has accepted that Jesus (ʿĪsā), in the case of a Christian, and Moses (Mūsā) and ʿUzayr, in the case of a Jew, were God's messengers. The fourth states that the convert has fulfilled the acts of ablution, purification, and prayer and has undertaken to fulfill the duties imposed on a Muslim. The fifth records his or her recognition that Islam abrogates (*nāsikh*) all other religions. In a second paragraph, the notary states that the conversion took place before a named magistrate, who might be the chief judge or any other judge, chief of police, chief of the town's administration, chief of the market's administration or chief of public complaints. All of these bureaucrats were men of medium rank in the legal hierarchy who were needed to testify regarding where and when the conversion took place and to date the document. The convert is required to testify that he or she understands and accepts all that is stated in the document. Further instructions are given to the notary indicating the phrase that should be used to describe the role of the witnesses. Finally, the year in which the document was prepared is to be recorded. Two copies must be made; although one authenticated document is sufficient, making several copies is preferable.

The second part of the conversion document was intended to provide the notary with legal appendices addressing the legal matters arising from the particular conditions of each conversion. These appendices consisted of commentary (*tafsīr*) and law (*fiqh*). The notary's task was to define how the status of the marriage was affected by the conversion, to inform the new convert and his or her spouse of their new status, and to produce a watertight legal document to that effect. He was instructed to carefully verify the spelling of the name of the official who accepted the conversion (*aslama ʿalā yaday*) because this person would be responsible for any necessary actions arising from changes to the status of the convert.

On the face of it, conversion appears to have been a straightforward legal matter not unlike any routine business transaction, which could be settled by a visit to a law clerk. Neither Ibn al-ʿAṭṭār nor the other notaries indicated in the deeds or in the commentaries that the notarial authentication of conversion was anything but routine. On the contrary, they noted that the deed used for conversion of a Christian woman could be used without any changes for that of a Jewish woman. Nonetheless, the different legal implications and consequences that could result from conversion in a variety of situations affected women's marriages, their property rights, and their relationships with their children, especially if conversion was imposed on them through the conversion of a husband or father. Conversion had serious legal consequences for women's status and fortunes.

The Legal Framework of Conversion

The first structural link between conversion and marriage was created at an early stage in the development of Islamic law. Ever since the establishment of the first Islamic communities in Mecca and Medina, conversion was a common and frequent event, and defining the convert's status was a continuous legal issue during the formative years of Islamic law. Because of its centrality to the nascent community, one might expect conversion to have been treated as an independent chapter in that part of the substantive law devoted to the creed. Instead, references to conversion were scattered, above all, throughout the section on marriage and also throughout various sections dealing with the practical implications of conversion for the individual's rights and obligations—an early indication that the doctrine underlying conversion would be centred on how conversion mattered to the family.

The first reference to women's conversion is found in the section on marriage in the eighth-century *Muwaṭṭaʾ*, the principal Maliki text. There, it consists of a set of five *ḥadīth*s addressing the status of the marriage of a polytheist husband (*mushrik*) in the aftermath of his wife's conversion to Islam and vice versa.[10] The *ḥadīth*s refer to pagan Arabs, all of whom were contemporaries and relatives of the Prophet Muḥammad, whose wives had converted before them and who were personally invited by the Prophet to join the Muslim community. The following legal rulings on the issue were articulated on the basis of these *ḥadīth*s, with the most central one addressing the differences between a married man and a married woman in conversion: in the case of a pagan woman's conversion, the marriage would not be annulled immediately.[11] Even though a Muslim woman could not be married to a pagan, if the pagan husband wanted to retain his marriage, he was given a delay of two to four months to convert as well, while his wife remained in the waiting period required after separation (*ʿidda*).[12] On the other hand, if the husband converted before his pagan wife, and she was offered the opportunity to convert but refused, the couple had to separate immediately.[13]

Saḥnūn (d. 854) edited and expanded the Maliki laws on marriage and divorce in the *Mudawwana*, where the subject of conversion and marriage in North Africa appears more comprehensibly.[14] Under the heading "Marriage with Non-Muslims," previous rulings from the *Muwaṭṭaʾ* and the episodes and *ḥadīth*s dealing with pagans were reported literally; however, a set of rules was added addressing the conversion of People of the Book (i.e., Jews and Christians), referred to as *dhimmī*s, as well as the conversion of slaves.[15] Both of these developments can be explained by a change in the identity of converts. Whereas converts had previously been pagans with various religious practices, who had no preferred status under Islamic law, they were now largely Jews and Christians, whose right to practice their religion freely was protected by treatises. As Saḥnūn stated: "The marriage of two slaves, Christian or Jewish, to one another is permitted. If the slave converts and his wife is a Christian or Jewish slave, she is forbidden to him unless she converts instantly (*makānan*), the same as for a pagan woman whose husband converts to Islam. If she converts instantly, she remains in the marriage since it is not appropriate (*lā yanbaghī*) for a Muslim slave to marry a Jewish female slave, the same as for a free Muslim. It is inappropriate for him to marry a Jewish or Christian female slave."[16]

More than a century later, Ibn Abī Zayd al-Qayrawānī's *Risāla* was considerably more laconic in addressing the issue.[17] A contemporary of al-ʿAṭṭār's *Kitāb al-Wathāʾiq*, the work treated briefly the issue of marriage and conversion. If two pagans converted together, their marriage remained valid, but if they converted separately, their marriage was dissolved without a divorce. If a man converted during his wife's waiting period and he was married to a woman of the Book (*kitābiyya*), the marriage remained valid. Nonetheless, there were some nuances in al-Qayrawānī's discussion. For example, a pagan wife who converted soon after her husband's conversion could remain married, but if she delayed her conversion, she could not. This may have been related to the fact that by the tenth century, the east of North Africa, where the *Risāla* was written, had been Islamized for all intents and purposes, meaning that the pace of conversions had slackened there.[18]

In al-Andalus, where more frequent conversions were still taking place at the time, the presence of detailed conversion deeds is not a surprise. Tenth-century al-Andalus, while not yet home to the homogenous society that some scholars have imagined,[19] was nonetheless a cultural and economically prosperous society whose practices coincided with what has been described in the literature as the peak of voluntary conversion to Islam in the Iberian Peninsula.[20] For Jews and Christians, the People of the Book referred to in the documents, there were many enticements for them to convert:[21] the period culminated in a robust economy, a new social order, a unique and sophisticated culture, and a sophisticated legal system that functioned smoothly.[22] However, the extant historical evidence relates more to the conversion of Christians than to that of Jews. Acculturation among the Mozarabs was strong, while Hebrew poetry and Jewish philosophy display Arab influences and reveal the inroads made among Jewish intellectuals.[23] The reasons for conversion included securing a political appointment, escaping tax liabilities or family complications, and overcoming individual alienation from one's community. There were also administrative reasons for the preponderance of notarial deeds treating conversion. Conversion had to take place before a magistrate, not merely for tax purposes but also because the sophisticated economy favoured the use of documents, meaning that the possession of a conversion certificate became necessary for family and commercial transactions.[24]

The subsequent absence of conversion documents from the notarial manuals of the twelfth century and afterward corresponded to the decline in voluntary conversions but not to a decline in religious zeal in the Muslim West, which would result in forced conversions from time to time, as happened during the Almoravid and Almohad invasions of Spain.[25] The polemical writings against Islam that appeared in the twelfth century suggest that both Muslims and non-Muslims living in al-Andalus and North Africa were open to discussions of the question of conversion. The Mozarab community did not fade away as a religious community, while Muslim converts to Christianity became visible from the eleventh century onward in tandem with the progress of the Reconquista.[26] The tension surrounding the issue of conversion continued unabated in the thirteenth and fourteenth centuries. The discovery of a "newly" reconstructed history of the conversion of the Berbers to Islam has revealed that as late as the fourteenth century, even such longstanding Muslims as the Berber intellectuals who wrote the new history of the Berber conversion were preoccupied with this question.[27]

The treatment of conversion and marriage in the fourteenth-century law books reflects the existing body of rules as well as changes in the historical environment, which were incorporated into an elaborate section of the family law. The historical scene had changed considerably in the period separating the early Maliki legal thinking on conversion, when Islam was expanding, and the fourteenth century, when it was in territorial decline. During this period, conversion to Islam did not come to a halt but assumed different characteristics.[28] Converts came mostly from within the established communities of Jews and Christians. Conversion no longer represented an entrance into an unknown world, as it had for the early converts, but occurred among individuals whose families had lived for generations among Muslims. Such conversions were isolated acts, not part of a mass conversion such as those seen during the earlier centuries. It could no longer be anonymous and would necessarily involve severing contacts with one's previous community.

An improved and superior organization of the material relating to conversion and marriage during the fourteenth century may be found in the legal manuals of Ibn Juzayy and Khalīl b. Isḥāq, which represent the Western and Egyptian branches of Malikism respectively. Ibn Juzayy devoted a full section to the issue of marriage and conversion in his comprehensive, detailed, comparative, and well-rounded doctrine on marriage:

> There are five marriage pillars (*arkān*): the husband, the wife, the legal guardian, the *ṣadāq*, and the contract form (*ṣīgha*). In the first pillar, that which regards the couple, seven characteristics (*awṣāf*) must be present, the first being Islam. Four modes are envisaged here, the first two of which are legitimate: (1) the marriage of a Muslim man and a Muslim woman; (2) the marriage of a nonbeliever (*kāfir*) and a female nonbeliever; (3) the marriage of a nonbeliever and a Muslim woman, which is not permitted and which all jurists agree should be terminated by divorce; and (4) the marriage of a Muslim man and a nonbeliever, which is allowed if the woman is from the People of the Book (*kitābiyya*)—marriage to any other female nonbeliever is not allowed. Mālik [Ibn Anas, founder of the Maliki school in eighth-century Medina] also condemned marriage to a woman from the people with whom the Muslims are engaged in war (*dār al-ḥarb*) because the child will remain in the abode of war.[29]

By incorporating early elements from the *Muwaṭṭa'*, Ibn Juzayy provided a schematic introduction to the doctrine of Islamic marriage, placing questions of marriage with non-Muslims in a fuller legal framework than had previously been attempted.

Khalīl b. Isḥāq addressed the issue of conversion and marriage in two sections of his chapter on marriage, one dealing with marriages between slaves and nonbelievers and the other with marriages between the converted and the sick. Khalīl's discourse is concise; he treated the issue of marriage to non-Muslims and conversion in a few short sentences. But he also provided new interpretations, such as the following: "If a wife converts to Islam, and her husband converts during her waiting period, even if he has divorced her before, the marriage is valid [since divorce in a non-Muslim court does not hold in a Muslim court]."[30] These two new interpretations, one lengthening the period during which a divorced non-Muslim woman could remain in her marriage after conversion and the other disqualifying a non-Muslim divorce, could be related to the contemporary conditions that the author witnessed, but there is no definitive explanation for their appearance at this juncture.

The most important concern following conversion to Islam, for women and jurists alike, was not how well versed converts were in their new religion but the status of their marriages. Certainly, questions regarding women's knowledge of their religion after conversion were asked and answered by jurists, and these will be discussed later in reviewing the related fatwas. But the issue was of secondary importance. Whether property rights remained in force or not was determined by whether a marriage remained valid or should be annulled following conversion.

Preservation and Annulment of Marriage Following Conversion

Once conversion had taken place, the notary was required to establish the status of the marriage in the deed itself and to elaborate the defining measures by which it was either validated or invalidated. Five conditions needed to be examined: (1) previous religious adherence, namely, pagan or as one of the People of the Book; (2) simultaneous or delayed conversion of the spouse; (3) civil status (i.e., free or unfree); (4) a forbidden degree of relationship between the spouses (e.g., blood relationship or affinities of mother's milk or marriage); and (5) consummation of the marriage. If the existing marriage was considered valid, the jurist did not insist on fulfillment of the usual legal requirements for an Islamic marriage, such as the presence of either a guardian or a *ṣadāq*.

Using the five conversion certificates under review, I have constructed a systematic chart showing how each of the conditions would affect the marriage status in the event of conversion both in cases where the husband had initiated the conversion and in cases where the wife was the initiator (Table 1).

The conclusion to be drawn from this chart is that the conversion to Islam of either spouse had the potential to provoke immediate changes in his or her status as a married person. As far as Islamic law was concerned, the conversion of only one spouse would not immediately bring about dissolution of the marriage except under specific conditions. Either spouse

Table 1
Preservation and annulment of marriage following conversion (kitābī = one of the People of the Book)

Conversion of a *kitābī* husband		Marriage
Married to:	Valid	Invalid
kitābī converted wife	x	
kitābī nonconverted wife	x	
kitābī converted slave wife		x
kitābī nonconverted slave wife		x
kitābī converted wife of the forbidden degree		x
kitābī nonconverted wife of the forbidden degree		x
pagan converted wife	x	
pagan nonconverted wife		x
Conversion of a *kitābī* wife		Marriage
Married to:	Valid	Invalid
kitābī converted husband	x	
kitābī nonconverted husband		x
pagan converted husband	x	
pagan nonconverted husband		x
Conversion of a pagan husband		Marriage
Married to:	Valid	Invalid
kitābī converted wife	x	
kitābī nonconverted wife		x
pagan converted wife	x	
pagan nonconverted wife		x
Conversion of a pagan wife		Marriage
Married to:	Valid	Invalid
kitābī converted husband	x	
kitābī nonconverted husband		x
pagan converted husband	x	
pagan nonconverted husband		x

could annul the marriage on his or her own if the condition that might invalidate it in Islamic law existed, e.g., if they were related to each other in the forbidden degree. As a result, while the conversion of both spouses by itself might have produced two good Muslims, it did not create a valid Islamic marriage. Thus, once conversion occurred, it set in motion a process in which the ensuing conditions could independently influence the status of the marriage and, in turn, determine the wife's acquisition of her marriage-related property rights.

Previous Religion and Simultaneous or Delayed Conversion of a Spouse

The first factor in the validation or annulment of a marriage was the presence of Islam. When either a *kitābī* or a pagan married woman converted to Islam without her *kitābī* or pagan husband, she set in motion a process that could end either in validation or annulment, depending on whether the husband chose to convert. The validation process unfolded in stages, each one decided according to the marriage law. In the first phase, after the wife converted, a situation was created where a Muslim woman was married to a non-Muslim man, and a separation or divorce was to immediately ensue. It did not matter whether the husband was a *kitābī* or a pagan since the law stipulated that a Muslim woman could not be married to a non-Muslim man.[31] However, if her husband converted at the same time, annulment would not occur. Indeed, his conversion would produce two Muslims married to one another. Such a marriage could later be invalidated on other grounds, but for the time being, it was considered valid: "In the event he converted with her, she is his wife, and their marriage is not quashed (*tanaqqada*)," said Ibn al-ʿAṭṭār.[32]

A second means of remaining in the marriage could be exercised during the wife's waiting period. In conformity with the Islamic law of divorce, the new Muslim wife whose husband had not converted with her, and who was thus divorced, could not remarry for a period of three menstrual cycles; consummation of a marriage meant the possibility of a pregnancy: "When a married woman converts [without her husband], her marriage is invalidated and she is told to enter the waiting period (*ʿidda*) . . . If he converts during her *ʿidda* and before she has had three menses from the time of her conversion, providing she is from among those who menstruate—three months if she is someone who does not menstruate—he will remain with her in a state of marriage."[33] If the husband converted after the waiting period, the couple was no longer considered married: "If her *ʿidda* elapsed before his conversion, he has no recourse to her and if he converted after that, he is available for marriage to others."[34] This stipulation was clear because the end of the waiting period signalled that the divorce was definitive under the law and that the woman and the man were thus available to marry other people.

Conversion within the marriage of two pagans was treated with a slight difference. Upon the conversion of either the husband or the wife to Islam, their marriage would immediately be dissolved since no Muslim, man or woman, could legally be married to a pagan.[35] In the legal portion of the conversion certificates that provided for a pagan man and a pagan woman, Ibn al-ʿAṭṭār explained that if either one embraced Islam and the other refused to accept it, the bond of marriage between them would be severed.[36] But the equality between the spouses ended here. Whereas a pagan husband could still remain in his marriage by a delayed conversion while his converted wife was in the waiting period, a delayed conversion of the pagan wife did not have this effect. She would no longer be considered his wife, and separation of the couple would automatically ensue. At the same time, if a pagan husband had not cohabited with his wife, even his delayed conversion would not preserve a marriage that had been annulled by the wife's conversion to Islam, and no waiting period was required from her. If he did not convert but did cohabit with her, then he could either divorce her immediately, restoring her rights as an unmarried woman, or allow the waiting period to lapse, initiating an automatic separation.

Free and Unfree Spouses

The almost impossible situation of a valid marriage according to Islamic law between a slave and a free individual arose if either of them converted to Islam. In the legal section of the conversion certificate for a Jewish male, Ibn al-ʿAṭṭār, probably following in the footsteps of Saḥnūn, discussed the case of a convert married to a slave.[37] The converted slave who was married to a free Jewish or Christian woman would remain married. However, the marriage would be annulled if the wife was unfree (*mamlūka*), because a Muslim cannot marry a Jewish or Christian slave.[38] The notary invoked a Qur'anic verse, quoted by previous and later authors as well: "On this day all things that are clean have been made lawful for you; and made lawful for you is the food of the People of the Book, as your food is made lawful for them. And lawful are the chaste Muslim women, and the women of the People of the Book who are chaste [for marriage], and not fornication or liaison, if you give them their dowries. Useless shall be rendered the acts of those who turn their back on their faith, and they will be among the losers in the life to come" (Q 5:5). This verse does not explain specifically why it was unlawful to marry a *kitābī* slave woman, whereas marriage to a *kitābī* free woman was lawful, but the reason becomes clear if one takes the conflicting property rights into account.

The issue of slavery and the question of civil status as the second condition for a valid marriage entered the doctrine in Ibn Juzayy's discourse:

> The second condition to be considered in marriage is slavery, and there are four characteristics here: (1) marriage of a free man to a free woman; (2) marriage of a male slave to a female slave, both of which are valid; (3) marriage of a male slave to a free woman, which is permitted if she wants it—if he has misled her [with regard to his status], she has the right to choose; and (4) marriage of a free man to a female slave, which is permitted on three conditions: first, that she is a Muslim; second, that the means (*ṭawl*) are absent, which is the *ṣadāq* of a free woman, or some say, the payment for maintenance (*nafaqa*); and third, that there has been fornication (*ʿanat*).[39] Do not make these latter two, fornication and means, requirements for the marriage of a slave and a slave woman.
>
> Slavery in marriage is subject to four conditions. First, that none of the spouses owns the other in mutual agreement and that one does not marry his son's female slave or his master's *umm al-walad* (a female slave who has borne her master's child), in which case the marriage becomes invalid and requires divorce. Second, if one of the spouses has bought the other, or part of him or her, the marriage is invalid because the buyer owns the slave or a part of him or her. Third, the male slave cannot marry without his master's permission—if his master allows him, then the marriage is valid. Fourth, if a free man marries a free woman in addition to being married to a female slave, or marries a female slave in addition to a free woman, the free woman can choose to remain or to have a legal divorce because it is her right to demand that he not form a link between her and a slave woman.[40]

By comparison, Khalīl dealt only briefly with the issue of conversion and marriage of a slave. But he did invoke the link between property status and conversion by saying that conversion should entail the manumission of the slave wife: "In the case of the conversion of a husband, his marriage to a Jewish or Christian slave would be valid *only if she is manumitted*."[41]

An array of marriage arrangements between Mamluk slaves and the slave girls of their masters provides examples of an Islamic society concerned with marriage between slaves of both genders, their conversion to Islam, and property.[42] Documents for charitable endowments (*waqf*) as well as literary sources show that in these instances marriages were arranged by the master of the Mamluk in question. While manumission and conversion to Islam were, in fact, taken for granted, they were specifically noted, as, for example, in *waqf* deed No. 3131, Ministry of Awqaf, Cairo, in order to guarantee the deed's legal status. Conversion was assumed from the Islamic names of both husband and wife, but manumission was stated separately, and the endowing woman's name was followed by the title "a freed slave" (*maʿtūqa*), as was the husband's name. Several authors have made the point that when an emir died, it was customary for his successor to inherit his title and marry his widow.

The Forbidden Degree

A further cause for the annulment of a marriage following the conversion of either spouse was the forbidden degree of relationship between spouses, which refers to a degree of blood relation that disallows their marriage to one another under the Muslim marriage law, as established in Q 4:23. As Ibn al-ʿAṭṭār stated: "If he is married to a sister or an aunt, whether on the mother's or the father's side, or married to [his] mother or [his] daughter, in his Christianity, or Judaism, or paganism, and whether or not his previous community considers this kind of marriage union lawful, the marriage is annulled with his conversion, as this marriage is considered unlawful in Islam."[43]

While annulment had to be enforced in such cases, the law did address some of the unfairness that it caused the wife by granting her the rights of a Muslim woman facing a divorce. Her former husband had to bear the cost of maintaining her until the end of the waiting period, at which time she became available for marriage to someone else. If she was pregnant, he would provide for her until she gave birth. The fourteenth-century jurists gave full exposure to the forbidden degree in their doctrines of marriage. Ibn Juzayy devoted a long chapter to it, five whole pages in the printed edition of his manual, providing a list of no less than forty-eight female relatives who were forbidden to a Muslim man, some forever, others temporarily:

> Twenty-five cases are termed "eternal" (*mu'abbadāt*), the first seven being those of one's descent (*nasab*): mother, daughter, paternal aunt, sister, maternal aunt, daughter of the brother, daughter of the sister, and others who are of a similar affinity created by ties of suckling (*riḍāʿ*). Four categories are created through marriage: the wife's mother, her daughter, the father's wife, and the son's wife. [Also forbidden are] those who shared suckling ties with them, the wives of the Prophet, the cursed woman, and the wife married during a waiting period. Altogether twenty-five. The other twenty-three cases are the apostate, the non-*kitābiyya*, the married woman, the one in a waiting period, the one divorced from him in an *ibrā'* divorce [a mutual renunciation of obligations], a slave woman held jointly, a pagan female slave, a Muslim female slave who experienced the full range (*ṭawl*) of marriage rights, the son's female slave, one's own female slave, one's mistress's slave, the mother of one's master, one that is forbidden during the Pilgrimage, the sick woman, the wife's sister, her paternal aunt, and her maternal aunt. The union

> between such is not allowed, nor is the union with a woman married on Friday afternoon [the day of rest], with one who was demanded in marriage after she had been promised to someone else, and with an orphan who is not legally of majority status.[44]

Khalīl referred to the forbidden degree when dealing with marriage between slaves and non-Muslims: "If the two converted together, their marriage is valid, unless they are related in the forbidden degree."[45]

Nonconsummation

Consummation being required for the validation of a marriage, a fourth factor that could invalidate a marriage following conversion was nonconsummation. Regardless of the religious persuasion of the spouse before conversion, if the marriage was not consummated, it was annulled. If the husband were also to convert, a new marrriage could take place without a waiting period: "He could marry her with her consent, in a new marriage ceremony, with a marriage guardian and a *ṣadāq*."[46]

The fourteenth-century jurists did not make an outright attempt to link nonconsummation and conversion in the formulation of the marriage doctrine. However, Ibn Juzayy referred to it when he wrote about conversion and marriage: "If the couple convert together, their marriage is valid; if the preliminary requirements of a marriage guardian and a *ṣadāq* are lacking, [proceed all the same], no attention need be paid to it. If the husband converted earlier, the marriage with a *kitābiyya* remains valid, as does a marriage with any other; if she converts after him [and] if it happens before cohabitation [consummation of the marriage], they should be divorced. If the wife converts after cohabitation and the husband convertes during her waiting period, the marriage remains valid."[47]

Children

Ibn al-ʿAṭṭār's first and only concern when addressing the fate of children of converts was their faith. From his exposé it is clear that the legal status of children of a spouse who converted to Islam could be affected in different ways depending on the individual circumstances of the converted spouse. Children of slaves, children born into a marriage between parents related in the forbidden degree, and children in the custody of a divorced mother had a different legal status and different relations with their mothers.

The dictum was that a child followed his father in religion and his mother in civil status, either freedom or slavery.[48] However, only a child under the age of seven, male or female, would become a Muslim (*dakhala fī Islām abīhi*) if his father converted.[49] A child over the age of seven retained his birth religion. The age of seven was selected here on the assumption that this was an age at which a child was capable of making a reasoned decision about religion; the legal term used was *yuʿqal dīnihi*.[50] A child who became Muslim under such circumstances, the jurist explained, could well become an apostate later on, when he reached the age of majority. He would then be held accountable for his actions and be liable for capital punishment, the penalty for renunciation of his religion. Others said that since he had not been born "in Islam," he should not be held accountable for apostasy. For instance, if the newly converted father of a child younger than seven did not convert him to Islam, but neglected him, or if the child reached the age of majority without converting to Islam, even if he had been invited to join time after time and had refused, he was not to be considered liable for capital punishment.[51] It seemed that the law, while encouraging the conversion of young children, did not deny them their right to make a choice regarding their religion, once they reached the age of seven. Indeed, the law respected the notion that the need to choose a religion should not be imposed on children whose parents converted.[52]

The law was equally compassionate toward children born of a man's marriage to a woman related in the forbidden degree. After the dissolution of the marriage, a child, if still a minor, became a Muslim. Such a child was attached (*yulḥaq*) to the father, considered fully legitimate, and unlike children born from an adulterous relationship, could inherit from him. This was the case, as Ibn al-ʿAṭṭār explained, because adultery (*zināʾ*) in Christianity was not as bad as adultery in Islam.[53] If a pregnant wife was of a forbidden degree, however, the law was less kind to her. She was forced to separate from her husband at the time of his conversion, but being entitled to the rights of a divorced Muslim wife, she received food and shelter until she gave birth. After the birth, her child was taken away from her and given to the father. It appears that a wife of the forbidden degree did not qualify for custody or guardianship of her young child, a right given by Maliki law even to a divorced Jewish or Christian mother.[54] In the case of the forbidden degree involving a female slave, the conversion of the master (father) determined the conversion of the biological child, but again only up the age of seven. A slave was assigned the legal status of a child upon conversion, with those under seven years of age becoming Muslim and the older ones retaining their original religions.

In conclusion, the mother who did not convert clearly did not have the same rights over the child as the converted father since she had no say in the religion of the child under the age of seven. Nonetheless, her rights as a mother included guardianship of the young child, and in most cases these rights were preserved when she separated from the child's father, regardless of whether she converted. This provision gave a mother actual custody of her young child, which could be used, if she so desired, to exercise some influence over his religious beliefs.

The dissolution of the marriage entitled both a converted unmarried woman and a converted married woman whose marriage had been annulled to contract an Islamic marriage. It entitled a woman to a marriage agent, a role that, Ibn al-ʿAṭṭār stated, automatically fell to the legal patron of conversion, namely, the person who had accepted her conversion, whether the qadi or another official, who also became her legal guardian. He was under an obligation to see that she was married, or remarried, in her new faith and in her new community. This provision was doubly important for the converted woman. First, no marriage was legally valid without a *walī*, making this provision a fundamental requirement. Second, to initiate the process of matrimony, a Muslim woman needed a *walī* because, as Ibn Juzayy put it, "a woman cannot contract a marriage for herself or for another woman, no matter to what social class she belongs."[55] Unlike a Muslim virgin woman getting married for the first time, a converted unmarried woman had to give her consent to the marriage: "If she is without a husband, the person who converts her becomes her *walī* in marriage, and he will marry her off with her consent (*bi-riḍāhā*)."[56]

In the case of a converted woman, there was, in addition to the legal requirements, a practical side to the provision. Under normal circumstances, the marriage agent would be a close male relative, such as the father. By comparison, the converted woman was not only a newcomer to the community, and thus likely to face difficulty finding someone to act as an agent, but also deprived of her former family's close relatives.[57] Appointing an agent at the moment of conversion helped to prevent a situation where the new Muslim woman might remain unmarried and a burden on the community. Also, since the Islamic legal system did not anticipate any real possibility of a single woman living on her own, in the absence of an unmarried women's community, unlike in the Christian context where institutional arrangements were available for unmarried women such as nunneries, a matrimonial arrangement after a woman had reached the age of majority was imperative.[58]

The Ṣadāq in Conversion

The absence of a *ṣadāq* would normally invalidate the Islamic marriage. Conversion, however, did not constitute normal circumstances since it affected the timing of the application of the rules for a valid marriage. A marriage concluded under Christian or Jewish law might or might not have involved a payment of some sort, a *ṣadāq*, but once an Islamic marriage had emerged, the Muslim jurist was legally concerned about its absence. Strictly within the realm of property rights, the *ṣadāq* constituted a fundamental right of the woman. When the marriage went through the validation process, the link between consummation and the *ṣadāq* had to be established; the Muslim wife could refuse consummation of the marriage if she had not received a *ṣadāq*. In a conversion case, according to Ibn al-ʿAṭṭār, the question of the nature of the *ṣadāq* became a contentious issue:

> If he did not consummate the marriage before he converted to Islam, he remains in the marriage with her if he gave her a *ṣadāq*. If he gave her a *ṣadāq* of [unlawful nature, if he gave her] wine or pigs, he should be forced to give her a *ṣadāq* of similar value, in dirhams or another lawful item. It is said that he should give her something less than what is estimated to be legal for deflowering, a quarter of a dinar,[59] and he should get rid of the unlawful items. If she has taken possession of the unlawful items, she should spoil it, spill the wine, and kill the pigs. It is said that she should get rid of it and not kill it, and he would remain married to her, but if he refused [to get rid of the unlawful items of the *ṣadāq*], they should be separated. If he gave her a *ṣadāq* of unlawful items and she accepted it and consummated the marriage and he converted after the consummation, he would remain married to her, and he would not have to pay anything in addition to the *ṣadāq*. This is so if it happened within the time frame in which it was allowed for him in his previous faith and which he thought constituted a legal marriage. However, if she did not take the *ṣadāq* from him before he converted, he had to pay her a *ṣadāq* like the one he had obligated himself to give her. If he consummated the marriage, all the wine that he had in his possession at the time should be spilled and all the pigs should be sent away, or, as others say, should be killed.[60]

According to this ruling, a *kitābī* wife, most probably a Christian, would have to relinquish her marriage payment, the equivalent of a *ṣadāq*, if it consisted of unlawful items, such as wine and pigs, even though she herself did not convert. The jurist could have well anticipated a situation where, in order to preserve a marriage, a converted husband would give into a wife who used the *ṣadāq* requirement as blackmail, agreeing to include unlawful items in her *ṣadāq*. Ibn Mughīth also discussed ways to handle the unlawful *ṣadāq*. According to him, the wife of a convert could not stipulate that she would remain with her husband on condition that he provide her with a *ṣadāq* consisting in part of wine. This would be unlawful, but he was to provide her with a *ṣadāq* of equivalent value.[61]

This problem of a *ṣadāq* consisting of "wine and pigs," unique to converts from Christianity, must have been of particular relevance during periods of frequent conversions since the issue of the *ṣadāq* and conversion was treated in two places in the *Mudawwana*. The first is in the section dealing with the *ṣadāq* given to women who convert to Islam but whose husbands decline to follow them; this particular ruling in the *Mudawwana* is attributed to Mālik:

> [In the case of] a Jewish, Christian, or pagan woman who converts to Islam and whose husband declines conversion, if he has given his wife a *ṣadāq*, part of it early, part deferred, and has consummated the marriage, she is entitled to receive both the early and the delayed *ṣadāq*. If he has not consummated the marriage and has not given her a *ṣadāq*, she has no right to it. If she has taken it from him, she has to give it back. This is because the reason for the dissolution of the marriage came from her, making it into an annulment (*faskh*), not a divorce (*ṭalāq*).[62]

The second ruling deals directly with the unlawful *ṣadāq*:

> Ibn al-Qāsim was asked about a Christian who married a Christian woman with a *ṣadāq* consisting of wine or pigs, or without a *ṣadāq*, or who made a condition that there should not be a *ṣadāq* because they considered this lawful in their religion, and who converted to Islam. He answered that he, Ibn al-Qāsim, had not heard anything from Mālik regarding this, but said that he was leaning toward deciding that if the husband consummated the marriage, the wife should get a *ṣadāq* of a similar value if she had not received any before cohabitation. If he has consummated the marriage and she has taken the *ṣadāq* before cohabitation, it is her *ṣadāq*, and she cannot be deprived of it, but she cannot claim anything in addition and remain married. If he has not consummated the marriage before conversion, and whether she has taken possession of the *ṣadāq* or not, Ibn al-Qāsim's opinion is that he has the power of choice about whether he wants to give her a *ṣadāq* of similar value. If he refuses, they have to be separated, and she has no claim over him.[63]

In fourteenth-century Granada, Ibn Juzayy continued to discuss this aspect of the Maliki marriage doctrine, including it in his outline of the *ṣadāq* issue in marriage. In the chapter on the *ṣadāq*, he stipulated three conditions for a valid *ṣadāq*, the first being that it should consist of items that can be lawfully owned and sold by a Muslim, unlike wine, pigs, and the like.[64] Khalīl, while expressing his reservations, admitted the unorthodox nature of the *ṣadāq*'s contents but insisted that the main concern was the actual existence of a *ṣadāq*.[65]

Annulment

The extreme consequence of conversion was the invalidation and termination of an existing marriage through "severance" of the marriage bond (*tanqaṭiʿ ʿuqdat al-nikāḥ*). In such cases, the couple did not divorce by way of *ṭalāq*; rather, the marriage was declared void (*yufsakh*).[66] The difference between divorce and annulment was reflected in the rights, conditions, and compensation applicable to the woman.[67] An annulment persisted for as long as the circumstances occasioning the annulment continued to exist. Despite the different legal status of an annulment, the immediate action that ensued was the same as for a regular divorce: the wife would enter the waiting period of three menstrual cycles, the *ʿidda*, during which she was entitled to shelter and maintenance.[68]

Ibn al-ʿAṭṭār gave instructions in two cases necessitating annulment. The first was when a Christian wife converted without her husband,[69] in which case,

> her marriage is annulled, and if the marriage has been consummated, she is told to enter the waiting period, and the husband has to provide her with shelter and food. If she is pregnant, he has to provide for her until she gives birth. If she is not pregnant, he does not have to pay maintenance (*nafaqa*). The husband has to pay for the rent of a different shelter for the duration of the waiting period if she is in rented premises. If she remains in his home, she should stay there until the end of the waiting period.[70]

In the second case, an annulment resulting from marriage with a woman of the forbidden degree, no matter whether the woman was *kitābī*, a slave, or a pagan, she would continue to receive lodging, clothes, and food during the waiting period until she gave birth, but she could not benefit from the right of custody of the child, which, as discussed earlier, was usually counted as a maintenance right since the female guardian was entitled to a payment for this service.[71] The jurist indicated that the child would be attached to the father, would carry his name, and would benefit from all the rights of a legitimate child. He indicated that a child born of an adulterous relationship (*zināʾ*) in Islam was deprived of these legal rights, but not the child born of *zināʾ* in another religion. In conversion, however, although inheritance from previous family members was not permitted, inheritance from husband and children became possible.

The Wife's Creed

One aspect of women's conversion to Islam was her creed. When writing out the conversion certificate, the notary was not required to verify or otherwise testify to the level of either the female convert's faith or her knowledge of the Islamic creed. Nonetheless, once there was a legal link between faith and the validity of marriage, one's faith could result in a marriage's dissolution under certain circumstances. Men were given the right to question their wives about their creed and, if the wives were found lacking in this respect, they could divorce them under the rule forbidding marriage between a Muslim man and a pagan woman.

Three fatwas were written in fifteenth-century Maghrib in response to a single question about whether suspicion regarding a wife's faith was a valid reason for the dissolution of the marriage. The second, by Abū ʿAbd Allāh Muḥammad Ibn Marzūq,[72] was written as an opinion concerning a earlier fatwa issued by a nameless jurist. In this first fatwa, the jurist had responded to the question of whether every married man should interrogate his wife about the state of her creed and, if she was found to be ignorant, have his marriage to her annulled on the grounds that she was an idolater.[73] The reader appears to have disagreed with or to have been confused by the view expressed in the answer that he received. In the new query, addressed to Ibn Marzūq, he requested confirmation of whether an interrogation of the wife was indeed necessary and whether the abovementioned opinion should be followed. He also wanted to know what level of understanding of the creed was required from a wife. He specifically asked whether the marriage should be annulled if the husband found out that his wife was ignorant about the faith, knowing only the profession of faith (*shahāda*), which was what most people knew. Ibn Marzūq replied that if such an interrogation was indeed required either before or after marriage, no woman who professed only the *shahāda* would be married. If, on the other hand, bad belief cropped up among some married women without their being asked about it, then the situation was to be examined according to the law. He advised that something of this nature might necessitate grave action if not disciplined.

The third fatwa was written by ʿAbd Allāh al-ʿAbdūsī (d. Fez, 1445–46) in response to a query about a man who had found an intolerable weakness (*fasād*) in his wife's creed and wanted to know whether he should leave her, thus dissolving the marriage.[74] Al-ʿAbdūsī replied that there were three potential degrees of weakness in one's creed. The first was what the community (*jamāʿa*) regarded as unbelief (*kufr*). The second was a bad innovation (*bidʿa*) in one's religious thought, such that the person strayed from the right path. The third was conduct leading to debate about whether one was truly guilty of unbelief.

A woman who was a nonbeliever by general consensus, was considered a pagan (*majūsī*) and was not permitted to be married to a Muslim. If she was married to someone who had ignored her status, their marriage was to be annulled. This had to be established with a document confirming the annulment, signed by herself and her husband. If her husband did not confirm the annulment, her word could not be accepted because she might have been deliberately attempting to achieve the annulment of her marriage in this way. The annulment was to be carried out honorably and cautiously and to be free of doubts.

Anything that was not considered unbelief by consensus did not automatically lead to an annulment, and the husband was expected to correct his wife's creed through instruction if none of her own relatives was qualified to do so.

In the case of a wife about whose creed there was a disagreement, a judge should question the couple. If he determined that there was no unbelief, she was allowed to remain in the marriage. If both spouses declared that there was unbelief, they were to separate. This applied especially if the husband urged it because proof of the wife's guiltlessness lay in his hands. If the husband claimed that there was no unbelief and the wife declared the contrary, the wife was to be forced to stay in the marriage, and the judge's ruling was expected to put an end to the conflict.

Al-ʿAbdūsī explained his opinion on the issue of a wife's creed and potential annulment as follows:

> We trust in the sincerity of converted women when they manifest their creed and their Islam. Only God knows their secrets. Unless a man is convinced that there is a weakness in his wife's belief, he should not interrogate her about this. He is encouraged to teach her what she is ignorant of in that respect. Some of the jurists, whose model of behaviour is followed, say that during the writing of the marriage contract, the witnesses should examine the creed of the woman because a weak creed is common among them. They should do that and so lead a large number of people to the true creed.[75]

Al-ʿAbdūsī regarded the strength of a wife's creed as a true concern for husbands and was planning to write a book addressing the issue. While books dealing with women's conduct were not uncommon,[76] this one, if it was written at all, did not survive.

Given the complete disappearance of Christians in the Maghrib after the Almohad period of the eleventh-thirteenth centuries and the lack of evidence that marriage with Christians in North Africa was ever common enough to provoke such problems,[77] these three responses from Maghribi jurists indicate either that female converts to Islam were living in the Maghrib after having come there with their husbands from Spain during increased migration in the fifteenth century or that the jurists were answering questions from Spain. The issue of weak credal knowledge may indicate that both men and women used this concern to invalidate or escape unwanted marriages. Or it may be that the jurists were concerned about pious men who found themselves married to pagan women, and thus living in a state of sin, because their wives were ignorant of the fundamentals of the Islamic creed.

A view of women's religious awareness that is analogous to the medieval one has been revealed in anthropological studies of marriage in contemporary Morocco.[78] In this context, the three fatwas provide insights into yet another dimension of the Muslim marriage.

Women's Conversion in Comparative Context

The conversion certificates of al-Andalus and the comprehensive legal framework discussed in the previous sections provide an answer to the question of how Islamic law articulated and defined the issues related to women's conversion or to the conversion of their spouses, but not to questions related to the historical context of women's conversion to Islam and its historical significance. We cannot answer the question of how, why, and when women converted, and yet their conversion's dynamics had important implications to such central historical questions as the demographic growth of the Islamic community in the earlier stages. Since the increase in the size of the Muslim community during the first three centuries of its existence came about mainly through conversion and less through internal growth, any attempt to discuss the size of the convert community in definitive terms hinges on knowledge of how many, when, and how women converted; whether women followed their husbands in conversion; whether for every converted man, there was a converted woman; and whether women and children could join the Muslim community.[79] Another question is that of motivation. In later centuries, from about the tenth century onward, established and stable Jewish and Christian communities lived in the midst of a Muslim majority; conversion to Islam can thus be interpreted either as a unique act of defiance both against community and against religion or as an act of convenience, as a way to obtain the privileges and benefits associated with the ruling majority. Did such motives lie behind women's conversion? Did women indeed choose conversion as an act of defiance? How important was the social aspect of conversion to women as opposed to men? And did women's conversion, or lack of it, indicate a better or worse adjustment and integration on their part?

The literature on voluntary conversion is not negligible as all historians, not only historians of religion, regard conversion as a valuable tool for historical investigation into legal, social, and economic dimensions of religion. Yet the motivation for conversion in the medieval period, a religious age, has essentially been treated in the literature as a male issue, since conversion histories have so far come from men. Their manner of writing is generally apologetic, argumentative, and couched in theological and philosophical polemics, which has sent the scholarly investigation in the direction of intellectual rather than social and legal terms and, in turn, further suppressed and discouraged any investigation into the female role in conversion.[80] With the absence of women's voices on the subject, the recent historiography of conversion has devised a framework for a debate from which the feminine perspective has been omitted.[81]

The information on women and conversion from non-Islamic sources, such as the Geniza documents, does not provide all the answers but is nonetheless significant. Through them we are able to detect women's reactions to their husbands' or related males' conversion to Islam, and discover whether or not they decided to follow their men in conversion, which was one of the questions raised in the conversion documents. This information will help us evaluate the dynamics behind conversion and examine whether gaining access to Islamic women's property rights could have been a key element in persuading women to convert to Islam. As is to be expected, however, all the information from non-Islamic sources about women and conversion to Islam deals with the aftermath of their husbands and male relatives' conversion, while information about women's independent conversion remains non-existent.

Shlomo Dov Goitein's evidence about Jewish conversion to Islam includes several cases that show Jewish women not following their men in conversion.[82] The first case is that of a wife of a renegade, mentioned in a list of alms' receivers from the Jewish community. While the alms list may be understood as an indication that the woman was reduced to living on charity from the Jewish community as a result of her husband's conversion, it does not preclude her having lived off of alms before; it does show nonetheless that she did not convert along with her husband. In another case, the renegade sons of a poor widow who died in Cairo came back to claim her inheritance—an indication that she remained Jewish. A third case concerns an Egyptian Jew who converted to Islam, but continued to live with his wife, who did not convert. When he planned to go abroad on a business trip, he refused to grant her a divorce. After ten years of his absence, she applied for a divorce from him, but the appeal was transferred from the Muslim jurisconsult to the Jewish court and was rejected. Another Jew, an India trader, converted to Islam in Aden following the breakup of his marriage. His wife, who did not convert, was given shelter by the Jewish merchant's representative until her father could come and collect her.

Goitein also provides a list of cases of Jewish converts to Islam, some of whom are well known and others of no particular distinction; since nothing is said about their womenfolk, we can only guess at their fate. One such case was the wife of the poet Isaac Ibn Ezra, the well-known Jewish convert from al-Andalus, who appears in the Geniza letters and who was married to the daughter of the poet Judah Halevi. He converted to Islam around 1140, but we do not hear whether his wife converted to Islam with him or whether she followed her husband on his peregrinations throughout the Middle East and Europe. On the other hand, we do know that the daughters of Abū l-Barakāt, Ibn Ezra's teacher who also converted to Islam around the same time, remained Jewish. In 1030 a Karaite man, whose marriage contract is found in the Geniza, gave his Jewish bride 100 dinars as a wedding gift and promised 200 dinars more in deferred dowry. In 1047, after the assassination of his father, he converted to Islam, later becoming vizier of the Fatimid empire, but the fate of his wife, who began her married life with so much opulence, is unknown.[83] Maimonides, himself a survivor of a forced conversion in the twelfth century, mentioned a man who gave his wife a provisional bill of divorce when he was leaving on a trip, in case he embraced Islam while he was gone. And in fourteenth-century Tlemcen, a Jewish physician attending to the Marinid sultan Abū l-Ḥasan was invited to embrace Islam but refused. We do not know whether he consulted his wife or whether she would have chosen to divorce him if he had converted.[84]

The point of presenting the above cases, however meager the evidence, is to emphasize how little we know and understand about women's conversion to Islam in the early medieval period, which makes the existence of the conversion certificates so very precious. The evidence does confirm that many Jewish women chose to remain in the Jewish religion, not following their husbands in conversion, and similarly there is evidence that Christian women in Islamic lands resisted conversion, suffering legal and financial distress as a result. In his chronicle, Michael, the twelfth-century Antioch Syriac patriarch, had to address this question of Christian conversion to Islam in contemporary Antioch when the Christian marriage of a young woman, whose father had converted to Islam, was challenged by the Muslim community.[85] On this occasion, Michael commented on conversion in the past and quoted the ninth-century chronicle of Denys of Tell Mahré, which confirms Michael's observation that Christian women resisted conversion to Islam to a far greater degree than did men.[86] During the Mamluk period, between the thirteenth and sixteenth centuries, highly-placed Copts were frequently pressured to convert, but their mothers, wives, and daughters remained Christian.[87]

After studying the conversion certificates, Pedro Chalmeta opines that young women in al-Andalus who converted did so for sentimental reasons, such as love for a man of another faith, while the conversion of married women was a means of achieving a quick and cheap divorce.[88] Other historians looking at the respective evidence have equally suggested that women might have used conversion for this benefit. The reasons given for the conversion of Greek women to Islam during the early Ottoman period as described in the court documents of Kandiye, between the seventeenth and eighteenth centuries, also lean in this direction:[89] While more men than women there converted to Islam, married women seemed to have converted in order to have their marriages dissolved and to gain control of their children.[90] The court documents in Kandiye provide examples of how the dissolution of one marriage was often followed by an instant marriage to a Muslim man.[91]

It would indeed be intriguing to find out whether the Islamic laws regulating property and conjugal rights were behind a woman's reason for choosing conversion.[92] Could the legal aspects of women's conversion help us to better define the broader question of the status of women in Islamic law and their property rights?

Had conversion been either encouraged or discouraged by simply giving or denying property rights to new converts, this would benefit greatly our understanding of early settlement patterns,[93] but conversion entailed an automatic switch from one legal and social system to another, which in itself brought changes both to family and conjugal arrangements as well as to men's and women's family and property rights. The existence of the conversion certificates might suggest that the promise of property rights could offset the heavily negative social outcome of conversion for women, but the latter was very severe. The seclusion of women in all three religious cultures made the father's household and the relatives on both sides crucial to a woman's social interactions. Even within their own religious community, women had little freedom of movement: we know, for example, that Jewish women of the Geniza period could not leave their house without their husband's permission, and that the number of times they could visit members of their families was limited.[94] A woman's conversion to another religious community meant entirely severing relations with her family; conversion to Islam thus did not increase a woman's freedom of movement, but impaired it even more. The Geniza documents provide instances where converts to Judaism moved into different communities; one can assume that similarly a convert to Islam was likely to move away from his or her previous community. The heavy price paid in cases of conversion, especially for women, often erased the benefit of acquiring new property rights.

The importance of a society's willingness to accommodate the law is equally visible in the differences between the Islamic attitude to converts and that of Christianity and Judaism. While Islamic law regarded conversion as a spiritual act, which eliminated all barriers between one who was born a Muslim and the convert to Islam, the Iberian Christian concept of conversion, namely, that conversion to Christianity did not affect the physical nature of the body and its capacity to transmit Jewish-ness and Muslimness in spite of conversion, meant that interfaith sexual contact and communal living of converted Jews and Muslims in the Aragonese and Castilian cities in the fourteenth and fifteenth centuries was condemned.[95] In much the same way, the forced conversion of Jews to Christianity, as occurred in Spain in 1391, created many couples the spouses of which were of different religion, a situation similar to that described in the Islamic legal sources. Responding to the lack of provision in the Talmud for divorcing a Jewish woman and an apostate, the Sephardic rabbinate adopted the principle that the sanctified marriage remained valid and highlighted the genealogical principle behind Judaism by emphasizing that even in a case of conversion, a person's Jewish-ness remained intact.[96]

The demand by converted Jews and Muslims for full rights of integration into Spanish society as they became more numerous was rejected on basis of the claim that their bodies were transmitting a non-Christian identity in perpetuity, a concept fundamentally opposed to the Islamic legal approach to women's bodies and to conversion. The Islamic view of the female body as carrying individual property rights was alone affected by its religious identity. The acquisition of these rights hinged on being "in Islam" while the racial aspect of reproduction was absent.

Conclusion

The discussion of the legal discourse on conversion has been undertaken here for several reasons. In particular, the issue of conversion was uniquely relevant to conditions in al-Andalus, where conversion to Islam was a historical occurrence. In the case of Granada, conversion had serious repercussions for the fate of the Islamic community contemporary with the terminus of our documents. Our discussion of Granadan women's property rights has been both historically and legally comprehensive because the legal discourse on conversion is actually about the validity of marriage and thus reflects jurists' concerns about women's property rights. In addition to understanding the centrality of marriage to the acquisition of women's property rights, we now see how acquisition ebbed and flowed according to the effects of conversion on marriage. Women's property rights were maintained in conversion if a set of requirements was met, and they were withdrawn if these requirements were not met.

The jurists' discussion of the conversion certificates helped to define the Islamic construct of marriage by linking it to a vast array of rights in the event of conversion. This discussion has demonstrated that the status of the marriage was the most important legal matter to be affected by conversion, and it has shown that conversion was subject to gender equality insofar as either spouse could bring about this important change single-handedly and without consulting the other.

Since women had a distinct legal persona with separate property rights, a woman's conversion was seen as an individual act requiring a different document than that used by males. The couple did not convert as a unit, or in a single act, precisely because rights were involved that were affected by conversion. The consequences of conversion indicate that the acquisition of women's property rights through marriage could be negated in a single act, making these rights ephemeral, not universal to women.

We have seen that the Islamic legislation on conversion originated as an offshoot of, and was linked to, the marriage law and that it was included in the marriage chapters of the legal manuals. As time progressed, conversion no longer entailed marriage simply to a nonbeliever, but also to Jews or Christians, who had a distinct legal status in terms of marriage, which changed some aspects of conversion. The conversion of one spouse immediately placed the other in a position where he or she had to react since the couple's legal status had changed. In such instances, even though conversion was an individual undertaking and the law regarded it as such, the consequences to the wife could be detrimental precisely in terms of her property rights. Moreover, as the literary evidence suggests, because social considerations were equally taken into account, property rights could be sacrificed in exchange for being allowed to remain in proximity to the birth family and community.

This brings us to the discussion of the social framework that weighed on the uses that women could make of their property rights in economic life. Goitein claims that the seclusion of women in Jewish society was the norm but that it did not interfere with their economic activity. As we have seen, Muslim women's property rights were more extensive than those of Jewish women.[97] The next chapter looks at the economic activity of Muslim women and at whether the fruits of their labour and commercial activities were protected legally and socially by their property rights.

Part Three

ECONOMY AND CLASS

Seven

LABOUR AND WAGES

The Historical Context

With the exception of remuneration for wet nursing, the subject of women's wages is not addressed in the Qur'an, even though the following dictum could be interpreted as securing a woman's right to labour and wages: "Men have a share in what they earn, and women have theirs in what they earn" (Q 4:32).[1] At the other end of the chronological spectrum, the Granadan collection does not contain any hiring contracts, either for men or for women. Nonetheless, the subject of women's wage labour deserves its place in a study of women's property rights because the historical effect of these rights is determined by the role that they allowed women to play in the economic sphere. Indeed, legal sources such as notarial documents and fatwas, but also the positive law (*fiqh*), speak abundantly about women's labour. And women's role as wage labourers in the manufacturing sector was considerable.

European historiography gives women's wage labour a crucial role in the modern family formation as well as in the rise of capitalism, making it a historical factor in its own right.[2] This raises the question of whether a similar role can be attributed to Muslim women's wage labour? The European data are relevant to our understanding of how Islamic law regulated female wage labour because they provide us with a wide thematic framework, as well as analysis, for comparison. A brief look at the historical background to women's wage labour in the Islamic lands, both its dimensions and the occupations that women filled, will help to establish the legal context of wage labour as a woman's property right.[3]

With the arrival of the Islamic era we note the completion of a transformation process in labour organization in the Middle East, as servile labour was replaced by wage labour in the rural and urban areas, and in Maliki Muslim Spain and North Africa large agricultural estates (*latifundias*) were replaced by private ownership of small parcels of land. The process was already underway when Islam began its spread throughout the Middle East and could be observed during the transition period from Roman to Byzantine rule around the Mediterranean. Remnants of the Roman system continued through the eighth and ninth centuries in North Africa, where large estates are reported to have employed slave cultivators.[4] Where the land was owned by the state, as in ninth-century Egypt, the papyri show that small parcels of land were leased to peasants and wage labourers were hired to cultivate them.[5] In the Near East the last colony of slaves was eliminated during the Zanj revolt of the Iraqi marshes in 883.[6] The transformation in the organization of agricultural labour resulted in the disappearance of slave labour as a significant factor in the labour market as a whole, and may have been related to reorganization of labour in the urban centers as well. This is not to say that slave labour disappeared altogether from the labour market in the Middle East but to point out that it no longer constituted the core of the labour force in either agricultural cultivation or manufacturing. How did the changes in the scope of slave labour affect productivity and women's labour?

Indications of a rise in productivity in the rural areas show that this transformation in the labour force not only failed to hinder productivity but actually enhanced it. The change in the nature of the labour force from servile to free provided an incentive to landowners to search for ways to improve the productivity of their land by intensified fertilization, improved irrigation, summer crop rotation, technological innovations, and changes to the ecological system.[7] Population growth in the countryside and migration to the towns helped to fuel the manufacturing industries there, which were working with raw materials supplied by a more productive hinterland. This impact was particularly felt in the textile industry, where female wage labour was the main beneficiary.

Evidence from the late medieval period, between the eleventh and fifteenth centuries, indicates that women's participation in the labour market was both considerable and diversified. An analysis of women's market-related economic activities shows that from the tenth century onward women's participation in the labour force, which remained constant in the rural areas, increased in the towns, where it came to dominate the textile industry through the monopolization of certain tasks. Gender division of labour was the prevalent rule in manufacturing, unlike other sectors of the economy, such as agriculture, with the strongest showing in the textile industry. Occupations monopolized by women included spinning, dyeing, and embroidery within what was the largest, most specialized, and most market-oriented industry of the Muslim cities.[8]

Spinning was primarily a female occupation, and female spinners and combers of different threads did their work at home, where they could combine housework and childrearing with wage labour. The restrictions on their movement in the public sphere, to be discussed later in this chapter, were demanded by zealous market supervisors and mostly concerned trips to the market to purchase raw materials. The spinning tools found in women's estates as well as remnants of cotton, flax, or wool, whether in crude or spun form, indicate that they were engaged in both wage labour and manufacturing for their private needs.[9]

Women's trades and occupations, their nonprofessional and unskilled tasks, and the services that they provided through the commercial activities surrounding the textile sector represented a high degree of participation, specialization, and division of feminine labour in comparative and absolute terms. The growing size and activity of the feminine labour force were bound to have implications for women's status as wage earners and for the status of wage labour as a woman's property right. As female wage labour became widespread and commonplace, it also became a consistent factor in women's lives. Yossef Rapoport has linked women's wages to such important issues as "the balance of power between husbands and wives," "frequent divorce" in Mamluk society, and "increased numbers of single women able to live independently on their earnings which were low but not insubstantial."[10] While each of the above needs more than the anecdotal evidence provided to substantiate it, the question of earnings was a constant with which society had to contend. Women's earnings might not have been substantial, but they had to be protected. Thus they were another property right that the jurists had to address.

The Legal Framework of Wage Labour

The Islamic law of hire is gender-blind and thus does not lend itself directly to answering gender-related questions, but the legal sources raise issues related to the right of females to engage in wage earning and to keep and control their wages, considerations that are essential to its status as a property right. Unlike the previous rights treated here, which were defined as women's property rights to begin with, the definition of wage labour as a woman's property right was dependent upon legal deliberations.[11]

The law books define hire (*ijāra*) as an act through which one person, whether male or female, cedes to another for a determined period of time the use of either a thing or his labour in return for payment.[12] Provisions for the law of *ijāra* also included: a section on *istiṣnāʿ* (a contract in which an artisan hired out his skills to manufacture a specific item); and a section on *kirāʾ* (rent), which applied only to items that could not be used up. According to Joseph Schacht, this three-pronged construct of the *ijāra* followed the model of the Roman *locatio conducto* (*l.c.*), and the three originally separate transactions of *kirā'* (corresponding to *l.c. rei*), *ijāra* proper (corresponding to *l.c. operarum*), and *juʿl* (wages) (corresponding to *l.c. operis*) were combined.[13]

Muslim jurists viewed the contract of hire as constituting a sale (*bayʿ*) and included the subject matter either in the chapter on sale or immediately following it. There were those who regarded hire as an illegal sale because it constituted a contract for the use of one thing in exchange for another of non-equivalent value and also because it involved a conditional promise, wherein the required effort was not determined in advance, but the payment was. Payment could be revoked when the element of certitude no longer existed. The idea of treating rent as a sale was particularly heinous; it was forbidden to sell "non-existent" things—that is, things that one no longer possessed, having already received payment for them. The pervasiveness of the disagreement over the legal nature of hire can be gauged from the continuous debate over it among the Andalusian jurists. The notaries rejected the notion that sale and hire were the same thing. In the positive law section of his manual, Ibn Mughīth devoted much space to distancing the two from each other, arguing that in essence they were utterly conflicting: "The rule (*ḥukm*) of hire (*ijāra*) is not the rule of sale (*bayʿ*) because the object of a sale becomes the property of the buyer, while the object of a hire does not."[14] The Granadan jurist Ibn Juzayy said in his manual that the hire was an irregular sale because the work to be done could, but also could not, be determined, yet the chapter that treated the law of hire was called "The Second Chapter on Contracts that are Similar to Sales."[15]

Wage labour was never seen or regulated as a means of livelihood for women. Providing for the needs of females was the duty of fathers and husbands.[16] An independent single or unmarried adult woman simply did not belong to any legally defined category in terms of property rights, and a father could not force a divorced daughter who was again living in his house to work for wages in order to support herself. A wife or a husband could not treat wage labour as part of or as replacement for the wife's maintenance. However, while the law of hire was gender-blind and did not address any of these issues, labour's transformation did bring questions of property rights to the fore. The basic skills used for domestic consumption could now be remunerated. Women now had tools that generated income. In turn, the legal system needed to address the host of questions that these changes provoked. Thus the issue cannot be defined solely on the basis of the law of hire but must be considered with reference to data in the notarial manuals, especially female hiring contracts, and in the fatwas.

It is not clear when or why a written contract was absolutely necessary for certain undertakings or when an oral contract was deemed sufficient. In the Middle East, apart from their relative abundance in the Egyptian papyri collections, hiring contracts are hard to find in the Islamic archives.[17] Hiring was a common and frequent transaction in al-Andalus, and the notaries there did have a considerable number of deeds that they could use.[18] However, women's remunerative work did not result in regular contracts, let alone specific ones intended to accommodate the different aspects of women's labour. There are only two model deeds for female employment in the Andalusian notarial manuals, one in Ibn Mughīth's *Muqniʿ* for a house maid, indicating that domestic service was not the domain of servile labour alone,[19] and the other in al-Jazīrī's *Maqṣad* for a wet nurse.[20] Their content and their mere existence indicate not so much that women's wage labour had a different legal status but that it was affected by special conditions relevant to women alone. Even if the law did not identify wage labour as a separate women's property right, it had become a separate entity.

Nevertheless, the lack of a block of model deeds for women, similar to the one that we have for men's occupations, particularly in the textile industry, is intriguing. Given the large share of female wage labour in the manufacture of textile products and given the sophisticated division of labour in that sector, this lack of contracts could be explained by the physical conditions of female labour and its organization. The fact that women worked at home made the use of contracts for their tasks redundant and impractical. However, the specific issues involved in women's wage labour indicate that the changes in the status of wage labour became a factor in a wife's relations with her husband and with society at large. These patterns are evident in the fatwas.

The Right to Wage Earning

The Hairdresser

The fatwas yield information about the challenges to the right of wage earning, about the origins of these challenges, and about how these challenges were perceived by the jurists. That most of the fatwas dealing with women's issues of wage labour were treated in chapters other than the one on the law of hire is an indication that the matter of wages was linked to other rights. Mostly, the fatwas came from the chapter on marriage (*nikāḥ*), where many of the issues related to women's property rights were debated.

The first fatwa to challenge a woman's right to engage in wage earning was addressed to the jurist Ibn ʿArafa, a contemporary of the historian and later Maliki judge in Cairo Ibn Khaldūn.[21] Written in fourteenth-century Eastern Maghrib, it describes the case of a hairdresser (*māshiṭa*) who entered a clause in her marriage contract to the effect that her husband would not prevent her from exercising her trade. The husband accepted the condition but later changed his mind and forbade his wife to work. The ruling was:

> The husband is not obligated to fulfill the condition stipulated in the marriage contract. If her trade is unlawful, then it is obvious that he can forbid her to pursue it, but if her trade is a lawful one, more than one jurist thought that it would be commendable for the husband to keep his word and fulfill the contracted obligation, and some public notaries supported and asserted it. However, my decision is similar to the ruling made in a case where the future wife stipulated that her husband could not force her to leave her hometown, which is similar to a ruling in the *Mudawwana* that denies the obligating clause.[22]

It is not clear why the husband wanted to prevent his wife from exercising her trade. As Ibn ʿArafa inferred, there was no social stigma that could have reflected badly on the wife or her husband attached to the exercise of this trade—hairdressing was much in demand and indispensable to the elaborate marriage ceremonies. Motives for the husband's refusal could have been his desire to control his wife's movements or his dislike of seeing her operating outside the home, in the public sphere. There could well have been an economic motive—for instance, if she had refused the husband's demand to appropriate her wages or to have a share of them, or if he had tried to blackmail her in this way. Regardless, Ibn ʿArafa allowed the husband to ignore the contract, drawing an analogy to a husband's noncompliance with the conditions stipulated in the marriage contract regarding nonremoval of the wife to another location, which previous authorities had sanctioned. The only explanation for the reasoning presented by Ibn ʿArafa and those who preceded him in his ruling can be found in the context of property rights.

In Chapter One we saw that the wife could offer property in exchange for negation of the husband's right to enforce on her a move from her hometown. Other rights that the husband could negate in exchange for property were his right to marry a second wife and his right to be paid for a divorce initiated by the wife (*khulʿ*). Similarly, he could also obtain relief from his obligation to pay the delayed portion of the *ṣadāq*. In the present case, the wife was not seen as having offered to compensate her husband for giving up his rights in the matrimonial regime. As a result, even though he initially agreed to her work without mentioning compensation, he was later able to change his position with impunity and reclaim his rights. Apparently, this sort of conduct on the part of husbands was not particularly rare; as the fatwa mentioned, the notaries and some jurists were opposed to it.

The Wet Nurse

The second fatwa challenging a woman's right to engage in wage earning dealt with a husband's claim to his wife's wages for wet nursing. The fatwa is attributed to a general authorship (*baʿḍ al-shuyūkh*), a phrase that usually suggests either a generally applicable rule or a leading principle.[23]

> A woman hired herself out as a wet nurse without her husband's consent, and he did not learn about it until later. His wife contested his demand for the wages that she had received for suckling a baby. The jurist answered, "The time that elapsed since the writing of the contract means that he has no claim, but he has the right to invalidate any future hiring (*ijāra*) contract. The husband is entitled to benefit only from the things of the interior (*al-ashyāʾ al-bāṭiniyya*), i.e., the chores that a woman has to perform inside her home for the household. He has no rights over her wages because she retained ownership of her rightful things, even if she sold them without his permission."[24]

Wet nursing was considered part of a woman's rights over her body, or as the fatwa says, part of "her rightful things." It might not have been the most common of women's occupations, but, unlike other women's jobs, it required a written contract. The detailed elaboration in the contract clauses shows why a verbal agreement was insufficient. Wet nursing's frequency and prolonged nature, the uncertainties, and the series of obligations and restrictions that resulted from it affected how the law conceptualized and articulated women's wages as a property right. The many parties to the transaction, from the nursing baby and its father to the wet nurse and her husband, also made a contract necessary.[25]

The Egyptian jurist Khalīl treated the wet nurse contract in his chapter on the law of hire, highlighting the rights and duties of the nurse's husband and stating that the contract was binding, although he also noted that the husband was entitled to cancel the contract if he had not authorized it. If the husband had co-signed the contract, he was forbidden to have intercourse with his wife.[26] In Granada breastfeeding was not something that women of high society practiced. Ibn Juzayy treated the hiring of a wet nurse as he did the hiring of a servant, namely, as a matter of social standing. If the mother's social class required it and if the husband could afford it, hiring a wet nurse formed part of the expenses to which the wife was entitled in marriage.

Two model notarial deeds are available for comparison, one a Maliki model provided by the Andalusian notary al-Jazīrī and the other a contract for hiring a wet nurse provided by the tenth-century Egyptian writer al-Ṭaḥāwī.[27] Placing the two side by side gives us a sense of the rights and obligations shared by the affected parties.

al-Jazīrī, Muslim Spain

This man hires this woman to breastfeed his son named thus in his house or in her house for the duration of two years, starting at the date of this contract, to clean what he passes, to wash his wrappings, and to bathe him in return for this amount of dinars to be paid monthly during the mentioned period. He will pay for her maintenance (*nafaqa*) and clothes if she stays in his house, and if she lives in her house, he will pay her maintenance monthly: two quarts of high quality milled flour, a fourth part of a quart of green, high-quality olive oil, and two quarts of charcoal. As far as clothes go, in winter [he will provide] a top coat from linen, a padded dress, a veil and head cover, and shoes. In summer, as well as for sleep wear, the same as agreed.

In the commentary section, al-Jazīrī added:

If she has a husband, you [the notary] should add: "The husband of the aforementioned woman testifies that he has no claim on her wages, agrees to all the conditions stipulated in the contract, and undertakes not to have intercourse with her." If he engages in intercourse with her, the baby's father has the right to cancel the contract. This is Mālik's and Ibn al-Qāsim's view, and this was the practice. Ibn al-Mājishūn opposed it. The husband

Al-Ṭaḥāwī, Egypt

When a man hires a woman as a wet nurse to breastfeed his son for a designated number of months, for a designated salary, and he wants to write a contract for it, he should write like this:

"So-and-so hired this woman so-and-so for such-and-such months beginning in this month in this year for a certain amount of gold dinars of a certain weight to breastfeed his son with no restrictions and nurse him and serve him." In the rest of the contract, he should mention what has been agreed between them regarding the wages and how they will be paid, identify the child to be breastfed, and identify whatever has been agreed will be done to him. If this wet nurse has a husband, he has the right to prevent her from hiring herself as a wet nurse, and the contract is void if she has concluded it on her own. If the wages are for her solely, with the permission of her husband, it is necessary that this be written in the contract before the witnesses have signed it. The form should read as follows: "So-and-so, the husband of so-and-so mentioned in this contract, had the contract read to him. He understood and acknowledged its clauses letter by letter and understands that his wife's wages mentioned in this contract are hers by his volition and hers by his permission, that he has given permission to her to receive them and has no further claims on them."

has the right to cancel his wife's contract if it was concluded without his permission.[28]

After this, the witnesses can sign. The thing to watch for in this contract is that the name of the locality where the breast-feeding is to take place and the place where the hirer lives will be mentioned, in anticipation that there will be disagreement between them over this. It is not necessary to impose as a condition that the wages will include the food of the wet nurse or her clothes, but other jurists object to this and claim that the contract cannot be valid until it is known exactly what her wages include.[29]

Like the law of hire in general, the Islamic contract for wet nursing was not original in its formulation of the duties and obligations of the job at hand. Contracts from Greco-Roman Egypt show that a basic contract for wet nursing specified the place, length of time, wages in money and kind, and lifestyle of the wet nurse, detailing not only her nutrition but also the limitations on her sexual activity, which was meant to prevent pregnancy.[30] The Islamic contracts—the Maliki one from Spain and the Hanafi one from Egypt—likewise required detailed description of the conditions of the wet nurse's service as well as an account of her duties and remuneration.

The fatwa on wet nursing shows two sets of property rights in collision: the right of the wife-cum-wet nurse to hire herself out for payment versus the husband's right to sexual relations with his wife, a right that he previously acquired with the payment of the *ṣadāq*. His wife's hiring contract effectively eliminated this right for two years, assuming the lactation period was to be carried to its end. Once the contract had been signed, the husband was forbidden to have intercourse with his wife. This consequence could be an impediment to her acquiring the right to engage in wet nursing, but if she did acquire this right, the husband had no right to her wages.[31] The prerogative of the husband to forbid his wife to wet nurse was similar to the prerogative of the hairdresser's husband to forbid her to work, and, as in that case, the husband was entitled to cancel his wife's hiring contract after the fact if he had not authorized it.

By including the husband in his wife's wage-labour contract, the law recognized his right to give or withdraw his consent regarding her employment but not his right to her wages, which she was entitled to enjoy without sharing.[32] Most Muslim jurists did not argue that the husband should have the right to his wife's wages since he was the ultimate cause of her ability to engage in breastfeeding in the first place and since he had supported her during her pregnancy and afterward. Instead, they recognized her right to derive income from the milk that her body produced. Nonetheless, not all jurists agreed with the husband's right to consent. Ibn Qudāma, a twelfth-century Hanbali jurist, did not allow a husband to break a contract that his wife had signed before the marriage or one in which she hired herself out as a wet nurse.[33] Ibn Qudāma's stand also contradicted Ibn ʿArafa's view, discussed earlier, that the hairdresser's husband could override her stipulation in their marriage contract that she was free to work.

The attitude of the jurists and their discussion of the wages for wet nursing demonstrate the strength of the concept of a woman's property rights in legal thought, particularly when her wages were threatened by her husband despite their having signed a contract. Notably, this was the case even though the wet nurse's wages were not protected in other circumstances. Again, the challenge to any denial of a woman's wages for wet nursing lay in the infraction of property rights. In a fatwa written in twelfth-century Tunisia, al-Qābisī (d. 1012) explained what happened to wet nursing wages when the baby's father died:

> The wages have now become part of the estate and are in the hands of the heirs. Does the law, when speaking about nursing (*riḍāʿ*), refer to the milk or to the wages? Can the heirs actually share in this part of the estate? They can use wages but not milk. Another answer was given by the jurist Abū Ḥafṣ al-ʿAṭṭār, who said that if the father had paid this debt while alive, the milk constituted the estate coming to the infant son, but if there was no money left and the wages were taken over by the heirs as part of the estate, they should give this son his share in the form of wages for nursing. They cannot take their share from the milk; that belongs to the child. If there is no estate and the wages have been paid, the jurists have agreed that this is indeed a calamity (*jāʾiḥa*) for the heirs. Another opinion was that the estate should cover the nursing fee if there is no other female willing to do it and give the heirs their share in the wages. If someone is willing to do so, however, then the heirs should receive their share from the wages as well.[34]

In this case, the rights of the wet nurse to her wages were thwarted by those of the heirs. Any wages that had not been fully paid at the time of the employer's death became part of the estate. If the wet nurse had been paid in full before the father's death, the heirs could not reclaim the money or a share in the milk even if the nursing period had not been completed. But if the wages had not been paid, they could be deducted from the baby's share in the estate if the wet nurse continued her job. However, another woman's stepping forward to breastfeed free of charge would end the existing contract.[35]

The Flax Spinner

In another fatwa, the right of women to engage in wage earning came under scrutiny when their work could potentially interfere with their religious duties on certain days:

> One of the jurists was asked about the validity of the Ramaḍān fast of a woman who spins flax, holding the threads in her mouth and moistening them with her saliva. He answered that if the flax was Egyptian, it was acceptable, but if it was *dimni*, from Dimna in Egypt, which has a strong taste, it was forbidden. This ruling is the same as that for all holders of trades (*dhawī al-ṣināʿāt*): if she is poor, she is allowed to continue, but if she is not needy, she is not permitted to spin during the month of Ramaḍān.[36]

In this particular instance, the threat to religious duty resulted from the techniques involved in the trade, namely, holding the threads in the mouth, which could invalidate the fast of Ramaḍān, one of the five pillars of Islam. However, the jurists agreed to accommodate working women, acknowledging their dire financial situation. They were familiar with the economic conditions and drew a distinction between wage earners and those women who spun for domestic use. The details reported in this fatwa about the nature of the particular thread are confirmed by Geniza records showing that a large amount of Egyptian flax was exported as raw material to Tunisia, where the fatwa originated, for finishing and that it was spun there.[37]

The Slave Singer

A fatwa dealing with the right of a slave girl to retain her wages rather than surrender them to her master is included in the *Miʿyār*'s chapter on the law of hire (*ijāra*):

> The jurist Abū Muḥammad b. Abī Zayd [d. tenth century, Qayrawān] was asked whether a man whose slave girl sang at weddings and births, and other such joyful events, had the right to benefit from what she received or whether he should leave what she was given for this in her hands. He answered that if she received wages (*ajr*) from singing and entertaining, he was not entitled [to them] and could not benefit from them. The same was true if she died: her inheritance was not lawful and he should return it to her relatives if he knew them, and if not, he should give the estate as alms (*taṣaddaqa bihi*).[38]

This ruling needs to be understood within the larger framework of the changing nature of labour, in particular slave labour, and of slaves' property rights in the law during the first three centuries of Islamic rule. Contemporary with Ibn Abī Zayd's fatwa above was the contract model drafted by Ibn al-ʿAṭṭār in Cordova for a *salam*, or forward buying, contract of merchandise and the exchange, at time of delivery, of one skilled slave for two unskilled ones.[39] Ibn al-ʿAṭṭār added that the same principle applied to female slaves, namely, one could exchange a cook or a baker for two unskilled female slaves.[40] The purpose was to recognize the value of a slave's skills in the market, yet the contract does not mention whether the issue was the slave's capacity to generate income for his or her master or to save on the expenses of hiring a professional to fulfill these tasks. Yet the employment of slaves in activities that generated income, as depicted above, may have created a new conundrum for the question of wage earning since "all the schools agree that the master can do as he likes with property in the possession of his slave and is at liberty to take it away from him."[41] However, the earning capacity of such slaves was recognized in the legal literature when it stipulated that a master could use his legal power to confer "economic rights" upon a slave to trade and to represent the master in business transactions, "entrusting him with a capital sum where necessary."[42]

In fourteenth-century Granada, Ibn Juzayy explained that there were two kinds of slaves: the authorized slave (*ʿabd maʾdhūn*), who was allowed to pursue trade and to dispose freely (*taṣarruf*) of what he gained in trading, like an empowered agent, and the unauthorized slave, who was not allowed to engage in any spending activities such as buying, gifting, almsgiving or manumission; his status was the same as the person under interdiction.[43] The above fatwa forbidding the female slave's master from using her earnings was dictated by the special standing of the Maliki law on gifts and bequests, which was different from that of the other schools.[44]

The situation discussed in the fatwa concerned that of a female slave singer. The notion of illicit profession followed this feminine trade. The fourteenth-century Egyptian market supervisor, Ibn al-Ukhuwwa, in his guide for fellow-market supervisors, recommended that a female slave "not be sold to a purchaser who proposes to employ her in singing."[45] As justification he quotes a Qur'anic interdiction on selling and training female singers and music players.[46] There are indications that music-making and singing in public, as well as receiving income from these activities, were seen as immoral, as a thirteenth-century Moroccan treatise advocating against it makes explicit.[47]

Obligations and Liabilities

The Silk Worker

Obligations were always associated with rights, and the legal rulings with regard to contracts for wage labour demonstrate that when women contracted either to receive wages or to pay them, they had also to assume the obligations that doing so created. Female wage earners were not treated differently than males in such cases, but since their labour organization and work conditions were different, the legal circumstances of their cases also differed. Two fatwas written by Muḥammad al-Saraquṣṭī (d. 1459) in Granada are contemporaneous with documents dealing with female wages in the city's textile manufacturing. The first fatwa deals with a female silk worker who had been wrongly accused of avoiding paying the taxes arising from the sale of her work.[48]

> A woman was accosted in her home by the *qā'id*, a government officer [probably tax collector], who fined her (*aghramahā*), demanding payments (*juʿl*), without there being any fault on her part. He threatened that if she did not pay him by the end of the day, he would punish her by flogging (*ḍarb bi 'l-siyāṭ*). Scared, the woman borrowed the amount demanded of her, contracting to repay it with silk. The *qā'id* received the money directly from the moneylender. Did the woman have a right to refuse payment because she was coerced and threatened? He replied: Because of the circumstances, she should not be held responsible for either the money or the silk.[49]

In this fatwa discussing the silk worker's taxes, it is evident that she acted under duress in contracting a loan to pay the official. Duress was a concern that affected the validity of contracts and was a subject of considerable deliberations by jurists of all schools, with the Maliki school adopting the stand demonstrated in al-Saraquṣṭī's reply that the silk worker in question should not be held responsible for the contracted loan.[50] In essence, the opinion upheld was that a contract depended on consent and that duress nullified it. The acts that constituted duress were a threat to life or limb, a threat of long confinement or severe beating, and confiscation of property, but in order for duress to be operative, the fear of reprisal had to be well founded and the danger imminent and present: "The victim must believe that the duressor is able and intends to carry out his threat and that the victim is unable to repel the threats."[51] The duressor's actions had to be unlawful, to the extent that he exerted undue pressure, and "whether the threat is serious enough to induce fear or not depends on the circumstances of the particular victim."[52] All of these conditions were present in this episode.

The historical conditions of silk production provide the background necessary for understanding the fatwa's request. Silk production was one of the sub-industries of Islamic textile manufacturing, which itself was the most diversified, specialized, highly productive, and best functioning of all the industries or manufacturing activities in many Islamic cities, including Granada.[53] Female workers were engaged in multiple and specialized tasks, from cultivating the silk worms to dyeing, weaving, and selling the finished product. Two early commentators, Ibn al-Bannā' and the North African market supervisor Yaḥyā Ibn 'Umar described some of the functions fulfilled by women. In his calendar of agricultural labour, Ibn al-Bannā' said, "The women put the eggs of the silk worm in small bags which they carry under their arms, thus providing it [the bag] with continuous warmth until the worms hatch." In his manual, *Aḥkām al-sūq*, Yaḥyā Ibn 'Umar described how women whitened the silk threads by using ashes (*ramād*).[54]

Wages were determined by supply and demand in the labour market, by the rise and fall of the population, by the supply of raw material, and by the size of the consumer market. The notaries who wrote contracts, the muftis who gave legal advice, the judges who ruled in labour-related disputes, and the market supervisors who supervised and regulated wages were all part of the legal framework of the silk industry. The market supervisor, appointed and paid by the state, also regulated standards of production, labour relations, and matters of consumer protection. The tax collectors, who differed in their organization from one region to another, constituted a group of their own and were charged with collecting the taxes and dues imposed on finished items produced and sold. Because of the size of silk production, the many separate tasks that it entailed, and the highly specialized division of labour, taxes had to be collected for each of its operations and semi-finished items.

Female spinners or weavers worked at home, while the distribution of work and raw materials, as well as tax collection, could be undertaken by both female and male brokers. Female spinners were actively employed in both urban and rural textile markets. Female brokers could easily enter their homes, buy and sell items for the household, and interact with other women. They marketed goods to and from women but were also known to serve as intermediaries in women's provision of services and goods for male customers.[55] In addition to labourers and brokers, the silk industry required the presence of entrepreneurs who could invest capital, resulting in an output system in practically every centre where silk was produced. A trader or wholesaler could handle the entire process by commissioning work, buying raw material, negotiating and contracting amounts, distributing the work among female workers, and determining delivery dates for the finished product.[56]

Egypt was one of the regions where a system of tax farming was in place, and the trader himself could also act as a tax farmer. Goitein has identified a Jewish tax farmer in the Geniza records, who in a contract dated 23 March 1138 ceded his rights to taxes on the dyeing and the sale of silk in certain quarters of Old Cairo. He reserved for himself the right to do business with seven women brokers, four of whom were Muslim and three Jewish. Two of these brokers were mentioned by name together with their female partners.[57] Eight other women, who obtained specific fabrics on credit or paid for them outright, were mentioned in a detailed day-to-day account of another textile merchant, and there, too, most of the names were Muslim. The efficiency of tax collecting from employed women, either silk weavers or dyers, was hampered by the fact that most female workers were confined to the home, and the employment of female tax farmers did not eliminate the problem altogether.[58]

Communal decrees preserved in the Geniza records reveal that the Jewish community in Egypt had to forbid women to dye silk at home, except with the permission of the person who farmed the government tax for the product.[59] In Granada, however, the tax system functioned differently. There the tax, named *tartīl*, was imposed at 11 per cent of the value of the item and was collected directly by the state administration rather than being farmed out. The Nasrid fiscal agents were called *ʿummāl* (sing. *ʿāmil*, although the offiial named in the fatwa discussing the silk workers taxes is a *qāʾid*).[60] The Granadan practice of not employing a tax farmer (*ḍāmin*) was similar to that in neighbouring Marinid Morocco.[61] Some accounts have led scholars to suggest that, following its initial period of growth, the Granadan silk production was in decline under Nasrid rule.[62] However, the number of fatwas dealing with silk production and its taxation dating from the Nasrid period, including the late fifteenth century, and the continuous taxation of the industry under the Christian administration might signal otherwise.

Labour organization in Granada followed the usual patterns, with women working at home, making tax collection difficult. The state's tax collector entered the silk worker's house by force to make his claim. As al-Saraqusṭī pointed out, the victim was unable to repel the threat by appealing to the sultan, seemingly because the tax collector represented the central administration. In all other cases, a victim could appeal to the sultan for relief, but the right of recourse to the sultan ceased when the sultan himself was the duressor.[63]

The appeal made by the woman to al-Saraqusṭī raises the additional question of why she did not appeal to the special grievances court (*maẓālim*) in Granada set up, among other reasons, to handle complaints against the administration. It was presided over by the monarch himself and was conducted before a public audience. The workings of this court are well known from contemporary Egypt, where it was presided over by the Mamluk sultan.[64] The Nasrid rulers, like their Moroccan Marinid contemporaries across the strait, held a daily public audience, which probably served as a *maẓālim* court setting, without actually employing the term.[65]

In this case, the silk worker may not have taken her case to the grievances court either because it was not functioning in Granada due to war conditions or because it simply did not deal effectively with such matters.

The Broker

In another fatwa, al-Saraqusṭī dealt with a question concerning a female broker:

> A woman broker sold household effects (*asbāb*) for a male customer on credit for a delayed payment. The man collected most of the money owed and asked the broker to collect the small amount outstanding. Should she be held liable for it? He replied: The guideline should be the local practice. If the practice was that the client collected the debt himself, then it is not up to the broker to collect it for him. If it pleased her, she might do so of her own free will, and she would then be entitled to a fee for her efforts in addition to the commission that she received for the sale. If the local custom was such that the broker was the one charged with collecting the proceeds, and the commission was for both services, then the collection would be her responsibility.[66]

The legal subject matter of such disputes was substitution or compensation, which would occur when contracts were deemed to have not been fulfilled. The broker's gender had no bearing on al-Saraqusṭī's decision in this matter, which referred instead to the local conditions. The female broker, like her male counterpart, was bound to fulfill the duties and the rights of brokers respecting their clients according to the *ʿādat al-nās*, or *ʿurf* (local custom), which was to apply side by side with the law of hire.

The Grandmother

A matter submitted to the jurist Abū l-Ḥasan al-Ṣaghīr (d. Fez, 1319) dealt with liability for damages against a grandmother who had hired a cupper to circumcise her grandson:

> He was asked about an incident where a father had a son born to him during his absence. The child's grandmother hired a cupper (*ḥajjām*) to circumcise the

> infant on the seventh day. The child was circumcised and died as a result. The question was: Should the grandmother or the cupper be held responsible? The answer was: The grandmother could not be held liable because her action followed the custom of the people (*ʿādat al-nās*), even though the circumcision on the seventh day was reprehensible and not recommended. Her liability was restricted to the word and did not extend to the act, since she did not touch the child. The cupper, who touched, had permission to do so, especially since he did not know that the father was absent, and so acted upon instructions. It is not conceivable to reason that a cupper would meet a boy and circumcise him without permission, since such an act would not be legally permissible. Compare similar cases—for instance, someone who slaughtered a sheep that belonged to someone else without permission because he realized that it was weak, and he was afraid that it would perish soon. He was not held liable. There is, however, a dissenting opinion: that he would not be liable only if he could provide proof for his claim that the animal was close to death. A shepherd who looked after the sheep, on the other hand, would be held responsible. In this case, there would be a breach of law (*taʿaddī*) because he was not permitted to slaughter the sheep. The cupper's situation may be compared to that of someone who harvested grain without the owner's permission, and the wind carried the grain away. Here, the question is whether this man could receive his wages, and, if the grain was carried by the wind, whether he should be held responsible.[67]

The circumstances of the grandmother's involvement in the baby's death, like those of the death of a baby caused by the mother's refusal to breastfeed discussed earlier,[68] invoke a reality, that of the frequency of child mortality and how the law handled the circumstances of such cases. In this case, the law of liability (*ḍamān* or *taḍmīn*) was used for interpretation and deliberation. The law of liability dealt with compensation for damages to "things" or persons entrusted to the care of professionals for treatment or as workers and was a component of the law of hire. Liability could result from the nonperformance of a contract, from an infraction (*taʿaddin*) or from a combination of both.[69] The person in a position of trust was not liable for accidental loss but would lose this privileged position as a result of illicit acts that were incompatible with the fiduciary relationship.

The liability law reflects the complexity of issues surrounding the professional activities of artisans and tradesmen and the need to protect them in the exercise of their trade from claims that could interrupt a smooth and well-regulated economic performance. In this particular case, even though the baby's death resulted from the combined action of the grandmother and the cupper, no liability could be determined for either of them because no malevolent intention could be established that would have made it a criminal offence. The jurist, al-Ṣaghīr, discharged the grandmother since she had not performed an unlawful act. She had summoned the cupper on the seventh day, a local practice that was nonetheless irregular, condemned, for example, by the Granadan Ibn Juzayy: "It is better to delay the circumcision until the youngster can say his prayers, that is between age seven and ten. This is the time when he begins performing his religious duties (*ʿibādāt*). It is a bad idea to circumcise the child on his day of birth or on the seventh day, as the Jews do."[70] However, it was not illegal, and the grandmother did not operate on the child.

The jurist could not hold the cupper responsible either because he had permission to operate and, as a professional, had immunity from liability for damages caused to objects in his care (*taḍmīn al-ṣunnāʿ*).[71] Even though the cupper seemed not to have received explicit verbal authorization from the father, the person with legal authority in this case, he was summoned by a person who nonetheless had a right of guardianship respecting the baby. As a result, the jurist opined that the intention behind the act was legitimate, and that the baby's death was an accidental death for which no liability could be proven.

The Landowner and the Sharecropper

The hiring contract, whether written or oral, created both obligations and liabilities for the employer. Two fatwas deal with women who hired journeymen and incurred liabilities under the law of hire. In the first fatwa, written in Cordova, a woman landowner signed a sharecropping contract (*muzāraʿa*) with a journeyman, which was converted mid-term into a land lease.

> The male partner changed his mind during the period of the contract, and since there was still much labour involved, the woman leased him the land for [the amount of] ten *mithqāl*s for a period of two years. The first year of the new rent contract was also the second year of the first contracted partnership. Ibn al-Ḥājj, a twelfth-century Cordovan mufti, ruled that for the first year, the lessee was entitled to reclaim half the rent that he had paid if he had advanced it. However, he was to pay the entire rent for the second year. If he wished to contest his payment of taxes for the entire two years, he could do so as well.[72]

This particular problem was brought before the mufti because the transaction, which had begun as a sharecropping contract—in fact, as a partnership, had dissolved into a lease mid-term, before the work had been completed. This change affected the owner regardless of gender. The *muzāraʿa* was a specific hiring contract for the purpose of agricultural cultivation in partnership, in which one party in the agreement provided the land, and the other provided the labour. It was somewhat reluctantly admitted by the jurists because of its uncertain components. For instance, remuneration was based on the division of crops, which remained an unknown factor at the time that the contract was concluded. Also the precise amount of labour, grain, or animals used could not be determined in advance.

The sharecropping contract was the most common arrangement for cultivation of private land and became the pattern for the modern system of sharecropping in the Middle East, North Africa, and al-Andalus.[73] Women's land ownership, which originated, as we saw earlier, with any of the acquired property rights—gifts, inheritance, and the *ṣadāq*, presented women with questions of cultivation that could be solved either by hiring a journeyman, as was the case here, or by hiring their husband or other family members, whose own property rights could create complications, as we shall see in the next fatwas.

Wages in Matrimony: Hiring One's Husband

Instances of women being represented in court in estate divisions and other transactions are common in the Granadan collection; cases of estate divisions are as numerous as cases wherein the husband argued the right to live rent-free in his wife's houses. Whereas generally wives opposed the custom of husbands' taking for granted that they should not pay rent, husbands opposed the practice of wives' taking for granted that their husbands should represent them without pay. Here two fatwas are presented concerning the status of work performed by the husband on his wife's behalf. In the first, the husband claimed wages for representing his wife in an estate division, which Ibn Lubb, a fourteenth-century Granadan mufti, denied.

> The husband claimed that he had obtained his wife's share in the estate for her and therefore was entitled to wages for his labour. However, since there was no hiring contract between them, whatever the wife gained without her husband investing much effort was hers, and he could not claim wages. If he invested a great deal of time and money on her behalf and suffered a loss in his business as a result, she should bear the expenses. If he undertook this job without claiming anything for it in advance, then he engaged himself knowingly and was not entitled to receive wages.[74]

Despite the separation of property in marriage and the independent legal status of the female persona, Ibn Lubb ruled that the husband had no legal claim since no hiring agreement, either written or oral, was signed between them and no wages were specified. No declaration of an offer was made, nor was its acceptance recorded, both of which were required for a valid contract according to the law of obligations. In his ruling, Ibn Lubb did not suggest the possibility that the husband was an unauthorized agent (*fuḍūlī*) for his wife, which would have meant that his right to remuneration could be approved even after the fact, in which case wages could be claimed.[75] He did not deny that the regime of separation of property between spouses meant that one could, in fact, justify the husband's claim, but there was a common practice of representation that could not be ignored, so his reason for not granting the husband's request was the absence of a contract.

In a second fatwa dealing with the husband's status regarding his wife's property, the cultivation of her land was debated.

> A jurist was asked about a woman who had died while her husband, who cultivated land belonging to her, was about to begin sowing it. Should he proceed with sowing, and would he owe rent for the land, which was about to be divided and handed over to the heirs?
>
> The jurist replied that if the cultivation of the land in question was done with his wife's knowledge and consent, and this had been confirmed, he has to pay rent. If, on the other hand, he had no proof (*bayyina*) of this, then the heirs had the right to take the land away from him. His cultivation of her land without her knowledge amounted to usurpation, and the value of his work was disregarded. Ploughing alone does not constitute an act of legitimation.[76]

The Granadan collection offers a sample document relevant to the present case. In a document presented upon estate division, a husband and son gave an account of the value of the work that they had performed on a wife's land.[77] While cultivation by husbands of their wives' land was common, problems could arise upon the wife's death. The land that the husband had cultivated immediately became part of the estate to be divided, without the value added by the husband being credited to him. In the estate division, the land would first be shared among all the wife's heirs, including the husband, but without favouring him. Notarial arrangements could be made in order to regularize the transaction between the husband and his wife's heirs, whether a hiring contract, a land lease, or a sharecropping contract. If there was a written agreement between husband and wife about the cultivation of land belonging to her, the husband was considered a regular wage labourer who had rented land for cultivation and was expected to have paid rent. The lack of a legal document confirming that the husband had been hired to cultivate the land in question amounted to his cultivating the land of a total stranger without a contract, which eliminated any claims for recognition of the value of his work. Had he been retained, the land would have remained in his care until the process of sowing was completed. The lack of agreement enabled the wife's heirs to divide the estate without recognizing the value of the work performed by the husband.

The framework of the evidence in these two fatwas derives from the relationship between wives and husbands. The struggle revolved around their respective property rights and involved power relationships within the extended family, with potential heirs staking claims to the couple's property. The jurists' strong protection of women's property rights, the separation of property in marriage, and the inheritance law all combined to produce a strong effect on the status of women's property and on wage labour. These measures reinforced the status of labour as a property right, but at the same time should be recognized for the obstacle that they presented to conjugal economic cooperation. The result was less economic gain, which affected the conditions of the household.

The Comparative Context

The issue of a wife's wages occupies a distinct place in a comparison of Islamic and Jewish law. While the Islamic practice of commercial wet nursing was not adopted by the Jewish communities, these communities did adopt the Islamic attitude toward wage labour and its place in the property relations between husband and wife. Initially, the Jewish doctors of law did not elaborate whether a wife has to work for wages and whether her wages belonged to her husband.[78] During the tenth and eleventh centuries, there were only rare instances of Jewish women working for wages: a document found in the Geniza records (11th to 13th centuries) referred to "a man making peace with his wife on condition she does her work at home and not outside."[79] That the practice was changing is indicated by a clause—"her earnings belong to her"—that starts appearing in the marriage contracts of Jewish women in the Geniza society beginning in the twelfth century.[80] More cases surface as the twelfth century drew on, and even more appear during the thirteenth century, by which time the Jewish marriage contract had begun to formally contain specific clauses consistent with the Islamic provisions stating that a husband could not extract his spouse's earnings from her and that, if she worked, her wages belonged to her. In other cases it was stipulated in the marriage contract that a wife should use her earnings for her clothing. From the thirteenth century onward, the stipulation regarding a wife's control over her earnings appeared frequently, stating either that the husband had renounced all claims to his wife's earnings or that she would provide her own clothing and food in return for her freedom to use her earnings for herself. Goitein suggests that these changes might have occurred because of the deteriorating economic conditions of an average Geniza family during the thirteenth century. However, the existence of a similar practice next door, with a successful rate of observance by the Islamic community, cannot be overlooked. Despite, and maybe because of, the lack of a separation of property in marriage, Jewish women felt the need to protect their earnings from their husbands and could do so by registering a clause to this effect in their marriage contracts, a practice, as we have seen earlier, common to the Islamic marriage contract. Besides the question of whether Islamic notions of women's wage labour were adopted by the Jewish communities in medieval Egypt, the phenomenon described here emphasizes two points argued in this book. First, that women's wage labour, either in the Islamic or Jewish society, was a property right, which needed to be articulated and enforced by legal means, and second, that women's property rights were more secure in Islamic law thanks to its comprehensive framework of such rights, chief among them the separation of property in marriage.[81]

At the other extreme, feminist and economic historians of modern Europe have associated women's wage labour with a consequential array of issues, giving rise to analysis and assessment that no study of the Islamic data, or for that matter any study of the data from any other society and culture, can afford to ignore. The main thrust of the European historiography of women's wage labour lies in debating the effect of wage labour on women's relationships with their families and on their status in society.[82] Far from defining the relationship of women to wage labour as a property right, as we have done here, and celebrating the jurists' protection of a woman's right to be employed and to retain her wages, the historical picture of women's wage labour in medieval Europe is associated with three economic institutions to which Muslim women had no access, namely, the family workshop, the guild, and the combination of production and trade—institutions that counteract property rights by limiting the control and benefit of one's wage labour.[83]

To begin with and in clear contrast with the Islamic case, historians have noticed early on a major decline in women's participation in the textile industry, the traditional manufacturing sector of female labour. During the early medieval period, the textile industry declined both in size and in sophistication from its peak during the Roman and Byzantine periods.[84] Moreover, women endured the stigmatizing view, inherited from the classical period, that female textile workers were harlots.[85] Women's role in the labour force went from their strong participation in, and even control of, family-unit workshops during the thirteenth century to their virtual elimination from the labour force under the guilds. Guilds and governments curbed women's economic activity by imposing severe restrictions, such as social segregation, home confinement, and lack of opportunities to develop skills.[86]

In the direct aftermath of the Black Death in the fourteenth century, European female wage labour suffered in terms of women's participation, status, and share of wage labour, particularly due to their further removal from common shops and relocation to the home.[87] David Herlihy has noted the decline in the number of female occupations on the hand of tax surveys at the end of the fourteenth century and the growing number of poor women and prostitutes in Florence in 1427.[88] The case of Renaissance Italy offers observations on women's wage labour and its relationship to property rights. Brown and Goodman maintain that by the beginning of the seventeenth century the number of women participating in Florence's textile industry had increased dramatically, in particular in the wool industry but also in the silk industry, and that these numbers remained high, constituting almost 38 percent of wool workers.[89] Joan Kelly, who studied the freedom of medieval women of the higher classes, e.g., court ladies, queens, and princesses, to engage in illicit and adulterous love affairs as reflected in troubadour poetry, associated the increased demand for chastity and submission to the husband with the lack of feudal structures in Renaissance Italy, which had previously allowed the economic and political power that enabled feudal noblewomen in eleventh- and twelfth-century France and England to engage in political and cultural activities, including extramarital love affairs.[90] Kelly linked the loss of sexual freedom of Renaissance Italian women to their loss of political power in the new economy of the vigorous Italian cities; it seems to me that it also reflects the lack of women's property rights over the body, those that enabled Muslim women to connect their sexuality and reproduction to the context of property rights, as discussed in Chapter Five.

Nonetheless, the most hotly debated issue has been the significance of European women's wage labour in terms of the emancipation of women during the development of industrial capitalism during the nineteenth century. Edward Shorter, for one, argues that women's wage labour was instrumental in the sexual revolution and that it gave rise to the modern family, as it liberated women both economically and sexually from the dominance of men: "Not only did paid labour give young women an inclination to escape the sexual restrictions of their parents and the town fathers, it also gave them the *possibility* of doing so."[91] While Shorter goes so far as to claim that women supported capitalism for their own advantage, seeing in it a liberating force, Louise Tilly and Joan Wallach Scott offer a different interpretation of women's massive participation in the industrialized labour force of the eighteenth and nineteenth centuries: "Wage labour in itself represented a change but not an improvement in women's social position and did not dramatically alter the relationship of women—as daughters, wives, and mothers—to their families."[92] Lawrence Stone sums up the situation in a long essay on the new history of the family: "The generally accepted theory is that married women withdrew from productive labour for status reasons by 19th century Europe. This withdrawal was very damaging to the status of women since their psychological independence, their self-esteem and their power within the family was directly related to their economic participation in production [. . . .] As for the poor, 12 hours of hard work are hard to see as contributing to women's respect and power in the home."[93]

During the same period in the Middle East, the benefits of women's wage labour were as minimal as in Europe but not for the same reasons. As Islamic societies entered the modern period, both the quality of women's wage labour as an economic asset and its significance as a property right declined. This meant that as a property right, wage labour was not consequential to women's property-holding or to their status in the family. The professional profile and sector identity of women's wage labour has not changed much: in seventeenth- and eighteenth-century Aleppo, craft production appears to have been the only option open to women for earning wages.[94] In nineteenth-century Damascus, women's wage labour was concentrated in the textile sector (and poorly paid). Spinning, weaving, embroidering, and stitching were all occupations concentrated in the silk industry and dominated by women who worked at home and who relied on a male-dominated system to sell their work.[95] Industrial wage labour appeared in Egypt for the first time in the mid-nineteenth century; this had dire consequences for the traditional family economy, as it caused the marginalization of women there.[96] Female wage earners were confined to working in occupations that men did not want, excluded from the guilds, and treated as a threat to men's livelihood. In the nineteenth century, cotton imports from Britain were blamed for the destruction of the Egyptian and Syrian textile industries and with it the livelihoods of the women engaged there. By the time the twentieth century's economic developments in the Middle East began to affect society's views of women, wage labour was clearly having a negative effect on lower-class women and only a marginally beneficial impact on the social standing of professional, upper-class women.[97] As with conditions in Europe, the correlation between wage labour, women's education, and social status has been measured. Statistical evidence suggests that as late as 1978, the low levels of female employment corresponded to the low level of their education and that both were typical of the low status of women in Muslim societies.[98]

The Islamic and European experiences seem to indicate that in terms of the benefit of property rights to economic progress, women's wage labour was a negligible factor. It is not obvious that the right of women to earn wages was instrumental in the new economic era, in the creation of capitalism, or in the great economic leap forward. Protected and regularly acquired by women, these wages certainly did not improve their material conditions, nor did they give them new options and new power.[99] On the contrary, the system mostly victimized them. Economic historians might claim that evidence of the deteriorating conditions of half the human population does nothing to harm the capitalist theory, being irrelevant to the great economic progress achieved during the nineteenth century. This does not mean that as a property right wage labour was inconsequential to women's property-holding or to their status in the family, as indicated by the financial aspects of wages and their effect on twentieth-century women. What, then, was the significance of a woman's property right to engage in wage labour and to keep the wages in the Islamic context?

The legal protection of women's property rights in the Islamic medieval period highlights mostly the interaction of the legal, social, and economic systems. The right to engage in wage labour was part of an entire system of women's property rights in Islam and was therefore protected by the jurists and the courts. As women's wage labour became an integral part of the economic system, particularly in the urban centres, the right to wages and their protection became significant to the power relationship within the family, particularly to the relationship between husband and wife. It is not clear whether wage labour in and of itself can be seen as having created wealth in the medieval economy.[100] In the cities of Ottoman Syria, as with Europe a century or two later, the evidence seems to suggest that wage labour could not, and should not, be seen as a meaningful tool for acquiring capital and, for that matter, as capable of altering a woman's economic status within the family and society. Yet even though wage labour has a limited effect as a tool for wealth creation during the medieval and modern periods, for both males and females, the existence of the right itself and its acquisition, when protected by law and society, were a form of empowerment in the conjugal relationship, as shown in the different case studies throughout this book.

In the Islamic world, wage labour as a women's property right was maintained, but with worsening economic conditions, it became less and less significant in the economic and social life of women. The role of economic decline in diminishing property rights and in emptying them of their content should be recognized, whether in the European or in the Islamic case.

Conclusion

The object of this chapter has been to examine, first, the legal issues related to women's wage labour, the right to engage in wage labour, and the right to keep the proceeds and, second, how wage labour both affected and was affected, controlled, and regulated by laws, status, and jurists. Remuneration for productive labour was acquired and retained whether in the context of silk spinning or wet nursing. The scale of women's employment in manufacturing and services, particularly in the textile industry, has provided a significant historical context for the legal issues, but so has the strict separation of spousal property in marriage. The jurists' decisions on these legal issues demonstrate that engaging in wage labour was seen as a woman's property right. The right to engage in wage labour was upheld by the jurists in absolute terms as a universal property right, but in practice the acquisition of this right appears to have been subject to additional considerations unique to the relationship of competing property rights. The right was mainly challenged when it collided with other property rights; challenges on the grounds that wage labour transgressed the mores of women's conduct were hardly ever accepted by the jurists as having a legal basis. The marriage contract, which had become a vehicle for articulating and guaranteeing arrangements of all sorts, was equally used for wage-labour issues but failed to protect women when the right to engage in wage earning was opposed to the husband's property rights.

At the same time, wage labour was affected by general economic conditions and by the massive employment of women in the textile industry during the medieval period, which made women's wages a common and regular event to which the legal system, jurists, courts, and the social scene all needed to adapt. Although the law did not consider wage labour a substitute for a husband's support, nor marriage for that matter, the fatwas settling disputes in this area show how much wage labour was a commonplace for women. There can be no doubt that the new history motivated by gender studies has opened up many of the old maxims regarding women's role in the economy and status in society to new interpretations, even though it is not yet fully agreed whether and how the new situation affected women's economic and personal status and their family relationships. The examination of women's wage labour as a woman's property right, however, might bring about a new interpretation of the relationship between women and the law and, as a result, a new social and economic history of Muslim women.

Wage labour was one of women's economic activities, which, although central as a property right, was not only matched but even dwarfed by another set of activities, women's involvement in commercial transactions, sales, loans, and trading. An examination of the evidence found in the court records relating to women's ability to exercise their property rights in ventures requiring capital is the subject of the next chapter.

Eight

SALES AND LOANS

The Granadan Transactions

On 14 April 1470 two women pooled their resources to purchase a store in Granada's marketplace (*qaysāriyya*), Nuʿayma, daughter of the late *qāʾid* (notable) and vizier Abū Surūr al-Mufaraj, and Umm al-Fatḥ, daughter of Abū Qāsim al-Jayān.[1] The seller was none other then the Nasrid Treasury itself, and the price, paid in equal shares by the two women, was 212 gold dinars. A witnessed estimate of the value of the store, its precise location in the marketplace, and the identity of the owner, the Treasury, were recorded in a separate document attached to the sale deed. The notary stated that the two women were not present at the signing of the deed but were represented by males. The first, a widow, was represented by the jurist (*faqīh*) Abū l-Qāsim Ibn Salmūn, and the other by her husband, Abū ʿAbd Allāh b. ʿAlī al-Ḥaṣṣār. The agent of the royal Treasury was also present and he confirmed that the sale price had been paid in full and that the Treasury did not have any claim on the store.

Despite the worsening civil and economic conditions in Granada during the years preceding the conquest in 1492, the registration of transactions involving property, land, and real estate continued in the courts at a steady rate, reflecting increased sale activities. Women were beneficiaries of these activities: between the years 1425 and 1496, nineteen deals were executed by women and registered by the court in twenty-one separate documents.[2] Two additional transactions were registered in 1425 and 1467 and were kept in another archive in the city.[3] We know the genders of the actors because each commercial transaction recorded this information, even though the law of sales, like the law of hire regulating wage labour, was gender-blind. The legal manuals of the two fourteenth-century Granadan jurists, Ibn Juzayy and Ibn Salmūn, insisted on full disclosure of the details of sales transactions, but make no mention of the need to disclose gender. Their requirements included ascertaining full knowledge of the quality of the item to be sold, establishing that there were no concealed defects, fixing the rate of exchange for prices quoted in one metal and paid with another, and documenting delayed payments. Equally, the section on sales (*buyūʿ*)

in each manual made no particular reference to females.[4] The basic condition for making a legal transaction was that of ownership. The seller had to be a property owner, the agent of an owner, or the guardian (*nāẓir*) of an owner, and the property owner had to have attained legal age and the maturity of mind (*rashīd*) needed to make a sale or to buy property.[5] Nonetheless, when it came to the execution of a deal, women were always identified in the transaction. The notary al-Jazīrī was conspicuous in this, including in his manual instructions that when writing a sale contract for a woman, the notary should use the feminine form and require the husband to witness the document "for fear that he might have rights to the property."[6] He advised that all others who might have a legitimate share in the property, such as a father, brother, or mother, should also witness the document. At the same time, al-Jazīrī also indicated that the married woman was entitled to sell and buy without the explicit permission of her husband and that the latter should not be allowed to prevent her from selling by refusing to witness the sale document.[7] Fatwas issued in response to disputes that occurred in the course of such transactions also begin by indicating that a female was involved.[8] These patterns were a constant in the Granadan collection and are borne out by the records reviewed here.

Nuʿayma and Umm al-Fatḥ made one of the largest purchases recorded in the collection, but the largest purchase made by a woman during the period of study was that of the Nasrid princess Fāṭima, daughter of Abū l-Juyūsh Naṣr, who purchased an orchard in the suburb of al-Fakhkhārīn worth 800 gold dinars on 26 October 1425.[9] The sale deed, registered in the court by her agent, revealed that the princess intended to pay for her purchase in four instalments spread over several months, with the final payment due on 10 March 1427. Another large purchase was made on 22 January 1458, when the chaste woman (*al-maṣūna*) Fāṭima bt. ʿUthmān b. Muḥammad b. ʿUthmān bought a house (*dār*) for 150 gold dinars of the current mint.[10] The house was bought from the Nasrid Treasury, to which it had been ceded in payment for the inheritance tax owed by the estate of Abū Jaʿfar Aḥmad b. Daḥnīn. Like the princess, Fāṭima bt. ʿUthmān did not go to court herself to sign the deed but was represented by Abū ʿAbd Allāh Muḥammad b. Saʿīd b. ʿAtīq. Another Granadan woman, Fāṭima bt. ʿAṭiyya, did go to court herself to register several financial deals that she had completed between 1464 and 1469.[11] We met Fāṭima earlier when she was dealing with the aftermath of her inheritance from her husband and her father-in-law and the law suit launched against her by her brother-in-law, ʿAlī al-Barīṭī.[12] But Fāṭima, who admitted to having kept some of the money that she was supposed to share, also informed the court that she had bought a *feddan* (parcel of land) from her brother, Ibrāhīm, with this money.[13] Her property relations with her brother continued after their mother's death and her estate division. The estate brought Fāṭima another *feddan*, of which she took possession on 25 May 1464.[14] On 23 November 1464 Fāṭima came to court again, this time to acknowledge a sum of money that her brother had given her, consisting of 32 dinars from one mint and 2 dinars from another.[15] She testified to having used this money to pay certain bills that she had incurred and therefore ceded to her brother half of a *feddan* in payment of her debt, the other half of which they owned jointly. Five years later, on 13 August 1469, Fāṭima finally sold the remaining half of this *feddan* to her brother.[16]

Couples who owned property in equal shares found it convenient to sell it as a whole to another couple willing to acquire it on the same terms. In a deal struck on 21 April 1467, Yūsuf b. ʿAlī al-Mudéjar and his wife, ʿĀʾisha bt. Saʿīd al-Muwaḥḥad, bought in equal shares a dwelling from Abū l-Hajjāj Yūsuf b. Muḥammad Awyanāt and his wife, Fāṭima bt. Ibrāhīm al-Shānashī, who also owned it in equal shares, for 45 gold dinars.[17] On 9 December 1480, Umm al-Fatḥ bt. Muḥammad al-Shalubānī, whom we met earlier signing the foster-parenting deeds for her nephew and niece, registered in court a notarized document confirming the purchase of a house from her stepfather, Abū l-Ḥasan ʿAlī al-Ḥusaynī, for 28 dinars.[18] She arranged to pay for this in instalments: 10 dinars immediately, 10 dinars in the second October from the date of sale, and the remaining 8 dinars in the third October. However, she managed to make these payments before they fell due and went on to purchase more assets. On 7 January 1481 she paid 66 silver dinars for the house and on the same date bought half of the lane leading to her newly purchased house for 6 gold dinars from her stepfather, paying for it on the spot.[19] On 13 July 1483 her brother-in-law, the seller's son Aḥmad, acknowledged in court, in his name and that of his brothers, that the house had been paid for in its entirety.[20] The widow ʿĀʾisha, daughter of Abū ʿAbd Allāh b. al-Khaṭīb, also arranged payment in instalments when she sold a house to Umm al-Fatḥ, daughter of Abū Sirḥān, for 110 gold dinars.[21] On 10 January 1483, having been appointed by her late husband to act as guardian to her son, Muḥammad, ʿĀʾisha received 60 dinars when the sale was concluded, another instalment of 35 gold dinars on 9 February 1484, and a third instalment comprising the balance, all from the buyer's husband, Abū ʿAbd Allāh Muḥammad al-Qumārashī.[22] On 28 September 1484 she acknowledged in court that the price had been paid in full.[23] On 25 December 1483 Maryam bt. Muḥammad b. Faraj bought from her son Muḥammad half of the house that he had just inherited from his father.[24] The other half went to her other son, ʿAlī, a minor under guardianship. The price of the half was fixed at 30 gold dinars, which she paid by offering her son a silk cloth of southern [Genoese] manufacture (*ḥarīr janūbī*). Another sale between a mother and a son took place on 27 November 1483, when Umm al-Fatḥ bt. ʿAlī al-Qarbāqī bought an enclosure owned by her son outside Baza for the sum of 202 silver dinars. She paid 30 dinars upon closing the deal and pledged to pay the rest to ʿAlī b. Abī [sic] l-Ḥakīm.[25] Even though she had paid only part of the purchase price, the document confers on Umm al-Fatḥ the right of ownership for the entire property.

When transactions involved properties located in Baza, the court required signed estimates of their value before the deal could be completed. These estimates had to be collected on the spot. In one case, four witnesses from Baza provided a written testimony of the value of the cultivation and construction work that had been carried out by Muḥammad al-Qirbilyānī in the vineyard owned by his wife, ʿĀʾisha bt. Ibrāhīm al-Ḥakīm. The witnesses estimated the value of the work and the buildings constructed on the property to be 134 new silver dinars.[26]

Land was a precious commodity even during the days preceding the fall of Granada. On 10 April 1491 five women each bought a parcel of land from a certain Abū l-Qāsim, who had divided one large piece of land into several parcels and sold them separately. Fāṭima bt. Muḥammad al-Siyāsī, together with her son from her first marriage, bought one parcel for 45 gold dinars and was represented by her husband Abū ʿAbd Allāh Muḥammad.[27] On the same day, 10 April 1491, another woman, Maryam bt. Abī ʿAlī Ḥasan al-Ḥammī, bought a parcel of land for 63 gold dinars in the same location on behalf of her son, who was under her guardianship, using the child's money and property and with no restraints or supervision imposed on her by the court.[28] Another land purchase from the same individual on behalf of a third woman also took place on that same day. Abū Muḥammad b. Abī Faraj bought a parcel of land in the same location for his wife, Fāṭima bt. Aḥmad ʿUlaylash, for 63 gold dinars, using her money and property (*mālihā wa-matāʿihā*).[29]

With the help of her husband and father, Fāṭima was clearly determined to take advantage of the fire sales in Granada. On 29 September 1491 her husband bought a parcel of land in the same location for 50 gold dinars on her behalf and using her money and property.[30] On 30 December 1491 she bought an entire village from Abū Qāsim b. Sūda, again represented by her husband, the vizier ʿAbd Allāh b. Abī Faraj.[31]

Women continued to do business with Christian Spaniards and Muslims after the fall of Granada, both buying and selling land, and their sales continued to be registered in the Islamic court. On 3 March 1492 Ibrāhīm b. Aḥmad al-Zuhrī sold land outside Granada on behalf of his wife, Umm al-Fatḥ bt. ʿAbd Allāh al-Ḥayyānī, whose authorization of the deal was given in the same document. The sale price was 450 silver dinars, 136 dinars of which he received immediately, while the rest was to be paid according to the specifications of the creditor. The buyer was the major-domo Alfonso de Toledo.[32] On 23 March 1492 Fāṭima bt. Abī l-Qāsim al-Abār sold to the "Christian commander, the judge of the Castilian kings, their scholar and statesman, Qandarūn," the entire orchard in the suburb of the Bāb al-Fakhkhārīn for 600 silver dinars.[33] On 12 December 1492, Shams al-Muhājira and her husband, Abū Isḥāq Ibrāhīm b. Aḥmad al-Madīnī, sold an entire vineyard that they owned in equal parts to Fernando Villalobos, Canon of Granada, for 252 Castilian riyals.[34] A certain Fāṭima bt. Ibrāhīm, represented by her son, bought a vineyard on 14 May 1492 for 71 silver dinars.[35] On 21 November 1492 there was confirmation of conveyance (*ḥiyāza*) of a house, in which a son, Qāsim b. Aḥmad ʿĀshir, and his mother, Qamar bt. ʿAlī al-Arjadhūnī, were equal owners.[36] Fāṭima bt. Abī l-Raḍī b. Daʿmūn sold a vineyard to Abū Jaʿfar Aḥmad on 9 December 1494, including the irrigation rights for the property, for 320 silver dinars.[37] Finally, the last sale deed from our records in Granada was signed on 5 September 1496, when Fāṭima bt. Ibrāhīm al-Shalubānī, "the old woman," sold her orchard outside Granada to Abū ʿAbd Allāh Muḥammad al-Aḥshan al-Fashkūrī for 69 Castilian silver riyals.[38]

The women's deeds surveyed here constitute a substantial enough sample for us to attempt to formulate some patterns that, while unique to Granada,[39] may point more generally to the role that property rights played in women's property ownership and in the medieval Islamic economy. The documents show a rise in the size of women's property ownership as well as in their share of the land and real estate market in the city: some registered more than one or two deals, while one transaction involved three generations of females in the same family. The upward surge in sales and purchases of land and real estate witnessed in Granada was no doubt related to the ravages of war and the final political event, the transfer of control to Christian monarchy, that had taken place there, but it does indicate both the presence of capital and property in the hands of women, which came to them through gifts and inheritance, and the availability of these sources of income for further investment. The documents also show that women were motivated to engage in commercial transactions and to invest in property with anticipation of further gain. We could link both the effect of property rights and their defence by the law and society with a mentality that permitted women not only to feel secure about their ownership, but also to show entrepreneurial skills, to take advantage of financial opportunities with confidence, and to seize the moment and engage in commercial deals involving extensive finances. The question at hand is whether similar conclusions can be applied to Muslim women living in different social and economic conditions.

The Granadan records also reveal patterns of women's transactions that were not unique. For instance, transactions by women were not anonymous but frequently took place in the family context, with sales and purchases of land and houses often being undertaken to facilitate ownership after inheritance. Women also purchased or sold shares in inherited property, transactions that were necessary to facilitate the legal status of a property and, when a minor was involved, to concentrate its control in one set of hands, usually that of the minor. According to the information in the sales records, the sellers and the buyers were women from all walks of life, although wives and daughters of members of the upper class, particularly royals and viziers, were more prominent, a reflection of their better economic status. Property transactions showed neither preferential nor discriminatory treatment of women. Some represented themselves, as they did in noncommercial transactions, but most of them used agents. The court documents and, through them, the notaries and agents, royal treasurers, and assorted male witnesses appear to have taken nothing but the most matter-of-fact approach to dealing with women and their property.

The evidence from Granada shows that the most common commercial transactions undertaken by Granadan women were buying and selling property. Although a few loans are mentioned as well, in terms of economic activities, women's involvement in loans was limited, as was their involvement in such activities as credit, investment, commerce, and trade, which seemed to have been outside the spectrum of women's affairs. In exploring the historical link between women's property rights and the economy, we need to consider the implications of the evidence in Granada of women's lack of engagement in other economic activities while also analyzing the legal and economic significance of their concentration in real estate deals. Was this concentration related to the war conditions then present in Granada, or does it represent a more general pattern of women's economic activities? What can it teach us about the cycle of acquisition and this cycle's relevance to the economy? Studying women's involvement in sales and loans separately and within comparative contexts will help us to answer these questions by enlarging the field of evidence.

Women's Sales in Comparative Context

The loss of political independence to the Christian West was a commonality of Muslims in twelfth-century Sicily and in fifteenth-century Granada, as was the loss of their religious freedom and legal rights to varying degrees.[40] The administrative records from Sicily that are used here were written well after the Norman conquest. They are known for their trilingual approach; in addition to an Arabic version, both a Greek equivalent and a Latin translation were included.[41] The sale deeds, which followed Islamic law, were written only in Arabic, however; they were registered by the Islamic authorities and appear to have been as legally binding as any other typical Islamic court deed.[42] The frequent appearance of Muslims before an Islamic court to register land transactions evidences the existence of a formal Islamic court with legal power similar to that of the Norman chancellery.

The sale transactions record the following: In 1113 ʿĀʾika[43] bt. Aḥmad registered a sale of land that she owned with her son,[44] while in 1137 another woman, Sayyida bt. Yūsuf al-Qaysī, registered the sale of a house that she owned in unequal shares with her son ʿAlī.[45] ʿĀʾika went to court herself rather than use a male representative, while Sayyida represented both herself and her two younger children Bulbula and ʿAbd Allāh, who owned shares in the property. This last sale attested to the presence of a qadi and to the performance, in the names of the children, of a conveyance act (*ḥiyāza*) respecting the property. The transaction involved taking the payment from the buyer, dividing the shares among the family members, and registering that a brother and an uncle, the other shareholders in the property, surrendered their shares to Bulbula as a wedding gift.[46] A sale in 1161 records Manjūma bt. ʿUmar and her sister being represented by Manjūma's husband in the sale of land that the two sisters owned with their brothers.[47] In April 1190, while being held in captivity, a woman from Palermo, Zaynab bt. ʿAbd Allāh al-Anṣārī, was helped by the Christian court to sell her house for 500 *rubāʿ*is in order to raise the ransom for her release.[48] This case is similar to one involving Umm al-Fatḥ bt. Abī ʿUthmān, who in 1488 had her house in Granada rented by the Islamic court while she was being held prisoner in Christian hands.[49] The Granadan court record shows that the house was valued at 14 gold dinars, that it was rented out for 10 dirhams a month, and that the rent was collected on her behalf and saved for her in anticipation of her return. It is of note that in both places, Granada and Sicily, the Christian conquerors bought property from Muslims, paid the full price for houses and land, and had the deeds registered in court, thus sealing their property rights through purchases. It is doubtful that this reflects respect for Muslim property rights; it is more likely due to specific historical conditions prevalent in the Mediterranean reconquest movement. We should not forget the importance of the law of conquest (*lego ratio*), which was invoked by the Crusader's nobles in twelth-century Syria to justify their claim to full property rights over their fiefdoms.[50]

Another society experiencing political conditions similar to those of Granada was Mamluk Egypt, where women were affected in a similar manner. A set of sale documents in fifteenth-century legal records of property endowment for the public good show some interesting patterns of women's property rights. The sale documents in question involved women from the upper echelons of Mamluk society: wives, daughters, and widows of sultans, emirs, chief justices, treasurers, officers, and high bureaucrats.[51] Among the many purchases recorded were the transactions conducted by Fāṭima, daughter of the emir Khāṣṣbāk al-Nāṣirī and wife of Sultan Qāʾitbāy (1468–96), which included bills for purchases (*buyūʿ*) made between 1488 and 1491 totalling 16,500 dinars and 10,000 dirhams. The file contains thirty-nine transactions executed on her behalf. Two-thirds of these pertained to commercial or rental buildings bought in Cairo or its environs and the other third to agricultural lands either in Gharbiyya of the Delta region or in Ashmunayn of Upper Egypt. Fāṭima's purchases were not unique, and like those made by a similar group of women who purchased similar properties in similar circumstances, they were paid for with large amounts of cash acquired either as gifts or as inheritance. A similarity between the Egyptian and Granadan women was that both groups benefited from their men's shorter life expectancy. The Mamluks, being professional soldiers, suffered a naturally higher attrition rate due to their lifestyle, but they also suffered due to the rapacity of the regime. The Mamluk emirs protected their ill-gotten gains from confiscation and protected themselves from premature death, assassination, dismissal, or imprisonment, in addition to making provisions for their shorter life expectancy, by passing these gains to their women, whose property rights made them an ideal repository of wealth. In the Egyptian case, the ways that women came to own the capital that they used for purchases, how capital and property were transferred, the legal mechanisms involved, and the fact that women exercised their commercial rights under the court's protection all highlight the historical significance of the entire system of women's property rights.

In the fifteenth and sixteenth centuries, wives and daughters from the Ottoman royal family also made considerable endowments for the public good, financing public kitchens, drinking fountains, and other municipal institutions through the purchase of properties. The capital that they used was acquired from the Ottoman administration, which provided royal females with income generated from taxes collected in the provinces as well as with land, received by virtue of their connection to the Ottoman sultan, the supreme paterfamilias par excellence. These royal females, who had Central Asian ethnic origins, are believed to have had better property status than non-royals because of their racial background: they benefited from "important elements of the Turco-Mongol political heritage, particularly the notion that all members of the dynasty were entitled to a share of the patrimony."[52] Historians have attributed to these women a higher level of social equality and integration than that of non-royals, which is an attractive theory, but it has one major weakness: the state of women's property rights there.[53] A recent study of the Mongol rule of China has demonstrated that one of the first actions taken after the Mongols conquered China was to deprive Chinese women of their property rights, which were quite similar to those of Muslim women.[54] Whether or not we accept the notion that the economic activites of royal females were an exception, it is more plausible and historically accurate to relate the Ottoman princesses' financial affairs to the Ottoman application of the Islamic legal system, with its formidable women's property rights. If we accept as normal the preponderance of endowment-making (*waqf*) among Ottoman princesses as a result of the influential Islamic culture, there is no need to explain the accumulation of wealth in women's hands with reference to another and alien cultural factor. Whether received as *sadāq*, a gift, or as inheritance, Ottoman women's acquisitions followed Islamic law.

The later Ottoman period's records from the Arab, Anatolian, and Balkan provinces are equally rich in examples of sales transactions by women. These records allow for statistical evaluations, thus offering a more accurate depiction of women's market share and property ownership. The combined evidence from the court records from Cairo, Damascus, Aleppo, and Kayseri between the seventeenth and nineteenth centuries shows both similarities and variables in the patterns of women's sales and purchases. Sales records from seventeenth-century Kayseri show that 39 per cent of land and property transfers involved at least one woman and that women sold land and real estate three times as frequently as they bought them.[55] In Cairo the *waqf* registers show that by the eighteenth century, purchases made by women belonging to the Mamluk class increased to include shops, workshops, warehouses, living units, mills, and watermills.[56] Sales transactions from Aleppo and Damascus also show that a greater variety of properties were bought and sold, reflecting the changing nature of the urban economy. Property sold and purchased by women included the basic family house, rental property, and commercial real estate. In addition, rights to conduct a commercial enterprise could be either leased or bought outright and leased to others.[57] In all places, such deals continued to be made with family members, such as husbands, sons, and daughters,[58] but the women in Damascus routinely bought houses from non-family members, and "when they sold houses it was to outsiders at least as often as to other members of their families."[59] Most of the property transactions concerned residential and rental properties, although "unlike residential properties, pre-emptive transfer of commercial properties to women was infrequent."[60] In the nineteenth century the dichotomy between the patterns of men's and women's property investments became more defined: men bought workshops, stores, and orchards, whereas women bought houses. While the detailed accounts of women's estates do not reveal commercial goods or money lending, an economic activity favoured by males, this should not be taken as proof that women were not involved in commerce or trade on a regular basis,[61] for representation of women in court by a third party was common. James Reilly has found some examples in nineteenth-century Damascus of women who went to court without agents, regardless of social class, but more often they were represented by men.[62]

How should the frequent appearance of women as sellers of property be interpreted? Ronald Jennings posits that the inheritance law, "which makes women heirs in greater numbers than men . . . explains their more frequent appearance in court . . . they tended to rid themselves of property they inherited," although he recognizes that "it is not clear what implications can be drawn from the differences in frequency of sales and purchases."[63] Both Reilly and Bruce Masters also caution against interpreting the numerous examples of women participating in sales transactions as an indication of a greater economic initiative. They appeared in court to sell their shares to males, engaging in the consolidation either of inheritance or of small fragments of property that did not benefit women's ownership since the men accumulated more properties in the process than did women.[64] Was women's high rate of participation in sales transactions, then, an indication that a process of property loss was underway?

When these records are compared to the evidence from Granada, there are general features of women's sales and purchases that confirm the effect of property rights on the frequency and regularity with which women became property owners. An analysis of what, how, why, to whom, and with whom transactions were made shows a continuity and gives us insight into the origin of the property sold. For one, the size and value of the properties varied according to the individual family's prosperity, ranging from very large to small. Most women did not go to court themselves to conclude a sale or purchase transaction but were represented by related or unrelated males, a class indicator more than anything else. When required, however, a woman's appearance in court to validate and conclude a sale transaction was considered nothing but routine. The norm was that sales and purchases were made with family members and that transactions with non-family were limited. One kind of property, real estate (mostly houses), dominated.

The evidence from Granada strongly suggests that while in many instances land and real estate purchases were made for future profit, purchases for reasons of inheritance consolidation occurred just as frequently. Similar interpretation of the Ottoman archival data is possible. Both suggest that class, individual and economic circumstances, and general economic conditions had an effect not so much on how women's property rights were used in property acquisition but on the property's dimensions, that is, the size and content. The sale records confirm the strength of one property right in particular, that of inheritance. The cycle of acquisition inaugurated by the act of *tarshīd* (release from guardianship) was completed when property derived from gifts and inheritance was incorporated into women's holdings. In this sense, sales and purchases carried out by women, which necessarily reflect the impact of property rights on the structures and execution of their economic activities, are the final test of the strength and protection of these property rights. Nonetheless, the question remains whether the preponderance of real estate transactions by women in Granada and elsewhere was a response to changing political, local, and personal conditions and circumstances or a response to a lack of access to other venues of investment. Given that conditions in Granada did not create patterns of women's commercial transactions, only highlighted and maybe favoured them, is it possible that women's purchases of land and real estate were an indicator of investment policy?

Women's Loans in Comparative Context

The second commercial activity undertaken by women is revealed by deeds found in the Granadan documents that register loans made by women; these are also revealed in records of estate divisions. On 22 February 1455 Abū ʿAbd Allāh b. Saʿīd al-Sulaymī registered a loan of 175.5 silver dinars made to him by his wife, Fāṭima bt. Muḥammad al-Khalīʿ.[65] With this money, he informed the court, he had bought articles for their daughter's trousseau (*shiwār*). In the deed, he itemized his purchases: a silk cloth and a new garment of yellow colour, six pearls, half an ounce of gold, a padded gown made of unadorned cotton, and six *rubʿ*s of washed wool. He had given these items to his daughter when she was married but had not yet repaid the loan, so in court he acknowledged the debt in his wife's presence and with her consent. Before signing the document, the witnesses testified that both husband and wife were in good physical and mental health. On 30 December 1488 another husband settled a loan that he had received from his wife. Ḥasan b. Saʿīd b. Zurayq testified in court that his wife, ʿĀʾisha bt. ʿAlī al-Maratashī, had given him 20 gold dinars as an interest-free loan.[66] He stated that he had spent the money on himself and on renovations to his house. In repayment of the loan, he now declared his wife half-owner of this house, situated near the stone oven in the Bayāzīn quarter. After naming the properties that bordered the house on four sides, the deed confirmed that ʿĀʾisha had complete ownership of half of the house, including the inside and the outside components, and the elimination of the debt was recorded. A loan made to a woman is recorded in the estate division of Umm al-Ḥasan bt. Abī l-Hajjāj Yūsuf b. Abī Ḥadīd, which also mentions a loan of 122 gold dinars, previously given to her on an unspecified date and in two parts: 60 dinars from her son, Muḥammad al-Baḥṭān, and the balance from her second husband, Aḥmad b. ʿAlī al-Minshālī. The loan itself had not been registered in court but fell due, upon the borrower's death, during the estate division on 11 February 1467.[67] The court was notified that, as collateral, she had left a house bordering certain specified properties and a vineyard, which, together with her clothes and the tools of her trade (*asbāb miḥnatihā*), were equal to the amount of the debt. Her son chose the vineyard and 4 gold dinars as his share, leaving the rest to his stepfather. (As we learn from another document, the son later returned to court to sue his stepfather for money belonging to his late sister Fāṭima, which he claimed had been given to him by his late mother for investment.)[68] Two final case studies are that of the estate division of Abū l-Ḥasan ʿAlī b. Aḥmad b. Abī l-Ḥasan al-ʿUndūq, which paid 115 dinars to his first wife, Umm al-Fatḥ, a sum that included the repayment of a loan she had given to her husband,[69] and that of a loan extended by a wife to a husband, recorded in the estate division of Abū ʿAbd Allāh Muḥammad b. Faraj, whose estate was divided on 17 March 1487.[70] The whole estate was valued at 1,175 and nine-tenths dinars, from which the notary deducted the debts, the customary portion of the wife's *ṣadāq*, and a loan of 285 dinars that she had made to him. (A debt of 10,000 dirhams that he owed to his wife was revealed in the estate division of a Jerusalem merchant.)[71]

Certain features appear common to all cases. All loans were taken from or given to close relatives, mostly husbands or children, and discharged at some time or another, usually upon estate division, if not earlier. The presence of heirs made notarial documentation necessary and required accurate recording of all loans. The loans made between family members seem to have been used to provide for shared family goals, such as buying a trousseau, providing for house renovations, buying a vineyard, or buying raw materials. Because there was no conjugal property, it was possible for wives to give loans to their husbands, but it was also necessary to record these loans very carefully to prevent bickering at the time of estate division. These conditions raise the question whether the reliance of the husband on his wife in financial matters might have influenced their relationship. When husbands lacked financial means, respectful and cautious behaviour toward their wives may have ensued.

Records found in the Geniza documents showing that Jewish women both gave and received loans bear testimony to their comparable use of credit within the family and the economy.[72] Jewish wives loaned their husbands money from their dowries and gold and silver coins to each other, and they used their property to guarantee loans given to their husbands or brothers. In the reverse situation, where they contracted loans from their husbands, collateral was required and regular payments were made, although loans to strangers were also registered. Jewish women were familiar with the use of credit in labour transactions. In Egypt some women took over the tax farming respecting spun threads or dyed silk, which meant that they had either advanced a certain amount of money or were able to wait for payment. At the same time, they could generate work and collect the finished merchandise for sale, thus accumulating enough money to cover the loans owed to them, perhaps even with a surplus. The silk industry, like the rest of the textile production industries, worked on the basis of farming out the work, so credit was regularly offered and charged.[73]

Between the seventeenth and nineteenth centuries, loans registered by and for women became more common, though there were still considerably less than those contracted by men. Jennings notes that women occasionally appeared as debtors and creditors in seventeenth-century Qayseri, the latter more often than the former; however, a larger body of evidence points to women who inherited a debt or credit from a relative and undertook to secure its collection through the court. Sometimes, a "forced lending" was reported, when individuals sold houses and merchandise but payment was not forthcoming. Loans, limited both in size and in number, were also made to family members and even to outsiders. Women lent money or gave credit, with substantial amounts going to other women.[74]

In seventeenth-century Aleppo, where moneylending was a favourite profit-making venture, Masters found a strong dichotomy between the involvement of men and women, where women extended almost no credit or loans on their own, but they did extend loans together with their husbands, as independent partners, and used their property as collateral; one woman was found to have lent money to peasants working her land, and another had lent money to city folks.[75] Typically, the debt owed to most women and registered in the estates in the various court registers was their delayed *mahr* (or *ṣadāq*).[76]

Women's investment or engagement in commerce or trade was not recorded in the Granadan court documents.[77] This lack of information was matched in the Granadan collection by the silence in the estate divisions about the presence of goods in transit or in quantities sufficient to indicate women's participation in local trade. More evidence is required if we are to evaluate the relationship of credit and loans to women's property rights. For a more complete picture of women's economic activities, their apparent lack of investment in trade needs to be taken into account. Because women were well aware of the role of credit, the limited scope of the activities that they financed reflects a limitation in their exposure to economic life.

Some information about women's involvement in trade comes from the accounts of the estate divisions from fourteenth-century Jerusalem collected by Huda Lutfi from the Ḥaram documents. There, a slight increase in women's commercial activities was reported. In some cases, especially textiles, the quantities of items shown suggest that the owners might have been engaged in commercial activities. For instance, inventories showing 21 pairs of footwear and 18 pieces of headgear,[78] 18 kerchiefs and 8 brass containers,[79] or 3 linen pieces, 3 dresses from Baʿlabakk, and 2 dresses from Mecca[80] conjure up an image of female peddlers selling inexpensive items, operating from home, and interacting only with other women.[81] The textual mention of female searchers posted at city gates or assigned to meet the boats, who were allowed to slip their hands into the waistbands of disembarking women in search of hidden merchandise for sale that the authorities wanted to tax, are also an indication that women undertook commercial activities.[82] Likewise, on the basis of information regarding loans extended by women in fourteenth-century Jerusalem and the report of the creation of a female partnership in the second half of the fifteenth century, Rapoport has concluded that women's exclusion from the control over land pushed them towards the credit market, and that the practice of lending money to husbands had become a standard feature of fifteenth-century marriages.[83] Changes in the urban economy during the premodern period did not bring any visible change in the limited female participation in trade and commerce. In seventeenth-century Aleppo none of the women whose estates are examined by Masters kept their wealth in commercial goods, "in contrast to men." However, Masters also makes the point that women were prevented from participation by "social custom which restricted women from being involved directly in business, and it further forbade them from traveling . . . only *muḍāraba* was left to them."[84]

The question of women's participation in credit investment through silent partnership (*muḍāraba*, or *qirāḍ*) is another form of women's commercial activities that we need to consider when investigating the question of the relationship of credit and loans to women's property rights. Three instances of such investment link Muslim women to the trading universe of the Mediterranean. All date from the twelfth century, and two are directly related to trade with Sicily, but they are sufficient to provide us with the patterns. One act of credit investment appears among the Sicilian/Norman documents. It mentions Ṣadaqa, who, together with her brother Maymūn and other Muslims from Cefalù, was engaged with the Norman "Sir William" to invest in trade.[85] Another instance occurs in a fatwa sent for consultation to al-Māzarī (d. 1141) involving a woman who had entrusted her jewellery—a gold ring and a large bracelet—to an agent to sell in Sicily. The proceeds were to be used to buy grain, which was to be sold for profit in Mahdia. The value of the deal was 11 dinars minus 1 *rubāʿī*, and the jurists' discussion revolved around the question of whether the deal was actually a *qirāḍ* transaction, in which case the woman and the trader would share the profit equally, or whether the agent had been hired to carry out the transaction, in which case the outcome of his efforts would determine his fees.[86] Another legal issue raised by the transaction was the difficulty involved in determining the precise value of the jewellery once it was converted into cash. This issue was unique to women, who frequently converted their cash into jewellery. The third record is from the Geniza documents and tells the story of a Jewish woman, al-Wuḥsha, who contributed small sums to the 800 dinars that her brother had invested in a partnership with another India trader.[87] When her brother died on the voyage, al-Wuḥsha claimed her share in the goods that were sold. She participated in another venture involving twenty-two camel loads weighing 11,000 pounds. For this deal, she was represented by an agent. Of 700 dinars, she had deposited 67 with another woman and had loaned 333, for which collateral was given and kept by her. An example of collateral given by a woman is a boat owned by the "sayyida, Umm mallāl, the aunt of Bādis, ruler of Ifriqiya," anchored in Mazara, Sicily, mentioned in a Geniza letter written in October 1056.[88]

Finally, documents detailing the trading activities of a family of Red Sea traders in the area of the Red Sea port of Quseir from mid-thirteenth century, show women of the household making investments and talking about tax collection money. They participated in long-distance business travels, actually physically traveling for either business or pilgrimage.[89] The documents also show women suppliers of flour to traders, and two women are mentioned as independent account holders alongside their male counterparts.[90]

The limited use of credit extended by Muslim women in market activities stands in great contrast to the data available about women's money-lending in medieval and premodern Europe. Women there played a larger and more discernible role in the economy, providing productive loans and credit.[91] They included widows who extended mortgages to peasants for real estate purchases and provided capital for the traditional industries, wives who were their husbands' business partners, and even nuns making credit investments in nunneries, all of which contributed to the acquisition of capital by generating profits, which in turn could be invested elsewhere.[92] William Jordan also sees women's trade investment as a component of their credit and loan activities. He examines examples of Italian women who invested in trade, which by the thirteenth century was "commonplace in the Italian economy,"[93] and observes that according to the evidence, women were much more active in this area in Europe than they were in Islamic regions, something that he attributes to the "strict control on public or business activity by Muslim women."[94] Olivia Constable also notes that Genoese women enjoyed considerable financial independence and often used their money to commercial advantage, investing it with family members, brothers, husbands, and sons. She judges Italian women to be "unique because there are no records of female investors in either Muslim or Jewish merchants' communities."[95] Indeed, the limited record currently available about Muslim women's participation in local and long-distance trading and commerce makes it difficult to address the question of their involvement in economic activities, particularly the use of credit. Yet this is one area where women's property rights facilitated female participation more than anywhere else.

Whether the result of social pressure furthered by the preaching of moral values, particularly by market supervisors, or the result of pressure applied by the family itself, Muslim women were not encouraged and often forbidden to venture into the public sphere.[96] This social segregation prevented their wide or full-scale engagement in trade by blocking their access to the communication channels that were needed to implement investment decisions. The hardships and dangerous travelling conditions that were part of long-distance trade in particular made it very difficult for women to physically participate. Nevertheless, this need not have discouraged them from investing small or large amounts of capital in long-distance trade with male family members; on the contrary, their property rights were particularly designed to enable them to do so.

Avram Udovitch has drawn attention to limitations and weaknesses of the Islamic credit institutions, blaming their shortcomings on their limited social context.[97] Based on information in the Geniza documents and the Hanafi law manuals, he observes that credit transactions for the purpose of trade were made primarily between parties who shared a similar social status and for whom personal relations were the norm. This circle of familiarity, or intrafamily nature of credit and trade transactions, favoured women's investment in trade. Investing money with family members not only meant that it would remain secure since it would eventually be inherited by those same members of the family, who thus had a vested interest in ensuring that its whereabouts remained known, it also solved the difficulty of obtaining market information. The circle of familiarity also relied on ethnic-group affiliation, thus avoiding in credit and trade activities the barriers of language and culture from which females frequently suffered. Their property rights enabled women to make use of investment techniques such as a third-party investment (*qirāḍ*, *muḍāraba*, or *sharika*), because they were familiar with the use of notaries and court registration and had ready access to these services. Not legal rules, but only the social pressure to stay away from public spaces, prevented women from making full use of money changing, merchant banking, investment partnership, pooling of resources, or pooling capital—yet all of these could be undertaken using family connections.

Islamic societies did not invent, nor were they the first or only society to adopt, an ideological stand that denied women access to the public sphere. Byzantine society held the belief, fostered by the church fathers, that women were morally inferior, and previously polytheistic Greek society held similar views.[98] The large number of surviving images of Byzantine women, their faces exposed and bodies richly dressed, and a somewhat more limited but nonetheless significant number of Islamic sources depicting women raise reasonable doubts about the actual restriction on women's public appearance in both societies. Surely, what mitigated the effect of misogyny in society were women's property rights. Male traders identified in the Geniza documents had parallel careers as doctors, scholars, and the like. They were frequently silent investors in long-distance trade, and there was no reason why women, "homemakers" and "caregivers," could not invest in this sector as well if they had the means. As Reilly points out, such networks did not exclude women and their property but incorporated them.[99] Udovitch points out how strictly Islamic law enforced the requirement that all transaction details of any legally valid commercial deal, from the most humble sale of a pair of shoes to the lucrative transactions of international trade, be fully disclosed.[100] This requirement favoured the use of the professional agents whose services women regularly used in court and elsewhere as a result of their social segregation.

Given the favourable legal and social framework surrounding women's property rights, women should have been investing in long-distance trade by providing credit to a greater degree than we have found in the sources. If we accept the lack of evidence as an effective sign of nonparticipation, there must have been other reasons why this did not occur. The potential for men and women to generate wealth depended on myriad social and cultural conditions, but mostly on economic conditions. The evidence from the modern period seems to indicate that women's participation in the markets and in economic life in general was linked to the amount of property that they acquired through their property rights but also tightly linked to the general economic conditions. Wealth was configured anew with each generation. For instance, Reilly observes that in the nineteenth century, the status of poor and rural women deteriorated, while that of urban middle-class women improved.[101] As the amount of property in the hands of this class increased, so did women's share in it: "The fact that middle- and upper-class women held property in their own names throughout this period meant that they were potential beneficiaries of capitalistic development."[102] Unlike for men, what women could do with property was dependent not only on their having property rights, but also on cyclical movements of the economy and on regional economic conditions that could restrict or enhance economic performance.[103] Historians who have tended to dismiss the notion that women created wealth, because they simply used inherited property and sold it, have adopted a narrow view of the issue, one that isolates women as non-actors and ignores the long-term patterns of the process in question. Property circulated in generational cycles from males to females and from females to males, regardless of the fact that inheritance was based on unequal shares. Each generation of males or females inherited property and left property in inheritance, and the wealth, land, or other property generated by each was recycled in the next round of estate division. Instead of focusing on women losing property, it should be recognized how well integrated women were in the system and how much economic integration benefited from women's property rights.

It should also be pointed out that the same circle of familiarity facilitated Italian women's participation in economic activity. Their investment patterns show that they invested only with family members, yet their investments, together with those of men, helped to trigger the "commercial revolution" and certainly did not limit the size of transactions and the scope of investment activities. If the Italian women's record was unique, it was probably related to factors other than their property rights.

Conclusion

Women's commercial activities were concentrated in selling and buying land and real estate; tax farming and brokerage, small local commerce, and investing in long-distance trade by supplying capital or credit lagged far behind. Women's financial transactions show similar patterns. Motivation, access to the markets, identity of partners, the size and nature of the property transacted, and frequency and legal complexities were consistent throughout. Because of the strong defence that the law extended to property rights, the Islamic patterns of credit-giving, as well as other economic activities, could safely benefit from women's investment because family cooperation was guaranteed and would have facilitated women's participation. As a result, when wives gave loans to husbands or allowed their property to stand as collateral for their husbands' business activities, their capital was secure.

Unlike in Europe, women did not have to wait to become widows in order to lend money, to place capital in the market, or to have a say in or control over their property, something that is demonstrated by the larger participation of widows there; the evidence presented throughout this study documents the positive effects of Muslim women's property rights on their capacity to invest once they were released from guardianship. By guaranteeing women's property rights within the marriage and preventing the husband's control over conjugal property, the law neutralized the domination of the family while at the same time it could be used to facilitate and encourage women's investment. Scholars who speak poorly of the intrafamily nature of commercial deals because they think that such deals limited women's participation in investment activities are assuming that free access to market information was so crucial that if it was missing, women did not invest. But in the medieval period, successful business enterprises, whether European or Islamic, flourished thanks to the circle of familiarity, which provided for the free flow of information. Intrafamily interaction did not protect against the hazards of investing, but, precisely because of the degree of security that it provided, it did ensure the trust and confidence needed for investment in business deals. Whether the phenomenon of transactions with family members reflects women's limited exposure to the market or instead a more secure way of doing business is a matter of interpretation. Any answer must adjust modern economic theory to medieval conditions while accounting for legal and regional variables as well as the economic structures of medieval Islamic society.

CONCLUSION

In this book I have offered a new perspective on the status of women, one of the more trying questions in Islamic history, by examining the legal and empirical evidence of their property rights in a single historical milieu: that of fifteenth-century Granada. Despite the unique circumstances of the city's political and military situation at that time, the legal structure of women's property rights in Granada were a common factor of Islamic law shared by other Muslim women in different times and places. Thus, while the social and economic conditions of the context that I have examined will differ from those of other contexts, analysis of the specifics presented in the chapters reveals the broader structures, constructs, rules, conditions, factors, and paradigms that shaped women's property rights under Islamic law.

This book's new perspective on the status of women consists of defining the female legal persona as someone with property rights in the abstract and in reality. Whether one can conclude from the evidence presented here that women's propertied identity played a historical role in enhancing a woman's status in family relationships is a matter of interpretation. The same is also the case for the impact of women's property rights on the economy. Evidence of the myriad ways in which the law articulated women's property rights and in which the jurists executed them is further supported by the absence of reference in the legal sources to any other constructs of the female persona. To my mind, the existence of property rights was central to the conjugal relationship. To propose that these rights mitigated the negative effects of patriarchy is not unreasonable.

This conclusion is based on the recognition that Muslim women's property rights were part of an integrated, interactive, and balanced system. Patriarchal property control, for instance, needs to be viewed for what it was. The law prolonged such control by accepting that guardianship over a daughter's property continued after marriage, but this arrangement also made gifting property to daughters more attractive to parents. Indeed, while prolonged guardianship deprived young wives of immediate property control, it also prevented their husbands from attempting to impinge on wives' property rights. Guardianship provided security for the property while giving very young brides several years in which to become accustomed to conjugal relations, family obligations, and exposure to the economic environment.

To balance this effect, guardianship had a defined date of termination. Once freed from guardianship, the presence of property and property rights guaranteed that wives were not helpless pawns in marriage. These rights enabled wives to deflect their husbands' power because a wife could trade her property rights in exchange for her husband's renunciation of his rights in marriage, such as the right to a divorce and the right to engage in polygamy. The division of property in marriage gave women not merely bargaining power in their conjugal relationships, but also the actual power to extend loans to husbands, to allow husbands to live rent-free, and to permit husbands to use wives' property.

The system of women's property rights was both balanced and, due to the inheritance law, safeguarded and secure. It was in the interest of future heirs that the property of their mothers, sisters, and daughters be recognized and protected because its unlawful dissipation would directly affect their share. Women's property rights were universal. They mandated that a woman could become a property recipient at any stage of life, from birth to just before death, as well as before, during, and after marriage. And acquisition was guaranteed, even if stretched over a woman's entire lifespan. Women's property rights were more than just a facet of the legal system; they were a legal philosophy and a pervasive paradigm that extended to the female body and to its power of procreation. Women's property rights made property ownership a normal construct of the Muslim woman's legal persona and a norm of their existence.

The comparative context in which I have examined women's property rights has served to highlight both the uniqueness and the limitations of the Islamic case. The Islamic inheritance law, for instance, imposed obligatory and fixed shares that were to be given to females. Daughters received only half the share given to sons, but, whether married or not, they could not be denied a share of the family patrimony. By comparison, European women were frequently excluded from inheriting if they had previously received their dowry. Furthermore, neither the *ṣadāq* nor gifts ever became shared matrimonial property. The Islamic marriage, although so much involved with women's property rights, did not create a conjugal economic unit, as it did in Europe. Instead, there was the wife's estate, or the husband's estate, or property that was owned in equal shares and that retained an independent existence throughout the marriage, watched over by an array of heirs, in addition to the children of the respective couple. Only a legal contract for a partnership holding, such as applies to commercial, labour, or investment transactions involving two equal partners, could define the property relationship between the couple. Whether a wife's property would be put to use to enhance the household income was, in fact, entirely at the wife's discretion. Whereas the husband was legally obliged to provide for her and the family, she did not have this oligation. However, the divine nature of Islamic law, in contrast to the "man-made" secular nature of European law, did adversely affect the Islamic context. Unlike the contemporary Italian cities, where the legal framework of women's property rights was constantly changing and evolving through legislation, Muslim women's property rights were, although stable, quite rigid, which prevented the entire system from adjusting to and accommodating changing social and economic conditions.

Women's property rights had a direct effect on the size of their property ownership and thus on their potential role in the economy. Timing was a crucial factor in acquisition and in realizing benefit from property. It also determined the economic potential of the property acquired and the size of any future gain that a woman and her family could expect. Prolonged interdiction meant that women might wait years before they could actually acquire property. In the meanwhile, the revenue derived from their property went to the patriarchal household's members. The length of time before an actual transfer took place also invited challenges to the legitimacy of gifts given to a minor. The desire to derive revenue from the wife's property required the husband to become her ally against other family members, partners, or hired labour, to represent her in estate division, and to exercise her rights on her behalf. Collaboration was indispensable, sometimes offering the husband small benefits for his continuing efforts.

Although women's social segregation had a damaging effect on the economy, their property rights benefited the economy by integrating and facilitating the movement of property and by securing property transmission between generations. The property mentioned in the sources, whether real estate, houses, stores, agricultural land, grains, orchards, groves, or irrigation rights, was in motion, both vertically and horizontally, with intergenerational and lateral transfers following blood lines and affinal links. The existence of these assets suggests that they were accumulated one generation at a time and that women's property rights played a role in ensuring that property was transferred within and outside the family in a regular and stable manner. These rights made women malleable instruments of property devolution, whether intergenerational or horizontal, thereby satisfying society's need for orderly property devolution against the background of changing political and economic conditions. Obviously, in a society in which private property was held, women from across the entire social spectrum owned property but in different amounts. On certain occasions, a significant portion of property appears to have been concentrated in the hands of women of higher classes, but during normal circumstances women's ownership would not have amounted to half the property in society at any given time.

Optimally applied, the legal construct of women's property rights offered to benefit conjugal, patriarchal, and economic relationships, but this potential could be undermined by misogyny and social segregation. Moreover, it is not clear that society as a whole recognized the legal persona of the propertied female with all its attributes.

The implementation of women's property rights was undertaken by the representatives of the legal system—the notaries, witnesses, judges, and muftis—all of whom were male and jurists. The historical evidence of their compliance with property law is strong, but at the same time, there is historical evidence that this compliance could have been challenged by ideology. We cannot, for example, ignore the impact of misogynous writings that were put together by individuals such as Ibn Ḥabīb in Spain and Ibn al-Jawzī in the East. It is plausible that the level of compliance varied according to economic conditions and to the degree of legal sophistication of individual societies.

Muslim Granada embraced women's property rights but other Islamic societies, those where there was a widespread dichotomy between law and society, might not have. General economic and political conditions also influenced compliance, as we have seen in the case of Granada. But a society's property rights contributed to its members' rational economic behaviour. As economies expand and retract, so, too, do the benefits of property rights, both for women and for men. The prosperity of Islamic societies would have affected the scope and size of women's property, but not the status of their property rights. Although the existence of women's property rights in Islamic societies did not establish gender equality, these rights certainly benefited women.

NOTES

Introduction

1. In preserving property-related documents, the Christian administration continued a pattern of postconquest respect for Islamic legal records and procedures, observed at other meeting points between the two cultures, such as Sicily and the Crusader states in the Holy Land; see Jeremy Johns, *Arabic Administration in Norman Sicily: The Royal Dīwān* (Cambridge: Cambridge University Press, 2002), 41 n. 56; Jonathan Riley-Smith, "The Survival in Latin Palestine of Muslim Administration," in *The Eastern Mediterranean Lands in the Period of the Crusades*, ed. P.M. Holt (Warminster: Aris and Phillips, 1977), 9–22; Salvatore Cusa, *I diplomi greci ed arabi di Sicilia* (Köln/Wien: Bohlau Verlag, 1982); and Pierre Guichard and Denis Menjot, "Les Emprunts aux vaincus: Les Conséquences de la 'reconquête' sur l'organisation institutionelle des États castilan et aragonais au Moyen Âge," in *État et colonisation au Moyen Âge et à la Renaissance*, ed. M. Balard (Lyon: La Manufacture, 1989), 379–96.

   For this book, I describe and analyze all the cases relevant to the subject from the Granadan collection; in addition, I have added samples of all the relevant cases reported from other collections, such as the Ḥaram collection from Jerusalem. After the book went to print, I came across references to additional notarial documents not included in the Granada collection published by Seco de Lucena. Once studied and published in their entirety, these additional documents will enhance the dimension and the significance of the notarial and juridical culture of fifteenth-century Granada; to the best of my knowledge, however, none contains information that either challenges the conclusions reached in this book or the use of the Granadan documents as a catalyst and a research engine for the subject of women's property rights in Islamic law and society.
2. For transactions concluded after the conquest, see *Documentos*, documents 79–95. See also note 3.
3. *Documentos*. On Seco de Lucena Paredes, the documents, and the Granada school of Islamic legal studies, see Francisco Javier Aguirre Sádaba, "Granada y los estudios de derecho islámico," *Revista del Centro de Estudios Históricos de Granada y su Reino* 13–14 (1999–2000): 461–93. Strangely, since their publication by Seco de Lucena Paredes, the whereabouts of eighty-three of the collection's ninety-five original documents has been reported as unknown (*paradero desconocido*); see Carmen Barceló and Ana Labarta, "Los documentos arabes del reino de Granada: Bibliografia y perspectivas," *Cuadernos de la Alhambra* 26 (1990): 117. Dr. Amalia Zomeño has informed me in a private correspondence that she is in the process of studying the Granadan documents, which might solve the mystery of those that have vanished: A. Zomeño, "Repertorio documental arábigo-granadino. Los documentos de la Biblioteca Universitaria de Granada," *Qurtuba* 6 (2001): 275–96.

4. See, for instance, the study of samples from Ottoman registers from Galata, 1729, 1769, and 1789, which revealed that women's transactions amounted to one-quarter of the total. Fatma Müge Göçek and Marc David Baer, "Social Boundaries of Ottoman Women's Experience in Eighteenth-Century Galata Court Records," in *Women in the Ottoman Empire. Middle Eastern Women in the Early Modern Era*, ed. Madeleine C. Zilfi (Leiden: Brill, 1997), 51.
5. Rachel Arié, *L'Espagne musulmane au temps des Nasrides* (Paris: Editions de Boccard, 1973; reprint, 1990), 339–40 and xxviii. On the demography of Muslim Spain, see Leonard P. Harvey, *Islamic Spain, 1250–1500* (Chicago: University of Chicago Press, 1990), 5–9. For estimates of population size for the Islamic Mediterranean, see Maya Shatzmiller, *Labour in the Medieval Islamic World* (Leiden: E.J. Brill, 1994), 55–68.
6. Arié, *L'Espagne musulmane*, 221.
7. Yoram Barzel, *Economic Analysis of Property Rights* (Cambridge and New York: Cambridge University Press, 1989).
8. I am referring above all to Douglass C. North and Robert P. Thomas's book *The Rise of the Western World: A New Economic History* (Cambridge: Cambridge University Press, 1973). North expanded his investigation of property rights to national economies and economic growth in his book *Structure and Change in Economic History* (New York: Norton, 1981) but revised some of his conclusions in *Institutions, Institutional Change and Economic Performance* (Cambridge: Cambridge University Press, 1990). In this last publication, more emphasis is put on economic institutions and their performance.
9. Farhat J. Ziadeh, "Property Rights in the Middle East: From Traditional Law to Modern Codes," *Arab Law Quarterly* 8 (1993): 4: "Is there really a general theory of property law in the *shari'a*? The answer is no."
10. Baber Johansen, *The Islamic Law on Land Tax and Rent* (London: Croom Helm, 1988).
11. In a previous publication I demonstrate how, in the case of the *waqf khayrī* (Islamic charitable foundation dedicated to a pious cause), institutional property rights were not secure and therefore led to abuse and misuse of public charity. This in turn was detrimental to property's economic performance, hampering returns on investments and causing dissipation of the assets; see Maya Shatzmiller, "Islamic Institutions and Property Rights: The Case of the 'Public Good' Waqf," *Journal of the Economic and Social History of the Orient* 44 (2001): 44–74.
12. Mainard P. Maidman, "Nuzi: Portrait of an Ancient Mesopotamian Provincial Town," in *Civilizations of the Ancient Near East*, ed. Jack Sasson et al., 4 vols. (New York: Scribner's, 1995), vol. 2, 944.
13. For details, see David M. Schaps, *Economic Rights of Women in Ancient Greece* (Edinburgh: Edinburgh University Press, 1979).
14. Thomas Kuehn, *Law, Family, and Women: Toward a Legal Anthropology of Renaissance Italy* (Chicago: University of Chicago Press, 1991), 197–238.
15. A woman named Babatha possessed assets in excess of 400 denarii in the form of four prosperous date orchards. Babatha lent her husband 300 denarii toward the 500 denarii dowry needed for his daughter by his first marriage, but after her hus-

band's death, when his estate was insufficient to pay either the loan or her own dowry, Babatha took possession (probably *de jure* since a widow was entitled to the return of her dowry) of her husband's date orchards; see N. Lewis, Y. Yadin, and J. Greenfield, eds., *Judean Desert Studies II: The Documents from the Bar Kokhba Period in the Cave of Letters* (Jerusalem: Israel Exploration Society, 1989), 24, documents 16–18 and 25. I thank Professor Timothy Barnes for drawing my attention to this publication.

16. Edith Ennen, *The Medieval Woman*, trans. Edmund Jephcott (Oxford: Basil Blackwell, 1989), 27ff.
17. For interpretation of the old and new property regimes of the Arabs, see among others, Maxime Rodinson, *Islam and Capitalism*, trans. Brian Pearce (New York: Pantheon Books, 1974); and Mahmoud Ibrahim, *Merchant Capital and Islam* (Austin: University of Texas Press, 1990).
18. W. Montgomery Watt, *Muhammad at Medina* (Oxford: Oxford University Press, 1956), "Excursus J.," 373–88.
19. Noel J. Coulson, "Regulation of Sexual Behavior under Traditional Islamic Law," in *Society and the Sexes in Medieval Islam*, ed. Afaf Lutfi al-Sayyid Marsot (Malibu, CA: Undena, 1979), 66–7. On filiation, see *Traité*, vol. 2, 17–22; and Watt, *Muhammad at Medina*, 374.
20. Joseph Schacht, *An Introduction to Islamic Law* (Oxford: Clarendon, 1964), 126. See also N. Tomiche, art. "Mar'a," in *EI*[2]; and Ma. Isabel Fierro, "La mujer y el trabajo en el Corán y el hadiz," in *La mujer en al Andalus: Reflejos históricos de su actividad y catgorías sociales*, ed. M.J. Viguera Molins (Madrid: Universidad Autónoma de Madrid; Seville: Editoriales Andaluzas Unidas, 1989), 35–51.
21. J. Roussier, "La Femme dans la société islamique: Droit malikite maghribin," *Recueils de la Société Jean Bodin* 11–12 (1959): 225. All quotations from non-English sources are my translations.
22. Barbara Freyer Stowasser, "Women and Citizenship in the Qur'an," in *Women, the Family, and Divorce Laws in Islamic History*, ed. Amira El-Azhary Sonbol (New York: Syracuse University Press, 1996), 34.
23. Sir Hamilton Gibb, "Women and the Law," in *Actes du Colloque sur la sociologie musulmane, 11–14 septembre 1961* (Bruxelles: Publications de Centre pour l'étude des problèmes du monde musulman contemporain, 1962): 233–48.
24. Linda Schatkowski Schilcher, "The Lore and Reality of Middle Eastern Patriarchy," in *Gegenwart als Geschichte: Islamwissenschaftliche Studien*, ed. A. Havemann and B. Johansen (Leiden: E.J. Brill, 1988): 496–512.
25. *Traité*, vol. 3, 144.
26. Michael Morony cites several cases of women buying estates in the last decades of the seventh century; see M.G. Morony, "Landholding and Social Change in Lower al-Iraq in the Early Islamic Period," in *Land Tenure and Social Transformation in the Middle East*, ed. Tarif Khalidi (Beirut: American University of Beirut, 1984), 211, 213–14, 217.
27. Adolf Grohmann, *From the World of Arabic Papyri* (Cairo: Al-Maaref Press, 1952), 154, 176, 189–91, 205; Gladys Franz-Murphy, "A Comparison of the Arabic and

Earlier Egyptian Contract Formularies. Part 1, The Arabic Contracts from Egypt, 3rd/9th–5th/11th Centuries," *Journal of Near Eastern Studies* 40 (1981): 203–25.

28. Manuela Marín, "Learning at Mosques in al-Andalus," in *Islamic Legal Interpretation: Muftis and Their Fatwas*, ed. M. Khalid Masud, B. Messick, and D.S. Powers (Cambridge, MA: Harvard University Press, 1996), 47–54.
29. Delfina Serrano Ruano, "La escuela de alfaquies Toledanos a través del Miʿyār de al-Wansharīsī," *Revista del Instituto Egipcio de Estudios Islámicos en Madrid* 30 (1998): 127–53.
30. Christian Müller, *Gerichtspraxis im Stadtstaat Córdoba: Zum Recht der Gesellschaft in einer mālikitisch-islamischen Rechtstradition des 5./11. Jahrhunderts* (Leiden: Brill, 1999).
31. Luis Seco de Lucena Paredes, "La escuela de juristas Granadinos en el siglo XV," *Miscelánea de Estudios Árabes y Hebraícos* 8 (1959): 7–28; José López Ortiz, "Fatwas Granadinas de los siglos XIV y XV," *Al-Andalus* 6 (1941): 72–127.
32. See Claude Cahen, "Considérations sur l'utilisation des ouvrages de droit musulman par l'historien," in *Atti del III Congresso di Studi Arabi e Islamici, Ravello, 1966* (Naples: N.p., 1967), 244.
33. *Qawānīn.*
34. I have used the Arabic text of Khalīl b. Isḥāq's *Mukhtaṣar* as well as the French translation, *Abrégé*, in which one can find the first attempts among French legal historians, including Jacques Berque, to write an Islamic legal anthropology.
35. *Mukhtaṣar*, 8: *mubyyinan limā bihi al-fatwā.*
36. *Qawānīn*, 6.
37. Mohammad Fadel, "Rules, Judicial Discretion, and the Rule of Law in Naṣrid Granada," in *Islamic Law: Theory and Practice*, ed. R. Gleave and E. Kermeli (London: I.B. Tauris, 1997), 51. Fadel attempted to measure the theory's development by using Khalīl's manual as the authoritative text but found that these Granadan muftis had deviated considerably (57).
38. *Mukhtaṣar*, 8–9.
39. *Qawānīn*, 6–7.
40. *Traité*, 9.
41. Fadel, "Rules," 74.
42. Ibid., 51–2.
43. Cahen, "Considerations," 240.
44. Monika Gronke, "La Rédaction des actes privés dans le monde musulman médiéval: Théorie et pratique," *Studia Islamica* 59 (1984): 159–74; Jeanette A. Wakin, *The Function of Documents in Islamic Law* (Albany: State University of New York Press, 1972), 37–72.
45. On the Andalusian notarial manuals, see Wilhelm Hoenerbach, *Spanisch-islamische Urkunden aus der Zeit der Nasriden und Moriscos* (Bonn: Selbstverlag des Orientalischen Seminars der Universität Bonn, 1965), which includes a list of works and authors at xxxx–xxxxiv. For a recent update, see Francisco Javier Aguirre Sádaba, "Notas acerca de la proyección de los 'kutub al-waṭā'iq' en el estudio social y económico de al-Andalus," *Miscelánea de Estudios Árabes y Hebraicos. Sección de árabe-islam* 49 (2000): 3–30.
46. *Kitāb al-Wathā'iq.*

47. *Muqniʿ*.
48. *Maqṣad*.
49. See Wael B. Hallaq, "Model *Shurūṭ* Works and the Dialectic of Doctrine and Practice," *Islamic Law and Society* 2 (1995): 109–34.
50. Huda Lutfi, "A Study of Six Fourteenth Century Iqrārs from al-Quds Relating to Muslim Women," *Journal of the Economic and Social History of the Orient* 26 (1983): 246–94; idem, *Al-Quds al-Mamlūkiyya: A History of Mamlūk Jerusalem Based on the Ḥaram Documents* (Berlin: Klaus Schwartz Verlag, 1985).
51. Maya Shatzmiller, "Women and Property Rights in al-Andalus and the Maghrib: Social Patterns and Legal Discourse," *Islamic Law and Society* 2 (1995): 219–57.
52. Fadel, "Rules," 52.
53. M. Khalid Masud, B. Messick, and D.S. Powers, eds., *Islamic Legal Interpretation: Muftis and Their Fatwas* (Cambridge, MA: Harvard University Press, 1996), 3.
54. López Ortiz, "Fatwas Granadinas," 74. See also Christian Müller, "Judging with God's Law on Earth: Judicial Powers of the Qāḍī al-Jamāʿa of Cordoba in the Fifth/Eleventh Century," *Islamic Law and Society* 7 (2000): 159–86.
55. López Ortiz, "Fatwas Granadinas," 90–127.
56. *Miʿyār*.
57. For the editorial process affecting the fatwas in *Miʿyār*, see Amalia Zomeño, *Dote y matromonio en al-Andalus y el Norte de Africa: Estudio sobre la jurisprudencia islámica medieval* (Madrid: Consejo Superior de Investigaciones Científicas, 2000), 46–53. For a history of the writing of fatwas, see Masud, Messick, and Powers, eds., *Islamic Legal Interpretation*, 3–32.
58. David S. Powers, "Fatwās as Sources for Legal and Social History," *Al-Qantara* 11 (1990): 295–341; idem, "The Maliki Family Endowment: Legal Norms and Social Practices," *International Journal of Middle East Studies* 25 (1993): 379–406, especially 382–86, 395, and 397 on women and *waqf*; idem, *Law, Society and Culture in the Maghrib, 1300–1500* (Cambridge: Cambridge University Press, 2002), 1–11; M.J. Viguera Molins, annotated bibliography, in "Estudio preliminar," in *La mujer en al-Andalus*, ed. Viguera Molins, 17–34; Zomeño, *Dote y matrimonio*, which is based exclusively on fatwas.
59. James M. Nichols, "The Concept of Woman in Medieval Arabic Poetry," *The Maghreb Review* 6 (1981): 85.
60. Hilary Kilpatrick, "Women as Poets and Chattels: Abū l-Faraj al-Iṣbahānī's 'al-Imā' al-shawā'ir,'" *Qauderni de Studi Arabi* 9 (1991): 161–76; Hilary Kilpatrick, "Some Late ʿAbbāsid and Mamlūk Books about Women: A Literary Historical Approach," *Arabica* 42 (1995): 56–78. The dense and copious monograph on women in al-Andalus by Manuela Marín offers a comprehensive history of Andalusian women; see Manuela Marín, *Mujeres en al-Ándalus* (Madrid: Consejo Superior de Investigaciones Científicas, 2000).
61. Louis Pouzet, "Vision populaire de la femme en Syrie aux VIe et VIIe/XIIe et XIIIe siècles," in *Proceedings of the 14th Congress of the Union Européenne des Arabisants et Islamisants, Budapest 1988*, ed. Alexander Fodor (Budapest: Eötvös Loránd University Chair for Arabic Studies, 1995), 295.
62. Huda Lutfi, "Al-Sakhāwī's *Kitāb al-nisā'* as a Source for the Social and Economic

History of Muslim Women During the Fifteenth Century A.D.," *The Muslim World* 71 (1981): 105.

63. See Ronald C. Jennings, "Women in Early 17th-Century Ottoman Judicial Records: The Sharia Court of Anatolian Kayseri," *Journal of the Economic and Social History of the Orient* 18 (1975): 53–114; Judith E. Tucker, *Women in Nineteenth-Century Egypt* (Cambridge: Cambridge University Press, 1985); Haim Gerber, "Social and Economic Position of Women in an Ottoman City, Bursa, 1600–1700," *International Journal of Middle Eastern Studies* 12 (1980): 231–44; Bruce A. Masters, *The Origins of Western Economic Dominance in the Middle East: Mercantilism and the Islamic Economy in Aleppo, 1600–1750* (New York: New York University Press, 1988); Abraham Marcus, *The Middle East on the Eve of Modernity: Aleppo in the Eighteenth Century* (New York: Columbia University Press, 1989); Madeleine C. Zilfi, ed., *Women in the Ottoman Empire. Middle Eastern Women in the Early Modern Era* (Leiden: Brill, 1997).
64. Gideon Libson, *Jewish and Islamic Law: A Comparative Study of Custom During the Geonic Period* (Cambridge, MA: Harvard University Press, 2003).
65. Michelle Lamarche Marrese, *A Woman's Kingdom: Noblewomen and the Control of Property in Russia, 1700–1861* (Ithaca and London: Cornell University Press, 2002); Bettine Birge, *Women, Property and Confucian Reaction in Sung and Yüan China (960–1368)* (Cambridge: Cambridge University Press, 2002).
66. Renée Hirschon, "Introduction: Property, Power and Gender Relations," in *Women and Property, Women as Property*, ed. Renée Hirschon (London and New York: Croom Helm and St. Martin's, 1984), 1–23. The treatment of women as property in Islamic law can be studied by comparing notarial models for the sale of an array of slave girls, such as a *jāriya* (singer), a *mamlūka* (a generic term for a slave girl), a *ṣabiyya* (ten-year-old slave girl), a slave girl with a suckling baby, a particularly beautiful slave girl, and an *umm walad* (concubine who had given the slave owner offspring), all of whom had distinct status; see *Muqniʿ*, 166–79. See also *Kitāb al-Wathāʾiq*, 33–4.
67. See the discussion in Tucker, *Women in Nineteenth-Century Egypt*, 6–7.
68. Carol M. Rose, "Women and Property: Gaining and Losing Ground," in *Property and Persuasion. Essays on the History, Theory, and Rhetoric of Ownership* (Boulder, CO: Westview, 1994), 233–63.
69. Rose, "Women and Property," 236.
70. North and Thomas, *The Rise of the Western World*, 19ff., explain the crucial role played by property rights in stimulating economic activity in the Western capitalist system. On women in the European economy, see M.J. Boxer and J.H. Quataert, eds., *Connecting Spheres: Women in the Western World, 1500 to the Present* (New York: Oxford University Press, 1987), 3–17. On women's labour, see David Herlihy, *Opera Muliebria: Women and Work in Medieval Europe* (New York: McGraw Hill, 1990). See also Elizabeth Ewan, "Scottish Portias: Women in the Courts in Medieval Scottish Towns," *Journal of the Canadian Historical Association* n.s. 3 (1992): 27–45.
71. *The Lawyers Weekly*, Ontario Lawyers Association Bulletin, 20 August 2004.
72. Alexandra J. Zolan, "The Effect of Islamization on the Legal and Social Status of Women in Iran," *Boston College Third World Law Journal* 7 (1987): 183–93. See also Ron Shaham, "Custom, Islamic Law, and Statutory Legislation: Marriage Registration

and Minimum Age at Marriage in the Egyptian Sharīʿa Courts," *Islamic Law and Society* 2 (1995): 258–81.

73. For an update on the progress made in women's conditions, we now have the *Arab Human Development Report 2002* (New York: United Nations Publications, 2002), 28. The ideological approach to women's issues is explored by Barbara Freyer Stowasser, "Women's Issues in Modern Islamic Thought," in *Arab Women. Old Boundaries, New Frontiers*, ed. Judith E. Tucker (Bloomington and Indianapolis: Indiana University Press, 1993), 3–28. A somewhat dated statistics publication that is nevertheless of great methodological significance is Elizabeth H. White, "Legal Reform as an Indicator of Women's Status in Muslim Nations," in *Women in the Muslim World*, ed. L. Beck and N. Keddie (Cambridge, MA: Harvard University Press, 1978), 52–68.
74. Abdullahi An-Na'im, "The Rights of Women and International Law in the Muslim Context," *Whittier Law Review* 9 (1987): 491–516.
75. See Nadia Wassef, "Masculinities and Mutilations: Female Genital Mutilation in Egypt," *Middle East Women's Studies Review* 8 (1998): 1–4.
76. See Vardit Rispler-Chaim, "Hasan Murad Mann: 'Childbearing and the Rights of a Wife,'" *Islamic Law and Society* 2 (1995): 92–9, on a modern day fatwa in which the woman's right to children is upheld by offering her the right to a *khulʿ* divorce from a sterile husband, albeit with the appeal that she respect his reputation by not acting on this right. On the misery and abuse inflicted on the childless woman, see Marcia C. Inhorn, "Population, Poverty, and Gender Politics: Motherhood Pressures and Marital Crisis in the Lives of Poor Egyptian Women," in *Population, Poverty and Politics in Middle East Cities*, ed. Michael E. Bonine (Gainesville: University Press of Florida, 1997), 186–207. On the debate on women's ultimate rights to children in Western societies, see Mary Warnock, *Making Babies: Is There a Right to Have Children?* (Oxford: Oxford University Press, 2002), who considers this a dubious right.
77. Barbara Freyer Stowasser, *Women in the Qur'an: Traditions and Interpretation* (Oxford: Oxford University Press, 1994); Amina Wadud, *Qur'an and Woman: Rereading the Sacred Text from a Woman's Perspective* (Oxford: Oxford University Press, 1999).

Chapter One. *The Ṣadāq*

1. *Documentos*, 104–6, document 61, tr. 113–14. On Seco de Lucena Paredes, the documents, and his role in the development of Islamic legal studies in Granada, see Aguirre Sádaba, "Granada y los estudios de derecho islámico," 471–74. For a description of the collection, see *Documentos*, vii–l of the introduction to the Spanish text.
2. On the battles and the civil war, see Arié, *L'Espagne musulmane*, 159–71. Arié estimates the population in Granada during the fifteenth century at 50,000 (340).
3. Fernando de la Granja, "Condena de Boabdil por los alfaqíes de Granada," *Al-Andalus* 26 (1971): 145–76.

4. For the fall of Granada and life under the Naṣrids, the last dynasty of Muslim Spain, see Arié, *L'Espagne musulmane*; and Harvey, *Islamic Spain.*
5. On the notarial tradition in al-Andalus, see Emile Tyan, *Le Notariat et le régime de la preuve par écrit dans la pratique du droit musulman*, 2nd ed. (Beirut: Hariss Impr. St.-Paul, 1959).
6. *Documentos*, 104–6, document 61, tr. 113–14.
7. See for instance, a marriage contract from Nablus, 1725, in Judith E. Tucker, *In the House of the Law: Gender and Islamic Law in Ottoman Syria and Palestine* (Los Angeles and Berkeley: University of California Press, 1998), 39.
8. Their *kunyas* (patronymics) disclose that his father's name was "potter" and that hers was "grain merchant," which does not necessarily refer to their current occupations. On traders and trade names, see Shatzmiller, *Labour*, 69ff.
9. On the variety of jewelry and cloth items worn by the Granadans, both men and women, see Arié, *L'Espagne musulmane*, 382–92. Jewelry and fine clothes were the standard items given to the bride; however, the jewelry given by the groom to the bride on this occasion may have been part of the monetary value of her *ṣadāq* or given to her independently as a gift. This difference could be of great significance in the future; see Amalia Zomeño Rodriguez, "Transferencias matrimoniales en el occidente Islámico medieval: Las joyas como regalo de boda," *Revista de Dialectología y Tradiciones Populares* 51 (1996): 87ff. On perfumes, see Lucie Bolens, "Les Parfums et la beauté en Andalousie médiévale (XIe–XIIIe siècles)," in *Les Soins de beauté: Actes du IIIe Colloque International, Grasse 1985* (Nice: Centre de la Méditerranée moderne et contemporain, 1985), 145–69.
10. The amount of land was sixteen *marjiʿ ʿamaliyy*. One *marajiʿ* equalled 500 square metres. On this land unit, see *Documentos*, 19 of the introduction to the Arabic text; and Arié, *L'Espagne musulmane*, 217.
11. *Documentos*, 8–9, document 4, tr. 7–8.
12. The documents allow us to reconstruct the existence in Granada of a community of several families from Baza who were related through marriage and whose women continuously refer to properties left behind. Baza fell to the Christians on 28 November 1489.
13. Seco de Lucea Paredes highlights the documents' contribution to understanding the monetary system prevalent in fifteenth-century Granada. Three types of dinars were legal tender in commercial transactions in Granada: the gold dinar proper; the silver dinar, not to be confused with the traditional silver coin, the dirham; and the dinar *ʿaynī*. There were also gold dinar doubles, called doblas; see *Documentos*, xlvii. Generally, prices were quoted in gold coins but paid in the other denominations. Thanks to another document in the collection, document 54, registered in 1485, Seco de Lucea Paredes was able to establish that 1 gold dinar was equal to 7.5 silver dinars, while document 65 establishes that 1 gold dinar was equal to 75 dirhams, indicating that 10 dirhams was equal to 1 silver dinar, hence the appellation dinar *ʿashrī* (dinar of ten). The relation between the three coins—gold dinar, silver dinar, and dirham—was therefore 1 gold dinar equalled 7.5 silvar dinars or 75 dirhams. However, Seco de Lucena Paredes was not able to establish the value

of either the dinar *ʿaynī* or the copper coins. For a comprehensive bibliography on Andalusian numismatics, see Alberto Canto and Tawfiq Ibrahim, *Moneda andalusí en la Alhambra* (Granada: Scriptorium, 1997), 235–76.

14. *Documentos*, 10–11, document 6, tr. 10, indicates that the father offered his house in Baza as collateral in a transaction using property belonging to his other daughter, Umm al-Fatḥ, property that she and Fāṭima had inherited from their mother and that he managed. Both sisters were minors and under his guardianship.
15. On the possibility that Fāṭima bt. Abī ʿAbd Allāh Muḥammad b. Abī l-Nuʿaym Riḍwān was the granddaughter of the famous vizier, see Harvey, *Islamic Spain*, 206–10.
16. *Documentos*, 18–19, document 7(e), tr. 17–19. The different deals undertaken by Fāṭima's aunt on her behalf and accounted for in the document reached the sum of 1,400 gold dinars and 39 silver dinars. These transactions are discussed in Chapter 4.
17. *Documentos*, 14, document 7(c), tr. 14–15.
18. The Ḥaram collection of court documents dating from fourteenth-century Mamluk Jerusalem likewise contained only a small number of marriage contracts; see Donald P. Little, *A Catalogue of the Islamic Documents from al-Ḥaram aš-šarīf in Jerusalem* (Beirut: Orient-Institut der Deutschen Morgenländischen Gesellschaft, 1984), 300–6.
19. The *ṣadāq*'s early development as a gift is discussed in Yossef Rapoport, "Matrimonial Gifts in Early Islamic Egypt," *Islamic Law and Society* 7 (2000): 1–36. Rapoport's contribution lies in documenting evidence in Egyptian marriage contracts of the *ṣadāq*'s early practice. His use of the Andalusian and North African material to supplement his argument is controversial. As we shall see, while the principle of *ṣadāq* remained intact, regional variations in its acquisition abound.
20. In Qur'an 4:4, known as "Sūrat al-nisā'" (The Women's Chapter), many women's rights are pronounced.
21. Abū Muḥammad ʿAbd Allāh b. Ibn Abī Zayd al-Qayrawānī, *Matn al-risāla* (Cairo and Beirut: Dār al-Fikr, 1980), 89–94.
22. The *Risāla* was credited with the spread and consolidation of Malikism in the Islamic West. On the author and his work, see H.R. Idris, art. "Ibn Abī Zayd al-Ḳayrawānī," in *EI*[2]. The *Risāla* also attracted early European attention; for French translations and analysis, see Emile Fagnan, *Abrégé de droit malékite et morale musulmane* (Paris: J. Carbonel, 1914); and Abū Muḥammad ʿAbd Allāh b. Ibn Abī Zayd al-Qayrāwānī, *La Risāla*, trans. L. Bercher (Alger: N.p., 1949). On the *mudejar* copies, see Harvey, *Islamic Spain*, 74.
23. A comprehensive analytical and comparative treatment of the law of the Islamic marriage can be found in *Traité*, vol. 2, where the unique Maliki stand on *ṣadāq* is discussed at pages 195–98. For a synthetical approach to the different aspects of the *ṣadāq* in Islamic law, see vol. 2, 199–255. For a general view of marriage in classical Islam, see J. Schacht, art. "Nikāḥ," and O. Spies, art. "Mahr," both in *EI*[2].
24. *Qawānīn*, 152.
25. Compare Tucker, *In the House of the Law*, 50; Annelies Moors, *Women, Property and*

Islam: Palestinian Experiences, 1920–1990 (Cambridge: Cambridge University Press, 1995), 85.

26. This "customary" arrangement was initially suggested by J. Schacht, art. "Nikāḥ," in *EI*[2]: "The essential features of the Muslim law of marriage go back to the customary law of the Arabs which previously existed." But links with the Byzantine legal developments predating Islamic Egypt are discussed by Rapoport, "Matrimonial Gifts," 28–31.
27. Rapoport, "Matrimonial Gifts," 5–9.
28. *Qawānīn*, 153.
29. *Muqniʿ*, 23. Also, compare *Kitāb al-Wathāʾiq*, 10; and *Maqṣad*, 13. Each of these notaries provided a legal commentary on the marriage contract; see *Kitāb al-Wathāʾiq*, 5–10; *Muqniʿ*, 19–37; and *Maqṣad*, 12–42.
30. *Muqniʿ*, 76–7.
31. Ibid.
32. *Kitāb al-Wathāʾiq*, 10.
33. Ibid., 10: *Kull al-abāʾ fī dhālika siwāʾ al-ʿadl al-ṣāliḥ al-mashhūr.*
34. Abū l-Walīd Muḥammad al-Qurṭubī Ibn Rushd, *Bidāyat al-mujtahid*, 4 vols. (Cairo: Dār Ibn Ḥazm, 1952), vol. 2, 28; Joseph Schacht, *The Origins of Muhammadan Jurisprudence* (Oxford: Clarendon, 1979), 193–94.
35. See Ibn Rushd's fatwa on the father's and husband's inheritance rights to the dead daughter's trousseau before consummation, in *Miʿyār*, vol. 3, 35–6.
36. Ibn Rushd, *Bidāyat al-mujtahid*, vol. 2, 25, provides a comparative view of the other schools. See also *Traité*, vol. 2, 232–33.
37. Zomeño Rodriguez, *Dote y matrimonio*, 83–6. In the Kayseri court records, Jennings found several cases of "girls who had been wed" as children and who went to court when they came of age to indicate formal consent to (or repudiation of) the marriage, probably as a prelude to the marriage's actual consummation; see Jennings, "Women in Early 17th-Century Ottoman Judicial Records," 77. See also Harald Motzki, "Child Marriage in Seventeenth-Century Palestine," in *Islamic Legal Interpretation: Muftis and Their Fatwas*, ed. M. Khalid Masud, B. Messick, and D.S. Powers (Cambridge, MA: Harvard University Press, 1996), 129–40.
38. On the guardianship and interdiction of the young wife, see Chapter 4.
39. Because of their location in the capital, the writings and rulings of the jurists of Cordova were crucial to the development of the legal institutions and the law itself. For an analysis of the work of the court and judges in Cordova, see Müller, *Gerichtspraxis.* See also M.J. Viguera Molins, "Los jueces de Cordoba en la primera mitad del siglo XI (análisis de datos)," *Al-Qanṭara* 5 (1984): 123–45.
40. *Miʿyār*, vol. 3, 221.
41. Ibid., vol. 3, 222.
42. Ibid., vol. 9, 150.
43. Ibid., vol. 3, 48.
44. Ibid., vol. 3, 89.
45. Abū l-Qāsim Ibn Salmūn, *al-ʿIqd al-munaẓẓam*, printed in the margin of Ibrāhīm b. ʿAlī Ibn Farḥūn, *Tabṣīrat al-ḥukkām fī uṣūl al-aqḍiyya wa-manāhij al-aḥkām*, ed. Ṭāhā

ʿAbd al-Raʾūf Saʿd, 2 vols. (Cairo: Maktabat al-Kullīyāt al-Azhāriyya, 1986), vol. 2, 83–4.

46. *Documentos*, 86–7, document 47, tr. 91–2.
47. *Documentos*, 48, document 23, tr. 49.
48. Fadel, "Rules," 72: "*Fatwās* from Granada given by al-Ḥaffār (d. 1408) and Ibn Sirāj (d. 1444) describe "lawsuits in which the children are suing the father for money owed to their deceased mother. In both cases the father, over the duration of the marriage, had exploited his wife's properties, apparently keeping the produce for himself . . . The implicit claim of the father in both is that his wife had forgiven him his debts, while the children deny this."
49. Lutfi, *Al-Quds al-Mamlūkiyya*, 286.
50. *Muqniʿ*, 338.
51. *Miʿyār*, vol. 5, 89.
52. Ibid., vol. 5, 99.
53. On the heirs' quest to claim the *ṣadāq*, see *Miʿyār*, vol. 3, 47; and on the wife's struggle against the heirs to recover the *kāliʾ*, see *Miʿyār*, vol. 3, 88–9.
54. *Miʿyār*, vol. 3, 90.
55. *Muqniʿ*, 68–9.
56. Ibid., 69–70.
57. *Documentos*, 59–60, document 31, tr. 62–5.
58. Ibid., 60.
59. For an example of the formula, see *Maqṣad*, 30.
60. The period a married woman may remain under guardianship is seven years, during which she is deprived of the power to manage her financial and property affairs. For a full treatment of the guardianship of married women, see Chapter 4.
61. *Qawānīn*, 167. Gifting the women's property rights to the husband in exchange for divorce also had early precedents; see Rapoport, "Matrimonial Gifts," 15, 21, 31–3.
62. *Kitāb al-Wathāʾiq*, 434–37.
63. Ibid., 422–27.
64. *Muqniʿ*, 337–38.
65. *Kitāb al-Wathāʾiq*, 434–37.
66. *Muqniʿ*, 70–2, 78–9; *Maqṣad*, 61–2.
67. *Muqniʿ*, 70: *ṭayyibatan bihi nafsihā shukran ʿalā jamīl suḥbatihi wa-ḥusn muʿāsharatihi lahā*.
68. Ibn Salmūn, *al-ʿIqd al-munaẓẓam*, vol. 1, 82.
69. On the *ḥiyāza*, see Chapter 2.
70. Tyan, *Le Notariat*, 56–8.
71. *Muqniʿ*, 71.
72. For more on the issue of monogamy and the husband's right to a concubine, see Chapter 6.
73. Jack Goody and S.J. Tambiah, *Bridewealth and Dowry* (Cambridge: Cambridge University Press, 1973), 37.
74. Rose, "Women and Property," 236. See also my discussion of Rose's feminist theory in the Introduction.
75. Hady R. Idris, "Le Mariage en occident musulman d'aprés un choix de fatwas

médiévales extraits du *Mi'yār* d'al Wansharisi," *Studia Islamica* 32 (1970): 157–67, continuation in *Revue de l'Occident musulman et de la Méditéranée* 12 (1972): 45–62; 14 (1974): 71–105; and 25 (1978): 119–38. On monetary evidence of the *ṣadāq* in the Middle East, see Lutfi, *Al-Quds al-Mamlūkiyya*, 286.

76. For details of these investments, see Chapter 4.
77. Women's *ṣadāq* investments are discussed in Chapter 8.
78. Lutfi, *Al-Quds al-Mamlūkiyya*, 286: "The dinar does not seem to have been as common as the dirham. For the most part the dinar appears in deferred dowries owed to wives by their husbands."
79. Svetlana Ivanova, "Muslim and Christian Women Before the Kadi Court in Eighteenth Century Rumeli: Marriage Problems," *Oriente Moderne* 18–19 (1999): 161–76.
80. Jennings, "Women in Early 17th-Century Ottoman Judicial Records," 86–7; Svetlana Ivanova, "The Divorce between Zubaida Hatun and Esseid Osman Ağa: Women in the Eighteenth-Century Sharia Court of Rumelia," in *Women, the Family, and Divorce Laws*, ed. Sonbol, 114; Ivanova, "Muslim and Christian Women," 163; Iris Agmon, "Muslim Women in Court According to the Sijill of Late Ottoman Jaffa and Haifa: Some Methodological Notes," in *Women, the Family, and Divorce Laws*, ed. Sonbol, 127–30.
81. Colin Imber collected a number of Ottoman fatwas, written between the years 1718 and 1730 and issued by the Ottoman *şeyhülislam* Yenişehirli Abdullah, that deal with issues related to marriage, including the *mahr*, or *ṣadāq*. These fatwas confirm the similarity of the Hanafi school's legal practice to that of the Malikis. However, Imber also makes the point that no historical data can be culled from these fatwas; see Colin Imber, "Women, Marriage and Property: *Mahr* in the Behcetü'l-Fetāvā of Yenişehirli Abdullah," in *Women in the Ottoman Empire: Middle Eastern Women in the Early Modern Era*, ed. Madeline C. Zilfi (Leiden: Brill, 1997), 81–104.
82. Ivanova, "The Divorce," 11; Ivanova, "Muslim and Christian Women," 165.
83. Jennings, "Women in Early 17th-Century Ottoman Judicial Records," 85; Ivanova, "The Divorce," 115–16; Ivanova, "Muslim and Christian Women," 165.
84. Jennings, "Women in Early 17th-Century Ottoman Judicial Records," 86.
85. Ibid., 82–4; Ivanova, "The Divorce," 116.
86. Richard P. Saller, *Patriarchy, Property and Death in the Roman Family* (Cambridge: Cambridge University Press, 1994), 204–7. Despite the difference between a bride-price and a dowry, Schacht refers to the *ṣadāq* throughout his text as a "dowry"; see Joseph Schacht, *An Introduction*, 161; and Schacht, art. "Nikāḥ," in *EI*[2].
87. Saller, *Patriarchy, Property and Death*, 204ff.
88. Libson, *Jewish and Islamic Law*, 10, 158–59.
89. Ibid. For a detailed study of Jewish marriage practices contemporary with the Islamic marriage contract, see Mordechai Akiva Friedman, *Jewish Marriage in Palestine: A Cairo Geniza Study*, 2 vols. (Tel-Aviv: Tel-Aviv University Press, 1980–81).
90. See Judith Romney Wegner, "The Status of Women in Jewish and Islamic Marriage and Divorce Law," *Harvard Women's Law Journal* 5 (1982): 1–33; and Libson, *Jewish*

and Islamic Law. Libson makes great use of the primary Hebrew and Islamic legal sources but little of the related historical material. Equally, Wegner's general comparative account should now be modified for historical accuracy to reflect evidence contained in the Geniza documents.

91. Art. "Dowry" (Heb. *nedunya*), in *Encyclopedia Judaica* (Jerusalem: Encyclopedia Judaica, 1972), vol. 6, 185–89.
92. On Jewish women appealing to Muslim courts, see Shlomo Dov Goitein, *A Mediterranean Society: The Jewish Communities of the Arab World as Portrayed in the Documents of the Cairo Geniza*, 5 vols. (Los Angeles and Berkeley: University of California Press, 1967–93), vol. 2, 301, 368, 399; and Shlomo Dov Goitein, *Jews and Arabs: Their Contacts Through the Ages* (New York: Schocken Books, 1974), 181–82. Similar conclusions on Jewish and Christian women bringing cases to the Islamic court could be reached on the basis of the court documents from eighteenth-century Galata, cf. Göçek and Baer, "Social Boundaries of Ottoman Women's Experience," 57: "We conjecture that women who were dissatisfied with the inheritance partitioning within the context of their local communities . . . brought cases to the Islamic court."
93. See Joseph Rivlin, *Shitre Kehilat Alyucena: Bills and Contracts from Lucena, 1020–1025 C.E.* (Ramat-Gan: Bar-Ilan University Press, 1994), 33.
94. Goitein, *A Mediterranean Society*, vol. 3, 346–52.
95. Diane Owen Hughes, "From Brideprice to Dowry in Mediterranean Europe," *Journal of Family History* 3 (1978): 266–71.
96. Ibid., 262–69. On the types of dowries and bridewealth systems, see Goody and Tambiah, *Bridewealth and Dowry*.
97. Hughes, "From Brideprice to Dowry," 281ff.; Thomas Kuehn, *Law, Family, and Women*, 238–57; Thomas Kuehn, "Person and Gender in the Laws," in *Gender and Society in Renaissance Italy*, ed. Judith Brown and Robert Davis (New York: Longman, 1998), 88: "In Renaissance Italy the dowry signified women's exclusion from their natal patrilineage."
98. Goody refers to the land that brides received from their husbands in England as "dower"; however, "this was the future endowment given to the bride at the church door, which she would use for support after her husband's death." In this case, "dowry and inheritance were alternative not cumulative"; see Jack Goody, "Inheritance, Property and Women: Some Comparative Considerations," in *Family and Inheritance: Rural Society in Western Europe, 1200–1800*, ed. J. Goody, J. Thirsk, and E.P. Thompson (Cambridge: Cambridge University Press, 1976), 17.
99. See in particular, Moors, *Women, Property and Islam*, 82–4; and Zomeño Rodriguez, *Dote y matrimonio*, 57–68. The Islamic anthropological approach was inspired by models studied in Goody and Tambiah, *Bridewealth and Dowry*, and expounded in Jack Goody, *The European Family: An Historico-Anthropological Essay* (Oxford: Blackwell, 2000), 15ff.

    In his book on the property of Mamluk women, Yossef Rapoport has argued that the "dowries," always household items in the form of a trousseau, were in fact premortem inheritance shares, which guaranteed women's independence. A claim that "dowries" (*jihāz*), which were neither registered in the marriage contract nor mandated by the law, tacitly subverted an explicit law of inheritance, needs more substantiation than currently available. While the *jihāz* given by Mamluk parents was rendered in cash, sometimes for a large amount, depending on their means, it was always given in the form of household items and cloth, never real estate; there is no evidence that when division of the estate took place—the Ḥaram documents quoted by Rapoport were not estate divisions but estimates of property at the moment of death—the inheritance law was circumscribed and disregarded in Mamluk Egypt. See Yossef Rapoport, *Marriage, Money and Divorce in Medieval Islamic Society* (Cambridge: Cambridge University Press, 2005), 6, 12–30, esp. 19.

100. Patterns of gifting at marriage are described at length in Zomeño Rodriguez, "Transferencias matrimoniales," but see for instance, Little, *Catalogue of Islamic Documents*, 300–6.
101. See Zomeño Rodriguez, *Dote y matrimonio*, 156–74 for a discussion of the many appeals by heirs concerning the status of properties given as marriage gifts with the *ṣadāq*.
102. See J. Kirshner and A. Molho, "The Dowry Fund and the Marriage Market in Early Quatrocento Florence," *Journal of Modern History* 50 (1978): 404–38. On the importance of the documents used in this article as a source for the history of women, see David Herlihy, *Women, Family, and Society in Medieval Europe: Historical Essays, 1978–1991*, ed. A. Molho (Providence, RI: Berghahn Books, 1995), 24.

Chapter Two. *The Inter Vivos Gift*

1. *Documentos*, 145, document 93, tr. 147–48. This gift deed is from the archives of the wife's family. Fāṭima's father, Aḥmad b. Musāʿid, appears in a barter transaction (*muʿāwaḍa*) that took place on 28 August 1461; see *Documentos*, 37, document 17, tr. 38–9.
2. For an item-by-item list of the capitulations, see Harvey, *Islamic Spain*, 314–23.
3. Jean-Pierre Molenat, "Les Musulmans de Tolède aux XIVe et XVe siècles," in *Les Espagnes médiévales: Aspects économiques et sociaux* (Nice: Publications de la Faculté des lettres et sciences humaines de Nice, 1983), 175–90.
4. On the Muslims of Granada in the aftermath of the conquest, see Leonard P. Harvey, *Muslims in Spain, 1500–1614* (Chicago: University of Chicago Press, 2005), 1–79.
5. *Documentos*, 51–2, document 25, tr. 53.
6. Ibid., 10, document 6, tr. 10.
7. Ibid., 36, document 16c, tr. 37–8.
8. On the Banigas family, see Harvey, *Islamic Spain*, 275ff.
9. The most comprehensive analysis of the inter vivos gift in Islamic law is provided in *Traité*, vol. 3, 311–411. The summary here incorporates the notions of the different legal schools but gives preference to the Maliki school's standing with regard to the issues of property transfers, which is crucial for understanding the Andalusian practice.

10. On the Hanafi practice, see Muḥammad b. Aḥmad al-Sarakhsī, *Kitāb al-Mabsūṭ*, 30 vols. (Beirut: Dār al-Maʿārif, A.H. 1398), vol. 12, 48.
11. For the Maliki legal stand on the inter vivos gift, see Ibn Abī Zayd al-Qayrawānī, *Matn al-risāla*, 116–21; and *Qawānīn*, 277–79. Both authors treat the *hiba* and endowments (*aḥbās*) as similar transactions, which they see as complete and full renunciations of one's property. The contract forms for each are conveniently placed next to each other in the notarial manuals; see *Kitāb al-Wathā'iq*, 217–32; *Muqniʿ*, 330–34; and *Maqṣad*, 298–310.
12. See for instance, *Muqniʿ*, 308.
13. For details, see *Abrégé*, vol. 3, 151.
14. This process of possession-taking was the same as that in the Hanafi school but unlike that in the other schools.
15. For the general nature and interpretation of the inter vivos gift, see Schacht, *An Introduction*, 157–58; *Traité*, vol. 3, 362ff.; and David S. Powers, "Parents and Their Minor Children: Familial Politics in the Middle Maghrib in the Eighth/Fourteenth Century," *Continuity and Change* 16 (2001): 179–81.
16. *Qawānīn*, 277.
17. One such case that highlighted a mother's ability and willingness to abuse her power of guardianship over a married daughter, thus depriving the daughter of control over and revenue from gifted property—in this case, a mill gifted to her as a minor in favour over her brother—is described in Powers, "Parents and Their Minor Children," 177–200.
18. For a variety of model deeds for giving gifts to minors, see *Kitāb al-Wathā'iq*, 211–31; *Muqniʿ*, 328–31; *Maqṣad*, 301–06; and Ibn Salmūn, *al-ʿIqd al-munaẓẓam*, vol. 2, 124.
19. See Shatzmiller, "Women and Property Rights," 227–31.
20. *Miʿyār*, vol. 9, 123.
21. On the *siyāqa* and the *niḥla*, see *Muqniʿ*, 37, 79–82; and *Maqṣad*, 30–2, 29–30. On the *siyāqa*, see also Zomeño Rodriguez, *Dote y matrimonio*, 151–74. On these terms, see Idris, "Le Mariage en occident musulman."
22. *Muqniʿ*, 79.
23. Ibid., 79–82: *rafaʿa lahā fī mahrihā muʿajjalahu wa-mu'ajjalahu.*
24. On the *siyāqa* and the *niḥla*, see Ibn Salmūn, *al-ʿIqd al-munaẓẓam*, vol. 1, 9, 11.
25. *Maqṣad*, 30.
26. This is the major theme in Zomeño Rodriguez's thesis; on the *siyāqa* as a fictitious gift, see Zomeño Rodriguez, *Dote y matrimonio*, 173.
27. Ibid., 151–63.
28. Zomeño Rodriguez, *Dote y matrimonio*, 173–74.
29. Ibid., 69–80.
30. Idris, "Le Mariage en occident musulman," 162.
31. *Documentos*, 93–7, documents 50–4, tr. 99–105.
32. Ibid., 77, document 42, tr. 81–2.
33. Ibid., 84, document 45, tr. 89–90. The insane were relegated to a permanent state of guardianship and therefore could never acquire property rights; see Michael W. Dols, *Majnūn: The Madman in Medieval Islamic Society*, ed. Diana E. Immisch (Oxford: Clarendon, 1992), 434–55.

34. For ʿĀʾisha's case, *Documentos*, 55, document 98, tr. 105–6; on the case involving Tāj al-Ūlā, see Chapter 4.
35. A model notarial deed was provided for a father who needed to pay female family members to look after his children in the aftermath of a divorce; see *Muqniʿ*, 124–25.
36. *Documentos*, 93, document 50, tr. 99.
37. Ibid., 94, document 51, tr. 100.
38. *Qawānīn*, 277.
39. *Documentos*, 94, document 51, tr. 100.
40. Ibid., 96, document 53, tr. 102–3.
41. Ibid., 90–1, document 48, tr. 96.
42. Ibid., 99–100, document 56, tr. 106–7.
43. Arié, *L'Espagne musulmane*, 171–72.
44. On Mamluk Egypt, see Werner Diem, "Vier arabische Rechtsurkunden aus dem Ägypten des 14 und 15 Jahrhunderts," *Der Islam* 72 (1995): 193–258.
45. On a woman's right to renounce the second *ṣadāq* instalment, see Chapter 1.
46. *Maqṣad*, 31–2.
47. Ibid., 34: *rifqan bihi wa-iḥsānan ilayhi wa-istijlāban minhu li-ḥusn al-ʿushra wa-karīm al-ulfa li-jawgihi al-madhkūra.*
48. Abū Saʿīd Faraj Ibn Lubb (d. Granada, c. 1381). On this jurist, the Andalusian fatwas, and their historical value, see López Ortiz, "Fatwas Granadinas," 73–84.
49. I am thankful to Delfina Serrano Ruano for bringing this information to my attention. On the issues of legal practice (*ʿamal*) in al-Andalus, see Delfina Serrano Ruano, "La práctica legal (*ʿamal*) en al-Andalus durante los siglos X–XII, a través de los *Madhāhib al-ḥukkām fī nawāzil al-aḥkām* de Muḥammad ibn ʿIyāḍ." *Qurṭuba* 1 (1996): 180.
50. *Miʿyār*, vol. 9, 150. Since the *ṣadāq* is legally a gift, some of the fatwas dealing with it are included in the *Miʿyār*'s ninth volume, which is devoted to the subject of gifts. On the life gift (*ʿumrā*) to the husband and on the house as a gift, see *Muqniʿ*, 331–35. On the nature of the *ʿumrā*, see Schacht, *An Introduction*, 158.
51. *Miʿyār*, vol. 3, 244–45.
52. *Qawānīn*, 167.
53. Ibid., 34–5.
54. *Miʿyār*, vol. 9, 127–28.
55. *Documentos*, 95, document 52, tr. 101–2. On Andalusian irrigation rights, see Thomas Glick, *Irrigation and Hydraulic Technology: Medieval Spain and Its Legacy* (Aldershot: Variorum, 1996).
56. *Documentos*, 99–100, document 56, tr. 106–7.
57. *Abrégé*, vol. 3, 151–52. See also *Traité*, vol. 3, 372.
58. Saller, *Patriarchy, Property and Death*, 155–56.
59. Susan Stuard, "The Dominion of Gender: Women's Fortunes in the High Middle Ages," in *Becoming Visibles: Women in European History*, ed. Renate Bridenthal, Claudia Koonz, and Susan Stuard (Boston: Houghton Mifflin Company, 1987), 153–71; R.M. Smith, "Women's Property Rights Under Customary Law: Some Developments in the Thirteenth and Fourteenth Centuries," *Transactions of the Royal Historical Society*,

5th series, 36 (1986): 165–94; Goody, *The European Family*, 86–99; Hirschon, "Introduction," 1–23.

60. Kuehn, "Person and Gender," 88. On the dowry in the Italian cities, see J. Kirshner, "Materials for a Gilded Cage: Non-Dotal Assets in Florence, 1300–1500," in *The Family in Italy, from Antiquity to the Present*, ed. David I. Kertzer and Richard P. Saller (New Haven: Yale University Press, 1991), 184–85.
61. Kirshner, "Materials for a Gilded Cage," 192, 196–97.
62. Ibid., 190–91.
63. Ibid., 191.
64. Ibid., 192ff.
65. Ibid., 192.

Chapter Three. *Inheritance*

1. *Documentos*, 142–44, document 92, tr. 144–47. See Amalia Zomeño, "Siete historias de mujeres. Sobre la transmisión de la propriedad en la Granada Nazarí," in *Mujeres y sociedad islámica: Una visión plural*, ed. M.I. Calero Secall (Malaga: Universidad de Málaga, 2006), 187–88.
2. The Arabic text of *Documentos* (142) indicates 75 silver dinars, while the Spanish translation (144) indicates 65 dinars.
3. This transaction was used to introduce Chapter 2, on gifts to minors.
4. On the different administrative patterns of the Islamic regions, see the list of estate inventories in Jerusalem's Mamluk court in Little, *Catalogue of Islamic Documents*, 59–186, documents 21–469. See also Donald P. Little, "Ḥaram Documents Related to the Jews of Late Fourteenth Century Jerusalem," *Journal of Semitic Studies* 30 (1985): 227–370; Donald P. Little, "Documents Related to the Estates of a Merchant and His Wife in Late Fourteenth Century Jerusalem," *Mamlūk Studies Review* 2 (1998): 93–193; Lutfi, *Al-Quds al-Mamlūkiyya*, 15–22; and Aharon Layish, "Bequests as an Instrument for Accommodating Inheritance Rules: Israel as a Case Study," *Islamic Law and Society* 2 (1995): 282–319.
5. The dates and document numbers for these estate divisions, as shown in *Documentos*, are: 1430 (7c), 1452 (7b, d, e), 1452 (8), 1457 (11), 1458 (12b), 1464 (19a–c, 19e–f), 1464 (20), 1466–68 (21, 22, 23), 1468 (24), 1476 (33a–d), 1482 (43), 1484 (40b), 1483 (47), 1485 (49), 1487 (58), 1490 (64a–b), 1493 (87), 1495 (95).
6. For prior mention of Fāṭima, granddaughter of Abū l-Nuʿaym Riḍwān, see note 15 in Chapter 1.
7. *Documentos*, 11–19, document 7a–f, tr. 11–20.
8. Khālid's bequest, signed on 15 December 1430, included money for food to be distributed to the poor, money for Muslim prisoners, and money for orphaned virgin girls from poor families, presumably for their trousseaus; see *Documentos*, 14–15, document 7c, tr. 14–15.
9. Ibid., 17–18, document 7e, tr. 17–19.
10. Ibid., 20–2, document 8, tr. 20–3.

11. Although the document does not specify which wife came first, I am presuming that Umm al-Fatḥ was the second wife in accordance with her being listed second in the document. On the basis of the Granadan collection she studied, Manuela Marín counted 44 women named Fāṭima, 42 named ʿĀ'isha, and 17 named Umm al-Fatḥ. While there were a few other names mentioned, she considers the names of Granadan women a special case because of the limited variety of first names. To her mind the appearance of the name Umm al-Fatḥ (lit. mother of the conquest) should be attributed to the political situation of 14th- and 15th-century Granada. See Marín, *Mujeres en al-Ándalus*, 70–3.
12. Court records of estate divisions frequently reveal loans made by wives to husbands or debts to wives incurred by husbands during marriage—for instance, when a wife contributed either to building or to renovating and improving a house. On other occasions, the debt was revenue gained by the husband through cultivation of the wife's land.
13. *Documentos*, 24–5, document 12, tr. 25–7; Zomeño, "Siete historias de mujeres," 192–95.
14. Ibid., 26–7, document 13, tr. 27–8.
15. Ibid., 108–10, document 64a–b, tr. 117–19.
16. Ibid., 74–6, document 40a–c, tr. 77–80.
17. Ibid., 75–6, document 40c, tr. 79–80.
18. Ibid., 64–5, document 33, tr. 67–8.
19. Ibid., 65, document 33c–d, tr. 68–9.
20. Ibid., 86–90, document 47a–b, tr. 91–5. I am assuming that this Aḥmad b. Muḥammad al-Ruffa, who died in 1483, was the son of Abū ʿAbd Allāh Muḥammad b. Aḥmad al-Ruffa, who died in 1476. The document does not specify their relationship.
21. Ibid., 89–90, document 47b, tr. 95.
22. Ibid., 41, document 19c, tr. 41–2; Zomeño, "Siete historias de mujeres," 185–87.
23. Ibid., 44–5, document 20, tr. 45–6.
24. Ibid., document 2, tr. 47–9; Zomeño, "Siete historias de mujeres," 189–92.
25. Ibid., 48, document 23, tr. 49–50.
26. Ibid.
27. Ibid., 55–6, document 27, tr. 57–8.
28. Ibid., 49–50, document 24, tr. 50–2; Zomeño, "Siete historias de mujeres," 183–85.
29. Ibid., 101–3, document 58, tr. 108–10.
30. ʿĀ'isha was probably the sister of Muḥammad b. Aḥmad al-Ashkar, whose *khulʿ* divorce act of 1474 was discussed earlier.
31. Lopez Ortiz, "Fatwas Granadinas," 84–7.
32. *Documentos*, 78–80, document 43, tr. 82–5.
33. Ibid.
34. Ibid., 105, document 61, tr. 113–14; 8–9, document 4, tr. 7–8; 10–11, document 6, tr. 10; 77, document 42, tr. 81–2; 84, document 45, tr. 89–90. The data on inherited property do not come solely from estate divisions but also from references to them in court documents of other transactions, such as references to property

previously inherited by females now involved in other transactions in Granada. Together, they contribute to analysis of the patterns of female inheritance.

35. The standard work on succession is Noel J. Coulson, *Succession in the Muslim Family* (Cambridge: Cambridge University Press, 1971), which contains a bewildering array of details on the calculation of the shares. A good and concise introduction to Islamic inheritance law is J. Brugman, "The Islamic Law of Inheritance," in *Essays on Oriental Laws of Succession* (Leiden: E.J. Brill, 1969), 88–91 (on women's inheritance, see 83–6). See also Schacht, *An Introduction*, 169–74. The early development of the Islamic inheritance law has been studied by David S. Powers, who devotes a large part of his book to the formulation of the law relating to the share alotted to females; see *Studies in Qur'an and Ḥadīth: The Formation of the Islamic Law of Inheritance* (Los Angeles and Berkeley: University of California Press, 1986). See also David S. Powers, "The Islamic Inheritance System: A Socio-Historical Approach," in *The Islamic Family Law*, ed. Chibli Mallat and Jane Conners (London: Graham and Trotman, 1990), 11–29.
36. Powers, "The Islamic Inheritance System," 29.
37. Coulson, *Succession*, 235.
38. Ibid., 213–34.
39. Ibid., 239.
40. Saller, *Patriarchy, Property and Death*, 159, 161–68.
41. On factors influencing marriage patterns of the Arab family, see Judith E. Tucker, "The Arab Family in History. 'Otherness' and the Study of the Family," in *Arab Women. Old Boundaries, New Frontiers*, ed. Judith E. Tucker (Bloomington: Indiana University Press, 1993), 195–207.
42. Maria Luisa Avila, "The Structure of the Family in al-Andalus," in *The Formation of al-Andalus*, ed. Manuela Marín, 2 vols. (Aldershot: Ashgate, 1998), vol. 1, 482.
43. Women in eighteenth-century Aleppo regularly assumed the role of property manager; see Margaret L. Meriwether, "The Rights of Children and the Responsibilities of Women: Women as Wasis in Ottoman Aleppo, 1770–1840," in *Women, the Family, and Divorce Laws*, ed. Sonbol, 228–30. Based on evidence from cases in the Aleppan court, the *maḥkama sharʿiyya*, the author provides a statistical illustration of the preference for females over males when males were alive but does not provide explicit reasons for this trend. See also Jennings, "Women in Early 17th-Century Ottoman Judicial Records," 71–5.
44. For an example of a female fulfilling the role of property guardian in Granada, see the case of Tāj al-ʿUlā in Chapter 4.
45. On payment of the deferred portion of the *ṣadāq*, see Chapter 1.
46. Kathryn A. Miller, "Muslim Minorities and the Obligation to Emigrate to Islamic Territory: Two Fatwās from Fifteenth-Century Granada," *Islamic Law and Society* 7 (2000): 267 (for the Arabic text of the fatwa in question, see 280). On the status of the converted or non-Muslim spouse's children, see Chapter 6.
47. For a similar kind of family archive in ninth-century Egypt, including records of economic transactions as well as a marriage contract, see Yūsuf Rāġib, *Marchands d'étoffes du Fayyoum au IIIe/IXe siècle d'après leurs archives (actes et lettres)*, vol. 1, *Les actes des Banū ʿAbd al-Muʾmin* (Cairo: Institut français d'archéologie orientale, 1982), 33–5.

48. On the stability of women's succession rights, see Johansen, *The Islamic Law on Land Tax and Rent*, 1–6.
49. On the Roman law of succession, see Saller, *Patriarchy, Property and Death*, 163–68.
50. For a summary of Roman inheritance rights in the XII Tables (451–50 B.C.) see Saller, *Patriarchy, Property and Death*, 163–68, which provides ample references; on the *Lex Voconia*, see 166–67, where the estates barred to women as heirs are described as "estates of the top property class (100,000 or more)."
51. Kuehn, "Person and Gender," 93; Kuehn, *Law, Family, and Women*, 238–57.
52. Kuehn, "Person and Gender," 94.
53. Layish, "Bequests as an Instrument."
54. On whether the Ḥaram documents, the fourteenth-century court documents from Mamluk Jerusalem, originated in the administration or in the court, see Lutfi, *Al-Quds al-Mamlūkiyya*, 8ff.
55. Compare Lutfi, *Al-Quds al-Mamlūkiyya*, 8–36; and Little, "Documents Related to the Estates of a Merchant and His Wife."
56. Jennings, "Women in Early 17th-Century Ottoman Judicial Records," 69–71; Colette Establet and Jean-Paul Pascual, "Women in Damascene Families around 1700," *Journal of the Economic and Social History of the Orient* 45 (2002): 319.
57. Establet and Pascual, "Women in Damascene Families," 318.
58. On the imam in the Hanafi legal sources, Johansen, *The Islamic Law on Land Tax and Rent*, 10–11.
59. A connection between a society at war and women's property rights has been suggested in the case of ancient Sparta in fourth-century B.C. There Sparta's conquest of its neighboring lands made it obligatory to provide women with property rights over agricultural land, so that women could supervise and manage land cultivation when their men were engaged in military activity. Women reportedly controlled 40 per cent of Sparta's total agricultural terrain. See Robert K. Fleck and F. Andrew Hanssen, "'Rulers Ruled by Women': An Economic Analysis of the Rise and Fall of Women's Rights in Ancient Sparta," http://www2.montana.edu/ahanssen/Papers/sw140.pdf.
60. On the multiple uses and forms of *waqf*-making throughout the Islamic world, see the multiauthor entry "Waḳf," in *EI*². Subsequent references to the *waqf* in this chapter are only to *waqf* issues that arise in the context of women's property rights. See Maria del Carmen Villanueva Rico, *Habices de las mezquitas de la ciudad de Granada y sus alquerias*, 2 vols. (Madrid: Instituto Hispano-Arabe de Cultura, 1961–66). On organization of the *waqf*'s administration in Fez, a neighbouring city in Marinid Morocco, see Maya Shatzmiller, *The Berbers and the Islamic State: The Marīnid Experience in Pre-Protectorate Morocco* (Princeton: Markus Wiener, 2000), 95–115.
61. Shatzmiller, "Islamic Institutions and Property Rights," 44–74.
62. Timur Kuran, "The Provision of Public Goods under Islamic Law: Origins, Impact, and Limitations of the Waqf System," *Law and Society Review* 35 (2001): 841–97.
63. Margaret L. Meriwether, "Women and *Waqf* Revisited: The Case of Aleppo, 1770–1840," in *Women in the Ottoman Empire: Middle Eastern Women in the Early Modern Era*, ed. Madeline C. Zilfi (Leiden: Brill, 1997), 140.
64. On the historical phenomenon of *waqf*-making by the wealthy women of Mamluk

Egypt, see Carl Petry, "A Paradox of Patronage During the Later Mamlūk Period," *The Muslim World* 73 (1983): 182–207; and idem, "Class Solidarity Versus Gender Gain: Women as Custodians of Property in Later Medieval Egypt," in *Women in Middle Eastern History: Shifting Boundaries in Sex and Gender*, ed. B. Baron and N. Keddie (New Haven and London: Yale University Press, 1991), 122–42.

65. Gabriel Baer, "Women and *Waqf*: An Analysis of the Istanbul *Tahrir* of 1546," *Asian and African Studies* 17 (1983): 9–27.
66. Powers, "The Maliki Family Endowment," 386. The fatwas Powers studied are collected in the *Miʿyār*.
67. Ibid., 385–86.

Chapter Four. *Delayed Acquisition*

1. For the cluster of documents recounting the story of Tāj al-ʿUlā, see *Documentos*, 11–20, documents 7a–f, tr. 11–20. I am grateful to Professor David Powers of Cornell University, who read a paper detailing some of the issues dealt with in this chapter and offered comments.
2. For a succinct explanation of *ḥajr*, see the art. "Ḥadjr" (Schacht) in *EI*[2].
3. *Documentos*, 8–9, document 4, tr. 7–8.
4. Ibid., 104–6, document 61: *wa-hiya bikr bāligh fī sanatihā yatīma muhmila.*
5. On the Islamic law of guardianship respecting minors, see *Traité*, vol. 3, 197–255 (respecting the interdiction of adults, see 259–304). On the *waṣī*, see Schacht, *An Introduction*, 173.
6. *Traité*, vol. 3, 201.
7. *Qawānīn*, 242–43.
8. Later generations of Malikis eliminated the obligation of seven years' marriage as a condition for release from guardianship; see *Traité*, vol. 3, 215–16, for one such jurist, the eighteenth-century Egyptian Dardīr, previously discussed for his commentary on Khalīl's *Mukhtaṣar*.
9. *Mukhtaṣar*, vol. 3, 62.
10. *Muqniʿ*, 24.
11. *Muqniʿ*, 294–95.
12. *Kitāb al-Wathāʾiq*, 339–40.
13. On insolvency (*taflīs*), see *Qawānīn*, 240–42. An interesting case of the emancipation of slaves by minors has been studied by Donald P. Little, "Two Fourteenth-Century Court Records from Jerusalem Concerning the Disposition of Slaves by Minors," *Arabica* 29 (1986): 16–49. There, the male minor emancipated the slaves on his deathbed; however, the Shafiʿi judge in Jerusalem rescinded the act because, even though the minor had officially attained majority (*bulūgh*), he had not attained the power of reason (*qabl rushdihi*), a direct reference to the official release from interdiction (*tarshīd*) (30).
14. *Mukhtaṣar*, vol. 3, 63.
15. Ibid., vol. 3, 64.
16. *Miʿyār*, vol. 9, 150.

17. *Miʿyār*, vol. 5, 242, dating approximately from the same period of the Granadan documents. On the two muftis, Ibn al-Sarrāj and al-Ḥaffār, see López Ortiz, "Fatwas Granadinas."
18. *Miʿyār*, vol. 5, 98. On al-ʿUqbānī and his manual for market supervisors (*ḥisba*), see Muḥammad al-ʿUqbānī, *Un Traité de hisba*, ed. A. Chénoufi (Damascus: Institut français d'archéologie orientale, 1967). On the *khulʿ* divorce and its relationship to women's property rights, see Chapter 1, and Schacht, *An Introduction*, 164.
19. See Goody, "Inheritance, Property and Women," 21.
20. In *Documentos*, 99–100, document 56, tr. 106–7, see the account given at the court of the work undertaken by Muḥammad b. Aḥmad al-Qirbilyānī and his sons in the vineyard of his wife, ʿĀʾisha bt. Ibrāhīm al-Ḥakīm, on 7 December 1485.
21. *Documentos*, 3–4, document 1a–b, tr. 3–5.
22. *Documentos*, 98–9, document 55, tr. 105–6.
23. Saller, *Patriarchy, Property and Death*, 181–203.
24. Ibid., 207.
25. On guardianship in the Florentine context, see Kuehn, *Law, Family, and Women*, 212–37.
26. Joan Kelly, "Did Women Have a Renaissance?" in Joan Kelly, *Women, History and Theory* (Chicago: University of Chicago Press, 1984), 19–50.
27. Kuehn, *Law, Family, and Women*, 237.
28. Kirshner, "Materials for a Gilded Cage," 192.
29. Caroline Brettell, "Kinship and Contract: Property Transmission and Family Relations in Northwestern Portugal," *Comparative Studies in Society and History* 33 (1991): 443–62.
30. On equality in marriage, see Farhat J. Ziadeh, "Equality (Kafāʾah) in the Muslim Law of Marriage," *American Journal of Comparative Law* 6 (1957): 503–17; and Amalia Zomeño Rodriguez, "Kafāʾa in the Mālikī School: A Fatwā from Fifteenth-Century Fez," in *Islamic Law: Theory and Practice*, ed. R. Gleave and E. Kermeli (London: I.B. Tauris, 1997), 87–106.

Chapter Five. *The Body as Property*

1. *Documentos*, 140, document 90, tr. 142. An "orphan" in Islamic law denotes a child who is fatherless.
2. *Documentos*, 46–9, documents 22, 23, tr. 47, 49. On her estate division, see Chapter 4.
3. *Documentos*, 76, document 41, tr. 80.
4. *Documentos*, 137, document 87, tr. 139–40.
5. E. Chaumont, art. "Yatīm," in *EI*[2]. Adoption, as understood today, was not permitted by the law, and the document itself, despite the title *Tabannī yatīm*, does not refer to adoption but to custody (*ḥaḍāna*). (On adoption in Islamic law and the lack of a specific provision regarding adoption, see *Traité*, vol. 3, 61–3.) It appears nevertheless that adoption was a common practice in Maliki North Africa; see *Traité*, vol. 3, 62. On the legal concept in early periods, see Ella Landau-Tasseron,

"Adoption, Acknowledgment of Paternity and False Genealogical Claims in Arabian and Islamic Societies," *Bulletin of the School of Oriental and African Studies* 66 (2003): 169–92. One could suggest that the payment for custody was in fact commonly practiced, as we shall presently see, and that it took care of orphans' needs. This would then explain the cases found by Landau-Tasseron of adoption by women (186–87). On adoption and the rights of children in modern-day Morocco based on interpretation of the Maliki law, see M. Abdelkebir Alaoui M'Daghri, "The Code of Children's Rights in Islam," in *Children in the Muslim Middle East*, ed. E. Fernea (Austin: University of Texas Press, 1995), 30–41; and Amira al-Azhary Sonbol, "Adoption in Islamic Society: A Historical Survey," in ibid., 45–67.

6. *Documentos*, 59, document 31, tr. 62–3. The *khulʿ* settlement document refers to two *ḥaḍāna* payments, one current and the other involving a future child in the event the wife was pregnant. In the latter case, if a male child was born, custody by the mother would last until his maturity (*bulūgh*), and if it were a female child, until consummation of her marriage, as is common in Maliki law. The document also confirmed that the daughter would remain in her mother's custody and that the father would pay maintenance for the child. Trading the right to custody payment in exchange for a *khulʿ* divorce was a common practice under Maliki law; see *Traité*, vol. 3, 152.
7. Noel Coulson's explanation that the concept of women's property rights in Islamic law arose in tandem with the equal rank women have come to occupy with males in generating filiation (*nasab*) has its corresponding dimension in the righs women acquired over the functions of their bodies. Coulson, "Regulation of Sexual Behavior," 67.
8. *Traité*, vol. 2, 25; see also 232ff.
9. On the relations between the first *ṣadāq* instalment and consummation, see Chapter 6.
10. *Traité*, vol. 2, 239.
11. Ibid., vol. 2, 60–5. The Hanafi stand on the female body is discussed in Baber Johansen, "The Valorization of the Human Body in Muslim Sunni Law," in *Law and Society* (Princeton: Markus Wiener, 1996), 71–112. On literary sources that treat issues of the female body, see Franz Rosenthal, "Fiction and Reality: Sources for the Role of Sex in Medieval Muslim Society," in *Society and the Sexes in Medieval Islam*, ed. Afaf Lutfi al-Sayyid Marsot (Malibu, CA: Undena, 1979), 2–22.
12. Zomeño Rodriguez, *Dote y matrimonio*, 90–4. On the existence of physical defaults and their effect on the validity of a marriage, see *Traité*, vol. 2, 182–91.
13. Zomeño Rodriguez, *Dote y matrimonio*, 89–94.
14. *Maqṣad*, 69.
15. *Traité*, vol. 2, 260–65.
16. *Traité*, vol. 2, 266.
17. The Hanafis drew a distinction between (sexual) maturity and puberty. The latter was seen to occur around the twelfth or thirteenth year, the former possibly appearing earlier and making sexual intercourse permissable as early as age nine. Cf. *Traité*, vol. 2, 266, note 9: ". . . the wife has to be capable of sexual relations, even

though she has not yet reached total puberty." For fourteenth-century Granada, see *Qawānīn*, 167. The Hanafi standpoint may not make much difference in terms of the girl's physical and mental aptitude for sexual relations, but would matter in terms of her property rights, since it enables her to receive maintenance. The declaration of maturity must be made by the girl's guardian; Harald Motzki, who studied child marriage in seventeenth-century Palestine, has highlighted the parents' financial motivations in concluding marriages for their minor daughters: Motzki, "Child Marriage in Seventeenth-Century Palestine," 129.

18. See Carl F. Petry, "Conjugal Rights Versus Class Prerogatives: A Divorce Case in Mamlūk Cairo," in *Women in the Medieval Islamic World*, ed. Gavin R.G. Hambly (New York: St. Martin's Press, 1998), 227–40.
19. Birth control in Islamic law and medicine is treated in Basim Musallam, *Sex and Society in Islam: Birth Control before the Nineteenth Century* (Cambridge: Cambridge University Press, 1983). The following discussion of this subject uses his findings. On the legal provisions for birth control, see 28–38. While pioneering in its comprehensiveness, Musallam was not the first to draw attention to the law's positive view of birth control. G.-H. Bousquet suggested in 1950 that voluntary limitation to reproduction goes hand in hand with Islamic theology and law and that it should become the official ideology of reproduction in modern-day Islamic societies; see G.-H. Bousquet, "L'Islam et la limitation volontaire des naissances," *Population* 5 (1950): 121–28. This approach of using the law as a tool for legitimation for planned parenthood has now been adopted by Muslim scientists; see Abdel Rahim Omran, *Family Planning in the Legacy of Islam* (London and New York: Routledge, 1992).
20. Cf. Ibn Juzayy, who wrote that, "as far as *ʿazl* is concerned, it is not permitted with a free woman without her permission. . . ." *Qawānīn*, 160.
21. Musallam, *Sex and Society*, 28–9.
22. On the female slave body, see Johansen, "The Valorization of the Human Body," 80–9.
23. On Ibn Qayyim's and Ibn Taymiyya's stand on female circumcision, see text at n. 113.
24. Musallam, *Sex and Society*, 31.
25. *Traité*, vol. 2, 149–51.
26. Musallam, *Sex and Society*, 33.
27. Batool Ispahany, trans., *Islamic Medical Wisdom: The Ṭibb al-Āʾimma*, ed. Andrew J. Newman (London: The Muhammadi Trust, 1991), 176. On the genre, see Emily Savage-Smith, "Medicine," in *Encyclopedia of the History of Arabic Science*, ed. Roshdi Rashed in collaboration with Régis Morelon, 3 vols. (London and New York: Routledge, 1996), vol. 3, 927–39.
28. *Documentos*, 68–9, document 36, tr. 72. Goitein reported finding in the Geniza documents many similar female slaves' names. The pattern of naming slaves after precious stones (*zumurrud* is an emerald in Arabic) and other such items distinguished the female slave from the free woman; see Goitein, *A Mediterranean Society*, vol. 1, 130–45.
29. Avner Giladi, *Infants, Parents and Wet Nurses. Medieval Islamic Views on Breastfeeding and Their Social Implications* (Leiden: Brill, 1999), 13–41, 68–106. See also Judith E.

Tucker's review of Giladi's *Infants, Parents and Wet Nurses* in *International Journal of Middle East Studies* 34 (2002): 162–65; Mohammed Hocine Benkheira, "Donner le sein, c'est comme donner le jour: La Doctrine de l'allaitement dans le sunnisme médiéval," *Studia Islamica* 92 (2001): 5–52; and Mohammed Hocine Benkheira, "Le Commerce conjugale gâte-t-il le lait maternel? Sexualité, médecine et droit dans le sunnisme ancien," *Arabica* 30 (2003): 1–78. For a comparative study, see *Traité*, vol. 3, 143–49.

30. Translation from *Al-Qur'ān. A Contemporary Translation by Ahmed Ali* (Princeton: Princeton University Press, 1984), 41.
31. Ibid., 491.
32. *Traité*, vol. 3, 144. The lack of unanimity on the matter was also noted by Giladi, *Infants, Parents and Wet Nurses*, 91.
33. *Traité*, vol. 3, 146. Giladi, *Infants, Parents and Wet Nurses*, 13–41, 68–106, provides a thorough discussion of the infant and the parents' rights and duties in this matter.
34. *Traité*, vol. 3, 146.
35. Ibid., 146–47.
36. *Qawānīn*, 167–68. The notarial deed from eleventh-century Toledo for hiring a female domestic helper specifies that weaving and spinning were among the duties of the person hired; see *Muqniʿ*, 206–8, and *Traité*, vol. 3, 147.
37. Most of the fatwas dealing with divorce appear in vol. 4 of the *Miʿyār*; see in particular on this issue pp. 8–9 and 22–31.
38. Ibid., vol. 4, 23–4. On this mufti, see Powers, *Law, Society and Culture*, 26–7.
39. Ibid., vol. 4, 97, 101.
40. Cf., for example, Giladi, *Infants, Parents and Wet Nurses*, 101, where he suggests that the welfare of the newborn and the subservient position of women to their husbands under the law affect the legal stand on breastfeeding. This would seem to be contradicted by a fatwa issued by the Moroccan jurist Abū l-Ḥasan al-Ṣaghīr in fourteenth-century Fez in the case of a baby's death after it was rejected by its mother for nonpayment of breastfeeding fees. The mother was not held responsible for the child's death because the jurists recognized her right to agree or refuse to breastfeed when she was divorced or separated and not being paid according to the rule. *Miʿyār*, vol. 4, 22–3.
41. For the wet nurse contract and the laws respecting women's wage labour, see Chapter 7.
42. See details in Chapter 7.
43. On the rights of children in the womb, see Coulson, *Succession*, 204–10.
44. *Muqniʿ*, 123: *Wathīqa fī iqrār al-rajul bi-ḥamli zawjatihi.*
45. Ibid., 340–41: *Wathīqat istihlāl mawlūd ṣarīḥan thumma māta.*
46. See María Arcas Campoy, "El testimonio de las mujeres en el derecho mālikī," in *Homenaje al Prof. Jacinto Bosch Vilá*, 2 vols. (Granada: Departamento de Estudios Semitícos, Universidad de Granada, 1991), vol. 1, 473–79. On the requirement to verify the identify of the woman for whom the notary is drawing up a contract, see Tyan, *Le Notariat*, 56.
47. Coulson, *Succession*, 207: "The child must be born alive"; and 208–9: "The child must have been conceived before the death of the *praepositus*" [i.e., the father].

48. These two notarial models were not mentioned by Landau-Tasseron in her otherwise comprehensive discussion of the issues related to paternity; see Landau-Tasseron, "Adoption," 169–92.
49. On *tabannī* ("adoption"), which is not permitted in Islamic law, see *Traité*, vol. 3, 61–3, and E. Chaumont, art. "Yatīm," in *EI*[2]. On the *ḥaḍāna*, see *Traité*, vol. 3, 150–76. The concise version in *EI*[2] by the same author—Y. Linant de Bellefonds, art. "Ḥaḍāna"—contains discrepancies with regard to property rights as formulated in *Traité*. Recent publications on custody do not deal with the property rights aspect of the institution. See Mahdi Zahraa and Normi A. Malek, "The Concept of Custody in Islamic Law," *Arab Law Quarterly* 13 (1998): 155–77; Rachid El Hour, "Algunas reflexiones acerca de la custodia en la escuela mālikī," *Miscelánea de Estudios Árabes y Hebraícos* 53 (2004): 143–53. One should note, however, that both the English term "custody" and the French term "garde de l'enfant" tend to obfuscate the Arabic association of the function with the female person.
50. *Muqniʿ*, 124: *Wathīqa bi-dafʿ al-rajul nafaqat wālidihi li 'l-ḥāḍina.*
51. Ibid., 301–2: *Wathīqa bi-dafʿ al-waṣī al-nafaqa li-ḥāḍinat al-yatīm.*
52. Ibid., 145: *Wathīqa fīmā bāʿat al-ḥāḍina*, and 147–48.
53. *Maqṣad*, 76.
54. On the order of preference, see *Traité*, vol. 3, 159. The Maliki and Hanafi schools always prefer the female relatives of the mother, while the Shafiʿi, Hanbali, and Imami schools accept male relatives in certain circumstances. For the Maliki order of entitlement, see Ibn Juzayy, *Qawānīn*, 169: "First the mother, then the maternal grandmother, then the maternal aunt, then the paternal grandmother, and if she falls ill, her sister, then the paternal aunt, then the niece, the paternal brother's daughter, and then those worthy among the paternal relatives."
55. *Traité*, vol. 3, 154, has a different view. For the diversity among the schools regarding wages, see below.
56. The only time custody occurs during marriage is on the rare occasions when a wife has a separate domicile from the father.
57. *Traité*, vol. 3, 151.
58. Ibid., 169–72.
59. On the issue of custody in Hanafi fatwas, see Tucker, *In the House of the Law*, 121–41.
60. *Muqniʿ*, 120–21, and al-Jazīrī's model document mentioned earlier.
61. Ibid., 375.
62. Cf. *Abrégé*, vol. 2, 141: "There is neither wages nor *nafaqa* [to the mother] for holding the charge."
63. *Miʿyār*, vol. 3, 277.
64. Ibid., vol. 3, 278.
65. Ibid. His fatwas and those of his son were summarized by Vincent Lagardère, *Histoire et Société en Occident Musulman au Moyen Âge. Analyse du Miʿyār d'al-Wansharīsī* (Madrid: Collection de la Casa de Velázquez, 1995), 130–31.
66. *Muqniʿ*, 339: *Wathīqa bi-maʿrifa tarbiya rajul li-l-laqīṭ iltaqaṭahu fa-rabbahu wa-nashā'a ʿindahu.*
67. On training received by the Muslim physician, see Sami Hamarneh, "Medical

Education and Practice in Medieval Islam," in *The History of Medical Education*, ed. C.D. O'Malley (Los Angeles and Berkeley: University of California Press, 1970), 39–71; and Gary Leiser, "Medical Education in Islamic Lands from the Seventh to the Fourteenth Century," *The Journal of the History of Medicine and Allied Sciences* 38 (1983): 48–75.

68. See Ann Ellis Hanson, "The Medical Writer's Woman," in *Before Sexuality: The Construction of Erotic Experience in the Ancient Greek World*, ed. D. Halperin, J. Winkler, and F. Zeitlin (Princeton: Princeton University Press, 1990), 311, where she points out that "Interest in the gynecological treatises of Greco-Roman antiquity is largely a phenomenon of the last ten to fifteen years." See also Lesley Dean-Jones, *Women's Bodies in Classical Greek Science* (Oxford: Clarendon, 1994); and Helen King, *Hippocrates' Women: Reading the Female Body in Ancient Greece* (London and New York: Routledge, 1998).
69. B. Ebbell, trans., *The Papyrus Ebers: The Greatest Egyptian Medical Document* (London: Oxford University Press, 1937).
70. See Heinrich von Staden, "Women and Dirt," *Helios* 19 (1992): 7–30.
71. See Dean-Jones, *Women's Bodies*; and Lesley Dean-Jones, "The Politics of Pleasure: Female Sexual Appetite in the Hippocratic Corpus," *Helios* 19 (1992): 72–91.
72. Dean-Jones, "The Politics of Pleasure," 73. In a recent publication, Mayhew suggests a new reading of Aristotle's work, correcting his misogynous view of women with reference to social conditions; see Robert Mayhew, *The Female in Aristotle's Biology: Reason or Rationalization* (Chicago and London: University of Chicago Press, 2004).
73. Ibn al-Jazzār, *Kitāb Siyāsat al-ṣibyān wa-tadbīruhum*, ed. Muḥammad al-Ḥabīb al-Hīla (Beirut: Dār al-Gharb al-Islāmī, 1984), 47. See also Gerrit Bos, "Ibn al-Jazzār on Women's Diseases and Their Treatment," *Medical History* 37 (1993): 296–312.
74. On the training of midwives, see M.S. Spink and G.L. Lewis, *Albucasis on Surgery and Instruments* (London: The Wellcome Institute of the History of Medicine, 1973), 468–70.
75. ʿArīb b. Saʿīd al-Qurṭubī, *Kitāb Khalq al-janīn wa-tadbīr al-ḥabālā wa 'l-mawlūdīn. Le Livre de la génération du foetus et le traitement des femmes enceintes et des nouveau-nés*, trans. H. Jahier and N. Abdelkader (Alger: Librairie Ferraris, 1956).
76. Ibn Khaldūn, *The Muqaddimah*, trans. Franz Rosenthal, 3 vols. (Princeton: Princeton University Press, 1958), vol. 2, 368–72.
77. Arcas Campoy, "El testimonio."
78. G.H.A. Juynboll, "Some Isnād-Analytical Methods Illustrated on the Basis of Several Woman-Demeaning Sayings from Ḥadīth Literature," in *Studies on the Origins and Uses of Islamic Hadith* (London: Variorum, 1996), 343–83. On the earliest Maliki *ḥadīth* collection dealing with the conduct recommended for women in al-Andalus, see ʿAbd al-Malik Ibn Ḥabīb, *Kitāb al-Ghāya wa 'l-nihāya aw-Kitāb Adab al-nisā' (De l'etique feminine)*, ed. Abdel-Magid Turki (Beirut: Dār al-Gharb al-Islāmī, 1992).
79. On sexuality in Greek medicine, see Dean-Jones, "The Politics of Pleasure."
80. The following discussion of female circumcision relies heavily on Jonathan P. Berkey, "Circumcision Circumscribed: Female Excision and Cultural Accommodation in the Medieval Near East," *International Journal of Middle Eastern Studies* 28 (1996): 19–38; on the threat of female sexuality, 30–4.

81. With regard to this important debate Linant de Bellefonds disputed on several occasions the claims of Muslim jurists that the *ḥadīths* and their prescriptions were authentic, but he had to admit that they had resulted in a legal interpretation that was impossible to shake. In his comparative study of Islamic law, he noted as a case in point the obligation to have an agent (*walī*) represent the woman in marriage; see *Traité*, vol. 2, 51.
82. Berkey, "Circumcision Circumscribed," 24–5, n. 34. For early *ḥadīths* on female circumcision, see Ibn Ḥabīb, *Kitāb al-Ghāya*, 221–22.
83. *Qawānīn*, 164. See also Ibn Abī Zayd al-Qayrawānī, *Matn al-risāla* (Cairo and Beirut: Dār al-Fikr, 1980), 84, 156.
84. Berkey, "Circumcision Circumscribed," 25–6.
85. Aurora Cano Ledesma, trans., "La aportación quirúrgica de Abū 'l-Qāsim al-Zahrāwī según el ms. 876 de El Escorial," *La Ciudad de Dios* 203 (1990): 476–77.
86. Spink and Lewis, *Albucasis*, 396–97.
87. According to Berkey, "Circumcision Circumscribed," 25, the early written traditions warn the practitioner against cutting too much.
88. Ibid., 25–6.
89. Ibid.
90. Schacht, *An Introduction*, 203–4. For a fatwa dealing with a baby's death as a result of a botched circumcision, see Chapter 7.
91. Michael W. Dols, *The Black Death in the Middle East* (Princeton: Princeton University Press, 1977), 114–15.
92. On the reprinting of misogynous medieval writings, including the recent reissue of Abū l-Faraj Ibn al-Jawzī, *Kitāb Aḥkām al-nisā' li 'l-Imām Abī l-Farāj al-Jawzī*, ed. Ziad Hamdān (Beirut: Dār al-Fikr, 1989), see Fatima Mernissi, *Le Harem politique: Le Prophète et les femmes* (Paris: Albin Michel, 1987), 124–26.
93. Berkey, "Circumcision Circumscribed," 29–31.
94. On Trota, the enigmatic author of the earliest medieval gynaecological treatise, see Monica H. Green, ed. and trans., *The Trotula: A Medieval Compendium of Women's Medicine* (Philadelphia: University of Pennsylvania Press, 2001), 48–52; on male practitioners, 48ff.
95. Hildegard of Bingen, *On Natural Philosophy and Medicine*, trans. Margaret Berger (Cambridge: D.S. Brewer, 1999).
96. Arié, *L'Espagne musulmane*, 368.
97. Michael McVaugh, "Islamic Medicine in the Kingdom of Aragon in the Early Fourteenth Century," *Bulletin of Islamic Medicine* 3 (1984): 64.
98. Goitein, *A Mediterranean Society*, vol. 1, 164; vol. 3, 127–30; on women in the medical profession, vol. 3, 64.
99. Ralph Jackson, *Doctors and Diseases in the Roman Empire* (Norman, OK: University of Oklahoma Press, 1988), 86–7.
100. Edward J. Kealey, *Medieval Medicus: A Social History of Anglo-Norman Medicine* (Baltimore: John Hopkins University Press, 1981), 35. No midwives appear in the records either. However, Jewish women in thirteenth- and fourteenth-century Provence studied and trained with relatives, fathers or brothers, and were required to pass an official exam before they could practice. The evidence led Joseph Shatzmiller

to suggest that their medical training and aptitude was equal to that of their male contemporaries and colleagues; see Joseph Shatzmiller, "Femmes médecins au Moyen Age. Témoignages sur leurs pratiques (1250–1350)," in *Histoire et Société. Mélanges offerts à Georges Duby*, 4 vols. (Aix-en-Provence: Publications de l'Université de Provence, 1992), vol. 1, 167–75.

101. Medical writings have not always been considered beneficial to the study of social history; see Franz Rosenthal, "The Physician in Medieval Muslim Society," *Bulletin of the History of Medicine* 52 (1978): 476, where is written: "Intellectual activity in medieval Muslim civilization tended towards abstract thought."

102. For a detailed discussion of the population decline in the medieval Near East, see Musallam, *Sex and Society*, 105–21. On the effects of demographics and population size on economic performance and division of labour, see Shatzmiller, *Labour*, 55–70.

103. See the conclusions reached on the Ḥaram documents in Lutfi, *Al-Quds al-Mamlūkiyya*, 256.

104. The families profiled in the Granada documents confirm the demographic portrait of the families depicted in Lutfi, *Al-Quds al-Mamlūkiyya*, 255–58. For additional sources related to the demographics of the region, see Shatzmiller, *Labour*, 55–70.

105. On the many male religious scholars (*ʿulamāʾ*) who reached the mature age of seventy-five, see Maria Louisa Avila, *La sociedad hispanomusulmana al final del califato* (Madrid: Consejo Superior de Investigaciones Científicas, 1985).

106. Avner Giladi, *Children of Islam: Concept of Childhood in Medieval Muslim Society* (New York: St. Martin's, 1992), 74ff.

107. Coulson believed that this idea, which gave equal weight to the female line in filiation, was nothing short of a revolution that transformed the inheritance system; see Coulson, "Regulation of Sexual Behavior," 67.

108. See Ann Ellis Hanson, "Conception, Gestation, and the Origin of Female Nature in the Corpus Hippocraticum," *Helios* 19 (1992): 31–71; Green, ed. and trans., *The Trotula*, 39–40.

109. On the concept of mutuality in procreation, see Bos, "Ibn al-Jazzār on Women's Diseases," 303. The problem was equally recognized by prophetic medicine. On chanting invocations as a remedy for difficulty in childbirth and as a remedy for a man's lack of children, see Ispahany, trans., *Islamic Medical Wisdom*, 43, 83, 120, 171.

110. See Joshua Russell, "Aspects démographiques du debut de la féodalité," *Annales* 20 (1965): 1124–25.

111. Musallam, *Sex and Society*, 46.

112. Konstantinos Kapparis, *Abortion in the Ancient World* (London: Duckworth Academic, 2002), 176–84.

113. Ibid., 184.

114. Hanson, "The Medical Writers' Woman," 331. Soranos held the idea that virginity was beneficial and that intercourse and pregnancy were not critical to a woman's health. Hanson ties this idea to a different social context where women had an increased presence in social, economic, and sexual matters, as well as to

the existence of smaller families and voluntary celibacy, which Soranos associated with an alternative way of life for women.

115. Green, ed. and trans., *The Trotula*, 42.
116. Renate Blumenfeld-Kosinki, *Not of Woman Born: Representations of Caesarean Birth in Medieval and Renaissance Culture* (Ithaca: Cornell University Press, 1990), 91–119. The misogynous attitude was based on a connection made between midwives and deviant sexual behaviour, which was attributed to women in general, resulting in their being indicted as witches and burned at the stake.
117. Goitein, *A Mediterranean Society*, vol. 1, 127; vol. 2, 282.
118. Musallam, *Sex and Society*, 11–13.
119. Ron Barkai, *A History of Jewish Gynaecological Texts in the Middle Ages* (Leiden: Brill, 1998).
120. Haskell D. Isaacs, *Medical and Para-Medical Manuscripts in the Cambridge Geniza Collection* (Cambridge: Cambridge University Press, 1994).
121. Goitein, *A Mediterranean Society*, vol. 1, 127.

Chapter Six. *Property Rights in Conversion*

1. Camilo Alvarez de Morales y Ruiz-Matas, *Muley Hacén, el Zagal y Boabdil: Los últimos reyes de Granada* (Granada: Editorial Comares, 2000), 86–93. Details of Zoraya's business transactions appear in documents recording the financial activities of a cluster of royal women during the last decades of Nasrid rule in Granada; see Luis Seco de Lucena Paredes, "La sultana madre de Boabdil," *Al-Andalus* 12 (1947): 359–90.
2. Harvey, *Muslims in Spain*, 29.
3. See ibid., 23–35, on the *elches* (recent converts to Islam) in Granada and the role that the issue of their potential reconversion to Christianity played in the final decision to force conversion on Granada's Muslims.
4. *Kitāb al-Wathā'iq*, 405–18. See Pedro Chalmeta, "Le Passage à l'Islam dans al-Andalus au Xe siècle," in *Actas del XII Congreso de la U.E.A.I., Málaga, 1984* (Madrid: Union Européenne des Arabisants et Islamisants, 1986), 161–83. The documents were also used to explore the assumed conversion of Maimonides to Islam; see Monserrat Abumalham, "La conversíon según formularios notariales andalusíes: Valoracíon de la legalidad de la conversíon de Maimónides," *Miscelánea de Estudios Árabes y Hebraícos* 32 (1985): 71–84. On the Maliki school, see N. Cottart, art. "Mālikiyya," and J. Schacht, art. "Mālik b. Anas," both in *EI*[2].
5. *Muqniʿ*, 344–46. Ibn Mughīth also provides a certificate for an apostate returning to Islam after having converted to Judaism or Christianity; see *Muqniʿ*, 346–47.
6. *Maqṣad*, 424–27.
7. Chalmeta, "Le Passage à l'Islam," 175–76.
8. *Kitāb al-Wathā'iq*, 415–16: *thumma taqūlu shahāda.*
9. See W. Montgomery Watt, art. "ʿAḳīda," in *EI*[2].
10. Mālik b. Anas, *al-Muwaṭṭa' li 'l-imām Mālik b. Anas (179/796), riwāyat Suwayd b.*

Sa'īd al-Ḥadathānī (240/854), ed. 'Abd al-Majīd Turkī (Beirut: Dār al-Gharb al-Islāmī, 1994), 268–70. This text is from the series *Corpus Juris Islamici.*

11. For early Islam, the term "pagan" is used in the sense of an idolater; for the later period it is used for someone who is not an adherent of a revealed religion.
12. Ibid.
13. Ibid.
14. Saḥnūn, *al-Mudawwana al-kubrā li 'l-imām Malik b. Anas*, 9 vols. (Beirut: al-Maktaba al-Shar'iyya, 1999), vol. 2, 297–315.
15. Ibid.
16. Ibid., vol. 2, 288.
17. Ibn Abī Zayd al-Qayrawānī, *La Risāla*, trans. Bercher, 180–81.
18. Richard Bulliet, *Conversion to Islam in the Medieval Period: An Essay in Quantitative History* (Cambridge, MA: Harvard University Press, 1979), 97.
19. The image of al-Andalus as home to a homogenous society was probably more of a myth than a reality; see the discussion in Maya Shatzmiller, "The Legacy of the Andalusian Berbers in 14th-Century Maghreb: Its Role in the Formation of Maghrebi Historical Identity and Historiography," in *Relaciones de la Península Ibérica con el Magreb, Siglos XIII–XVI, Actas del coloquio, Madrid, 17–18 diciembre 1987*, ed. M. García-Arenal and M.J. Viguera Molins (Madrid: Instituto Hispano-Árabe de Cultura, 1988), 205–36.
20. Bulliet, *Conversion to Islam*, 117.
21. Could the conversion document for a "pagan" male and a "pagan" female actually refer to the existence of religious affiliations other than Jewish and Christian in al-Andalus? Whether a pagan's lack of legal status in Visigothic Spain survived into the Islamic period is a historical question to which there is no clear answer. The conversion document for a *majūsī*, a term reserved for a Zoroastrian, does not make much sense in the historical background of tenth-century al-Andalus, as there is no evidence for the existence of Zoroastrians there. The term is most probably used here due to reproduction of the original version found in the eighth- and ninth-century Maliki works that are quoted above.
22. In addition to Bulliet, *Conversion to Islam*, see Michael G. Morony, "Landholding in Seventh Century Iraq: Late Sasanian and Early Islamic Patterns," in *The Islamic Middle East, 700–1900: Studies in Economic and Social History*, ed. A.L. Udovitch (Princeton: Darwin Press, 1983), 135–72; and idem, "The Age of Conversions: A Reassessment," in *Conversion and Continuity: Indigenous Christian Communities in Islamic Lands, Eighth to Eighteenth Centuries*, ed. M. Gervers and R.J. Bikhazi (Toronto: Pontifical Institute of Medieval Studies, 1990), 135–50. See also Maya Shatzmiller, "Professions and Ethnic Origin of Urban Labourers in Muslim Spain: Evidence from a Moroccan Source," *Awrāq* 5 (1983): 149–64, where I suggest the existence of a correlation between conversion and economic prosperity in al-Andalus based on a document describing synchronization of the ethnic origins, religions, and occupations of Andalusians.
23. See Thomas E. Burman, *Religious Polemic and the Intellectual History of the Mozarabs, c. 1050–1200* (Leiden: E.J. Brill, 1994), 13–37. In a collection of essays devoted to

religious minorities in medieval Spain, several authors, such as Mikel de Epalza and Angel Sáenz-Badillos, provide a synthesis of the historical experience of acculturation in the Christian and Jewish communities in Muslim Spain, and some also address aspects of conversion to Islam; see Manuela Marín and Joseph Pérez, eds., *Minorités religieuses dans l'Espagne médiévale. Revue du monde musulman et de la Méditerranée* 63–4 (Aix-en-Provence, 1992).

24. Chalmeta, "Le Passage à l'Islam," 174, supports the idea that conversion peaked in the ninth century with reference to the case of a dignitary who was obliged to display a conversion certificate. He also challenges Lévi-Provençal's dates for mass conversion in the eighth century, at 176–77. On al-Andalus's mercantile activity, see Olivia R. Constable, *Trade and Traders in Muslim Spain: The Commercial Realignment of the Iberian Peninsula, 900–1500* (Cambridge: Cambridge University Press, 1994).
25. On the Jewish chronicles of the forced conversions under the Almohads in North Africa and Spain, see M. Shatzmiller, art. "Muwaḥḥidūn," in *EI*[2]. In the East, religious persecution against Christians and Jews culminated in forced conversions during the tenth century under the Fāṭmid caliph al-Ḥākim.
26. Hanna E. Kassis, "Roots of Conflict: Aspects of Christian-Muslim Confrontation in Eleventh-Century Spain," in *Conversion and Continuity,* ed. Gervers and Bikhazi, 151–60.
27. Elsewhere, I have studied attempts by the Berbers to claim an earlier conversion to Islam than is attributed to them while also looking at the circumstances of the Berber case in the context of the "official" historiography of conversion; see Maya Shatzmiller, "Une source méconnue de l'histoire des Berbères: Le Kitāb al-ansāb li-abī Ḥayyān," *Arabica* 30 (1983): 73–9; also "Le Mythe d'origine berbère: Aspects historiographiques et sociaux," *Revue de l'Occident Musulman* 35 (1983): 145–56; and "The Legacy of the Andalusian Berbers," all of which are now grouped together in Maya Shatzmiller, *The Berbers and the Islamic State.*
28. See Linda S. Northrup, "Muslim-Christian Relations during the Reign of the Mamlūk Sultan al-Manṣūr Qalāwūn, A.D. 1278–1290," 253–61; and Donald P. Little, "Coptic Converts to Islam during the Baḥrī Mamlūk Period," 263–88, both in *Conversion and Continuity*, ed. Gervers and Bikhazi.
29. *Qawānīn*, 148–49.
30. *Abrégé*, vol. 2, 35–6.
31. *Traité*, vol. 2, 124–25.
32. *Kitāb al-Wathā'iq*, 416.
33. Ibid.
34. Ibid.
35. Ibid., 413–14.
36. Ibid., 414 and 417, respectively.
37. Ibid., 410. There is practically no information on Jewish slaves in Muslim Spain or North Africa, but see the fatwa by Ibn Sahl, an eleventh-century Granadan jurist, which dealt with a case of a young slave owned by a Jew who seemingly converted him to Judaism. The young man approached the Muslim judge, claiming that he was born a Muslim to Muslim parents; see Thami El Azemmouri, ed.,

"Les *Nawāzil* d'Ibn Sahl: Section relative à l'*iḥtisāb*," *Hespéris-Tamuda* 14 (1973): 74–5. Jews were entitled by their own religion to own non-Muslim slaves and, according to the Jewish law, were expected to convert them to Judaism. On slaves and slave girls owned by Jews in North Africa, see H.J. Hirschberg, *Toldot ha-yehudim be-Afrika ha-tsefonit*, 2 vols. (Jerusalem: Mosad Bialik, 1965), vol. 1, 134–35 (rev. Engl. transl. *A History of the Jews in North Africa*, Leiden: E.J. Brill, 1974).

38. *Kitāb al-Wathā'iq*, 410: *li-anna al-muslim yatazawwaj al-naṣrāniyya wa 'l-yahūdiyya, wa-lā tanqaṭiʿ ʿuqdat al-nikāḥ baynahumā bi-islām al-zawj illā an takun al-zawja mamlūka fa-yuf-sakh al-nikāḥ baynahumā*. Both *ama* (slave girl) and *mamlūka* (of unfree status) are used in the text.
39. The two somewhat obscure terms *ṭawl* and *ʿanat* refer to the Qur'anic verse 4:25, wherein are laid down conditions for marriage to slave women.
40. *Qawānīn*, 149. *Traité*, vol. 2, 150–51, makes the important observation that the law does not permit a marriage with one's slave, Muslim or non-Muslim, as the two sets of rights, matrimony and property, contradict each other in this case.
41. *Abrégé*, vol. 2, 35–6, emphasis in the original.
42. Fay, "Women and Waqf," 41–5.
43. *Kitāb al-Wathā'iq*, 412. On the fate of children born into such a union before conversion, see below.
44. *Qawānīn*, 155.
45. *Abrégé*, vol. 2, 36; on the forbidden degree as an impediment to marriage, vol. 2, 29–32.
46. *Kitāb al-Wathā'iq*, 416.
47. *Qawānīn*, 149.
48. *Kitāb al-Wathā'iq*, 411.
49. Ibid.
50. Ibid.
51. A fatwa dealing with the fate of a child who converted to Islam on his own and was later convinced by his father to return to his previous faith is included in Ibn Sahl's collection of fatwas; see David Wasserstein, "A Fatwā on Conversion in Islamic Spain," in *Studies in Muslim-Jewish Relations* (Oxford: Oxford Centre for Postgraduate Studies, 1993), vol. 1, 177–89. I thank Kathryn Miller for drawing my attention to this publication.
52. The Islamic attitude to a child's choice regarding conversion was fundamentally different from the attitude prevailing at the time in Spain. In 633 the Fourth Council, under the presidency of St.-Isidore of Seville, repeated the principle that religion was a matter of persuasion and personal conviction and that forcible conversion was improper, yet children of apostates were to be taken from their parents and reared as Christians. See Joseph F. O'Callahan, *A History of Medieval Spain* (Ithaca: Cornell University Press, 1975), 71ff. As O'Callahan notes, the church of Visigothic Spain, by means of the *Collectio Hispana*, a collection of canons attributed to St.-Isidore, deeply influenced the development of canon law in the West.
53. *Kitāb al-Wathā'iq*, 412. The reference in the text is to Christianity, but earlier all three possibilities, Christian, Jewish and pagan, are mentioned in the same section,

so it is possible that Ibn al-ʿAṭṭār is simply referring to a common perception of adultery among non-Muslims under the umbrella of Christianity.

54. According to the Maliki school, females remained in the custody of their mother until marriage, male children until they reached the age of majority. On the right of custody, see Chapter 5; Y. Linant de Bellefonds, art. "Ḥaḍāna," in *EI*[2]; *Qawānīn*, 169–70; and *Traité*, vol. 3, 150ff.
55. *Qawānīn*, 150.
56. *Kitāb al-Wathā'iq*, 416.
57. In the Andalusian Maliki school, the best synthesis of the issue of the converted woman as a newcomer to the community can be found in *Qawānīn*, 150–52. On the conditions required for fulfilling the role of marriage agent, see *Abrégé*, vol. 2, 17ff. For a comparison of the *walī* requirement among the different schools, see *Traité*, vol. 2, 48ff. In the law books, the reason given for requiring a *walī* was the intellectual and moral weakness of the woman.
58. See Ibn Mughīth on this issue, in *Muqniʿ*, 345–46. Marriage to recent converts or to their sons was a legal issue of some relevance for the Hanafi school, where a debate raged on the fate of converts and their deficiency as potential marriage partners. In Islamic law, and particularly among the Hanafis, a woman can only marry someone of an equal or higher status, making a man of lower status ineligible. Initially, dissimilarity of religion, in terms of social standing, was a cause for the annulment of a marriage in the case of recent conversion and marriage to Arabs. Thus the condition is unique to non-Arabs. Those who recently converted to Islam could not marry a wife whose parents had been Muslims for many generations unless the union was approved by her *walī*. The question debated by the Hanafi school was how many generations removed a conversion had to be before such a man was fit to marry a longstanding Muslim woman. According to Abū Yūsuf, it was sufficient for the father of the man to be a Muslim, but the general opinion was that the grandfather had to be a Muslim; see *Traité*, vol. 2, 175.
59. This is the minimum payment for a *ṣadāq*; see Ibn Abī Zayd al-Qayrawānī, *La Risāla*, trans. Bercher, 172–73.
60. *Kitāb al-Wathā'iq*, 411–12.
61. *Muqniʿ*, 345.
62. Saḥnūn, *al-Mudawwana*, vol. 2, 232.
63. Ibid., 297.
64. *Qawānīn*, 152–53.
65. *Abrégé*, vol. 2, 36–7.
66. *Kitāb al-Wathā'iq*, 410.
67. *Traité*, vol. 2, 307–11.
68. *Kitāb al-Wathā'iq*, 412.
69. Ibid., 416.
70. Ibid., 412. It is not clear, however, how feasible it would have been for a qadi to enforce these provisions in the case of a non-Muslim male.
71. Ibid., 412; *Traité*, vol. 3, 164–65.
72. Died Tlemcen, A.H. 842/A.D. 1438–39.

73. *Miʿyār*, vol. 3, 86.
74. Ibid., vol. 3, 87–8.
75. Ibid., vol. 3, 88.
76. For instance, Ibn Ḥabīb, *Kitāb al-Ghāya.*
77. I have not encountered fatwas from earlier centuries mentioning such marriages.
78. Marjo Buitelaar, "Between Oral Tradition and Literacy: Women's Use of the Holy Scriptures in Morocco," *The Arabist* 9 (Budapest: Budapest Studies in Arabic, 1994): 225–39.
79. For a critical evaluation of the methodology and numerical estimates of converts in Bulliet, *Conversion to Islam*, see Morony, "The Age of Conversions."
80. Moshe Perlmann, "The Medieval Polemics between Islam and Judaism," in *Religion in a Religious Age*, ed. Shlomo Dov Goitein (Cambridge, MA: Association for Jewish Studies, 1973), 103–38. An illustration of the male's conversion discourse is provided by a twelfth-century Maghribi Jewish convert to Islam. See *Samaw'al al-Maghribī's (d. 570/1175) Ifḥām al-yahūd. The Early Recension*, ed. I. Marazka, R. Pourjavady, and S. Schmidtke (Wiesbaden: Harrassowitz, 2006). See also Gervers and Bikhazi, eds., *Conversion and Continuity*, 15–103; and, for a sociologist's view on conversion, Lewis R. Rambo, *Understanding Religious Conversion* (New Haven: Yale University Press, 1993).
81. Omission of the feminine perspective altogether from the historiography of conversion is demonstrated by the lack of interest in the subject among the participants at the conference on conversion and converts to Islam held in Toronto in 1986; see Gervers and Bikhazi, eds., *Conversion and Continuity.* In recent years, women's conversion has been studied as a spiritual experience within their own faith, not in terms of conversion to another faith, and mostly with reference to its literary treatment; see Virginia L. Brereton, *From Sin to Salvation: Stories of Women's Conversions, 1800 to the Present* (Bloomington: Indiana University Press, 1991).
82. The following examples are taken from Goitein, *A Mediterranean Society*, vol. 2, 299–303.
83. Ibid., vol. 3, 135–36.
84. Maya Shatzmiller, "Les Juifs de Tlemcen au XIVᵉ siècle," *Revue des Etudes Juives* 137 (1978): 171–77; Shatzmiller, *The Berbers and the Islamic State*, 55–69.
85. Cyril Jalabert, "Les Conversions à l'Islam chez Michel le Syrien," paper presented at the annual meeting of the French Association of Islamic Studies, Perpignan, 7 July 1995, 7.
86. Ibid., 8.
87. Little, "Coptic Converts to Islam," 273–74.
88. Chalmeta, "Le Passage à l'Islam," 177.
89. Molly Green, *A Shared World: Christians and Muslims in the Early Modern Mediterranean* (Princeton: Princeton University Press, 2000), 93–4.
90. Ibid., 146–56.
91. Ibid., 147, 155.
92. Susan Carol Rogers, "Woman's Place: A Critical Review of Anthropological Theory," *Comparative Studies in Society and History* 20 (1978): 124.

93. Morony, "Landholding in Seventh-Century Iraq."
94. Mordechai Akiva Friedman, "The Ethics of Medieval Jewish Marriage," in *Religion in a Religious Age*, ed. Goitein, 83–102.
95. David Nirenberg, "Conversion, Sex, and Segregation: Jews and Christians in Medieval Spain," *The American Historical Review* 107 (2002): 1065–93.
96. David Nirenberg, "Mass Conversion and Genealogical Mentalities: Jews and Christians in Fifteenth-Century Spain," *Past and Present* 174 (2002): 15–16, 18–19.
97. Shlomo Dov Goitein, "The Status of Women According to the Cairo Geniza Documents" (in Hebrew), in *The 4th World Congress of Jewish Studies*, 2 vols. (Jerusalem: Ha-Igud ha-'Olami le-Mada'e ha-Yahadut, 1968), vol. 2, 177–79, English summary, 192.

Chapter Seven. *Labour and Wages*

1. Where the Qur'an does not provide completely clear text (*naṣṣ*), it is subject to considerable interpretation by Muslim jurists. For a Western scholar's view on the difficulty of consulting the Qur'an for actual judicial decisions, see *Traité*, vol. 3, 144. For a general view of Islamic law, see Schacht, *An Introduction*, esp. 126–27 on the legal position of women, 134–43 on property, and 161–69 on the family.
2. Wage labour has been portrayed both as providing sufficient economic independence for the liberation of women and as the great villain that deprived women of power and status within the family and in society in general; see Louise A. Tilly, "Industrialization and Gender Inequality," in *Islamic and European Expansion: The Forging of a Global Order*, ed. Michael Adas (Philadelphia: Temple University Press, 1993), 243–310.
3. In previous publications, I have dealt in great detail with the historical records of women's labour, with women's occupations, and with the role women played in the labour force from the eighth to fifteenth century; see Maya Shatzmiller, "Aspects of Women's Participation in the Economic Life of Later Medieval Islam: Occupations and Mentalities," *Arabica* 35 (1988): 36–58; and Shatzmiller, *Labour*, 347–69.
4. M. Talbi, "Law and Economy in Ifriqiya (Tunisia) in the Third Islamic Century: Agriculture and the Role of Slaves in the Country's Economy," in *The Islamic Middle East: Studies in Economic and Social History*, ed. A.L. Udovitch (Princeton: Darwin Press, 1981), 209–49.
5. See Adolf Grohmann, ed., *Arabic Papyri in the Egyptian Library*, 6 vols. (Cairo: Cairo Egyptian Library Press, 1934–74), vol. 2 (legal texts), 27–35 (land leases), 101–6 (hire of journeymen).
6. Alexandre Popovic, *La révolte des esclaves en Iraq au IIIᵉ/IXᵉ siècle* (Paris: P. Geuthner, 1976) (Engl. transl. *The Revolt of African Slaves in Iraq in the 3rd/9th Century*, Princeton: Markus Wiener, 1999); Ghada Talhami, "The Zanj Rebellion Reconsidered," *The International Journal of African Historical Studies* 10 (1977): 443–61.
7. On the Islamic agricultural revolution, see Andrew M. Watson, *Agricultural Innovation in the Early Islamic World: The Diffusion of Crops and Farming Techniques, 700–1100*

(Cambridge: Cambridge University Press, 1983). For a description of the duties of a slave girl in an Egyptian village, see Grohmann, *From the World of Arabic Papyri*, 172, 176.

8. See Shatzmiller, *Labour*, 118–24 on the different occupations and trades in the textile industry, 215 on the percentage of women in the manufacturing sector and their occupations, and 240–49 on organization of the industry.
9. Lutfi, *Al-Quds al-Mamlūkiyya*, 297–300. Eighty-four women, or 31 per cent of the women sampled in the Jerusalem study, were engaged in manufacturing for their private needs. However, we cannot be sure that all were engaged in wage earning.
10. Rapoport, *Marriage, Money and Divorce*, 32, 36.
11. The debate on female labour in premodern and modern Europe has not examined it as an issue of property rights, even though the subject is clearly related to the question of a society's economic performance, probably because historians there have been preoccupied mostly with the role of female labour within the family.
12. *Qawānīn*, 207–10; E. Tyan, art. "Id̲j̲āra," in *EI*^{2}; David Santillana, *Istituzioni di diritto musulmano malichita con riguardo anche al sistema sciafiita*, 2 vols. (Rome: Instituto per l'oriente, 1925–38), vol. 2, 254–75; Schacht, *An Introduction*, 154–55; Abū 'l-Walīd Muḥammad al-Qurṭubī Ibn Rushd, *al-Muqaddamāt*, 2 vols. (Beirut: Dār al-Gharb al-Islāmī, 1988), vol. 2, 123–82.
13. Schacht, *An Introduction*, 21–2. His speculation that these models were acquired in Iraq was later challenged by Patricia Crone, *Roman, Provincial and Islamic Law: The Origins of the Islamic Patronate* (Cambridge: Cambridge University Press, 1987), chap. 1.
14. *Muqniʿ*, 190–92.
15. *Qawānīn*, 207: *al-qism al-thānī fī'l ʿuqūd al-mushākila li'l-buyūʿ*.
16. For a detailed discussion of the obligation of family members to provide for women and the lack of obligation on the part of women to earn a livelihood, see *Traité*, vol. 3, 127–29. On the debate among Muslims, theologians, and historians on the duty of men to engage in active life and earn a living, see Shatzmiller, *Labour*, 369–98.
17. On the legal and historical sources for the history of labour, see Shatzmiller, *Labour*, 69–98. For hiring contracts from early Islamic Egypt, see Grohmann, ed., *Arabic Papyri*, vol. 2, 101–6.
18. *Kitāb al-Wathā'iq*, 457–83, limited hiring contracts, but see *Muqniʿ*, 189–226, on hiring a teacher, mason, well-digger, shepherd, artisan, shoemaker, tanner, mosque attendant, plougher, and an orphan for apprenticeship training.
19. *Muqniʿ*, 206–8: *Wathīqat istiʾjār imraʾtan li-khidmat al-bayt.*
20. *Maqṣad*, 246–7.
21. On Ibn Khaldūn and his contribution to the history and historiography of the medieval Islamic West, see Maya Shatzmiller, *L'Historiographie mérinide: Ibn Khaldun et ses contemporains* (Leiden: E.J. Brill, 1982); and Shatzmiller, *The Berbers and the Islamic State*, 5–39.
22. *Miʿyār*, vol. 3, 278–79.
23. Normally, the *Miʿyār* allows us to establish a fatwa's time and place by naming the

jurist; however, the author's identity is sometimes concealed because of the editing process to which the fatwas were submitted. On this process, see Zomeño Rodriguez, *Dote y matrimonio*, 46–53. On the important Cordovan legal school, see Viguera Molins, "Los jueces de Cordoba," 123–45, which thoroughly investigates individual scholars; and María J. Viguera Molins, "La 'historia de alfaquies y jueces' de Aḥmad b. 'Abd al-Barr," *Revista del Instituto Egipcio de Estudios Islámicos en Madrid* 23 (1985–86): 49–61.

24. *Miʿyār*, vol. 8, 285.
25. On the rights and obligations of the parents of a child wet nursed by another woman, see Giladi, *Infants, Parents and Wet Nurses*, 90–114. On contemporary wet nursing practices in Europe, see the case of fourteenth-century Florence in Christiane Klapisch-Zuber, *Women, Family and Ritual in Renaissance Italy* (Chicago and London: University of Chicago Press, 1985), 143ff.
26. *Abregé*, vol. 3, 129–30. See also *Traité*, vol. 3, 29.
27. Jeanette Wakin makes the point that the contract formulas drafted by al-Ṭaḥāwī were drawn up in a way that would make the contract valid in all regions and accepted by all schools in order to avoid the dreaded *ikhtilāf* (diversity of opinion) among legal scholars on details of positive law. Al-Ṭaḥāwī's approach is actually a significant indicator of local influences on legal practice. See Wakin, *The Function of Documents*, 32.
28. *Maqṣad*, 246–47: *ʿaqd ijārat ẓiʾr*.
29. Abū Jaʿfar Aḥmad b. Muḥammad al-Ṭaḥāwī, *al-Shurūṭ al-ṣaghīr*, ed. Rawḥī Ūzjān, 2 vols. (Baghdad: Riʾāsat Dīwān al-Awqāf, 1974), vol. 1, 453.
30. Keith R. Bradley, "Sexual Regulations in Wet-Nursing Contracts from Roman Egypt," *Klio* 62 (1980): 321–25. On Egypt in the Roman period, see Allan C. Johnson, *Roman Egypt to the Reign of Diocletian* (Baltimore: Johns Hopkins University Press, 1936), 286–90. On wage labour in pre-Islamic Mesopotamia with regard to the Jewish practice, see Meir Ayali, *Poalim ve-umanim: Melachtam u-ma'amadam be-sifrut hazal* (Givatayim: Masada, 1987), 43–61.
31. *Abregé*, vol. 3, 130.
32. As observed earlier, Muslim jurists followed Roman law in recognizing spouse's rights respecting each other's body; see Chapter 5.
33. Quoted in Giladi, *Infants, Parents and Wet Nurses*, 99–100. See George Makdisi, art. "Ibn Ḳudāma," in *EI*².
34. *Miʿyār*, vol. 8, 259. On these jurists, see J. Schacht, art. "Ibn al-Ḳāsim," and H.R. Idris, art. "al-Ḳābisī," both in *EI*².
35. *Abregé*, vol. 3, 129–30.
36. *Miʿyār*, vol. 1, 422.
37. Goitein, *A Mediterranean Society*, vol. 1, 128.
38. *Miʿyār*, vol. 5, 188.
39. *Kitāb al-Wathāʾiq*, 55.
40. Ibid., 56. The same principle applied to a slave who was a trader (*tājir*), who could be exchanged for two non-trading slaves.
41. R. Brunschvig, art. "ʿAbd," in *EI*², 28.

42. Ibid., 29.
43. *Qawānīn*, 219.
44. Brunschvig, art. "ʿAbd," in *EI*[2], 28: "Nevertheless the Mālikīs take up the remarkable position [. . .] of recognizing the slave's "ownership" (*milk*) of his *peculium*, whose source is mainly from gifts or bequests which it is permissible for him to accept on his own account, although the ownership here is precarious and may not be disposed of without consent."
45. Ibn al-Ukhuwwa, *Maʿālim al-qurba fī aḥkām al-ḥisba*, ed. R. Levy, E.J.W. Gibb Memorial Series, new series, vol. 12 (London: Luzac, 1938), 153, tr. 50. For hiring contracts for female dancers and musicians from Roman Egypt, see Johnson, *Roman Egypt*, 299, 307.
46. On musicians and musical training, see Shatzmiller, *Labour*, 281–84.
47. Ibid., 283.
48. The fatwa does not specify whether the woman was a breeder of silk worms, a spinner of silk thread, or a silk weaver. However, since spinning was the most common occupation, it would be reasonable to assume that the woman in question was a spinner. On the Granadan jurist al-Saraqusṭī, see Seco de Lucena Paredes, "La escuela," 14.
49. *Miʿyār*, vol. 5, 237–38. A similar case was submitted to al-Saraqusṭī's master, Ibn Sirāj, in which the *qāʾid* imposed an exorbitant tax (*maghram*) on a man who had been denounced to him by another worker. See López Ortiz, "Fatwas Granadinas," 96–7; on the Granadan fatwas dealing with labour contracts for breeding silk worms, 113–19. On Ibn Sirāj, see Seco de Lucena Paredes, "La escuela," 12.
50. M. El-Fatih Hamid, "Duress and Its Effect on Contracts in Islamic Law," *The Sudan Law Journal* (Faculty of Law, University of Khartoum, 1971): 334–44.
51. Ibid., 338.
52. Ibid., 340–41.
53. See Shatzmiller, *Labour*, 240–49 on the textile industry, and 347–68 on women's labour in the textile and other industries.
54. Ibn al-Bannāʾ, *Le Calendrier d'Ibn al-Bannâ de Marrakech*, ed. and trans. H.P.J. Renaud (Paris: Larose, 1948), 34; H.H. ʿAbd al-Wahhāb and F. al-Dashrawī, eds., *Aḥkām al-sūq li-Yaḥyā b. ʿUmar* (Tunis: al-Sharika al-Tūnisiyya li 'l Tawzīʿ, 1975), 124.
55. Goitein, *A Mediterranean Society*, vol. 1, 129, 169.
56. On the organization of textile production put in place and operated by Egyptian traders as early as the ninth century, see the papyri from al-Fayyum published and analyzed by Rāġib, *Marchands d'étoffes*.
57. Goitein, *A Mediterranean Society*, vol. 1, 161.
58. Lutfi, *Al-Quds al-Mamlūkiyya*, 298, and Appendix B, 345–47. Estate inventories from mid-fourteenth-century Mamluk Jerusalem confirm the extent to which female textile workers were confined to the home and can in all likelihood be considered valid for the entire Islamic medieval period.
59. Goitein, *A Mediterranean Society*, vol. 2, 67. By working at home, women and men could theoretically hide their work. However, because of the output system, it would have been difficult to deprive the tax farmer (*ḍāmin*) of his rightful income. The

tax farmer contracted out the work of silk spinning and weaving to women and collected the tax from the sale of their products, which he had previously advanced to the government.

60. On Granada's silk industry, see Arié, *L'Espagne musulmane*, 217–18, 218 n. 2, 221–22. The tax on the silk industry continued to be collected by the Catholic kings after the conquest; see Arié, *L'Espagne musulmane*, 355–56. On silk-labour contracts from Spain, see J. Madurell y Marimon, "El arte de la seda en Barcelona entre Judios y conversos," *Sefarad* (1965): 247–81.
61. Shatzmiller, *The Berbers and the Islamic State*, 128–32.
62. Constable, *Trade and Traders in Muslim Spain*, 173–77, 223–27.
63. Ibid., 338.
64. On this tort court, see J.S. Nielsen, *Secular Justice in an Islamic State: Maẓālim under the Baḥrī Mamlūks, 662/1264–789/1387* (Istanbul: Nederlands Historisch-Archaeologisch Instituut, 1985).
65. The details of the work of the *maẓālim* court in the Islamic West are not fully documented. Its existence was not mentioned by the twelfth-century Sevillan market supervisor Ibn ʿAbdūn when describing the court system, and Emile Tyan, historian of the legal institutions, concluded that if this court existed in Muslim Spain during this period, it was different from that of the East; see Emile Tyan, *Histoire de l'organisation judiciaire en pays d'Islam*, 2nd ed. (Leiden: E.J. Brill, 1960), 521ff., 523: "En revenche, les litiges qui, en Orient, étaient portés naturellement devant le souverain ou tout autre titulaire de la charge des *maẓālim*, on les voit en Espagne deférés au tribunal du magistrat ordinaire." This might explain why the silk worker's complaint ended up with al-Saraqusṭī. However, Christian Müller, in his study of the magistrate in tenth-century Cordova, found ample evidence for the existence of a fully functioning *maẓālim* court there; see Müller, *Gerichtspraxis*. For the later centuries, see Arié, *L'Espagne musulmane*, 292; and Shatzmiller, *The Berbers and the Islamic State*, 77–8.
66. *Miʿyār*, vol. 5, 238–39. The two fatwas appear in the chapter on sales (*buyūʿ*) and commutative contracts (*muʿāwaḍāt*) in the *Miʿyār*, not in the hiring (*ijāra*) section.
67. *Miʿyār*, vol. 8, 344. On this mufti, whom he calls al-Ṣughayyir, see Powers, *Law, Society and Culture*, 109–10.
68. On the obligation to breastfeed or the lack thereof, see Chapter 5.
69. On liability in Islamic law, see Schacht, *An Introduction*, 147–48, where liability is described as "one of the most intricate subject-matters in Islamic law," as, indeed, the deliberations occasioned by this particular case show.
70. *Qawānīn*, 146. On this and other questions related to jurists' attitudes toward circumcision, see Chapter 5; and Alfonso Carmona González, "El marco jurídico del ejercicio de la medicina en el mundo islámico medieval," in *Actas XVI Congreso UEIA*, ed. Concepción Vázquez de Benito and Miguel Ángel Manzano Rodríguez (Salamanca: Agencia Española de cooperación internacional, 1995): 117–24.
71. Abū ʿAlī al-Ḥasan Ibn Raḥḥāl al-Maʿdānī al-Tādilī, *Kashf al-qināʿ fī taḍmīn al-ṣunnāʿ*, trans. Jacques Berque as *Taḍmīn aṣ-ṣunnāʿ. De la responsabilité civile de l'artisan* (Alger: Éditions Carbonel, 1949).

72. *Miʿyār*, vol. 8, 166. This fatwa is analysed in Hadi R. Idris, "Contribution à l'étude de la vie économique en occident musulman médiéval: Glanes de données chiffrées," in *Mélanges Roger Le Tourneau*, 2 vols. (Aix-en-Provence: Revue de l'occident musulman et de la Méditerranée, 1972), vol. 2, 84.
73. On cultivation methods in the Muslim medieval West, see Watson, *Agricultural Innovation*; Lucie Bolens, "La Révolution agricole andalouse du XIe siècle," *Studia Islamica* 47 (1978): 121–41; and Maya Shatzmiller, "Unity and Variety of Land Tenure and Cultivation Patterns in the Medieval Maghreb," *The Maghreb Review* 8 (1984): 24–8. For samples of notarial models for cultivation contracts, see *Kitāb al-Wathā'iq*, 66–90.
74. *Miʿyār*, vol. 8, 368.
75. Schacht, *An Introduction*, 159–60.
76. *Miʿyār*, vol. 8, 167.
77. *Documentos*, 99–100, document 56, tr. 106–7.
78. Nevertheless, Goitein defined the practice as a statutory law: Goitein, *A Mediterranean Society*, vol. 3, 133, 134.
79. Ibid., vol. 1, 128.
80. Ibid., vol. 3, 132.
81. See also Rapoport, *Marriage, Money and Divorce*, 37.
82. On the historiography of women's labour, see Boxer and Quataert, eds., *Connecting Spheres*, 3–17.
83. For a useful summary of women's labour in the medieval period, see Herlihy, *Opera Muliebria*.
84. Molly Fulghum Heintz, "Work: The Art and Craft of Earning a Living," in *Byzantine Women and Their World*, ed. Ioli Kalavrezou (Cambridge, MA: Harvard University Art Museums; New Haven: Yale University Press, 2003), 139–61.
85. This was the view of women espoused by the Sevillan jurist Ibn ʿAbdūn; see Shatzmiller, *Labour*, 360–61. For a detailed study of the various social stereotypes of women and textile work, see Herlihy, *Opera Muliebria*.
86. On women's labour in medieval Paris, see Diane Frappier-Bigras, "L'Artisanat parisien du XIIIe siècle," 2 vols. (Ph.D. diss., Université de Montréal, 1984); and Herlihy, *Opera Muliebria*, 186, based on the same documents from Paris. For women's labour organization in medieval England, see Helen M. Jewell, *Women in Medieval England* (Manchester: Manchester University Press, 1996).
87. On conditions from the fifteenth to seventeenth century in Germany and Holland, see Merry E. Weisner, *Working Women in Renaissance Germany* (New Brunswick: Rutgers University Press, 1986); and Martha C. Howell, *Women, Production and Patriarchy in Late Medieval Cities* (Chicago: University of Chicago Press, 1986).
88. Herlihy, *Opera Muliebra*, 157–60: "It is not unlikely that the great loss of 1348 opened up many occupations to women, but the gains were temporary and were quickly erased once stability was restored."
89. Judith C. Brown and J. Goodman, "Women and Industry in Florence," *Journal of Economic History* 40 (1980): 73–80.
90. Kelly, "Did Women Have a Renaissance?," 19–50.

91. Edward Shorter, *The Making of the Modern Family* (New York: Basic Books, 1975), 260–61, emphasis added.
92. Louise A. Tilly and Joan W. Scott, *Women, Work and Family* (New York and London: Holt, Rinehart, and Winston, 1978), 2.
93. Lawrence Stone, "Family History in the 1980s: Past Achievements and Future Trends," in *The New History: The 1980s and Beyond. Studies in Interdisciplinary History*, ed. T. Rabb and R. Rotberg (Princeton: Princeton University Press, 1982), 65–6.
94. Masters, *The Origins of Western Economic Dominance*, 176–77.
95. James A. Reilly, "Women in the Economic Life of Late-Ottoman Damascus," *Arabica* 42 (1995): 92–6.
96. See the detailed analysis in Tucker, *Women in Nineteenth-Century Egypt*. See also Margaret L. Meriwether, "Women and Economic Change in Nineteenth-Century Syria. The Case of Aleppo," in *Arab Women. Old Boundaries, New Frontiers*, ed. Judith E. Tucker (Bloomington and Indianapolis: University of Indiana Press, 1993), 65–83.
97. Judith E. Tucker, "Gender and Islamic History," in *Islamic and European Expansion: The Forging of a Global Order*, ed. M. Adas (Philadelphia: Temple University Press, 1993), 58, 62–5.
98. White, "Legal Reform As an Indicator of Women's Status," 52–68.
99. See Tilly and Scott, "Industrialization and Gender Inequality," 243–310.
100. For detailed information on prices and wages, see Eliyahu Ashtor, *Histoire des prix et des salaires dans l'Orient medieval* (Paris: SEVPEN, 1969).

Chapter Eight. *Sales and Loans*

1. *Documentos*, 52–5, documents 26a–e, tr. 54–7.
2. The twenty-one documents are in ibid., 22, document 9, tr. 23; 24–6, document 12, tr. 40–4; 39–43, document 19, tr. 40–4, document 20, tr. 45–6; 46–7, document 22, tr. 47–9; 48–9, document 23, tr. 49–50; 52–5, document 26, tr. 54–7; 71–4, document 39, tr. 75–7; 81–3, document 44, tr. 86–9; 86–90, document 47, tr. 91–5; 99–100, document 56, 106–7; 102, document 62, tr. 115; 107, document 63, tr. 116; 113–14, document 66, tr. 122–23; 116, document 69, tr. 124–25; 120–21, document 73, tr. 127k–28; 127–28, document 79, tr. 131–32; 128–29, document 80, tr. 132–34; 132, document 82, tr. 136; 141, document 91, tr. 143; and 147, document 95, tr. 149.
3. Luis Seco de Lucena Paredes, "Documentos árabes Granadinos I: Documentos del Colegio de Niñas Nobles," *Al-Andalus* 8 (1943): 415–29; and "Documentos árabes Granadinos II: Documentos de las Comendadoras de Santiago," *Al-Andalus* 9 (1944): 121–40.
4. *Qawānīn*, 185–206. Pedro Cano Ávila, "Contratos de compraventa en el reino Nazarí de Granada, según el tratado notarial de Ibn Salmūn," *Al-Qantara* 9 (1988): 323–51.

5. *Qawānīn*, 186.
6. *Maqṣad*, 146.
7. Ibid., 148.
8. The fatwas collected in the volume on sales in al-Wansharīsī's *Miʿyār* contain numerous cases showing women involved in sales transactions; see *Miʿyār*, vol. 5, *Nawāzil al-muʿāwaḍāt wa 'l-buyūʿ*. Indeed, as a result of the practice of naming the gender when a woman was involved, the fatwas in this volume could help in a detailed study of women's sales.
9. Seco de Lucena Paredes, "Documentos árabes Granadinos II, where "Fajjārīn."
10. *Documentos*, 25–6, document 12b, tr. 25–7.
11. Ibid., 39–45, documents 19a–g, 20, tr. 40–6.
12. Ibid., 39–40, document 19c, tr. 41–2. See Chapter 3 for the earlier reference to Fāṭima's case.
13. Ibid., 41, documents 19b–c, tr. 41–2.
14. Ibid., 44–5, document 20, tr. 45–6.
15. Ibid., 42–3, document 19f, tr. 43–4.
16. Ibid., 43, document 19g, tr. 44.
17. Seco de Lucena Paredes, "Documentos árabes Granadinos I."
18. *Documentos*, 71–2, document 39a, tr. 75–6.
19. Ibid., 72–3, documents 39b–c, tr. 76–7. With regard to the 66 silver dinars for the debt of 28 (gold) dinars, the documents only say about the gold dinar that it was from the current mint; there is nothing about the value of the silver dinar. Since this payment took care of the debt, it must have been the equivalent.
20. Ibid., 73, document 39d, tr. 77.
21. Ibid., 82–3, document 44b, tr. 87–8.
22. Ibid., 84, document 44c, tr. 88.
23. Ibid., 84, document 44d, tr. 89.
24. Ibid., 89–90, document 47b, tr. 95.
25. Ibid., 90–1, document 48, tr. 96. The Ḥakīm family was originally from Baza and frequently appeared in court since they had migrated to Granada; see Chapter 2.
26. Ibid., 99, document 56a, tr. 106–7.
27. Ibid., 113–14, document 66, tr. 122–23.
28. Ibid., 116, document 69, tr, 124–25.
29. Ibid., 120, document 73b, tr. 127. The land sales made from this property are also known from Castilian documents, which identified Fāṭima's father as a spy in service of the Catholic king and their collaborator in Granada. See Luis Seco de Lucena Paredes, "El musulman Aḥmad Ulaylaš, espia de los reyes catolicos en la corte Granadina," *Miscelánea de Estudios Árabes y Hebraícos* 9 (1960): 157–60.
30. *Documentos*, 127, document 79, tr. 131–32.
31. Ibid., 121, document 73e, tr. 127–28.
32. Ibid., 128–29, documents 80a–b, tr. 132–34.
33. Ibid., 131, document 81, tr. 133–34.
34. Ibid., 135, document 85, tr. 138.

35. Ibid., 132, document 82, tr. 136.
36. Seco de Lucena Paredes, "Documentos árabes Granadinos I," 425.
37. *Documentos*, 131, document 91, tr. 143.
38. Ibid., 147, document 95, tr. 149.
39. The entire evidence displayed earlier, namely, the inheritance shares and the large number of women in the entire collection—about 90 percent of the documents deal with women as compared to the usual numbers of 25 to 30 percent in Ottoman archival studies—point to Granada being a unique case.
40. On the Sicilian documents, see Johns, *Arabic Administration in Norman Sicily*.
41. See Alex Metcalfe, *Muslims and Christians in Norman Sicily: Arabic Speakers and the End of Islam* (London and New York: Routledge, Curzon, 2003).
42. Cusa, *I diplomi greci ed arabi di Sicilia*. The documents in question have solicited great interest among historians; see Olivia R. Constable, "Cross-Cultural Contracts: Sales of Land between Christians and Muslims in 12th-Century Palermo," *Studia Islamica* 85 (1997): 67–84; and Johns, *Arabic Administration in Norman Sicily*, 204.
43. The transcription ʿĀ'ika appears thus in Cusa's edition.
44. Cusa, *I diplomi greci ed arabi di Sicilia*, 610–13; Constable, "Cross-Cultural Contracts," 70–1.
45. Cusa, *I diplomi greci ed arabi di Sicilia*, 61–7; Constable, "Cross-Cultural Contracts," 71.
46. The sale documents follow the Islamic notarial protocol of Egypt rather than of the Islamic West. On the notarial style of the Sicilian documents, see Antonio D'Emilia, "Diplomi arabi sicilliani di comprevendita del secolo VI Egira e loro raffronto con documenti egiziani dei secoli III–V Egira," *Annali Instituto Universitario Orientale de Napoli* 14 (1964): 83–109.
47. Cusa, *I diplomi greci ed arabi di Sicilia*, 101–6; Constable, "Cross-Cultural Contracts," 71–2.
48. Cusa, *I diplomi greci ed arabi di Sicilia*, 44–6; Constable, "Cross-Cultural Contracts," 72–3.
49. *Documentos*, 107, document 63, tr. 116.
50. On the law of conquest as a legal argument for refusing to surrender land to the church or the king, who was Frederic II in this case, see Jean d'Ibelin, quoted in Jonathan Riley-Smith, *The Feudal Nobility and the Kingdom of Jerusalem, 1174–1277* (Hamden, Conn.: Archon Books, 1973), 138.
51. On Mamluk wives and property, see Petry, "A Paradox of Patronage," 182–207; Petry, "Class Solidarity Versus Gender Gain," 122–42; and Sylvie Denoix, "Pour une exploitation d'ensemble d'un corpus des waqfs mamelouks du Caire," in *Le Waqf dans l'espace islamique, outil de pouvoir socio-politique*, ed. Randi Deguilhem (Damascus: Institut français de Damas, 1995), 29–44.
52. Leslie P. Peirce, *The Imperial Harem: Women and Sovereignty in the Ottoman Empire* (Oxford and New York: Oxford University Press, 1993), 213.
53. Denoix, "Pour une exploitation d'ensemble," 35–6. On the status of pre-Islamic Turkish women, see Jennings, "Women in Early 17th-Century Ottoman Judicial Records," 99–101, 113; and Peter Jackson, "Sulṭān Raḍiyya Bint Iltutmish," in

Women in the Medieval Islamic World, ed. Gavin R.G. Hambly (New York: St. Martin's, 1998), 181–99.

54. Birge, *Women, Property and Confucian Reaction.*
55. The frequent appearance of women in transactions in which they were not the primary actors is noted in Jennings, "Women in Early 17th-Century Ottoman Judicial Records," 99.
56. Fay, "Women and Waqf," 35–7. Fay's text incorporates evidence culled by André Raymond, *Artisans et commercants au Caire*, 2 vols. (Damascus: Institut français d'archéologie orientale, Damas, 1974). For statistics on *waqf*-making by women, see Fay, "Women and Waqf," 36–7.
57. Reilly, "Women in the Economic Life," 81–2.
58. Ibid., 83, 86, and compare to cases from Granada discussed in Chapters 3 and 4.
59. Ibid., 81.
60. Ibid., 84.
61. Masters, *The Origins of Western Economic Dominance*, 175–81; Establet and Pascual, "Women in Damascene Families," 319.
62. For cases of women who represented themselves in court, see Reilly, "Women in the Economic Life," 83–6.
63. Jennings, "Women in Early 17th-Century Ottoman Judicial Records," 99–101.
64. Reilly, "Women in the Economic Life," 81; Masters, *The Origins of Western Economic Dominance*, 179–80.
65. *Documentos*, 22, document 9, tr. 23.
66. Ibid., 106, document 62, tr. 115.
67. Ibid., 46–7, document 22, tr. 47–9.
68. Ibid., 48, document 23, tr. 49–50.
69. Ibid., 20–2, document 8, tr. 20–3.
70. Ibid., 101–3, document 58, tr. 108–10.
71. Little, "Documents Related to the Estates of a Merchant and His Wife," 111–12. The Ḥaram documents also show that a small amount of money was loaned to a peasant near Jerusalem in the fourteenth century, a transaction that appears in the estate division of Fāṭima, a baker's wife. These loans involved a somewhat wider credit operation: two villagers owed her 30 dirhams each, another owed her 350 dirhams, a bean maker owed her 500 dirhams, and her husband owed her 1,000 dirhams as his second instalment of her *ṣadāq*. See Lutfi, *Al-Quds al-Mamlūkiyya*, 319; also Rapoport, *Marriage, Money and Divorce*, 25.
72. Goitein, "The Status of Women According to the Geniza Letters," vol. 2, 177–79; Goitein, *A Mediterranean Society*, vol. 3, 346–52.
73. See Goitein, *A Mediterranean Society*, vol. 1, 160.
74. Ronald C. Jennings, "Loans and Credit in Early 17th Century Ottoman Judicial Records: The Sharia Court of Anatolian Kayseri," *Journal of the Economic and Social History of the Orient* 16 (1973): 194–97.
75. Masters, *The Origins of Western Economic Dominance*, 179–80.
76. Ibid., 180, and Table 11 at 168. On the delayed dower as a credit transaction, see Chapter 1.

77. On the Granadan markets, see Arié's study of fatwas (dealing with the sale of spices and dyes while mixing good and bad ingredients, with raising pigs, with the private domain of the sultan [*mustakhlaṣ*], with division of rights to irrigation water, and so forth), in Rachel Arié, "Considérations sur la vie économique dans l'Espagne musulmane au cours de bas Moyen Age," in idem, *Etudes sur la civilisation de l'Espagne musulmane* (Leiden: E.J. Brill, 1990), 68–79, and the fatwas that were used.
78. Lutfi, *Al-Quds al-Mamlūkiyya*, 290; Little, *Catalogue of Islamic Documents*, 132.
79. Lutfi, *Al-Quds al-Mamlūkiyya*, 290; Little, *Catalogue of Islamic Documents*, 178.
80. Lutfi, *Al-Quds al-Mamlūkiyya*, 290; Little, *Catalogue of Islamic Documents*, 160–61.
81. Lutfi, *Al-Quds al-Mamlūkiyya*, 290–91.
82. Ibn al-Mujāwir (A.H. 601–91/A.D. 1204–91), quoted in Hassan S. Khalilieh, *Islamic Maritime Law: An Introduction* (Leiden: Brill, 1998), 83. On the appointment of Jewish women as searchers in fourteenth-century Tlemcen, see Shatzmiller, "Les Juifs de Tlemcen," 171–77.
83. Rapoport, *Marriage, Money and Divorce*, 24–5.
84. Masters, *The Origins of Western Economic Dominance*, 181.
85. Cusa, *I diplomi greci ed arabi di Sicilia*, 502–4.
86. *Miʿyār*, vol. 9, 78. See also Hadi R. Idris, "Commerce maritime et *kirāḍ* en berbérie orientale," *Journal of the Economic and Social History of the Orient* 4 (1961): 235; Hadi R. Idris, *La Berbérie orientale sous les Zirides (X–XIIe siècles)*, 2 vols. (Paris: Adrien Maisonnueve, 1962), vol. 2, 667.
87. Goitein, *A Mediterranean Society*, vol. 3, 346–52; for a case of a woman suing her husband's partner, vol. 3, 280.
88. Moshe Gil, *In the Kingdom of Ishmael: Studies in Jewish History in Islamic Lands in the Early Middle Ages*, 4 vols. (Tel-Aviv: Tel-Aviv University Press, 1997), vol. 1, 547.
89. Li Guo, *Commerce, Culture and Community in a Red Sea Port in the Thirteenth Century. The Arabic Documents from Quseir* (Leiden: Brill, 2004), 8–9.
90. Ibid., 18, 26.
91. William C. Jordan, *Women and Credit in Pre-Industrial and Developing Societies* (Philadelphia: University of Pennsylvania Press, 1993).
92. Ibid., 60; on the role of widows, 67–9.
93. Ibid., 59.
94. Ibid., 60. At the same time, we must acknowledge the importance of specific historical events in facilitating women's involvement in trade investments—for example, "the uniquely empowering situation of war for wealthy women" (56), which is not unfamiliar to us from the Granadan context (see 56–60).
95. Constable, *Trade and Traders in Muslim Spain*, 103–4.
96. Even the more liberal Ibn Juzayy prescribed against males being in the position to view unrelated females; see *Qawānīn*, 341–42.
97. Avram L. Udovitch, "Reflections on the Institutions of Credit and Banking in the Medieval Islamic Near East," *Studia Islamica* 31 (1975): 5–23, based on the Hebrew Geniza documents and the Islamic legal manuals.
98. On a Byzantine Homiletic treatise from Egypt advising women to avoid interaction with men in the public sphere, see Heintz, "Work: The Art and Craft of Earning a Living," 145–46. On the ancient Greek view of women, see Chapter 5.

99. Reilly, "Women in the Economic Life," 99.
100. Avram L. Udovitch, "Islamic Law and the Social Context of Exchange in the Medieval Middle East," *History and Anthropology* 1 (1985): 445–65.
101. Reilly, "Women in the Economic Life," 99, and Chapter 7 above.
102. Reilly, "Women in the Economic Life," 106.
103. Udovitch, "Islamic Law and the Social Context of Exchange."

BIBLIOGRAPHY

Encyclopedia Judaica. 16 vols. Jerusalem: Encyclopedia Judaica, 1972.
Dowry (Heb. *nedunya*), vol. 6, 185–89.
The Encyclopaedia of Islam. New Edition. 12 vols. Leiden: Brill, 1950–2004.
ʿAbd (R. Brunschvig)
ʿAḳīda (W. Montgomery Watt)
Ḥaḍāna (Y. Linant de Bellefonds)
Ḥadjr (J. Schacht)
Ibn Abī Zayd al-Ḳayrawānī (H.R. Idris)
al-Ḳābisī (H.R. Idris)
Ibn al-Ḳāsim (J. Schacht)
Ibn Ḳudāma (G. Makdisi)
Idjāra (E. Tyan)
Mahr (O. Spies)
Mālik b. Anas (J. Schacht)
Mālikiyya (N. Cottart)
Marʾa (N. Tomiche)
al-Muwaḥḥidūn (M. Shatzmiller)
Nikāḥ (J. Schacht)
Ṣaghīr (A. Giladi)
Waḳf (multi-author)
Yatīm (E. Chaumont)

ʿAbd al-Wahhāb, H.H., and F. al-Dashrawī, eds. *Aḥkām al-sūq li-Yaḥyā b. ʿUmar* (Tunis: al-Sharika al-Tūnisiyya liʾl Tawzīʿ, 1975.

Abumalham, Monserrat. "La conversíon según formularios notariales andalusíes: Valoracíon de la legalidad de la conversíon de Maimónides." *Miscelánea de Estudios Árabes y Hebraícos* 32 (1985): 71–84.

Agmon, Iris. "Muslim Women in Court According to the Sijill of Late Ottoman Jaffa and Haifa: Some Methodological Notes." In *Women, the Family and Divorce Laws in Islamic History*, ed. Amira El Azhary Sonbol, 126–40. Syracuse: Syracuse University Press, 1996.

Aguirre Sádaba, Francisco Javier. "Granada y los estudios de derecho islámico." *Revista del Centro de Estudios Históricos de Granada y su Reino* 13–14 (1999–2000): 461–93.

———. "Notas acerca de la proyección de los 'kutub al-waṯāʾiq' en el estudio social y económico de al-Andalus." *Miscelánea de Estudios Árabes y Hebraícos. Sección árabe-islam* 49 (2000): 3–30.

Alaoui M'Daghri, M. Abdelkebir. "The Code of Children's Rights in Islam." In *Children in the Muslim Middle East*, ed. E. Fernea, 30–41. Austin: University of Texas Press, 1995.

Alvarez de Morales y Ruiz-Matas, Camilo. *Muley Hacen, el Zagal y Boabdil: Los Ultimos Reyes de Granada.* Granada: Editorial Comares, 2000.
Amar, Emile, trans. *Consultations juridiques des faqihs du Maghreb (Choix des fatwas du Mi'yar d'al-Wansharisi).* Archives Marocaines nos. 12–13. Paris: Honoré Champion, 1908–09.
An-Na'im, Abdullahi. "The Rights of Women and International Law in the Muslim Context." *Whittier Law Review* 9 (1987): 491–516.
Arab Human Development Report 2002. New York: United Nations Publications, 2002.
Arcas Campoy, María. "El testimonio de las mujeres en el derecho mālikī." In *Homenaje al Prof. Jacinto Bosch Vilá,* 2 vols., vol. 1, 473–79. Granada: Departamento de Estudios Semitícos, Universidad de Granada, 1991.
'Arīb b. Sa'd al-Qurṭubī. *Kitāb khalq al-janīn wa-tadbīr al-ḥabālā wa'l-mawlūdīn. Le Livre de la génération du foetus et le traitement des femmes enceintes et des nouveau-nés.* Ed. and annotated by Henri Jahier and Noureddine Abdelkader. Alger: Librairie Ferraris, 1956.
Arié, Rachel. "Considérations sur la vie économique dans l'Espagne musulmane au cours de bas Moyen Age." In idem, *Etudes sur la civilisation de l'Espagne musulmane,* 68–79. Leiden: E.J. Brill, 1990.
———. *L'Espagne musulmane au temps des Nasrides.* Paris: Editions de Boccard, 1973; reprint, 1990.
Ashtor, Eliyahu. *Histoire des prix et des salaires dans l'Orient medieval.* Paris: SEVPEN, 1969.
Avila, Maria Luisa. *La sociedad hispanomusulmana al final del califato.* Madrid: Consejo Superior de Investigaciones Científicas, 1985.
———. "The Structure of the Family in al-Andalus." In *The Formation of al-Andalus,* ed. Manuela Marín, 2 vols., vol. 1, 469–83. Aldershot: Ashgate, 1998.
Ayali, Meir. *Poalim ve-umanim: Melachtam uma'amadam be-sifrut hazal.* Givatayim: Masada, 1987.
Baer, Gabriel. "Women and *Waqf*: An Analysis of the Istanbul *Tahrir* of 1546." *Asian and African Studies* 17 (1983): 9–27.
Barceló, Carmen, and Ana Labarta. "Los documentos arabes del reino de Granada: Bibliografia y perspectivas." *Cuadernos de la Alhambra* 26 (1990): 113–19.
Barkai, Ron. *A History of Jewish Gynaecological Texts in the Middle Ages.* Leiden: Brill, 1998.
Barzel, Yoram. *Economic Analysis of Property Rights.* Cambridge and New York: Cambridge University Press, 1989.
Benkheira, Mohammed Hocine. "Le commerce conjugale gâte-t-il le lait maternel? Sexualité, médecine et droit dans le sunnisme ancien." *Arabica* 30 (2003): 1–78.
———. "Donner le sein, c'est comme donner le jour: La doctrine de l'allaitement dans le sunnisme médiéval." *Studia Islamica* 92 (2001): 5–52.
Berkey, Jonathan P. "Circumcision Circumscribed: Female Excision and Cultural Accommodation in the Medieval Near East." *International Journal of Middle Eastern Studies* 28 (1996): 19–38.
Birge, Bettine. *Women, Property and Confucian Reaction in Sung and Yüan China (960–1368).* Cambridge: Cambridge University Press, 2002.
Blumenfeld-Kosinki, Renate. *Not of Woman Born: Representations of Caesarean Birth in Medieval and Renaissance Culture.* Ithaca: Cornell University Press, 1990.

Bolens, Lucie. "Les Parfums et la beauté en Andalousie médiévale (XIe–XIIIe siècles)." In *Les Soins de la beauté: Actes du IIIe Colloque International, Grasse 1985*, 145–69. Nice: Centre de la Méditerranée moderne et contemporain, 1985.

———. "La Révolution agricole andalouse du XIe siècle." *Studia Islamica* 47 (1978): 121–41.

Bos, Gerrit. "Ibn al-Jazzār on Women's Diseases and Their Treatment." *Medical History* 37 (1993): 296–312.

Bousquet, G.-H. "L'Islam et la limitation volontaire des naissances." *Population* 5 (1950): 121–28.

Boxer, M.J., and J.H. Quataert, eds. *Connecting Spheres: Women in the Western World, 1500 to the Present.* New York: Oxford University Press, 1987.

Bradley, Keith R. "Sexual Regulations in Wet-Nursing Contracts from Roman Egypt." *Klio* 62 (1980): 321–25.

Brereton, Virginia L. *From Sin to Salvation: Stories of Women's Conversions, 1800 to the Present.* Bloomington: Indiana University Press, 1991.

Brettell, Caroline. "Kinship and Contract: Property Transmission and Family Relations in Northwestern Portugal." *Comparative Studies in Society and History* 33 (1991): 443–62.

Brown, Judith C., and J. Goodman. "Women and Industry in Florence." *Journal of Economic History* 40 (1980): 73–80.

Brugman, J. "The Islamic Law of Inheritance." In *Essays on Oriental Laws of Succession*, 82–91. Leiden: E.J. Brill, 1969.

Buitelaar, Marjo. "Between Oral Tradition and Literacy: Women's Use of the Holy Scriptures in Morocco." *The Arabist* 9 (Budapest: Budapest Studies in Arabic, 1994): 225–39.

Bulliet, Richard W. *Conversion to Islam in the Medieval Period: An Essay in Quantitative History.* Cambridge, MA: Harvard University Press, 1979.

Burman, Thomas E. *Religious Polemic and the Intellectual History of the Mozarabs, c. 1050–1200.* Leiden: E.J. Brill, 1994.

Cahen, Claude. "Considérations sur l'utilisation des ouvrages de droit musulman par l'historien." In *Atti del III Congresso di Studi Arabi e Islamici, Ravello, 1966*, 239–47. Naples: N.p., 1967.

Cano Ávila, Pedro. "Contratos de compraventa en el Reino Nazarí de Granada, según el tratado notarial de Ibn Salmūn." *Al-Qantara* 9 (1988): 323–51.

Cano Ledesma, Aurora, trans. "La aportación quirúrgica de Abū 'l-Qāsim al-Zahrāwī según el ms. 876 de El Escorial." *La Ciudad de Dios* 203 (1990): 89–110, 451–84.

Canto, Alberto, and Tawfiq Ibrahim. *Moneda andalusí en la Alhambra.* Granada: Scriptorium, 1997.

Carmona González, Alfonso. "El marco jurídico del ejercicio de la medicina en el mundo islámico medieval." In *Actas XVI Congreso UEIA*, ed. Concepción Vázquez de Benito and Miguel Ángel Manzano Rodríguez, 117–24. Salamanca: Agencia Española de cooperación internacional, 1995.

Chalmeta, Pedro. "Un formulaire notarial hispano-arabe du IV/Xe s. Glanes économiques." *Rev. Inst. Egipcio de Estudios Islamicos* 23 (1985–86): 181–202.

———. "El matrimonio según el Kitāb al-Wathā'iq de Ibn al-ʿAṭṭār (s. X). Análisis y observaciones." *Anaquel de Estudios Árabes* 6 (1995): 29–70.

———. "Le Passage à l'Islam dans al-Andalus au Xe siècle." In *Actas del XII Congreso de la U.E.A.I., Málaga, 1984*, 161–83. Madrid: Union Européenne des Arabisants et Islamisants, 1986.

Chehata, Chafik (Shehata, Shafik). *Etudes de droit musulman*. Paris: Presses Universitaires de France, 1971.

Constable, Olivia R. "Cross-Cultural Contracts: Sales of Land between Christians and Muslims in 12th-Century Palermo." *Studia Islamica* 85 (1997): 67–84.

———. *Trade and Traders in Muslim Spain: The Commercial Realignment of the Iberian Peninsula, 900–1500*. Cambridge: Cambridge University Press, 1994.

Coulson, Noel J. "Regulation of Sexual Behavior under Traditional Islamic Law." In *Society and the Sexes in Medieval Islam*, ed. Afaf Lutfi al-Sayyid Marsot, 63–8. Malibu: Undena, 1979.

———. *Succession in the Muslim Family*. Cambridge: Cambridge University Press, 1971.

Crone, Patricia. *Roman, Provincial and Islamic Law: The Origins of the Islamic Patronate*. Cambridge: Cambridge University Press, 1987.

Cusa, Salvatore. *I diplomi greci ed arabi di Sicilia*. Köln/Wien: Bohlau Verlag, 1982.

Dean-Jones, Lesley. "The Politics of Pleasure: Female Sexual Appetite in the Hippocratic Corpus." *Helios* 19 (1992): 72–91.

———. *Women's Bodies in Classical Greek Science*. Oxford, Clarendon, 1994.

D'Emilia, Antonio. "Diplomi arabi sicilliani di comprevendita del secolo VI Egira e loro raffronto con documenti egiziani dei secoli III–V Egira." *Annali Instituto Universitario Orientale de Napoli* 14 (1964): 83–109.

Denoix, Sylvie. "Pour une exploitation d'ensemble d'un corpus des waqfs mamelouks du Caire." In *Le Waqf dans l'espace islamique, outil de pouvoir socio-politique*, ed. Randi Deguilhem, 29–44. Damascus: Institut français de Damas, 1995.

Diem, Werner. "Vier arabische rechtsurkunden aus dem Ägypten des 14 und 15 Jahrhunderts." *Der Islam* 72 (1995): 193–258.

Dols, Michael W. *The Black Death in the Middle East*. Princeton: Princeton University Press, 1977.

———. *Majnūn: The Madman in Medieval Islamic Society*. Ed. Diana E. Immisch. Oxford: Clarendon, 1992.

Ebbell, B., trans. *The Papyrus Ebers: The Greatest Egyptian Medical Document*. London: Oxford University Press, 1937.

El Azemmouri, Thami. "Les *Nawāzil* d'Ibn Sahl: Section relative à l'*iḥtisāb*: Introduction et texte arabe." *Hespéris-Tamuda* 14 (1973): 7–107.

El-Fatih Hamid, M. "Duress and Its Effect on Contracts in Islamic Law." *The Sudan Law Journal* (Faculty of Law, University of Khartoum, 1971): 334–44.

Ennen, Edith. *The Medieval Woman*. Trans. Edmund Jephcott. Oxford: Basil Blackwell, 1989.

Establet, Colette, and Jean-Paul Pascual. "Women in Damascene Families around 1700." *Journal of the Economic and Social History of the Orient* 45 (2002): 302–19.

Ewan, Elizabeth. "Scottish Portias: Women in the Courts in Medieval Scottish Towns." *Journal of the Canadian Historical Association* n.s. 3 (1992): 27–45.

Fadel, Mohammad. "Rules, Judicial Discretion, and the Rule of Law in Nasrid Granada."

In *Islamic Law: Theory and Practice*, ed. R. Gleave and E. Kermeli, 49–87. London: I.B. Tauris, 1997.

Fagnan, Emile. *Abrégé de droit malékite et morale musulmane.* Paris: J. Carbonel, 1914.

Fay, Mary Ann. "Women and Waqf: Property, Power and the Domain of Gender in Eighteenth-Century Egypt." In *Women in the Ottoman Empire: Middle Eastern Women in the Early Modern Era*, ed. Madeline C. Zilfi, 28–47. Leiden: Brill, 1997.

Fierro, Ma. Isabel. "La mujer y el trabajo en el Corán y el hadiz." In *La mujer en al Andalus: Reflejos históricos de su actividad y catgorías sociales,* ed. M.J. Viguera Molins, 35–51. Madrid: Universidad Autónoma de Madrid; Seville: Editoriales Andaluzas Unidas, 1989.

Fleck, Robert K. and F. Andrew Hanssen. "*'Rulers Ruled by Women': An Economic Analysis of the Rise and Fall of Women's Rights in Ancient Sparta.*" http://www2.montana.edu/ahanssen/Papers/sw140.pdf

Franz-Murphy, Gladys. "A Comparison of the Arabic and Earlier Egyptian Contract Formularies. Part 1, The Arabic Contracts from Egypt, 3rd/9th–5th/11th Centuries." *Journal of Near Eastern Studies* 40 (1981): 203–25.

Frappier-Bigras, Diane. "L'Artisanat parisien du XIIIe siècle." 2 vols., PhD diss., Université de Montreal, 1984.

Friedman, Mordechai Akiva. "The Ethics of Medieval Jewish Marriage." In *Religion in a Religious Age*, ed. Shlomo Dov Goitein, 83–102. Proceedings of Regional Conferences Held at the University of California, Los Angeles, and Brandeis University, April 1973. Cambridge MA: Association for Jewish Studies, 1973.

———. *Jewish Marriage in Palestine: A Cairo Geniza Study.* 2 vols. Tel-Aviv: Tel-Aviv University Press, 1980–81.

Gerber, Haim. "Social and Economic Position of Women in an Ottoman City, Bursa, 1600–1700." *International Journal of Middle Eastern Studies* 12 (1980): 231–44.

Gervers, M., and R.J. Bikhazi, eds. *Conversion and Continuity: Indigenous Christian Communities in Islamic Lands, Eighth to Eighteenth Centuries.* Toronto: Pontifical Institute of Medieval Studies, 1990.

Gibb, Sir Hamilton. "Women and the Law." In *Actes du Colloque sur la sociologie musulmane, 11–14 septembre 1961*, 233–48. Bruxelles: Publications de Centre pour l'étude des problèmes du monde musulman contemporain, 1962.

Gil, Moshe. *In the Kingdom of Ishmael: Studies in Jewish History in Islamic Lands in the Early Middle Ages.* 4 vols. Tel-Aviv: Tel-Aviv University Press, 1997.

Giladi, Avner. *Children of Islam: Concepts of Childhood in Medieval Muslim Society.* New York: St. Martin's, 1992.

———. "Gender Differences in Child Rearing and Education: Some Preliminary Observations with Reference to Medieval Muslim Thought." *Al-Qantara* 16 (1995): 291–308.

———. *Infants, Parents and Wet Nurse: Medieval Islamic Views on Breastfeeding and Their Social Implications.* Leiden: Brill, 1999.

Glick, Thomas. *Irrigation and Hydraulic Technology: Medieval Spain and Its Legacy.* Aldershot: Variorum, 1996.

Göçek, Fatma Müge, and Marc David Baer. "Social Boundaries of Ottoman Women's

Experience in Eighteenth-Century Galata Court Records." In *Women in the Ottoman Empire. Middle Eastern Women in the Early Modern Era*, ed. Madeline C. Zilfi, 48–65. Leiden: Brill, 1997.

Goitein, Shlomo Dov. *Jews and Arabs: Their Contacts Through the Ages*. New York: Schocken Books, 1974.

———. *A Mediterranean Society: The Jewish Communities of the Arab World as Portrayed in the Documents of the Cairo Geniza*. 5 vols. Los Angeles and Berkeley: University of California Press, 1967–93.

———, ed. *Religion in a Religious Age*. Proceedings of Regional Conferences Held at the University of California, Los Angeles, and Brandeis University, April 1973. Cambridge MA: Association for Jewish Studies, 1973.

———. "The Status of Women According to the Geniza Letters." (In Hebrew). In *World Congress of Jewish Studies, 4th (1965)*, 2 vols., vol. 2, 177–79. English summary, 192. Jerusalem: Ha-Igud ha-ʿOlami le-Madaʾe ha-Yahadut, 1968.

Goody, Jack. *The European Family: An Historico-Anthropological Essay*. Oxford: Blackwell, 2000.

———. "Inheritance, Property and Women: Some Comparative Considerations." In *Family and Inheritance: Rural Society in Western Europe, 1200–1800*, ed. J. Goody, J. Thirsk, and E.P. Thompson, 10–36. Cambridge: Cambridge University Press, 1976.

———, and S.J. Tambiah. *Bridewealth and Dowry*. Cambridge: Cambridge University Press, 1973.

Granja, Fernando de la. "Condena de Boabdil por los alfaqíes de Granada." *Al-Andalus* 26 (1971): 145–76.

Green, Molly. *A Shared World: Christians and Muslims in the Early Modern Mediterranean*. Princeton: Princeton University Press, 2000.

Green, Monica H. "The Transmission of Ancient Theories of Female Physiology and Disease through the Early Middle Ages." PhD diss., Princeton University, 1985.

———, ed. and trans. *The Trotula: A Medieval Compendium of Women's Medicine*. Philadelphia: University of Pennsylvania Press, 2001.

Grohmann, Adolf. *From the World of Arabic Papyri*. Cairo: al-Maaref Press, 1952.

———, ed. *Arabic Papyri in the Egyptian Library*. 6 vols. Cairo: Cairo Egyptian Library Press, 1934–74.

Gronke, Monika. "La Rédaction des actes privés dans le monde musulman médiéval: Théorie et pratique." *Studia Islamica* 59 (1984): 159–74.

Guichard, Pierre, and Denis Menjot. "Les Emprunts aux vaincus: Les Conséquences de la 'reconquête' sur l'organisation institutionelle des États castilan et aragonais au Moyen Âge." In *État et colonization au Moyen Âge*, ed. M. Balard, 379–96. Lyon: La Manufacture, 1989.

Guo, Li. *Commerce, Culture and Community in a Red Sea Port in the Thirteenth Century. The Arabic Documents from Quseir*. Leiden: Brill, 2004.

Hallaq, Wael B. "Model *Shurūṭ* Works and the Dialectic of Doctrine and Practice." *Islamic Law and Society* 2 (1995): 109–34.

Hamarneh, Sami. "Medical Education and Practice in Medieval Islam." In *The History of Medical Education*, ed. C.D. O'Malley, 39–71. Los Angeles and Berkeley: University of California Press, 1970.

Hanson, Ann Ellis. "Conception, Gestation, and the Origin of Female Nature in the Corpus Hippocraticum," *Helios* 19 (1992): 31–71.

———. "The Medical Writer's Woman." In *Before Sexuality: The Construction of Erotic Experience in the Ancient Greek World*, ed. D. Halperin, J. Winkler, and F. Zeitlin, 309–38. Princeton: Princeton University Press, 1990.

Harvey, Leonard P. *Islamic Spain*, 1250–1500. Chicago: University of Chicago Press, 1990.

———. *Muslims in Spain, 1500–1614*. Chicago: University of Chicago Press, 2005.

Heintz, Molly Fulghum. "Work: The Art and Craft of Earning a Living." In *Byzantine Women and Their World*, ed. Ioli Kalavrezou, 139–61. Cambridge, MA: Harvard University Art Museums; New Haven: Yale University Press, 2003.

Herlihy, David. *Opera Muliebria: Women and Work in Medieval Europe*. New York: McGraw Hill, 1990.

———. *Women, Family, and Society in Medieval Europe: Historical Essays, 1978–1991*. Ed. A. Molho. Providence, RI: Berghahn Books, 1995.

Hildegard of Bingen. *On Natural Philosophy and Medicine*. Trans. Margaret Berger. Cambridge: D.S. Brewer, 1999.

Hirschberg, H.J. *Toldot ha-yehudim be-Afrika ha-tsefonit*. 2 vols. Jerusalem: Mosad Bialik, 1965 (rev. Engl. transl. *A History of the Jews in North Africa*. Leiden: E.J. Brill, 1974).

Hirschon, Renée. "Introduction: Property, Power and Gender Relations." In *Women and Property, Women as Property*, ed. Renée Hirschon, 1–23. London and New York: Croom Helm and St. Martin's, 1984.

———, ed. *Women and Property, Women as Property*. London and New York: Croom Helm and St. Martin's, 1984.

Hoenerbach, Wilhelm. *Spanisch-islamische Urkunden aus der Zeit der Naṣriden und Moriscos*. Bonn: Selbstverlag des Orientalischen Seminars der Universität Bonn, 1965.

Howell, Martha C. *Women, Production and Patriarchy in Late Medieval Cities*. Chicago: University of Chicago Press, 1986.

Hughes, Diane Owen. "From Brideprice to Dowry in Mediterranean Europe." *Journal of Family History* 3 (1978): 262–96.

Ibn Abī Zayd al-Qayrawānī, Abū Muḥammad ʿAbd Allāh. *Matn al-risāla*. Cairo and Beirut: Dār al-Fikr, 1980.

———. *La Risala*. Trans. L. Bercher. Alger: N.p., 1949.

Ibn al-ʿAṭṭār, Muḥammad b. Aḥmad. *Kitāb al-Wathāʾiq: Formulario notarial hispano-árabe por el alfaqui y notario cordobes*. Ed. Pedro Chalmeta and Francisco Corriente. Madrid: Instituto Hispano-Árabe de Cultura, 1983.

Ibn al-Bannāʾ. *Le Calendrier d'Ibn al-Bannâ de Marrakech*. Ed. and trans. H.P.J. Renaud. Paris: Larose, 1948.

Ibn Ḥabīb, ʿAbd al-Malik. *Kitāb al-Ghāya wa 'l-nihāya aw Kitāb Adab al-nisāʾ (De l'etique feminine)*. Ed. Abdel-Magid Turki. Beirut: Dār al-Gharb al-Islāmī, 1992.

Ibn al-Jawzī, Abū l-Farāj. *Kitāb Aḥkām al-nisāʾ li 'l-Imām Abī 'l-Farāj al-Jawzī*. Ed. Ziad Hamdān. Beirut: Dār al-Fikr, 1989.

Ibn al-Jazzār al-Qayrawānī. *Kitāb Siyāsat al-ṣibyān wa-tadbīruhum.* Ed. Muḥammad al-Ḥabīb al-Hīla. Beirut: Dār al-Gharb al-Islāmī, 1984.

Ibn Juzayy, Muḥammad b. Aḥmad. *Al-Qawānīn al-fiqhiyya.* Beirut: N.p., 1967.

Ibn Khaldūn. *The Muqaddimah.* Trans. Franz Rosenthal. 3 vols. Princeton: Princeton University Press, 1958.

Ibn Mughīth al-Ṭulayṭulī, Aḥmad. *Al-Muqniʿ fī ʿilm al-shurūṭ: Formulario notarial.* Ed. Francisco Javier Aguirre Sádaba. Madrid: Consejo Superior de Investigaciones Científicas, 1994.

Ibn Rushd, Abū l-Walīd Muḥammad al-Qurṭubī. *Bidāyat al-mujtahid.* 4 vols. Cairo: Dār Ibn Ḥazm, 1952.

———. *Al-Muqaddimāt.* 2 vols. Beirut: Dār al-Gharb al-Islāmī, 1988.

Ibn Salmūn, Abū l-Qāsim. *Al-ʿIqd al-munaẓẓam.* Printed in the margin of Ibrāhīm b. ʿAlī Ibn Farḥūn, *Tabṣīrat al-ḥukkām fī uṣūl al-aqḍiyya wa-manāhij al-aḥkām,* ed. Ṭāhā ʿAbd al-Raʾūf Saʿd, 2 vols. Cairo: Maktabat al-Kullīyāt al-Azhāriyya, 1986.

Ibn al-Ukhuwwa. *Maʿālim al-qurba fī aḥkām al-ḥisba.* Ed. R. Levy. E.J.W. Gibb Memorial Series. New series, vol. 12. London: Luzac, 1938.

Ibrahim, Mahmoud. *Merchant Capital and Islam.* Austin: University of Texas Press, 1990.

Idris, Hadi R. *La Berbérie orientale sous les Ẓirides (X–XIIe siècles).* 2 vols. Paris: Adrien Maison, 1962.

———. "Commerce maritime et *kirāḍ* en berbérie orientale." *Journal of the Economic and Social History of the Orient* 4 (1961): 225–39.

———. "Contribution à l'étude de la vie économique en occident musulman médiéval: Glanes de données chiffrées." In *Mélanges Roger Le Tourneau,* 2 vols., vol. 2, 75–87. Aix-en-Provence: Revue de l'occident musulman et de la Méditerranée, 1972.

———. "Le Mariage en occident musulman d'aprés un choix de fatwas médiévales extraits du *Miʿyār* d'al Wansharisi." *Studia Islamica* 32 (1970): 157–67; continuation in *Revue de l'Occident musulman et de la Méditéranée* 12 (1972): 45–62; 14 (1974): 71–105; and 25 (1978): 119–38.

Imber, Colin. "Women, Marriage and Property: *Mahr* in the Behcetü'l-Fetāvā of Yenişehirli Abdullah." In *Women in the Ottoman Empire: Middle Eastern Women in the Early Modern Era,* ed. Madeline C. Zilfi, 81–104. Leiden: Brill, 1997.

Inhorn, Marcia C. "Population, Poverty, and Gender Politics: Motherhood Pressures and Marital Crisis in the Lives of Poor Egyptian Women." In *Population, Poverty and Politics in Middle East Cities,* ed. Michael E. Bonine, 186–207. Gainesville: University Press of Florida, 1997.

Isaacs, Haskell D. *Medical and Para-Medical Manuscripts in the Cambridge Geniza Collection.* Cambridge: Cambridge University Press, 1994.

Ispahany, Batool, trans. *Islamic Medical Wisdom: The Ṭibb al-Āʾimma.* Ed. Andrew J. Newman. London: The Muhammadi Trust, 1991.

Ivanova, Svetlana. "The Divorce between Zubaida Hatun and Esseid Osman Ağa: Women in the Eighteenth-Century Sharia Court of Rumelia." In *Women, the Family, and Divorce Laws in Islamic History,* ed. Amira El Azhary Sonbol, 112–26. Syracuse: Syracuse University Press, 1996.

———. "Muslim and Christian Women before the Kadi Court in Eighteenth Century Rumeli: Marriage Problems." *Oriente Moderno* 18–99 (1999): 161–76.

Jackson, Peter. "Sulṭān Raḍiyya Bint Iltutmish." In *Women in the Medieval Islamic World*, ed. Gavin R.G. Hambly, 181–99. New York: St. Martin's, 1998.

Jackson, Ralph. *Doctors and Diseases in the Roman Empire*. Norman, OK: University of Oklahoma Press, 1988.

Jalabert, Cyril. "Les Conversions à l'Islam chez Michel le Syrien." Paper presented at the annual meeting of the French Association of Islamic Studies, Perpignan, 7 July 1995.

al-Jazīrī, ʿAlī b. Yaḥyā. *Al-Maqṣad al-maḥmūd fī talkhīṣ al-ʿuqūd*. Ed. Asunción Ferreras. Madrid: Consejo supeior de investigaciones científicas, 1998.

Jennings, Ronald C. "Loans and Credit in Early 17th Century Ottoman Judicial Records: The Sharia Court of Anatolian Kayseri." *Journal of the Economic and Social History of the Orient* 16 (1973): 168–216.

———. "Women in Early 17th-Century Ottoman Judicial Records: The Sharia Court of Anatolian Kayseri." *Journal of the Economic and Social History of the Orient* 18 (1974): 53–114.

Jewell, Helen M. *Women in Medieval England*. Manchester: Manchester University Press, 1996.

Johansen, Baber. *The Islamic Law on Land Tax and Rent*. London: Croom Helm, 1988.

———. "The Valorization of the Human Body in Muslim Sunni Law." In *Law and Society*, 71–112. Princeton: Markus Wiener, 1996.

Johns, Jeremy. *Arabic Administration in Norman Sicily: The Royal Dīwān*. Cambridge: Cambridge University Press, 2002.

Johnson, Allan C. *Roman Egypt to the Reign of Diocletian*. Baltimore: Johns Hopkins University Press, 1936.

Jordan, William C. *Women and Credit in Pre-Industrial and Developing Societies*. Philadelphia: University of Pennsylvania Press, 1993.

Juynboll, G.H.A. "Some Isnād-Analytical Methods Illustrated on the Basis of Several Woman-Demeaning Sayings from Ḥadīth Literature." In *Studies on the Origins and Uses of Islamic Ḥadīth*, 343–83. London: Variorum, 1996.

Kapparis, Konstantinos. *Abortion in the Ancient World*. London: Duckworth Academic, 2002.

Kassis, Hanna E. "Roots of Conflict: Aspects of Christian-Muslim Confrontation in Eleventh-Century Spain." In *Conversion and Continuity: Indigenous Christian Communities in Islamic Lands, Eighth to Eighteenth Centuries*, ed. M. Gervers and R.J. Bikhazi, 151–84. Toronto: Pontifical Institute of Medieval Studies, 1990.

Kealey, Edward J. *Medieval Medicus: A Social History of Anglo-Norman Medicine*. Baltimore: John Hopkins University Press, 1981.

Kelly, Joan. "Did Women Have a Renaissance?" In Joan Kelly, *Women, History and Theory*, 19–50. Chicago: University of Chicago Press, 1984.

Khalīl b. Isḥāq. *Abrégé de la loi musulmane selon le rite de l'imām Mālek*. Trans. G.-H. Bousquet. 4 vols. Alger/Paris: Adrien Maisonneuve, 1961.

———. *Mukhtaṣar*. Ed. Aḥmad Naṣr. Cairo: Dār Ihyāʾ al-Kutub al-ʿArabiyya, 1988.

Khalilieh, Hassan S. *Islamic Maritime Law: An Introduction*. Leiden: Brill, 1998.

Kilpatrick, Hilary. "Some Late ʿAbbāsid and Mamlūk Books about Women: A Literary Historical Approach." *Arabica* 42 (1995): 56–78.

———. "Women as Poets and Chattels: Abū l-Faraj al-Iṣbahānī's 'al-imā' al-shawā'ir.'" *Qaderni de Studi Arabi* 9 (1991): 161–76.
King, Helen. *Hippocrates' Women: Reading the Female Body in Ancient Greece.* London and New York: Routledge, 1998.
Kirshner, J. "Materials for a Gilded Cage: Non-Dotal Assets in Florence, 1300–1500." In *The Family in Italy, from Antiquity to the Present,* ed. David I. Kertzer and Richard P. Saller, 184–207. New Haven: Yale University Press, 1991.
———, and A. Molho. "The Dowry Fund and the Marriage Market in Early Quatrocento Florence." *Journal of Modern History* 50 (1978): 404–38.
Klapisch-Zuber, Christiane. *Women, Family and Ritual in Renaissance Italy.* Chicago and London: University of Chicago Press, 1985.
Kuehn, Thomas. *Law, Family, and Women: Toward a Legal Anthropology of Renaissance Italy.* Chicago: University of Chicago Press, 1991.
———. "Person and Gender in the Laws." In *Gender and Society in Renaissance Italy,* ed. Judith Brown and Robert Davis, 87–106. New York: Longman, 1998.
Kuran, Timur. "The Provision of Public Goods under Islamic Law: Origins, Impact, and Limitations of the Waqf System." *Law and Society Review* 35 (2001): 841–97.
Lagardère, Vincent. *Histoire et Société en Occident Musulman au Moyen Âge. Analyse du Mi'yār d'al-Wansharīsī.* Madrid: Collection de la Casa de Velázquez, 1995.
Landau-Tasseron, Ella. "Adoption, Acknowledgment of Paternity and False Genealogical Claims in Arabian and Islamic Societies." *Bulletin of the School of Oriental and African Studies* 66 (2003): 169–92.
The Lawyers Weekly. Ontario Lawyers Association Bulletin. 20 August 2004.
Layish, Aharon. "Bequests as an Instrument for Accommodating Inheritance Rules: Israel as a Case Study." *Islamic Law and Society* 2 (1995): 282–319.
Leiser, Gary. "Medical Education in Islamic Lands from the Seventh to the Fourteenth Century." *The Journal of the History of Medicine and Allied Sciences* 38 (1983): 48–75.
Lewis, N., Y. Yadin, and J. Greenfield, eds. *Judean Desert Studies II: The Documents from the Bar Kokhba Period in the Cave of Letters.* Jerusalem: Israel Exploration Society, 1989.
Libson, Gideon. *Jewish and Islamic Law: A Comparative Study of Custom During the Geonic Period.* Cambridge, MA: Harvard University Press, 2003.
Linant de Bellefonds, Y. *Traité de droit musulman comparé.* 3 vols. The Hague: Mouton, 1965–73.
Little, Donald P. *A Catalogue of the Islamic Documents from al-Ḥaram aš-šarīf in Jerusalem.* Beirut: Orient-Institut der Deutschen Morgenländischen Gesellschaft, 1984.
———. "Coptic Converts to Islam during the Baḥrī Mamlūk Period." In *Conversion and Continuity: Indigenous Christian Communities in Islamic Lands, Eighth to Eighteenth Centuries,* ed. M. Gervers and R.J. Bikhazi, 263–88. Toronto: Pontifical Institute of Medieval Studies, 1990.
———. "Documents Related to the Estates of a Merchant and His Wife in Late Fourteenth Century Jerusalem." *Mamlūk Studies Review* 2 (1998): 93–193.
———. "Ḥaram Documents Related to the Jews of Late Fourteenth Century Jerusalem." *Journal of Semitic Studies* 30 (1985): 227–370.
———. "Two Fourteenth-Century Court Records from Jerusalem Concerning the Disposition of Slaves by Minors." *Arabica* 29 (1986): 16–49.

López Ortiz, José. "Fatwas Granadinas de los siglos XIV y XV." *Al-Andalus* 6 (1941): 72–127.

Lutfi al-Sayyid Marsot, Afaf, ed. *Society and the Sexes in Medieval Islam.* Malibu, CA: Undena, 1979.

Lutfi, Huda. *Al-Quds al-Mamlūkiyya: A History of Mamlūk Jerusalem Based on the Haram Documents.* Berlin: Klaus Schwartz Verlag, 1985.

———. "Al-Sakhāwī's *Kitāb al-nisā'* as a Source for the Social and Economic History of Muslim Women during the Fifteenth Century A.D." *The Muslim World* 71 (1981): 104–24.

———. "A Study of Six Fourteenth Century Iqrārs from al-Quds Relating to Muslim Women." *Journal of the Economic and Social History of the Orient* 26 (1983): 246–94.

McVaugh, Michael. "Islamic Medicine in the Kingdom of Aragon in the Early Fourteenth Century." *Bulletin of Islamic Medicine* 3 (1984): 62–7.

Madurell y Marimon, J. "El arte de la seda en Barcelona entre Judios y conversos." *Sefarad* (1965): 247–81.

Maidman, Mainard P. "Nuzi: Portrait of an Ancient Mesopotamian Provincial Town." In *Civilizations of the Ancient Near East*, ed. Jack Sasson et al., 4 vols., vol. 2, 931–47. New York: Scribner's, 1995.

Mālik b. Anas. *Al-Muwaṭṭa' li 'l-imām Mālik b. Anas (179/796), riwāyat Suwayd b. Sa'īd al-Ḥadathānī (240/854).* Ed. 'Abd al-Majīd Turkī. Beirut: Dār al-Gharb al-Islāmī, 1994.

Marazka, Ibrahim, Reja Pourjavady, and Sabine Schmidtke, eds. *Samaw'al al-Maghribī's (d. 570/1175) Ifḥām al-yahūd. The Early Recension.* Wiesbaden: Harrassowitz, 2006.

Marcus, Abraham. *The Middle East on the Eve of Modernity: Aleppo in the Eighteenth Century.* New York: Columbia University Press, 1989.

Marín, Manuela. "Learning at Mosques in al-Andalus." In *Islamic Legal Interpretation: Muftis and Their Fatwas*, ed. M. Khalid Masud, B. Messick, and D.S. Powers, 47–54. Cambridge, MA: Harvard University Press, 1996.

———. *Mujeres en al-Ándalus.* Madrid: Consejo Superior de Investigaciones Científicas, 2000.

———, and Rachid El Hour. "Captives, Children and Conversion: A Case from Late Naṣrid Granada." *Journal of the Economic and Social History of the Orient* 41 (1998): 453–73.

———, and Joseph Pérez, eds. *Minorités religieuses dans l'Espagne médiévale. Revue du Monde musulmane et de la Méditerranée* 63–4. Aix-en-Provence, 1992.

Marmon, Shaun E. "Domestic Slavery in the Mamlūk Empire: A Preliminary Sketch." In *Slavery in the Islamic Middle East*, ed. Shaun E. Marmon, 1–24. Princeton: Markus Wiener, 1999.

Marrese, Michelle Lamarche. *A Woman's Kingdom: Noblewomen and the Control of Property in Russia, 1700–1861.* Ithaca and London: Cornell University Press, 2002.

Masters, Bruce A. *The Origins of Western Economic Dominance in the Middle East: Mercantilism and the Islamic Economy in Aleppo, 1600–1750.* New York: New York University Press, 1988.

Masud, M. Khalid, B. Messick, and D.S. Powers, eds. *Islamic Legal Interpretation: Muftis and Their Fatwas.* Cambridge, MA: Harvard University Press, 1996.

Mayhew, Robert. *The Female in Aristotle's Biology: Reason or Rationalization.* Chicago and London: University of Chicago Press, 2004.

Meriwether, Margaret L. "The Rights of Children and the Responsibilities of Women: Women as Wasis in Ottoman Aleppo, 1770–1840." In *Women, the Family, and Divorce Laws in Islamic History*, ed. Amira El-Azhary Sonbol, 219–35. Syracuse: Syracuse University Press, 1996.

———. "Women and Economic Change in Nineteenth-Century Syria. The Case of Aleppo." In *Arab Women. Old Boundaries, New Frontiers*, ed. Judith E. Tucker, 65–83. Bloomington and Indianapolis: University of Indiana Press, 1993.

———. "Women and *Waqf* Revisited: The Case of Aleppo, 1770–1840." In *Women in the Ottoman Empire: Middle Eastern Women in the Early Modern Era*, ed. Madeline C. Zilfi, 128–52. Leiden: Brill, 1997.

Mernissi, Fatima. *Le Harem politique: Le Prophète et les femmes.* Paris: Albin Michel, 1987.

Metcalfe, Alex. *Muslims and Christians in Norman Sicily: Arabic Speakers and the End of Islam.* London and New York: Routledge, Curzon, 2003.

Miller, Kathryn A. "Muslim Minorities and the Obligation to Emigrate to Islamic Territory: Two Fatwās from Fifteenth-Century Granada." *Islamic Law and Society* 7 (2000): 256–88.

Minkov, Anton. *Conversion to Islam in the Balkans: Kisve Bahasi Petitions and Ottoman Social Life, 1670–1730.* Leiden: Brill, 2004.

Molenat, Jean-Pierre. "Les Musulmans de Tolède aux XIVe et XVe siècles." In *Les Espagnes médiévales: Aspects économiques et sociaux*, 175–90. Nice: Publications de la Faculté des lettres et sciences humaines de Nice, 1983.

Moors, Annelies. *Women, Property and Islam: Palestinian Experiences, 1920–1990.* Cambridge: Cambridge University Press, 1995.

Morony, Michael G. "The Age of Conversions: A Reassessment." In *Conversion and Continuity: Indigenous Christian Communities in Islamic Lands, Eighth to Eighteenth Centuries*, ed. M. Gervers and R.J. Bikhazi, 135–50. Toronto: Pontifical Institute of Medieval Studies, 1990.

———. "Landholding and Social Change in Lower al-Iraq in the Early Islamic Period." In *Land Tenure and Social Transformation in the Middle East*, ed. Tarif Khalidi, 209–22. Beirut: American University of Beirut, 1984.

———. "Landholding in Seventh Century Iraq: Late Sasanian and Early Islamic Patterns." In *The Islamic Middle East, 700–1900: Studies in Economic and Social History*, ed. A.L. Udovitch, 135–172. Princeton: Darwin Press, 1983.

Motzki, Harald. "Child Marriage in Seventeenth-Century Palestine." In *Islamic Legal Interpretation: Muftis and Their Fatwas*, ed. M. Khalid Masud, B. Messick, and D.S. Powers, 129–40. Cambridge, MA: Harvard University Press, 1996.

Müller, Christian. *Gerichtspraxis im Stadtstaat Córdoba: Zum Recht der Gesellschaft in einer mālikitisch-islamischen Rechtstradition des 5./11. Jahrhunderts.* Leiden: Brill, 1999.

———. "Judging with God's Law on Earth: Judicial Powers of the Qāḍī al-Jamāʿa of Cordoba in the Fifth/Eleventh Century." *Islamic Law and Society* 7 (2000): 159–86.

Musallam, Basim. *Sex and Society in Islam: Birth Control before the Nineteenth Century.* Cambridge: Cambridge University Press, 1983.

Nichols, James M. "The Concept of Woman in Medieval Arabic Poetry." *The Maghreb Review* 6 (1981): 85–8.

Nielsen, J.S. *Secular Justice in an Islamic State: Maẓālim under the Baḥrī Mamlūks, 662/1264–789/1387.* Istanbul: Nederlands Historisch-Archaeologisch Instituut, 1985.

Nirenberg, David. "Conversion, Sex, and Segregation: Jews and Christians in Medieval Spain." *The American Historical Review* 107 (2002): 1065–93.

———. "Mass Conversion and Genealogical Mentalities: Jews and Christians in Fifteenth-Century Spain." *Past and Present* 174 (2002): 3–41.

North, Douglass C. *Institutions, Institutional Change and Economic Performance.* Cambridge: Cambridge University Press, 1990.

———. *Structure and Change in Economic History.* New York: Norton, 1981.

———, and Robert P. Thomas. *The Rise of the Western World: A New Economic History.* Cambridge: Cambridge University Press, 1973.

Northrup, Linda S. "Muslim-Christian Relations during the Reign of the Mamlūk Sultan al-Manṣūr Qalāwūn, A.D. 1278–1290." In *Conversion and Continuity: Indigenous Christian Communities in Islamic Lands, Eighth to Eighteenth Centuries*, ed. M. Gervers and R.J. Bikhazi, 253–261. Toronto: Pontifical Institute of Medieval Studies, 1990.

O'Callahan, Joseph F. *A History of Medieval Spain.* Ithaca: Cornell University Press, 1975.

Omran, Abdel Rahim. *Family Planning in the Legacy of Islam.* London and New York: Routledge, 1992.

Peirce, Leslie P. *The Imperial Harem: Women and Sovereignty in the Ottoman Empire.* Oxford and New York: Oxford University Press, 1993.

Perlmann, Moshe. "The Medieval Polemics between Islam and Judaism." In *Religion in a Religious Age*, ed. Shlomo Dov Goitein, 103–38. Proceedings of Regional Conferences Held at the University of California, Los Angeles, and Brandeis University, April 1973. Cambridge, MA: Association for Jewish Studies, 1973.

Petry, Carl F. "Class Solidarity Versus Gender Gain: Women As Custodians of Property in Later Medieval Egypt." In *Women in Middle Eastern History: Shifting Boundaries in Sex and Gender*, ed. B. Baron and N. Keddie, 122–42. New Haven and London: Yale University Press, 1991.

———. "Conjugal Rights versus Class Prerogatives: A Divorce Case in Mamlūk Cairo." In *Women in the Medieval Islamic World*, ed. Gavin R.G. Hambly, 227–40. New York: St. Martin's Press, 1998.

———. "A Paradox of Patronage during the Later Mamlūk Period." *The Muslim World* 73 (1983): 182–207.

Popovic, Alexandre. *La révolt des esclaves en Iraq au IIIe/IXe siècle.* Paris: P. Geuthner, 1976 (Engl. transl. *The Revolt of African Slaves in Iraq in the 3rd/9th Century*, Princeton: Markus Wiener, 1999).

Pouzet, Louis. "Vision populaire de la femme en Syrie aux VIe et VIIe/XIIe et XIIIe siècles." In *Proceedings of the 14th Congress of the Union Européenne des Arabisants et Islamisants, Budapest 1988,* ed. Alexander Fodor, 295–302. Budapest: Eötvös Loránd University Chair for Arabic Studies, 1995.

Powers, David S. "Fatwās as Sources for Legal and Social History." *Al-Qantara* 11 (1990): 295–341.

———. "The Islamic Inheritance System: A Socio-Historical Approach." In *The Islamic Family Law*, ed. Chibli Mallat and Jane Conners, 11–29. London: Graham and Trotman, 1990.

———. *Law, Society and Culture in the Maghrib, 1300–1500.* Cambridge: Cambridge University Press, 2002.

———. "The Maliki Family Endowment: Legal Norms and Social Practices." *International Journal of Middle East Studies* 25 (1993): 379–406.

———. "Parents and Their Minor Children: Familial Politics in the Middle Maghrib in the Eighth/Fourteenth Century." *Continuity and Change* 16 (2001): 177–200.

———. *Studies in Qur'an and Ḥadīth: The Formation of the Islamic Law of Inheritance.* Los Angeles and Berkeley: University of California Press, 1986.

Rāġib, Yūsuf. *Marchands d'étoffes du Fayyoum au IIIe/IXe siècle d'après leurs archives (actes et lettres).* Vol. 1, *Les actes des Banū ʿAbd al-Muʾmin.* Cairo: Institut français d'archéologie orientale, 1982.

Rambo, Lewis R. *Understanding Religious Conversion.* New Haven: Yale University Press, 1993.

Rapoport, Yossef. *Marriage, Money and Divorce in Medieval Islamic Society.* Cambridge: Cambridge University Press, 2005.

———. "Matrimonial Gifts in Early Islamic Egypt." *Islamic Law and Society* 7 (2000): 1–36.

Raymond, André. *Artisans et commercants au Caire.* 2 vols. Damascus: Institut français d'archéologie orientale, Damas, 1974.

Reilly, James A. "Women in the Economic Life of Late-Ottoman Damascus." *Arabica* 42 (1995): 79–106.

Riley-Smith, Jonathan. *The Feudal Nobility and the Kingdom of Jerusalem, 1174–1277.* Hamden, Conn.: Archon Books, 1973.

———. "The Survival in Latin Palestine of Muslim Administration." In *The Eastern Mediterranean Lands in the Period of the Crusades*, ed. P.M. Holt, 9–22. Warminster: Aris and Phillips, 1977.

Rispler-Chaim, Vardit. "Ḥasan Murād Mannāʿ: 'Childbearing and the Rights of a Wife'." *Islamic Law and Society* 2 (1995): 92–9.

Rivlin, Joseph. *Shitre Kehilat Alyucena: Bills and Contracts from Lucena, 1020–1025 C.E.* In Hebrew. Ramat-Gan: Bar-Ilan University Press, 1994.

Rodinson, Maxime. *Islam and Capitalism.* Trans. Brian Pearce. New York: Pantheon Books, 1974.

Rogers, Susan Carol. "Woman's Place: A Critical Review of Anthropological Theory." *Comparative Studies in Society and History* 20 (1978): 123–62.

Rose, Carol M. "Women and Property: Gaining and Losing Ground." In *Property and Persuasion. Essays on the History, Theory, and Rhetoric of Ownership*, 233–63. Boulder, CO: Westview, 1994.

Rosenthal, Franz. "Fiction and Reality: Sources for the Role of Sex in Medieval Muslim Society." In *Society and the Sexes in Medieval Islam*, ed. Afaf Lutfi al-Sayyid-Marsot, 2–22. Malibu, CA: Undena, 1979.

———. "The Physician in Medieval Muslim Society." *Bulletin of the History of Medicine* 52 (1978): 475–91.

Roussier, J. "La Femme dans la société islamique: Droit malikite maghribin." *Recueils de la Société Jean Bodin* 11–12 (1959): 223–36.

Russell, Joshua. "Aspects démographiques du début de la féodalité." *Annales* 20 (1965): 1118–27.

Saḥnūn. *Al-Mudawwana al-kubrā li 'l-imām Malik b. Anas.* 9 vols. Beirut: Al-Maktaba al-Sharʿiyya, 1999.

Saller, Richard P. *Patriarchy, Property and Death in the Roman Family.* Cambridge: Cambridge University Press, 1994.

Santillana, David. *Istituzioni di diritto musulmano malichita con riguardo anche al sistema sciafiita.* 2 vols. Rome: Instituto per l'Oriente, 1925–38.

al-Sarakhsī, Muḥammad b. Aḥmad. *Kitāb al-Mabsūṭ.* 30 vols. Beirut: Dār al-Maʿārif, A.H. 1398.

Savage-Smith, Emily. "Medicine." In *Encyclopedia of the History of Arabic Science,* ed. Roshdi Rashed, 3 vols., vol. 3, 927–39. London and New York: Routledge, 1996.

Schacht, Joseph. *An Introduction to Islamic Law.* Oxford: Clarendon, 1964.

———. *The Origins of Muhammadan Jurisprudence.* Oxford: Clarendon, 1979.

Schaps, David M. *Economic Rights of Women in Ancient Greece.* Edinburgh: Edinburgh University Press, 1979.

Schilcher, Linda Schatkowski. "The Lore and Reality of Middle Eastern Patriarchy." In *Gegenwart als Geschichte: Islamwissenschaftliche Studien,* ed. A. Havemann and B. Johansen, 496–512. Leiden: E.J. Brill, 1988.

Seco de Lucena Paredes, Luis. "Documentos árabes Granadinos I: Documentos del Colegio de Niñas Nobles." *Al-Andalus* 8 (1943): 415–29.

———. "Documentos árabes Granadinos II: Documentos de las comendadoras de Santiago." *Al-Andalus* 9 (1944): 121–40.

———. "La escuela de juristas Granadinos en el siglo XV." *Miscelánea de Estudios Árabes y Hebraícos* 8 (1959): 7–28.

———. "El musulman Aḥmad Ulaylaš, espia de los reyes catolicos en la corte Granadina." *Miscelánea de Estudios Árabes y Hebraícos* 9 (1960): 157–60.

———. "La sultana madre de Boabdil." *Al-Andalus* 12 (1947): 359–90.

———, ed. and trans. *Wathā'iq ʿarabiyya gharnāṭiyya: Documentos arábigo-granadinos.* 2 vols. Madrid: Instituto de Estudios Islámicos, 1961.

Serrano Ruano, Delfina. "La escuela de alfaquies Toledanos a través del Miʿyār de al-Wansharīsī." *Revista del Instituto Egipcio de Estudios Islámicos en Madrid* 30 (1998): 127–53.

———. "La práctica legal (*ʿamal*) en al-Andalus durante los siglos X–XII, a través de los *Madhāhib al-ḥukkām fī nawāzil al-aḥkām* de Muḥammad ibn ʿIyāḍ." *Qurṭuba* 1 (1996): 171–92.

Shaham, Ron. "Custom, Islamic Law, and Statutory Legislation: Marriage Registration and Minimum Age at Marriage in the Egyptian Sharīʿa Courts." *Islamic Law and Society* 2 (1995): 258–81.

Shatzmiller, Joseph. "Femmes médecins au Moyen Age. Témoignages sur leurs pratiques (1250–1350)." In *Histoire et Société. Mélanges offerts à Georges Duby*, 4 vols. (Aix-en-Provence: Publications de l'Université de Provence, 1992), vol. 1, 167–75.

Shatzmiller, Maya. "Aspects of Women's Participation in the Economic Life of Later Medieval Islam: Occupations and Mentalities." *Arabica* 35 (1988): 36–58.

———. *The Berbers and the Islamic State: The Marīnid Experience in Pre-Protectorate Morocco.* Princeton: Markus Wiener, 2000.

———. *L'historiographie mérinide: Ibn Khaldun et ses contemporains*. Leiden: E.J. Brill, 1982.

———. "Islamic Institutions and Property Rights: The Case of the 'Public Good' Waqf." *Journal of the Economic and Social History of the Orient* 44 (2001): 44–74.

———. "Les Juifs de Tlemcen au XIVe siècle." *Revue des Etudes Juives* 137 (1978): 171–77.

———. *Labour in the Medieval Islamic World.* Leiden: E.J. Brill, 1994.

———. "The Legacy of the Andalusian Berbers in 14th-Century Maghreb: Its Role in the Formation of Maghrebi Historical Identity and Historiography." In *Relaciones de la Península Ibérica con el Magreb, Siglos XIII–XVI, Actas del coloquio, Madrid, 17–18 diciembre 1987*, ed. M. García-Arenal and M.J. Viguera, 205–36. Madrid: Instituto Hispano-Árabe de Cultura, 1988.

———. "Marriage, Family, and the Faith: Women's Conversion to Islam." *Journal of Family History* 21 (1996): 235–66.

———. "Le Mythe d'origine berbère: Aspects historiographiques et sociaux." *Revue de l'Occident Musulman* 35 (1983): 145–56.

———. "Professions and Ethnic Origin of Urban Labourers in Muslim Spain: Evidence from a Moroccan Source." *Awrāq* 5 (1983): 149–64.

———. "Une source méconnue de l'histoire des Berbères: Le Kitāb al-ansāb li-abī Ḥayyān." *Arabica* 30 (1983): 73–9.

———. "Unity and Variety of Land Tenure and Cultivation Patterns in the Medieval Maghreb." *The Maghreb Review* 8 (1984): 24–8.

———. "Women and Property Rights in al-Andalus and the Maghrib: Social Patterns and Legal Discourse." *Islamic Law and Society* 2 (1995): 219–57.

———. "Women and Wage Labour in the Medieval Islamic West: Legal Issues in Economic Context." *Journal of the Economic and Social History of the Orient* 39 (1997): 1–33.

Shorter, Edward. *The Making of the Modern Family.* New York: Basic Books, 1975.

Smith, R.M. "Women's Property Rights Under Customary Law: Some Developments in the Thirteenth and Fourteenth Centuries." *Transactions of the Royal Historical Society*, 5th series, 36 (1986): 165–94.

Sonbol, Amira. "Adoption in Islamic Society: A Historical Survey." In *Children in the Muslim Middle East*, ed. E. Fernea, 45–67. Austin: University of Texas Press, 1995.

———, ed. *Women, the Family, and Divorce Laws in Islamic History*. Syracuse: Syracuse University Press, 1996.

Spink M.S., and G.L. Lewis, trans. *Albucasis on Surgery and Instruments.* London: The Wellcome Institute of the History of Medicine, 1973.

Staden, Heinrich von. "Women and Dirt." *Helios* 19 (1992): 7–30.

Stone, Lawrence. "Family History in the 1980s: Past Achievements and Future Trends." In *The New History: The 1980s and Beyond. Studies in Interdisciplinary History*, ed. T. Rabb and R. Rotberg, 51–87. Princeton: Princeton University Press, 1982.

Stowasser, Barbara Freyer. "Women and Citizenship in the Qur'an." In *Women, the Family, and Divorce Laws in Islamic History*, ed. Amira El-Azhary Sonbol, 23–38. New York: Syracuse University Press, 1996.

———. *Women in the Qur'an: Traditions and Interpretation.* Oxford: Oxford University Press, 1994.

———. "Women's Issues in Modern Islamic Thought." In *Arab Women. Old Boundaries, New Frontiers*, ed. Judith E. Tucker, 3–28. Bloomington and Indianapolis: Indiana University Press, 1993.

Stuard, Susan. "The Dominion of Gender: Women's Fortunes in the High Middle Ages." In *Becoming Visibles: Women in European History*, ed. Renate Bridenthal, Claudia Koonz, and Susan Stuard, 153–71. Boston: Houghton Mifflin Company, 1987.

al-Tādilī, Abū ʿAlī al-Ḥasan Ibn Raḥḥāl al-Maʿdānī. *Kashf al-qināʿ fī taḍmīn al-ṣunnāʿ*. Trans. Jacques Berque as *Taḍmīn aṣ-ṣunnāʿ. De la responsabilité civile de l'artisan.* Alger: Éditions Carbonel, 1949.

al-Ṭaḥāwī, Abū Jaʿfar Aḥmad b. Muḥammad. *Al-Shurūṭ al-ṣaghīr*. Ed. Rawḥī Ūzjān, 2 vols. Baghdad: Riʾāsat Dīwān al-Awqāf, 1974.

Talbi, M. "Law and Economy in Ifriqiya (Tunisia) in the Third Islamic Century: Agriculture and the Role of Slaves in the Country's Economy." In *The Islamic Middle East: Studies in Economic and Social History*, ed. A.L. Udovitch, 209–49. Princeton: Darwin Press, 1981.

Talhami, Ghada. "The Zanj Rebellion Reconsidered." *The International Journal of African Historical Studies* 10 (1977): 443–61.

Tilly, Louise A. "Industrialization and Gender Inequality." In *Islamic and European Expansion: The Forging of a Global Order*, ed. Michael Adas, 243–310. Philadelphia: Temple University Press, 1993.

———. *Women, Work and Family.* New York and London: Holt, Rinehart and Winston, 1978.

Tucker, Judith E. "The Arab Family in History. 'Otherness' and the Study of the Family." In *Arab Women: Old Boundaries, New Frontiers*, ed. Judith E. Tucker, 195–207. Bloomington: Indiana University Press, 1993.

———. "Gender and Islamic History." In *Islamic and European Expansion: The Forging of a Global Order*, ed. M. Adas, 37–73. Philadelphia: Temple University Press.

———. *In the House of the Law: Gender and Islamic Law in Ottoman Syria and Palestine.* Los Angeles and Berkeley: University of California Press, 1998.

———. Review of Giladi's *Infants* in *International Journal of Middle East Studies* 34 (2002): 162–65.

———. *Women in Nineteenth-Century Egypt.* Cambridge: Cambridge University Press, 1985.

———, ed. *Arab Women. Old Boundaries, New Frontiers.* Bloomington and Indianapolis: Indiana University Press, 1993.

Tyan, Emile. *Histoire de l'organisation judiciaire en pays d'Islam.* 2nd ed. Leiden: E.J. Brill, 1960.

———. *Le Notariat et le régime de la preuve par écrit dans la pratique du droit musulman*. 2nd ed. Beirut: Hariss Impr. St.-Paul, 1959.

Udovitch, Avram L. "Islamic Law and the Social Context of Exchange in the Medieval Middle East." *History and Anthropology* 1 (1985): 445–65.

———. "Reflections on the Institutions of Credit and Banking in the Medieval Islamic Near East." *Studia Islamica* 31 (1975): 5–23.

al-ʿUqbānī, Muḥammad. *Un Traité de hisba*. Ed. A. Chénoufi. Damascus: Institut français d'archéologie orientale, 1967.

Viguera Molins, María J. "Estudio preliminar." In *La mujer en al-Andalus: Reflejos históricos de du actividad y categorías sociales*, ed. M.J. Viguera Molins, 17–34. Madrid: Universidad Autónoma de Madrid; Seville: Editoriales Andaluzas Unidas, 1989.

———. "La 'historia de alfaquies y jueces' de Aḥmad b. ʿAbd al-Barr." *Revista del Instituto Egipcio de Estudios Islámicos en Madrid* 23 (1985–86): 49–61.

———. "Los jueces de Cordoba en la primera mitad del siglo XI (análisis de datos)." *Al-Qanṭara* 5 (1984): 123–45.

———, ed. *La mujer en al-Andalus: Reflejos históricos de su actividad y categorías sociales*. Madrid: Universidad Autónoma de Madrid; Seville: Editoriales Andaluzas Unidas, 1989.

Villanueva Rico, María del Carmen. *Habices de las mezquitas de la ciudad de Granada y sus alquerias*. 2 vols. Madrid: Instituto Hispano-Arabe de Cultura, 1961–66.

Wadud, Amina. *Qur'an and Woman: Rereading the Sacred Text from a Woman's Perspective*. Oxford: Oxford University Press, 1999.

Wakin, Jeanette A. *The Function of Documents in Islamic Law*. Albany: State University of New York Press, 1972.

al-Wansharīsī, Aḥmad b. Yaḥyā. *Al-Miʿyār al-muʿrib wa 'l-jāmiʿ al-mughrib ʿan fatāwā ʿulamā' ifrīqiya wa 'l-andalus wa 'l-maghrib*. Ed. M. Ḥājjī et al. 13 vols. Beirut: Dār al-Gharb al-Islāmī, 1981–82.

Warnock, Mary. *Making Babies: Is There a Right to Have Children?* Oxford: Oxford University Press, 2002.

Wassef, Nadia. "Masculinities and Mutilations: Female Genital Mutilation in Egypt." *Middle East Women's Studies Review* 8 (1998): 1–4.

Wasserstein, David. "A Fatwā on Conversion in Islamic Spain." In *Studies in Muslim-Jewish Relations*, vol. 1, 177–89. Oxford: Oxford Centre for Postgraduate Studies, 1993.

Watson, Andrew M. *Agricultural Innovation in the Early Islamic World: The Diffusion of Crops and Farming Techniques, 700–1100*. Cambridge: Cambridge University Press, 1983.

Watt, Montgomery W. *Muhammad at Medina*. Oxford: Oxford University Press, 1956.

Wegner, Judith Romney. "The Status of Women in Jewish and Islamic Marriage and Divorce Law." *Harvard Women's Law Journal* 5 (1982): 1–33.

Weisner, Merry E. *Working Women in Renaissance Germany*. New Brunswick: Rutgers University Press, 1986.

White, Elizabeth H. "Legal Reform As an Indicator of Women's Status in Muslim Nations." In *Women in the Muslim World*, ed. L. Beck and N. Keddie, 52–68. Cambridge, MA: Harvard University Press, 1978.

Ziadeh, Farhat J. "Equality (Kafā'ah) in the Muslim Law of Marriage." *American Journal of Comparative Law* 6 (1957): 503–17.

———. "Property Rights in the Middle East: From Traditional Law to Modern Codes." *Arab Law Quarterly* 8 (1993): 3–12.

Zolan, Alexandra J. "The Effect of Islamization on the Legal and Social Status of Women in Iran." *Boston College Third World Law Journal* 7 (1987): 183–93.

Zomeño Rodriguez, Amalia. *Dote y matrimonio en al-Andalus y el norte de África: Estudio sobre la jurisprudencia islámica medieval.* Madrid: Consejo Superior de Investigaciones Científicas, 2000.

———. "Kafā'a in the Mālikī School: A Fatwā from Fifteenth-Century Fez." In *Islamic Law: Theory and Practice*, ed. R. Gleave and E. Kermeli, 87–106. London: I.B. Tauris, 1997.

———. "Repertorio documental arábigo-granadino. Los documentos de la Biblioteca Universitaria de Granada." *Qurtuba* 6 (2001): 275–96.

———. "Siete historias de mujeres. Sobre la transmisión de la propriedad en la Granada Nazarí." In *Mujeres y sociedad islámica: Una visión plural*, ed. M.I. Calero Secall, 175–97. Malaga: Universidad de Málaga, 2006.

———. "Transferencias matrimoniales en el occidente islámico medieval: Las joyas como regalo de boda." *Revista de Dialectología y Tradiciones Populares* 51 (1996): 79–96.

INDEX

N.B. Owing to the frequency of their occurrence, the following have not been indexed: fatwas, *ṣadāq*, Granada, acquisition, property rights. The notes have also not been included in the index.

ʿAbbasid court 13
al-ʿAbdūsī (mufti) 27, 29, 137, 138
Abortion 16, 95, 114
Abrahen Alcaysi (Toledan Muslim) 42
Abū ʿAbd Allāh Muḥammad b. Aḥmad al-Ruffa 64
Abū ʿAbd Allāh Muḥammad al-Aḥshan al-Fashkūrī 180
Abū ʿAbd Allāh Muḥammad al-Fakhkhār 19
Abū ʿAbd Allāh Muḥammad b. Faraj 66, 187
Abū ʿAbd Allāh Muḥammad b. Marzūq 137
Abū ʿAbd Allāh Muḥammad al-Qumārashī 178
Abū ʿAbd Allāh Muḥammad b. Saʿīd b. ʿAtīq 177
Abū ʿAbd Allāh b. ʿAlī al-Ḥaṣṣār 176
Abū ʿAbd Allāh b. Saʿīd al-Sulaymī 186
Abū l-Ḥajjāj Yūsuf b. Muḥammad Awyanāt 178
Abū l-Ḥajjāj Yūsuf Ibn al-Sharāj 42
Abū Ḥanīfa see Hanafi school
Abū l-Ḥasan ʿAlī al-Ḥusaynī 178
Abū l-Ḥasan ʿAlī al-ʿUndūq 62, 187
Abū l-Ḥasan al-Lakhmī 105
Abū l-Ḥasan al-Ṣaghīr 164
Abū Isḥāq Ibrāhīm b. Aḥmad al-Ḥakīm 20
Abū Isḥāq Ibrāhīm b. Aḥmad al-Madīnī 180
Abū Isḥāq Ibrāhīm al-Tūnisī (mufti) 27, 55
Abū Jaʿfar Aḥmad b. Dughnayn (Daḥnīn) 63, 177
Abū Jaʿfar Aḥmad b. Muḥammad al-Fakhkhār 1
Abū Jaʿfar Aḥmad b. Muḥammad al-Mughannī 50–51
Abū Jaʿfar Aḥmad b. ʿUthmān al-Gharūj 42
Abū Muḥammad b. Abī Faraj 179
Abū Muḥammad al-Zawāwī (mufti) 106
Abū l-Qāsim b. Riḍwān Banigash 42
Abū Qāsim b. Sūda 179
Abū ʿUthmān Saʿīd al-Sulaymī 85
Abū Yazīd Khālid Jāʾ al-Khayr 21, 62, 77
Aḥmad b. ʿAlī al-Minshālī 65, 187
Aḥmad b. Muḥammad al-Ruffa 28
Aḥmad al-Shuwaykh 65
ʿĀʾika bt. Aḥmad (Sicilian Muslim) 182
ʿĀʾisha bt. Abī ʿAbd Allāh b. al-Khaṭīb 178
ʿĀʾisha bt. ʿAbd Allāh b. Mufaḍḍal 21
ʿĀʾisha bt. Abī Jaʿfar Aḥmad 42
ʿĀʾisha bt. Abī ʿUthmān Saʿd b. Aḥmad 30, 48, 94
ʿĀʾisha bt. Aḥmad al-Ashkar 66
ʿĀʾisha bt. Ḥakīm b. Ibrāhīm Ghālib 41–42
ʿĀʾisha bt. Ibrāhīm al-Ḥakīm 51–52, 85, 103, 179
ʿĀʾisha bt. Ibrāhīm b. Thābit 85

ʿĀʾisha bt. Muḥammad b. Naṣīr 63
ʿĀʾisha bt. al-Martushī (al-Maratashī) 63, 187
ʿĀʾisha bt. Saʿd b. Ḥasan 64
ʿĀʾisha bt. Saʿīd al-Muwaḥḥad 178
Albaicín 19; see also Bayāzīn
Albergotti (Italian jurist) 59
Aleppo 74, 172, 184, 189–190
Alfonso de Toledo (Major-domo) 180
Algeciras 56, 104
ʿAlī b. Ibrāhīm al-Ḥakīm 51–52, 179
ʿAlī b. Muḥammad al-Barīṭī 64, 177
ʿAlī b. Mūsā al-Lakhmī 42
Anatolia, Anatolian provinces 34, 184
Andalusian biographical dictionaries 68
Andalusian society 1, 5, 68
ʿAqīda see Creed
ʿArīb b. Saʿd 108
Assets
  control of 32, 78, 84
  in the hands of women 34, 40, 87
  separation in matrimony 3
ʿAzl see *Coitus interruptus*

Bāb al-Fakhkhārīn (quarter) 177, 180
Baer, Gabriel 74
Balkan provinces 34, 184
Bayāzīn (quarter) 41, 187
Bayt al-māl (state treasury) 63, 77, 176
Baza 20–21, 50–52, 68
Berbers 123
Berkey, Jonathan 110
Birth control 10, 16, 114–115
Black Death 171
Blumenfeld, Renate 115
Boabdil 2, 19
Bousquet, G.-H. 7
Breastfeeding 10, 94, 99, 100–101, 115–116
Brideprice 35, 37
Buliyāna (village) 20
Byzantine
  legacy 107
  Mediterranean 149, 170
  wet nurse contract 101
  women in society 192
Caesarean birth, section 103, 115
Cahen, Claude 6
Capitulations (of 1492) 41, 118
Catholic kings 42
Chalmeta, Pedro 142
Child marriage 26, 97
Childrearing, childcare 104, 105, 116, 150
  wages for 10, 94
China (Chinese women) 184
Christian(-s, -ity)
  armies 19, 93, 118
  chronicles 42
  communities 123, 139
  conversion (wife) 136
  conversion certificates 11
  conversion in the East 141
  court (Sicily) 182
  disappearance from North Africa 138
  Europe 13, 115
  forbidden degree 132
  Iberian concept of conversion 143
  kings 22
  marriage 133
  slave 128–129
  West 182; see also Europe
Christian Spain
  administration 1
  conquest 1, 22
  monarchy 180
Circle of familiarity 192–193
Coitus interruptus (*ʿazl*) 97, 99, 115
Constable, Olivia 191
Consummation (of marriage) 22, 24–26, 84, 95–97, 104, 127, 131, 134–135
Conveyance (*ḥiyāza*) 21, 31, 43–44, 60, 83, 180, 182
Copts 142
Cordova 5, 11, 25, 31, 56, 166
Coulson, Noel 4

Court (of law)
cases 24
documents 21, 34, 71, 85, 109, 118
Granada 1, 8, 51, 61–62, 75, 77, 99, 178, 180, 182, 189
Islamic 15, 19, 36–37, 40–42, 105, 119, 125, 173–174, 182, 185–186
Kandiye 142
notary 52
records, registers 28, 175, 189, 192
role in acquisition 14
Credit 12, 164, 181, 188–189, 191–193; see also Loans
Creed (*ʿaqīda*) 120, 137
Crusader's nobles 183
Custody (*ḥaḍāna*) 93–94, 103, 105–106, 131, 136

Damascus 71–72, 172, 184, 185
Demographic
conditions Granada 1, 2, 67
decline 10, 113–114
growth 139
Dhū l-Nūn b. Aḥmad b. ʿAbd Allāh b. Lubb 66
Doña Hebiba (Toledan Muslim) 42
Dower, dowry, Christian 31, 35, 37–39, 58, 86, 128, 188; see also Europe
Duress 161

Economic(s)
history 2, 33
performance 2, 15
theory 2, 195
Egypt 15, 23, 34, 36, 38, 57, 72, 74, 80, 97, 101, 112, 115, 150, 153, 157, 163, 172, 183
Endowment see *Waqf*
Estates 28–29, 31, 44–45, 49, 53, 61–76, 78, 81, 106, 151, 159, 169, 190, 198
division 28, 48–50, 52, 54–55, 57, 61–76, 113, 167–168, 178, 187–189, 193, 199
Europe, European 35, 38, 70–71, 86–87, 170, 194, 198
dowry 9, 38, 40, 70, 198
historiography 149
women 3, 14, 58, 198

Fadel, Mohammad 7
Farda (outer garment) 20–21
Farming out 188
Fāṭima bt. Abī ʿAbd Allāh Muḥammad b. Abī l-Nuʿaym Riḍwān 21, 33, 62, 77–78
Fāṭima bt. Abī Jaʿfar Aḥmad Musāʿid 41, 61
Fāṭima bt. Abī l-Juyūsh Naṣr (Nasrid princess) 177
Fāṭima bt. Abī l-Qāsim al-Abār 180
Fāṭima bt. Abī l-Raḍī b. Daʿmūn 180
Fāṭima bt. Aḥmad b. ʿAjīb 51
Fāṭima bt. Aḥmad b. ʿAṭiyya 64–65, 177–178
Fāṭima bt. Aḥmad al-Sharqī 30
Fāṭima bt. Aḥmad al-Shūbarī 66
Fāṭima bt. Aḥmad ʿUlaylash 179
Fāṭima bt. ʿAlī (or ʿUbayd Allāh) al-Lakhmī 20, 42, 78
Fāṭima bt. ʿAlī b. Zāfir 64
Fāṭima bt. Ibrāhīm al-Layṭī 65
Fāṭima bt. Ibrāhīm al-Shalubānī 180
Fāṭima bt. Ibrāhīm al-Shānashī 178
Fāṭima bt. Khāṣṣbāk al-Nāṣirī (Mamluk princess) 183
Fāṭima bt. Muḥammad b. ʿAmr 66
Fāṭima bt. Muḥammad al-Khalīʿ 186
Fāṭima bt. Muḥammad al-Siyāsī 179
Fāṭima bt. Saʿd b. Lubb 61, 66
Fāṭima bt. ʿUthmān b. Muḥammad b. ʿUthmān 63, 177
Female circumcision 11, 15, 95, 110–112, 116, 117
Female hiring contract 152, 155, 157

Female physicians
Jewish 112
Muslim 112
Roman 113
see also Trota
Female sexuality 111
Fernando Villalobos (Canon of Granada) 180
Fez 27
Fī ḥajr see Interdiction
Filiation see *Nasab*
Fiqh see Law manuals
Florence 38, 58, 86, 171

Gender division of labour 150
Geniza (documents) 35–36, 113, 115, 140–143, 159, 163, 169–170, 188–190, 192
Genoese women 191
German marriage gift (*Morgengabe*) 37
Germanic law 3
Gibb, Hamilton 4
Goitein, Shlomo Dov 36, 112, 115, 140–141, 145, 163, 170
Goody, Jack 37
Granadan family 67, 77
Greece 38
Greek
logic 107
medicine 107–109, 112–113, 115
physicians 11
society 192
translation 182
women's conversion 142
Green, Monica 115
Guilds 172

Ḥaḍāna see Custody
al-Ḥaffār (mufti) 83
Ḥakīm b. Ibrāhīm Ghālib 41, 61
Hanafi school, law, Abū Ḥanīfa 34, 43, 72–74, 79, 95, 97, 100, 104–105, 157, 192
Hanbali school, law 6, 98, 100, 105, 111, 158
Hanson, Ann Ellis 115
Ḥaram al-Sharīf (documents of) 113, 189
Ḥasan b. Saʿīd b. Zurayq 63, 187
Hellenic period 3
Herlihy, David 171
Hiba (gift) 43, 45, 51, 60
Hippocratic medical corpus 11
Hippocratic view 115
Hisba manuals 110
Hughes, Diane Owen 37

Ibn Abī Zayd al-Qayrawānī (jurist) 22, 122, 159–160
Ibn ʿArafa (mufti) 154, 158
Ibn ʿAttāb (mufti) 56
Ibn al-ʿAṭṭār 8, 25, 31, 80–81, 118–121, 127–128, 130–134, 136, 160
Ibn Ezra (poet) 141
Ibn Ḥabīb (jurist) 109, 200
Ibn al-Ḥājj (mufti) 166
Ibn al-Jawzī 200
Ibn al-Jazzār 108
Ibn Juzayy 6, 7, 23–24, 30, 44, 55, 79, 81, 100, 110, 124, 129–131, 133, 135, 152, 155, 160, 166, 176
Ibn Khaldūn 108, 154
Ibn Lubāba (mufti) 26
Ibn Lubb 54, 82, 167–168
Ibn al-Mājishūn (jurist) 156
Ibn al-Makwī (mufti) 45–46
Ibn Mughīth 8, 25, 28 32, 47, 80, 102 103, 105, 109, 118, 133, 152 153
Ibn al-Qāsim (jurist) 7, 135, 156
Ibn Qayyim al-Jawziyya 111
Ibn Qudāma 111, 158
Ibn Rushd 7, 25–26, 54, 110
Ibn Salmūn, Abū l-Qāsim (jurist and notary) 28, 31, 48, 176
Ibn al-Sarrāj 82
Ibn Taghrībirdī 112

Ibn Taymiyya 111–112
Ibn al-Ukhuwwa 111, 160
Ibn Yūnis 7
Ibrāhīm b. Aḥmad al-Zuhrī 180
Idris, Hady 33, 50
Ijmāʿ 7
Imtāʿ 55–56
Inheritance law, succession law 3, 10, 44, 49, 52, 62, 67, 69, 75–76, 81, 85, 88, 114, 185, 198
Inheritance state bureau 63
Inheritance tax 177
Instalment(-s) (of the *ṣadāq*) 9, 23–24, 27–29, 32–33, 37, 84
  payment for purchase 177–178
Intercourse 94, 98–99, 101, 103
Interdiction (*maḥjūra, fī ḥajr*) 27, 29, 45, 77–90, 96, 199
Intrafamily 12, 76, 192, 194
Irrigation rights 43, 56, 180, 199
ʿĪsā b. Mahdī 93–94
Islamic capitalism 4
Islamic economic structures 13
Islamic gynaecology 109
Islamic medicine 11, 107, 114
Islamic Mediterranean 113
Italian Renaissance cities 13, 37, 58, 70–71, 86–88, 171, 199
Italian women 37, 86, 171, 191, 193
ʿIyāḍ (qadi) 54

al-Jabāsin (quarter) 20
al-Jazīrī 8, 31, 47, 53–54, 56, 96, 104, 118, 153, 156, 177
Jennings, Ronald 185, 188
Jerusalem 28, 71–72, 113, 187, 189
Jewish
  communities, society 13, 115, 123, 139–141, 143, 163, 169, 191
  conversion to Islam (without her husband) 135
  conversion certificates 11
  law and legal system 13, 37–38, 169
  marriage 134
  marriage contract (*ketubbah*) 35–36
  marriage gifts (*nedunia*) 36, 38
  notarial model 36
  rabbinical courts 36
  seclusion of women 145
  slave 128–129
  state of Israel 71
  women 3, 116, 142, 188
Jihāz, also *shiwār* see Trousseau
Johansen, Baber 2, 72
Joint usufruct 64
Jordan, William 191
Judah Halevi (poet) 141
Judge (*qāḍī*) 6, 26, 101, 111, 120, 133, 182, 200
  Granadan 8
Jurists
  Andalusian 8, 152
  Cordovan 54
  discourse 9, 94
  female, lack of 112
  Imami 100
  Italian 58–59, 70
  Maliki 24, 110
  Muslim 5, 26–27, 40, 44, 46, 55, 84, 89, 95–97, 101–102, 106–107, 109, 111, 117, 119, 125, 131–132, 134, 138, 153, 157, 166, 173–174
  North African 50, 139, 190
  role in acquisition 40
  upholding the rights 11
Juynboll, G.H.A. 109

Kāliʾ (second *ṣadāq* instalment) 23–24, 27–32, 34, 53, 56, 84
Karaite 141
Kayseri 34–35
Kelly, Joan 87, 171
Khalīl b. Isḥāq 6–7, 57, 80–81, 124, 129, 131, 135, 155
Khulʿ divorce 10, 30, 35, 48–49, 53, 83, 94, 97, 103, 154

Kirshner, Julius 59, 87
Kitābī, Kitābiyya 122, 124, 126–128, 130–131, 134, 136
Kuehn, Thomas 87
Kutub al-wathā'iq see Notarial manuals

Land taxation 2
Law manuals, legal manuals, positive law (*fiqh*) 2, 7–8, 23, 100, 107, 110, 117, 149, 176
Layish, Aharon 71
Legal
  advisory boards, *shūras* 5
  community 7
  discourse 95–96, 115
  documents 6, 8, 88
  entitlements of women 1
  framework 9
  history of Muslim Spain 5
  historians 4
  historical sources 6
  institutions 3, 86
  mechanisms 5, 21, 60
  norms 9, 101
  practice in al-Andalus 6–7
  procedure 1, 12
  provisions 2
  records 9, 12, 39
  rules 7
  sources 7, 95, 102, 111, 116
  status of the female body 114
  status of women 11
  studies 5
  system 86, 118, 123, 133, 174
  theory 8
Libson, Gideon 35
Literary sources 12, 100, 110
Linant de Bellefonds, Yvon 5, 7, 99, 104
Loan(-s) 33–34, 175–176, 181, 186–188, 191, 194, 198; see also Money lending
López Ortiz, José 8
Lucena 36
Lutfi, Huda 13, 189
al-Mahdiyya (Mahdia) 27, 55, 190
Mahjūna bt. Ibrāhīm al-Ḥakīm 50–52, 85, 113
maḥjūra see Interdiction
Maimonides 141
Mālik Ibn Anas 124, 135
Maliki school 6, 82, 100, 161
  legal sources 12, 22, 121
  marriage doctrine 135
  norms 23
  notarial norms 19
  rule, law 26, 43, 50, 56, 73–75, 77, 79–80, 104, 123, 132
Manjūma bt. 'Umar (Sicilian Muslim) 182
Market place (*qaysāriyya*) 176
Marinids 141, 163
Marriage
  ambiguity 10
  children's 26
  contract 20–24, 27, 29, 31, 37, 39, 47–50, 56, 138, 154, 169–170
  cultural perceptions 9
  economic paradigms 14
  patterns 68–69
  standards of conduct 11
Maryam bt. Abī 'Alī Ḥasan al-Ḥammī 179
Maryam bt. Abī Yaḥyā b. Jubayr 63
Maryam bt. Muḥammad b. Faraj 28, 178
Maryam bt. Nabīl 62–63
Masters, Bruce 185, 189–190
Maẓālim (grievances court) 97
Mazara (Sicily) 190
al-Māzarī (mufti) 7, 55, 190
Means of production 14
Meccan society 3
Meriwether, Margaret 74
Mernissi, Fatima 112
Michael the Syrian 141–142
Middle East 3, 37, 113, 149–150, 153, 167, 172

Midwife, midwives 96, 102, 107–109, 113, 115
Milk bond 95
Misogyny, misogynous 107, 109, 111–112, 115, 192, 200
Money lending 185, 189, 191, 194
Mozarabs 123
Muḍāraba, qirāḍ 190, 192
al-Mudawwana 122, 135, 154
Mudejar 22, 41
Mufti(s) 6, 8, 26–27, 38, 82–83, 96, 106, 111, 166, 200
Muḥammad b. Aḥmad al-Ashkar 30
Muḥammad b. Aḥmad al-Qirbilyānī 52, 179
Muḥammad b. ʿAlī al-Barīṭī 65
Muḥammad b. Ḥayy 64
Muḥammad b. Ibrāhīm al-Ṣanāʾ 64
Muḥammad b. Muḥammad Baḥṭān 28, 65, 69, 93, 187
Muḥammad b. Muḥammad al-Ḥajjām 64
Muḥammad al-ʿUqbānī (market supervisor) 83
Mundualdus (legal guardian) 86–88
Musallam, Basim 98
al-Muwaṭṭaʾ 121–122, 124

Nafaqa (maintenance) 35, 93, 95, 100, 129, 136, 152
Naqd (cash; first *ṣadāq* instalment) 23–24, 27, 30
Nasab (filiation) 4, 37, 106, 114, 117, 130
Nasrid, family 2, 62, 72, 177
  treasury 176–177
Nāẓir (property guardian) 177
Niḥla (marriage gift) 20–21, 43, 47–50, 53, 56, 60
Norman conquest (of Sicily) 182
Notarial
  act 77
  Andalusian 19, 45
  deeds 81, 106, 123
  formulas, models 101, 105, 107, 123
  manuals (*kutub al-wathāʾiq*) of Muslim Spain 6–9, 24, 103, 152
  manuals of the Middle East 8, 152
Notary(-ies) 32–33, 61, 63, 80, 87, 96, 102, 109, 111, 116, 118, 152, 162, 181, 187, 192, 200
Nuʿayma bt. Abī Surūr al-Mufaraj 176–177
Nuzi (city) 3

Ottoman empire 72, 173
  archives 13, 186
  courts 34, 38
  historians 34
  royal women 183–184

Pagan
  conversion certificates 11, 118
  female slave 130
  legal status of marriage in conversion 126–128
  marriage to a Muslim 138
  women's conversion 121, 126, 135
Palermo (Sicily) 182
Palestine 34
Papyri 5, 153
Patriarchy, patriarchal 4–5, 14–15, 197, 199–200
Polygamy, polygamous marriage 62, 68, 198
Population
  Granada 1–2
  explosion 16
  growth 150; see also Demographics
Portugal, Portuguese 88
Possession taking see *Qabḍ*
Pouzet, Louis 13
Pronatalism 112–113, 117
Property executor see *Waṣī*
Property ownership 86
  collective 3
  control 21
  devolution 9

role of property rights in women's 180
separation in marriage 10, 55, 88–90, 168, 170, 174
women's 5, 68, 74
Powers, David 67, 74

Qabḍ (possession taking) 43–44, 47–48, 57, 60
al-Qābisī (mufti) 158
Qadi see Judge
Qafṣa 55
Qamar bt. ʿAlī al-Arjadhūnī 180
Qandarūn (commander of the Christian kings' army) 180
Qarbasāna al-Qanb (village) 20
Qāsim b. Aḥmad ʿĀshir 180
Qayseri 188
Qirāḍ see *Muḍāraba*
Quseir (Red Sea port) 191

al-Rammāḥ (mufti) 106
Rapoport, Yossef 151, 189
Reconquista 19, 123
Reilly, James 185, 192–193
al-Risāla (by Ibn Abī Zayd) 22
Roman law 3, 58, 70, 86, 114, 117, 151
Roman legacy 107
Roman Mediterranean 35, 38, 149
Rose, Carole 14, 15, 33, 59
Roussier, Jules 4
Rumelia 34–35

Saʿd b. Aḥmad al-Muʾadhdhin 30
Ṣadaqa (gift) 43, 60
Saḥnūn 122, 128
al-Saraqusṭī, Muḥammad (mufti) 161, 164
Sayyida bt. Yūsuf al-Qaysī (Sicilian Muslim) 182
Schacht, Joseph 4, 151
Schatkowski Schilcher, Linda 5
Seco de Lucena Paredes, Luis 1
Shafiʿi school, law, jurists 6, 97, 100, 105
Shams al-Muḥājira 180
Shariʿa 15, 34, 54
Shiʿi school, law 97–98
Shiwār see Trousseau
Shorter, Edward 171
Shuhūd, ʿudūl (professional witnesses) 25, 44, 46, 80, 93, 200
Sicily 182, 190
Siyāqa (marriage gift) 47–49
Slave(-s) 21, 24, 57, 65, 77, 98
children of 131, 132
conversion of 122, 128
labour 149, 150, 153, 160
marriage 129
marriage to nonbelievers 124
Slave women 98–99, 111–112, 130, 160
Spinning 150–151, 172
Status of women 16, 142, 170, 172, 197
Stone, Lawrence 172
Stowasser, Barbara 4
Syria 72, 172–173, 183

al-Ṭaḥāwī, Aḥmad b. Muḥammad 156
Taḥbīs (making an endowment) 82
Tāj al-ʿUlā bt. Abī l-Nuʿaym Riḍwān 51, 62, 77–78, 85
Tajrīd (release) 80–81
Talmud 143
Tarshīd (declaration of mental maturity) 79–80, 186
Tax farming 12, 163, 194
Textile industry 151, 153, 161–162, 170, 188
employment of women in 12, 150, 172, 174
Third (of the estate) see *Thulth*
Thulth (unencumbered third of the estate) 21, 51, 62, 71, 73, 81, 88
Tlemcen 83, 141

Toledo 41–42
Trade 33, 175, 181
  local 12, 189, 191, 194
  long distance 12, 191–194
Transactions
  business 41
  commercial 1, 32, 88, 155, 175–176, 180
  conjugal 57
  deathbed 81
  family 1, 31
  financial 12
  gift 44, 55
  land 12, 166
  legal 86
  non-commercial 181, 186, 194
  property 2, 29, 47, 68, 88, 176–95
  public 89
  women's 181
Trota, the Trotula 112, 115
Trousseau (*jihāz*, *shiwār*) 24–26, 33–34, 71, 186, 188
Turco-Mongol (heritage) 184

Udovitch, Avram 192–193
Umm al-Fatḥ bt. ʿAbd Allāh al-Ḥayyānī 180
Umm al-Fatḥ bt. Abī Bakr al-Shaqwashī 64
Umm al-Fatḥ bt. Abī l-Ḥasan al-Qarbāqī 179
Umm al-Fatḥ bt. Abī l-Qāsim al-Ḥannāt 19, 24, 33, 37, 78
Umm al-Fatḥ bt. Abī Qāsim al-Jayān 176–177
Umm al-Fatḥ bt. Abī Sirḥān 178
Umm al-Fatḥ bt. Abī ʿUthmān 182
Umm al-Fatḥ bt. ʿAlī al-Lakhmī 42
Umm al-Fatḥ bt. Faraj 62–63
Umm al-Fatḥ bt. Muḥammad al-Shalubānī 93, 99, 178
Umm al-Fatḥ bt. Yūsuf b. Ḥadīd 93
Umm al-Ḥasan bt. Abī l-Ḥajjāj Yūsuf b. Abī Ḥadīd 187
ʿUmrā (life gift) 43, 82

Virginity 95–96, 99

al-Waghlīsī (mufti) 28
Wakīl (agent) 87
al-Wansharīsī, Aḥmad b. Yaḥyā 9, 55
Waqf (endowment) 13, 68, 71–73, 75–76, 129, 183–184
Waṣī (property executor) 21, 51, 69, 79, 82
Wet nurse, wet nursing 99–101, 107, 114, 149, 153, 155–157
Women's contract 3
Women's status 112, 115, 121, 173
  in Greek society 108
al-Wuḥsha (Jewish woman) 190

Yaḥyā b. ʿUmar (market supervisor) 162
al-Yaznasānī (mufti) 100
Yūsuf b. ʿAlī al-Mudéjar 178
Yūsuf al-Qirbilyānī, 52

al-Zaghal 19
al-Zahrāwī, Abū l-Qāsim 108, 110
Zanj revolt 150
Zaynab bt. ʿAbd Allāh al-Anṣārī 182
Ziadeh, Farhat 2
Zomeño Rodriguez, Amalia 50, 96
Zoraya (Nasrid princess) 118
Zawīla 27, 55